Don Morris is a family man, and a retired veteran social worker. Retirement is fun-filled, with fourteen super-active grand kids. He relaxes with family and friends at local coffee shops all over their coastal paradise. Don's professional experience integrates counselling, program management, organisational improvement, leadership development, teaching at university and TAFE, and running his consulting business. Don is people-focused, a big-picture thinker and a change agent. He is passionate about people, values, social justice and critical analysis of human issues. Don is incisive, articulate, solution-focused and innovative. He tackles issues with originality, clarity, and tenacity. In this book, Don drills down into 'inconvenient truths', synthesizers complex and diverse macro and micro issues, and proposes ways to prioritise and build a network of dignity, rationality, integrity and accountability in individuals, relationships, communities, cultures, and in our global human and environmental ecologies.

I dedicate this book to two people. My amazing, late, Uncle Bob; who encouraged me to be interested in societal issues, to ask lots of questions, to think critically, and to love through dignity, kindness and integrity. And my dear wife, Desiree, who believes in me, and is always confirming, encouraging and gracious.

Don Morris

CAN WE DO BETTER?

Can Humankind Do Better than our
Man-made History of Abuse,
Exploitation and Harm?

AUSTIN MACAULEY PUBLISHERS™

LONDON * CAMBRIDGE * NEW YORK * SHARJAH

A CIP catalogue record for this title is available from the British Library.

ISBN 9781398464025 (Paperback)
ISBN 9781398464032 (ePub e-book)

www.austinmacauley.com

First Published 2022
Austin Macauley Publishers Ltd®
1 Canada Square
Canary Wharf
London
E14 5AA

Thank you — Romina Jamieson-Proctor for your feedback and encouragement; Julieann Wallace for your generosity of time and very helpful suggestions; Kirk Williamson for your generosity in proof-reading and critiquing; and my dear Desiree, thank you for your unwavering confirmation and encouragement.

Can We Do Better?

Can we humans do better than fantasies and wilful ignorance?

Can we be decent, factual, rational and integrous?

Can we be accountable for how we treat each other, our fellow species and the earth?

In all this, can we do better?

Don Morris

Annotated Chapter Headings

1. **The Bloke Who Wrote This Book**
   Meet an ordinary 'Australian bloke' who has decided that it's time to confront some big issues, to challenge some sacred cows, and to propose a values-based future that can bring safety, dignity and rationality to humankind, and that can help us heal and restore the planet.

2. **A Quick Look Ahead**
   The first three-quarters of this book is a detailed look at age-old roadblocks to empowering values such as reverence, dignity, factuality and critical thinking. The final quarter of the book suggests a rational, pragmatic path to prioritise and apply these values.

3. **Human Destructiveness**
   The issues described in this chapter are my reason for writing this book.

4. **Too Many and Too Few**
   There is a relatively small number of narcissistic and sociopathic power-brokers who wantonly and sadistically exploit and harm. There are many of us who see issues, but do nothing. And, there a small number who systematically and strategically stand-against abuse of power, and exploitation and harm; who strive to bring dignity and justice to the greatest number; and who strive to nurture and build a sustainable future.

5. **Patriarchy and Chauvinism – The Domains of Male Dominance**
   These two systemic anachronisms are critiqued and called-out as historical and contemporary drivers of harm and suffering.

6. **Enough Redundant Man-Made Dogma**
   It's time for us humans to move on from anachronistic, man-made assumptions, ideas and institutions.

7. **Slow Down**

This chapter is the first of several that might help us process the tough reality-checks of this book; and to reprioritise our values and aspirations.

8. **Where to Look for Peace, Clarity and Direction — and Where Not to Look**

Peace and clarity are not found in religion, politics, economics, new-age fantasies and conspiracy paranoia; but are found in a carefully chosen internal locus of priorities, values and principles.

9. **A Way to Slow Down and Become More Peacefully Aware**

Here is a rationale for a meditative process that can help us become aware, clear-minded and constructive.

10. **Personal Benefits of Breath Meditation**

Breath Meditation can help us be calm, present, aware and sensitive.

11. **Societal, Big Picture Benefits of Breath Meditation**

The calm and clarity of Breath Mediation can help us better understand big picture issues such as the indignities and suffering of social disadvantage, injustice and environmental damage.

12. **A Process for Listening to the Rhythm of Your Breath**

This chapter explains the practical process of Breath Meditation.

13. **Reality and Possibility**

This chapter explains the interdependent relationship between reality and possibility.

14. **The Jekyll and Hyde Species**

We humans do a lot of amazingly clever and commendably good things. However, we also do far too many terrible things that harm ourselves, our fellow species and our earthly home. As a species, we are noticeably sadomasochistic. We are the Jekyll and Hyde species.

15. **Us Quixotic Humans — Another Expression of Mr Hyde**

We humans tend to react against those who are different from us as individuals, and who are different from our tribe. We tend to jump at shadows, to act out and to lash out. In this, we 'tilt at windmills. These tendencies profile us as quixotic (pronounced … 'keyoitic').

16. **Liminality – Betwixt Jekyll and Hyde**

The poem in this chapter summarises and synthesises the first sixteen chapters. It brings our contradictions, dissonance, dissociations and incongruities into sharp focus.

17. Forthcoming Questions and Reflections

The next group of chapters are devoted to an array of questions that might help you explore the issues we've covered so far in this book?

18. Forks in the Road

Each question in chapters 22-34 places us at a fork in the road; with dignity and reason in one direction, and with aspects of egoic dysfunctionality and ignorance in the other direction. Each fork in the road is an invitation to discern and choose to move toward dignity and rationality, or to default to more and more egoic ignorance, dysfunctionality and recalcitrance. Remember — rational is, as rational does; and does and does and does. Stupid is as stupid does and does and does.

19. Counter-Intuitive Questions are Next

Many of the questions in ensuing chapters will seem counter-intuitive. Throughout this book there are lots of counter-intuitive questions that will challenge your assumptions, preconceptions, beliefs, opinions and alleged common sense.

20. Questions about You and Me

This chapter asks you to identify examples of when you have changed your mind on the basis of an encounter with dignity, logic, data, facts and/or critical thinking.

21. Questions about Design, God, Eternity and Creation

These questions challenge many sacred-cows. They ask you to identify an array of arbitrary assumptions and beliefs; and to rethink them.

22. Questions about Faith, Meaning and Purpose

Do we mistake presumption for faith? Do we contrive and concoct meaning to make us feel special? Do we bolster our ego by inflating our sense of purpose with fantasies and esoteric confabulations?

23. Questions about Imagination, Speculation and Fantasy

This chapter shows the relationship between the arbitrariness of misguided imagination, fanciful speculation, whims, fads, myths, and delusions. It contains lots of counter-intuitive questions.

24. Questions about Presumption, Pretention and Pontification

It's very short step from presumption to pretention, and then another tiny step to baseless, misguided and misleading pontification.

25. **Questions about Ego and God**

What is the difference been ego and God?

26. **Questions about Story-Making**

What might our thinking, speaking and acting look and sound like if we minimise contrived stories and fanciful confabulations?

27. **Questions about Evolution, Chemistry and Biology**

This chapter suggests that evolution, chemistry and biology are highly desirable alternatives to fantasies, myths and dogma; and are vastly preferable to arbitrarily made-up opinions and delusional beliefs.

28. **Questions about the Human Brain**

Does the human brain prefer confabulation to facts, reason and rationality? Does the brain resist facts and confound reality by making-up myths and fantasies? Can the human brain become predominantly factual and rational? Can we nurture and consolidate critical thinking?

29. **Questions about Violence and Degradation**

This chapter is about the degradation and violence that first arose from the agricultural era, and then greatly increased due to religion, industrialisation, colonisation, neo-liberal politics, capitalism and communism?

30. **Questions about Our Conflicted Nature**

Can we humans do better than our typical fanciful, fragmented, conflicted incongruence? Can we minimise our Dr Jekyll-Mr Hyde conflictedness, anomalies, aberrations and abominations?

31. **Questions about the Spirituality of Reverence, Dignity and Rationality**

Might core values, such as reverence, dignity and critical thinking, become the essence of 'grounded spirituality'?

32. **Questions about Possible Ways Forward**

What best equips you and me to appreciate ramifications of the questions in previous chapters? Remember the title and intent of this book – Can We do Better? Questions can help us evolve and do better.

33. **Sitting with these Questions**

I invite you to sit with and ponder the questions in the previous chapters for hours, days, months, years and decades. Let them speak to you as you reflect, learn and mature throughout the remainder of your life.

34. Ignorance

This chapter looks at three types of ignorance. Various aspects of ignorance are explored in the next several chapters.

35. A Snapshot of the Timeline of Ignorance

Even in the 21st century, the irrationalities and indignities of ignorance flourish due to antiquated political and religious presumption, tribalism and all sorts of exceptionalism. Ignorance also thrives due to the inanities of new-age faddism, social media psychobabble, conspiracy disinformation and populist 'big lies'.

36. Ignorance and Arbitrariness

Arbitrariness is rife in the mind of 21st century humankind. It arises from misguided imagination, whims and habituated confabulations. Arbitrariness proliferates fancies, fads, disinformation and lies. Arbitrary subjectivity is a major aspect of ignorance. Some interconnected enmeshments of arbitrariness are clarified in this chapter.

37. The Lure of Romantic Ignorance, Intrigue and Drama

There are also strong interconnections and enmeshments between ignorance, romantic idealism, fantasy, intrigue and drama. The egoic human mind loves drama, intrigue and romanticism.

38. Bullshit, Lies and Ignorance

It is one short step from fantasies to bullshit. Then, one more little step to wilful ignorance. Then, one further step to the deliberate deception of 'big lies', fraud and the deceptions of agnotology.

39. Our Choice – Wilful Ignorance – or – Intentional Reverence, Dignity, Reason and Honesty

This chapter contrasts wilful ignorance against intentional and purposeful values; including intentional reverence, dignity, sensitivity, rationality, integrity and accountability.

40. Another Poem About Us Humans

The poem in this chapter suggests that a web blind spots, contradictions, incongruities, anomalies, irony and paradox combine to form a mirror that reflects and reveals the rarely detailed shadow of the human ego.

41. A Look at Ego Through the Eyes of Eastern Philosophy

The following collection of chapters are about 'ego' and its role in creating and driving the arbitrariness, ignorance, fantasy and dishonesty of culture, politics, religion, big business, popular culture and quixotic conspiracy cults.

42. **Ego – The Voice in Your Head**

Ego is sound of the voice in your head and the voice in my head. It is the sound of mind-made confabulated stories, narratives and justifications that we tell ourselves over and over. It is the egoic fluff that we tell anyone who will listen and be sympathetic to our self-serving fanciful perceptions, opinions, beliefs, interpretations and biased versions of people, circumstances and events.

43. **Levels of Egoic Unawareness / Unconsciousness**

Egoic unawareness ranges from minor, semi-inconsequential unawareness to destructive, pathological unawareness.

44. **Strategic Ecological Wisdom vs the Self-leveraging Me**

This chapter compares relational and ecological wisdom with self-serving, self-leveraging control and coercion.

45. **Realising Potential Through Sentient Awareness-aka-Mindfulness**

Sensitive, alert awareness is the key to mindful, reverent, rational intentionality.

46. **More on What Ego Looks Like and Sounds Like**

Here are some more ways that ego manifests.

47. **The Virtual World of Ego**

This chapter provides a computer analogy that highlights the virtual, 'goggled-unawareness' of ego.

48. **Ego and Bullshit**

Ego causes us to 'think shit', 'believe shit', 'talk shit' and to do 'shitty things'; and for some, to be 'full of shit'; thereby, to be egoic 'shitheads'.

49. **Ego and Arbitrariness**

Egoic thinking is arbitrary. That is to say, it is whimsical, wishful, fantastical, irrational, illogical and self-serving.

50. **Presumptions, Pretentions, Opinions and Beliefs — Where 21st Century Ego Hides and Abides**

Ego is semi-invisible in our presumptions, pretentions, ill-informed opinions and arbitrary beliefs.

51. **Projection — Ego's Most Prominent Ploy**

We see the egoic-mind when we understand and embrace this chapter.

62. **A Few More Radical Reality-checks**

This is a critique of other aspects of arbitrariness, pretention, fantastical imagination and anthropocentric myth-making.

63. **Populism, Our Most Recent Expression of Dumb and Dumber**

An escalating, toxic political culture is catapulting 21st century humans back to pre-WWII levels of big-lies, propaganda, conspiracy madness, mass ignorance, societal dysfunction, political danger and the horrors of war.

64. **Destabilisation – The Hallmark of Populism**

Populism is destabilising the world, and threatening the earth and all its species with calamity.

65. **The Mad and the Bad**

There is a global mishmash of crazy, dangerous and destructive leaders, cults, cultures, governments and states. I refer to these as 'mad and bad'.

66. **Sanity and Dignity**

This chapter contrasts dignity and rationality against mad-bad theocratic and secular criminal, populist and totalitarian extremisms and extremists.

67. **More on Russia and China – Their Expressions of Mad and Bad**

The title speaks for itself.

68. **Yours and My Place in Big Picture Issues and Future Possibilities**

From this point onward, we will explore hope, possibilities, options and alternatives that can help us nurture reverence, dignity and rationality in personal, relational, societal, institutional, national and global domains.

69. **Dignity, Reason and Character – In Contrast to Ego**

Here is a profile of egoic misguidedness and misadventure.

70. **Alan — A Person of Character, Grace and Dignity**

Here is a role model of grace, dignity, reason and competence.

71. **Michael and Joan**

Michael and Joan are role models of humility, vision, success, and unpretentious normality.

72. **Alan, Bill, Michael and Joan – Four Excellent Role Models**

This chapter summarises the learnings from everyday egoic self-servingness; and from three exemplars of lived-values and mindful normality.

73. **Uncle Bob**

This chapter is very close to my heart. Uncle Bob is a role model who exemplifies grace, dignity, reason and strategic discipline.

74. **From Now On, Values and Rationality**

Reverence, dignity, integrity, rationality and accountability are at the forefront of a network of values, principles and priorities that contribute greatly to our hope and potential for personal and societal evolution.

75. **Envisage**

Envisage and envision yourself, relationships, society and humankind in a future that prioritises dignity, reason, integrity and accountability.

76. **A Revolutionary, Mindful, Enlightened and Evolved Culture**

This is the first of several chapters about First Nation mindfulness.

77. **Practical Learning from Australia's First Peoples**

This chapter summarises sixty thousand years of mindful awareness, values, principles, priorities and disciplines that Australia's First Peoples combined to ensure their 'perpetual continuance within the oneness of the ecology of life'.

78. **Principles, Priorities and Aspirations**

If we can open our minds and our hearts, First Peoples can educate and enlighten us in the ways of mindful reverence, relationship, community, ecology and sustainability. First People wisdom can revolutionise contemporary human existence.

79. **Women's Voices and Women Role Models**

It is time to hear the iconic voice of 'the-feminine' and 'the archetypal mother'; and to be guided by women stewards, leaders and elders toward a future of Yin-based dignity and reason.

80. **My Acknowledgements and Commitments**

Read and consider.

81. **Your Acknowledgements**

Read, consider and respond.

82. **An Internal Locus**

Mindful capacities and priorities must come from the inside; from an internal locus of sentience, reverence, dignity, reason, integrity, character and accountability.

83. **A Final Recap of Some Principles for Values and Rationality**

This chapter summarises the key values, principles, priorities and possibilities of Can We do Better.

84. Be the Difference to Make a Difference

A final encouragement: 'Be the difference to make the difference'.

Definition of Terms

This section at the end of the book provides an explanation of what I mean by many of the terms and concepts used throughout the book.

The Bloke Who Wrote this Book

It is likely that you and I were strangers until our encounter with this book. Now we are connected by my urge to write about the issues and themes flagged in the title, the synopsis and the chapter headings; and by your urge to read about them. Perhaps we are joined by deep concerns about what we see in the world of fundamentalist religion, populist politics, new-age counter culture, social media fads and conspiracy madness. Maybe you and I are joined by hope for reverence, dignity and responsibility through greater decency, rationality, integrity and accountability. Concern, decency, rationality and the hope that we humans can do better, are core themes in this book. They are my motivation for writing. The pressing and urgent need for greater decency, reason, integrity and accountability are also the reason why I have been so direct.

Putting More Cards on the Table

There are some things I want to clarify before you forge ahead. The first is that I am an ordinary, everyday Australian man; an 'Aussie bloke' who loves family, sport, riding my motorbike, coffee with friends and having a 'couple' of beers while watching the sunset over our local river. Ask my family and friends and they will assure you that I am not an academic, an expert, a guru, a mystic or a saint; especially not a saint! I am not religious. I have no particular political alliance. Nor am I a disciple of new-age pop-psychology. I am not an idealist, a conspiracy boffin, a cynic or an aggressive revolutionary. To be honest, however, I confess that I am an something of an iconoclast. I plead guilty to that charge.

Just like you, I put on my shorts one leg at a time. Every day, my inconsistencies look back at me from the mirror. Daily, I see the yawning gap between the values and principles in this book and the reality of my not so gracious attitudes and behaviours. My incongruities and short comings are in plain view for all to see. I'm not trying to impress you. Nor do I claim to be someone or something that I am not. Similar to you, I am a person of irony and frailty; an ordinary person who is replete with paradox, contradiction and blind spots.

As is the case for billions of people, I deal with all sorts of first world stuff — health concerns, a minefield of family politics, and the usual assortment of money issues. Just like you, most nights, my senses are bombarded by stark realities that we see on the television news, including environmental destruction, war, atrocities, terrorism, mass murders, epidemics, climate change urgency and denial, terrible injustices, abuses, degradations, exploitations, criminality, mad-bad politicians and greedy corrupt industrialists. Often, I'm horrified at the short-sightedness, ignorance, callousness and dishonesty of governments and corporations in their oblivion and disregard for the issues and needs of the poor and the powerless. I am also blown away by widespread citizenry ignorance, indifference and cynical disregard for the plight of our fellow species and the planet.

All in all, I am staggered by the scale and consequences of 'man-made' disasters that are being mismanaged by shallow, ambitious, unscrupulous and disturbed politicians; who are manipulated by greedy, opportunistic, unprincipled corporations and billionaires. There are so many issues, and so many drivers of. complex and dire macro problems of today's world. Sometimes, I respond peacefully to this stuff. But other times I react out of fear, frustration and anger. Often, I catch myself reacting with harsh judgement. Just like every human on this planet, I am a person under the sway of ego. All my ungracious reactions are classically egoic.

An Ordinary Person Writing an Unusual Book

In the face of my admissions and candour, perhaps you might like to spend some time with a writer who isn't a dry academic; a glib, religious fundamentalist; a strident ideologue; a shallow new-age faddist; or a nutcase conspiracy theorist. You might enjoy a book that isn't an expression of some underlying narcissistic, attention seeking pathology. You may feel inclined to read a book written by an ordinary person doing his best to live peacefully, integrously, realistically and effectively. You might be drawn to an author who is trying to make sense of confronting, perplexing and testing societal and global issues. It might be timely for you and engage with a writer who challenges assumptions; and who asks penetrating questions; some of which, are confronting and may be 'politically incorrect'. By writing this book, I'm putting myself out there; as we say in Australia, 'having a crack'. Perhaps, in speaking out, I am 'throwing myself under the bus'. That's a risk I'm prepared to take; come what may.

Critiques, Questions and Invitations

As seen in the Synopsis, this book strongly critiques popular culture, politics, religion and toxic masculinity. I don't hold back. There aren't any 'no-go zones'. I ask lots of piercing questions about a wide range of issues. I challenge lots of religious, ideological and new-age sacred cows. In doing so, I implore us to get our heads out of the clouds of baseless, arbitrary beliefs and made-up opinions; and to get our feet on a foundation of data-based, science-based factual reality, critical thinking and values-based decency. I offer a network of priorities, values and principles that might help us be more decent and rational. I offer lots of invitations to move a little farther from arbitrariness, assumption, pretention, ignorance and fantasy; which I suggest are systemic egoic barriers to decency and rationality. I hope that many of us can edge a little closer to awareness, sensitivity, concern, personal and citizenry responsibility, constructive community engagement, and accountability for what we say and do.

I offer lots of invitations for readers to pause, rethink, reprioritise, to choose afresh and to start-over. Frequently, I offer invitations to embrace self-reflection, self-awareness and self-honesty in relationships, roles, stewardship, endeavours, citizenship and leadership. I do this because reflection, self-awareness and self-honesty are the basis of relational and societal sensitivity and responsibility. These priorities are the foundations of dignity, rationality, intelligent educated citizenship and mindful accountability. Reflect on and envisage the possibility of a revolution and evolution of intelligent, educated, accountable citizenship that is guided by dignity, facts and critical thinking.

A Wide Net

As said before, this book casts a wide net. It shows the nuances and connections between a kaleidoscope of micro issues and a web of macro issues. You might find reading this mix of stuff to be challenging; perhaps, to be a bit personally confronting. If you do, don't hurry, read a little at a time, and keep going. I hope that what I have written will be worthy of your goodwill, faithfulness and persistence. I empathise with you if you find this book

22

challenging; and, at times, provocative. It is a big read that involves lots of heavy lifting in terms of self-reflection, self-honesty, critical thinking and accountability.

Be Curious

The key to reading this book is to be curious. So, be curious about what inspired or urged an ordinary Australian bloke to write about a mix of — arbitrariness, masculinity and ignorance; fictions and fads; deception, exploitation and violence; sensitivity, integrity and accountability; critical thinking and compassion; simplicity, contentment and gratitude; reason and rationality. As you read, be inquisitive about the interconnections among this unusual network of themes and topics.

As the book unfolds, I will do my best to clarify these connections. In the meantime, the short answer is that, all these macro and micro themes are interconnected. Each and all of them are highly relevant to you and me; and to each of 7.9 billion of the us who comprise the human world. This network of themes is relevant to all human relationships, communities, institutions, enterprises and governance. Ultimately, the themes and questions posed in this book relate to how the world can do better by reducing human suffering, devastation of species and environmental destruction. From various viewpoints, the book asks what you and I and humankind can do better than the web of shitty, destructive stuff that we humans continue to do in the 21st century? Surely, we can do better than the devastating war in Ukraine and the destruction of the biosphere.

So — be curious; be open; wonder; and question. Look in the mirror; reflect; examine yourself. Examine and critique your assumptions, opinions, beliefs and judgements. Think relationally, communally and ecologically. Embrace systems-thinking. Stay with me as I link personal micro themes to big-picture, collective, macro, systems themes. See and appreciate the systems connections between individual persons, citizenship, relationships, community, institutions, governance, history, human psychology, societal issues, ignorance, ego, stewardship, custodianship, leadership and eldership. Get ready to join a big bunch of dots that you may not have joined before reading this book.

You and I need to grasp and map the linkages between facts, values, possibilities, priorities and hope. If we want things to be different and better, we need to think, speak and act differently and better. We need to see and appreciate that we humans need to ditch some of the arbitrary, fanciful, ill-informed, ignorant and shitty stuff we believe, say and do. We need to embrace some new and better ways to exist on this planet; better ways to treat to each other and our fellow species; and better ways to treat the Earth, our Mother, and our home.

Dignity, Reverence, Reason, Critical Thinking and Accountability

My thesis is that the way forward toward a better world is through the combination of dignifying right hemisphere values, facts, rationality / critical thinking, integrity and accountability; not through more and more arbitrary fantasies and beliefs; nor through dogmatic religious and political ideologies. My thesis is that evolving dignifying core values needs to be our unified purpose, our common focus; our shared priority; our community intention; our societal purpose. A network of dignifying values needs to become our clarity, our intention, our means and our ends.

Therefore, prioritising and nurturing values that promote reverence, decency, honesty and critical thinking, are the core themes of this book. Dignifying values, in tandem with integrous, intelligent critical thinking, are the heart, head and the gut behind the question and title of this book: 'Can We Do Better'. My conclusion is that accountability for dignifying, integrous Yin-based values and commitment to critical thinking are our only way forward toward a decent, rational and sustainable human future. The only hopeful future is through decency toward each other, our fellow species, and the earth. This would be a revolutionary way to be human. Enshrining dignifying values and critical thinking would revolutionise our existence.

My thesis is that the adoption of any one of a tapestry of values will build and nurture the other values. Feel free to choose any one of the values from the those that keep popping up throughout the book. I encourage you to choose the value that resonates strongly for you. Latch onto it. Embrace your chosen, preferred value as your constant; as your ever-present priority, benchmark and guide. Whichever value you choose, will lead you to the other values. Ultimately, all the values emphasised in this book are interwoven and mutually reinforcing. Each and all of these values will help you nurture and role model dignity and rationality.

Is it possible for dignifying values and rationality to become the abiding personal and collective priority, revolution and reality for an increasing number of people; perhaps of a critical mass of 7.9 billion of us?

For a critical mass of us, can reverence, dignity, rationality, integrity and accountability evolve to become the new normal; the new common way of thinking, speaking, relating, prioritising, choosing, deciding, making policy, solving problems and evaluating outcomes.

Can strategically-chosen values and critical thinking evolve to become the new and prominent way of creating a kind, rational, empowering, just and sustainable future?

2020 and 2022

I started this book in about 2016, and was writing it throughout 2020–2021 and in early 2022. The complexities and machinations of Coronavirus, the Me-too and Black Lives Matter movements, domestic terrorism in the USA and climate change urgency were front and centre while I was writing. And then, Russia invaded Ukraine. We saw many horrible images and heard a plethora of heart-breaking accounts of murder, extreme violence and unconscionable, insane destruction. As well, in 2020, in Australia, the USA, and in other countries, we experienced by far our most devastating bushfire season in history. In early 2021, Australia's macho culture of gross disrespect for woman was exposed, scrutinised and challenged; including in Australia's Parliament House.

These situations highlighted the very best of human values and rationality, and exposed the very worst attitudes, beliefs, insensitivities and behaviours. Many citizens and professionals showcased dignity and rationality, kindness and generosity. But — too many people and groups displayed the darker aspects of our humanness. Selfishness, arbitrariness, ignorance, disrespect, cultism, big lies, crazy spurious conspiracy ideas, extreme irrationality, dishonesty, and callous disregard for others were too common.

In 2020-2022, people typified the contrasting themes and thesis of the book, decency, intelligence, and rationality – versus – egocentricity, ignorance, stupidity, extreme callousness, dishonesty and irrationality to the point of madness. As you read, remember the 2020-2022 goings-on of opportunistic, self-invested politicians, greedy Machiavellian industrialists, obnoxious selfish citizens, science deniers, conspiracy extremists, and junk medicine quacks. Remember the 2022 murderous violence and devastating destruction by Putin and his military in Ukraine. And, remember the dedicated and clear minded Ukrainian leaders and military. Remember clear-minded emergency workers, medical staff, fire fighters and a myriad of support workers and citizens. Use these examples to see the contrasts between dignifying values, rationality and self-sacrifice — versus, selfish motives, spurious wacko beliefs and sociopathic Machiavellian intent. Reflect on 2020-2022 COVID machinations and Putin's 2022 invasion of Ukraine. Reflect with the intention to become aware of humankind's contrasting expressions of the sanity and decency of Dr Jekyll, versus the sociopathic madness and extreme, deplorable harms of Mr Hyde. Decency and sociopathy are stark contrasts of humanness. These contrasts are emphasised and made prominent throughout this book.

Cherry Picking and Connections

Feel free to read the chapters that catch your eye and arouse your curiosity. However, I would be honoured if you follow my thesis from the beginning to the conclusion of the book. I encourage you to read slowly and sensitively. As said before, do your best to be open, transparent, brave and accountable. Map issues, egoic drivers and possible solutions, from chapter to chapter. Note the connections between the following extensive web of stuff — human destructiveness, patriarchy, chauvinism, man-made dogmas and institutions, arbitrariness, fantasies, confabulations, narratives, projections, ignorance and ego. Make the connections between values, rationality and accountability; between relational, communal and ecological systems priorities; and between the potential hope in feminine and First People to show us a different way to be human. Weave these dots and threads into a tapestry of awareness, understanding, wisdom, enlightenment, reality and hope.

My Hope and Purpose

My hope and purpose are that this book will stimulate a revolution of courageous personal reflection. It would be fantastic if this book is a catalyst for constructive, forward-thinking discussions, and for the networking of grounded, hopeful, intelligent, integrous, reasoned, creative and strategic minds. Contact me if you want to chat about issues, and to network understandings, ideas, possibilities and strategies for human evolution.

Idiosyncrasies of My Writing

As your read, don't be distracted by the idiosyncrasies of my writing; nor by typos and bloopers that proofreading has missed. Irrespective of expression and style, the thesis is clear enough to be discerned and understood. I hope and trust that his book is a treasure-trove of gems that are ready to be gleaned. So, glean absorb and respond to what resonates; and leave the rest for another time.

As you progress through the book, note various groupings of words. Be aware that I deliberately group powerful words to highlight points that I consider are particularly important. From time to time, I will ask you to reread sentences and paragraphs. When I do this, please, pause, reread, reflect and absorb their impact. Let slow, mindful reading, word groupings and the rereading of sentences and paragraphs speak to you. Let them impact you and sober you. Let them jolt you toward greater awareness of the nature and importance of dignity and rationality. These two core themes are emphasised many times as the book unfolds.

Definitions and explanations of terms are in Appendix 1 at the end of the book.

Some Terms

Throughout this book, I often refer to 'man-made', 'masculine, masculinised', Yang-based and left hemisphere. These are a web of macro and micro issues that are associated with long-standing patterns of patriarchal, chauvinistic and misogynistic male-dominance attitudes and actions. For me, Yang, means — an orientation of overt masculine ethos; valuing and asserting strength, wilful power, ambition, control, force, judgement and justification. In contrast, right hemisphere includes is Yin-oriented, motherly, relational and ecological awareness and dispositions. A Yin disposition is inclusive, disposed to grace, inclusion, empathy and compassion. A Yin orientation is consciously welcoming, inclusive, negotiable, empathic, compassionate, sensitive, gracious, kind and a wise-motherly disposition. These explanations will be clarified, amplified, nuanced and contextualised as the book unfolds; beginning with the next chapter.

Imagine and Envisage

Imagine if an ever-increasing number of people from diverse walks of life got together and began networking right-hemisphere values, knowledge and strategies that might nurture dignity, integrity, critical thinking and accountability for the betterment of humankind, for the protection of our fellow species, and for the healing of planet. Envisage yourself contributing to this network of values and critical thinking. Envisage yourself playing an active role in a revolution and evolution of a critical mass of love-in-action.

These invitations signal one of these themes of this book go forward.

A Quick Look Ahead

The First Three-Quarters of This Book — Yin and Yang Issues

The first three-quarters of this book involves comprehensive problem-definition — chapter by chapter, issue by issue, driver by driver, context by context. Accordingly, it's not by chance that in the first three-quarters of the book, I have written in detail about the egoic left hemisphere as the shadow of human history.

Why the 'left hemisphere'?

Because — for millennia, prior to agriculture, Australia's First Peoples were highly effective right hemisphere custodians of the community and the earth. Throughout 60,000 years, First Peoples evolved a 'wise and loving mother' model of community, custodianship, leadership and eldership. Australian First People Mother Model prioritised a holistic, big-picture, very long-term, ecological systems awareness and perspective of human existence. The First People systems mother model sees humans as integral to nature, 'with' nature and within nature.

Australia's First Peoples are 60,000-years exemplars of the efficacy of a Yin-based ecological systems model. First Peoples are strategically oriented to right hemisphere ecological systems holism. This is how the right hemisphere perceives, thinks, prioritises, values and relates. For First Peoples — with-and-within architectural, relational, right hemisphere holism enshrines the sanctity and functionality of the oneness and wholeness of diversity among humans, among our fellow species, and between humans, our fellow species, habitats, ecologies, endowments and the earth.

In complete contrast, the left hemisphere is oriented toward cognitive and intellectual muscularity, drivenness, ambition, mechanical thinking, stern obedience to rules, and a 'controlling, authoritarian masculine orientation. The left hemisphere is oriented to quantity over quality, things over people, and results over values. The left hemisphere prefers goals, steps, data, parts, roles, rules, transactions, rigid hard-edged logic, strength, force, power and measurable outcomes. Left hemisphere preferences and skills are those of bean-counting, number-crunching and calculating.

In contrast, the right hemisphere is guided.by humanistic and ecological values and principles. The right hemisphere strives to be an enlightened, mindful, holistic visionary, humanistic, relational and ecological. In idealistic situations, the left hemisphere is the analogous a highly intelligent engineering genius that has the dispositions and skills to implement technical and structural aspects of the right hemisphere vision and humanistic values of the right. The left is a brilliant doer and problem-solver, but, if unchecked, tends to fixate on rules, parts, linear steps and ends; and too often at the expense of values: for example; dignity, reverence, respect, compassion, kindness and accountability in human relationships; and too often at the expense of relationships with each other and our fellow species and ecologies.

By analogy, the right hemisphere perceives the Yin beauty, holism and common good that the processes of physics can create for peoples and ecologies. In contrast, the left tends to be restricted to prioritisation of Yang-focussed laws and goals. In another analogy; the right hemisphere relishes the wonder and bounty of the Yin systems-holism of the chemistry and biology of the earth. While, the left hemisphere is attuned to how to use Yang knowledge to explain cause and effect, to make thing happen, to control 'things', and to be effective and efficient; but not necessarily to promote the greater good of the environment or humankind. The left hemisphere is vulnerable to left hemisphere religious, political and economic fundamentalisms and conservatisms.

The Decline of Yin and the Rise of Yang

When agricultural humans transitioned away from First Peoples Yin-feminine perspective; and away from right hemisphere relational systems thinking; eventually, ultimately, their following generations adopted a mechanical, masculinised ends-driven agricultural left hemisphere model. Over thousands of years, progressively the mechanical, masculinised Yang-oriented left hemisphere assumed and gained control of a swage of Anglo-European humankind within several thousand years.

Beginning a few thousand years later, and continuing until present times, the controls and power of masculine, the mechanical left hemisphere was reinforced and bastardised by the encroachment and enmeshment of institutionalised religion, politics, commercialism, economics, materialism and consumerism. When this happened, the right hemisphere faded into relative oblivion, and the left became the master of Anglo-European world. Hard-edged left hemisphere mechanisms and controls were never and are not on the radar of the relational right hemisphere of pre-agricultural First Peoples.

The Loss of Systems Priorities and the Rise Institutional Controls

Thus, from about 10,000 years ago, First Peoples systems awareness and systems holism was increasingly supplanted by Yang-based mechanical reductionism. Relationships and ecologies were supplanted by institutionalised controls and societal transactions. Being one-with nature was superseded by being over nature. Ecological thinking was replaced by aggressive drives to exploit nature for human gain. Humankind moved away from a love of nature and devolved toward institutionalised, mechanical abuse of nature and each other. The results of these shifts became the norms of the dominance and exploitation of man-made, left hemisphere history; from the agricultural era until now.

I have explained this so that, potentially, you and I can be aware of the shadowy left hemisphere proclivities and constraints that have formed us humans and damaged the planet over the past 10,000 years. Man-made left hemisphere mechanisms devolved us, corrupted our thinking, stole our relative innocence, obliterated our mindfulness and compassion, and harm us, our fellow species and the planet. When you and I are aware of what stifles and disallows relational and ecological priorities, such as dignity toward each other and reverence toward nature, we may be better able to choose and commit to consciously replace demeaning and exploitative left hemisphere proclivities with respectful, holistic, strategic right hemisphere priorities, principles, values and processes.

As you begin each new chapter, be open to recognise and understand another bunch of factors in an extensive and interconnected web of masculine, left hemisphere influences, constraints and consequences. Every chapter reinforces our awareness of ego and ignorance, but also calls for hope through an unwavering commitment to and focus on dignifying values and accountability for the application of respectful, factual, rational processes My argument is that the purposeful application of mindful right hemisphere priorities, principles, values and ecological rationality is a viable way out of the web of man-made left hemisphere issues that are mapped throughout this book.

Therefore, the primacy of a network of core relational and ecological values and of critical thinking will be mentioned again and again; from chapter to chapter, from context to context, from them to theme. As well, three crucial words will pop up again and again — priorities, principles and values. By the conclusion of the book, these core themes will be burned into your consciousness as the elements of right hemisphere 'mindfulness'.

For the purpose this book, the priorities of mindfulness include intentional awareness, intentional dignity, intentional reverence, intentional decency, intentional integrity and intentional accountability. Together, these primacies are a purposeful basis for rekindling Yin-based relationship, community and systems ecology. Across a wide range of macro and micro contexts, the themes and imperatives in this paragraph will be emphasised many times throughout the book.

The issues explained in this chapter will come into sharp focus in Chapter 4.

The Final Quarter of the Book

The chapters in the final quarter of the book suggest ways by which individual and collective humans can be less discordant in relationships and ecologies; and less harmful. In particular, if we want things to be different and better, we must be less egoic — less self-serving, less arbitrary and less ignorant — and more aware, sensitive and relational. To this end, the final quarter of the book frequently highlights a range of revolutionary right hemisphere priorities, principles and values through which we can build 'the greater good' for 'the greater majority' — for us humans, for our fellow species, and for the earth.

Actioning Yin-based priorities, principles and values is the key to birthing and nurturing hope and possibility. Ultimately, hope and possibility will emerge as we care for peoples and Country through mindful relationship, citizenship, custodianship, stewardship, leadership, eldership and education. Our ultimate work throughout ensuing years and decades is to consciously prioritise, nurture an evolve a network of values-bases symbiosis and homeostasis among humans, between us humans and our fellow species, between us and our biological ecologies, and between us and the ultimate ecology — Mother Earth. The final quarter of the book explores ways that we can do this.

Country

The term, 'Country', appears throughout this book. My understanding is that for Australian First Peoples, Country is 'Mother'; the giver of life. 'She', Country, is 'the one' who forms us, births us, feeds us, carries us, sustains us, nurtures us, protects us, teaches us, evolves us. Country is Mother's womb, Mother's breasts, Mother's arms, Mother's embrace, Mother's voice, Mother's kiss, Mother's touch, Mother's unconditional love, Mother's sustenance, Mother's protection, Mother's nurturance, guidance and discipline. Keep the symbolism and profundity of this explanation with you as you read this book, especially when you consider issues of degradation of Country and violence against our Mother Earth. This book encourages us to be aware of the sacredness and power of 'the feminine', the Yin, of women and of the Feminine Mother. The pivotal importance of mindful reverence for the iconic, formative feminine, and universal Mother, will be revealed and reinforced as the book unfolds.

Some Questions

Are you up for a very different and blunt take on the best and worst of humankind?

Are you ready for some no-holds-barred observations of historical and contemporary messy, arbitrary, irrational, destructive situations that we humans have made; especially us men?

Are you ready to explore ways for us humans to move beyond the messy situations we have made?

I hope so, because here they come, ready or not.

Imagine and Envisage

Imagine and envisage a great number of us becoming committed to the steady evolution of Yin-based, right hemisphere awareness through eldership, leadership, stewardship, custodianship, citizenship and education.

Imagine if many of us harnesses the revolutionary power of dignifying values, systems-awareness and critical thinking — for ourselves, our families, for our peers, for our local and global communities, for our fellow species, for our ecologies, and for our Mother Earth.

Sit with the possibility of these becoming liberating and empowering ways to be human.

Human Destructiveness

This chapter expresses my strongest motivation for writing. If it were not for the issues summarised in this chapter, there would be no need to write; and no need to ask: 'Can We Do Better'? If it were not for the following web of enormous indignities and extreme irrationality, this book would almost be irrelevant and unnecessary. But, the size, pervasiveness, interconnectedness and historical continuity of the issues listed in this chapter drive me to write. And, I hope these issues will drive you to read, question, and to search for new ways for us humans to move forward with dignity and rationality. The blunt tone of this book matches the horror of the following entangled web of diabolical stuff that we humans have done over and over and over for thousands of years; and continue to do in the 21st century. The following are some of our litany of past, present and ongoing human horrors:

- War (Think of Ukraine, Afghanistan, Yemeni, and Syria in 2020-2022. Be aware that there are more than twenty wars and conflicts across the globe in early 2022)
- Religious, sectarian and ideological violence
- Terrorism
- Genocide and ethnic cleansing
- Decimation of First Peoples, their cultures, families, and the mass murders of many millions of persons
- Exploitation and degradation of the powerless
- Human and environmental harms caused by religious, political and corporate corruption and criminality
- Prolific levels of violence and an array of abuses committed by men on women and children

- Widespread abuse of power that enables a small percentage of mega rich and powerful men to control, exploit and repress the rest of us
- Obscene levels of preventable poverty, starvation and disease in the midst of unprecedented education, scientific discovery, burgeoning knowledge, economic growth and increasing prosperity of corporations, industries and governments
- Rapidly escalating extinction of species
- Exponentially increasing pollution and destruction of ecosystems and environments; and
- Imminent risk of catastrophic and possibly irreparable climate change damage to the entire planet and its atmosphere.

Reread these dot-points, slowly and carefully. Note that war, genocide, murder, violence, abuse, exploitation, degradation and decimation have been inflicted on billions of people throughout the thousands of years of recorded history; and escalated throughout 400 years of colonisation. Despite many recent post WWII social, health and economic improvements, these issues continue to affect billions of disadvantaged and disempowered people in the 21st century. In developing countries, poverty and starvation are by far the most common unconscionable causes of man-made suffering and preventable, premature death. Globally, in the 21st century, poverty and starvation are unacceptable, immoral injustices and extreme indignities. Global statistics of abuse of women and children are indicative of unrelenting toxic masculinity. All these dot-point issues are man-made.

What do we need to do to change in this situation?

What can we do; right now; in the immediate future; and going forward?

Pause, Reflect and Absorb

Don't rush ahead. Take a moment to make a meaningful mental list of the massive and widespread harms, injustices and suffering that arise globally for individuals and communities from each of the following:

War …

Religious, sectarian and ideological violence …

Terrorism …

Genocide and ethnic cleansing …

Decimation of aboriginal peoples and their cultures ...

Degradation and exploitation of the powerless ...

Religious, political and domestic dysfunction, corruption and criminality ...

Violence and abuse committed by men on women and children ...

Widespread abuse of power by mega rich and powerful men ...

Obscene levels of preventable poverty, starvation and disease ...

Escalating decimation of species ...

Escalating pollution, extinctions, and destruction of ecosystems and environments, and ...

Catastrophic damage to the entire planet and it's atmosphere ...

Clarity, sobriety, concern, and a conscious intention to do better can emerge as you and I take the time to be present to each of these enduring and stark realities. We need to become vividly aware of their interconnected and cumulative effects on humankind — past, present and emerging. We need to absorb these realities into our consciousness, and into our conscience.

Man-Made Problems

I hope you are asking: "How can this abhorrent situation continue into the 21st century"?

The short and blunt answer is that Yang-based cultural, religious, political, ideological, industrial, corporate, bureaucratic and military men have carried out the same indignities and irrationalities for thousands of years; and do so in the present century. Family men have abused women and children for thousands of years; and do so in present times. As has been the case for millennia, masculine dysfunctionality continues to impact all peoples, all species, all ecosystems, and the entire planet. Despite many impressive post-WWII social, educational and health improvements, a web of terrible man-made issues remains real and stark for billions. Because of Putin's threat to incite WWIII and to use of nuclear weapons. Because of Xi's subjugation of Hong Kong, his menacing intention to invade Taiwan and his establishment of military outposts in the South Pacific. And, because of a fast-approaching critical mass of damage to the biosphere — the need for stark, sobering, jolting, confronting books such as this one, is urgent.

Compared with men — women have played a tiny role in religious, political, cultural, economic, colonial, industrial and corporate criminality, corruption, violence, exploitation, injustice, and environmental destruction. For the most part, women are not perpetrators of crime, domestic violence and sexual abuse of children. Predominantly, historically and currently, it is powerful, masculine empires, powerful, chauvinistic men and dominant domestic men, who cause large-scale and widespread harm and suffering. For the most part, women are the victims of man-made issues, abuses and harms. More specifically, women are victims of masculine malignance and masculine toxicity; historically, and into the 21st century.

The long and short is that dysfunctional 'Yang-based, left hemisphere masculinity' is the thread that connects all historical, present and emerging issues; including those described in Chapter 4 – 7. Even in the 21st century, we face a wide and interconnected web of harmful left hemisphere, masculine dysfunctionality. We will look at a range of harms, and show how they intersect and connect to form the big picture of the man-made mess that we humans and our fellow species face right now, and into the future. Your job is to do your best to see and understand each part and each thread of the web of our human situation; and to do your best to profile and map the whole, entangle situation; including the negative, systemic roles of misguided masculinity and toxic masculinity.

The next paragraph is long because the situation it profiles and maps is vast. It consists of many interconnected parts.

The 'men' I refer to are the approximately 2% of toxic powerful men who have orchestrated the vast majority of the harms of history. In addition to the 2% of powerful, tyrannical male despots, there are many hundreds of millions of men who have been willing puppets of tyrants and despots; such as the Russian soldiers in Ukraine. Plus, there are countless millions of religious men who have oppressed and harmed innumerable alleged 'wrong-believers' and defenceless women and children. Plus, many millions of military men who have committed murder and atrocities in the name of religion, ideology, nationalism and power. Plus, countless millions of husbands and family men who have perpetrated family violence and sexual abuse on women and children. Plus, many tens of millions of men who may not have been perpetrators, but have condoned or tuned a blind eye to genocide, mass murder, global violence, decimation of First Nation peoples, exploitation of the poor and the powerless, and abuses within families. Plus, many millions of murderous and abusive colonising, empire-building men. Plus, many more millions of colonial and contemporary urban and agricultural men who have contributed to the decimation of lands, waterways, cultures, communities, families and spirituality. There is also an extensive array of several centuries of industrial and corporate men who have pillaged the earth, poisoned the atmosphere, caused the extinction of hundreds of species, and greatly harmed billions of people. These are some of the groups of 'men' to whom I refer throughout this book. This is what I mean when I say that the bulk of family, community, environmental and global issues and harms are 'man-made'.

The sentence after the next one, is also long. It lists and links an array of components of man-made issues. Harms listed in this chapter are perpetrated through a combination of: masculine empire building; masculine exercise of power; masculine aggression; arbitrary, masculine, male-dominated religions; contrived masculine political ideologies; masculine greed; contrived masculine economic models that amass capital and wealth as measures of status and success for a few elite, rich and powerful men; assumed, disrespectful, masculine superiority over women and children; spurious masculine rationalisations for genocide and theft of lands; a litany of heinous masculine crimes against humankind, other species and the earth; concocted masculine justifications for all the abominations mentioned in this paragraph and elsewhere in the book; and, irrational, stubborn, ignorant masculine refusal to be aware, contrite and accountable — historically, presently and into the future. Again, this is what I mean by an extensive and continuous litany of 'man-made' issues and harms. All these examples are the stuff of a global web of historical, contemporary and emerging toxic masculinity. All problematic masculinity arises from the Yang-based left hemisphere.

The following poem summarises and highlights the domains in which we see aberrant masculinity

The Reality of Too Many Malignant Men — Then and Now

For too long, too many egoic, malignant men have plighted peoples, our fellow species and the earth.
Men whose malignance manifests as malevolence and callous disregard for the pain and suffering they cause, enable and ignore.
Not all men, not even the majority of men; but, nevertheless, too many men in so many realms, over too long a time.
Too many malignant agricultural men.
Too many malignant religious men.
Too many malignant cultural men.
Too many malignant aristocratic men.

Too many malignant political men.
Too many malignant rich and powerful men.
Too many malignant ambitious men.
Too many malignant institutional men.
Too many malignant colonial men.
Too many malignant industrial men.
Too many malignant corporate men.
Too many malignant economic men.
Too many malignant business and commerce men.
Too many malignant oligarchical men.
Too many malignant military men.
Too many malignant bureaucratic men.
Too many malignant boss men.
Too many malignant conservative men.
Too many malignant fundamentalist men.
Too many malignant corrupt men.
Too many malignant criminal men.
Too many malignant police men.
Too many malignant husband and partner men.
Too many malignant father men.
Too many malignant sibling men.
Too many malignant boyfriend men.
Reality says that for too long, too many malignant men have done too much harm in too many ways.
Not all men, but too many men, in so many roles, in every place, through millennia of history.

Men and Women

Men — do your best not to be indignant, hurt or defensive about this. The reality is that, to a large extent, history is a record of vast range of dysfunctional and harmful stuff that we men have done for thousands of years. Feel free to be surprised or shocked. Feel free to be concerned and contrite. Feel free to want to help us men to do much better than the abhorrent stuff outlined so far.

Women — try not jump to judgment. Feel free to be very clear and forthright, but also to be empathic, rational and constructive. Now, is not the time to rub salt in the wound, as tempting and as gratifying as that might feel. Now is the time for women to help us men to nurture awareness, honesty, empathy, reverence, dignity, rationality, integrity and accountability — in families, workplaces, and in small and large communities. Now is the time for women to help reform man-made governments, institutions, industries, corporations, structures and policies. Now is the time for women to role model and nurture mindfully dignified and rational relational, communal and ecological leadership; mindfully responsible stewardship; and mindfully enlightened and wise eldership.

Women-Lead Solutions to Man-made Problems

My guess is that women will need to lead and drive much more than fifty percent of the right hemisphere reverence, reason, intelligence, understanding, leadership, education, envisioning and strategizing for the resolution of a vast, entangled web of local and global man-made issues. Healing historical and contemporary wounds of humanity will need to arise from women role models, women visionaries, women educators, women stewards, women custodians, women leaders, and women elders. We men have had at least 3,000 years to generate the terrible web of problems and harms that now beset 21st century humans, other species, and the planet. This century can be the beginning of new ways to create 'female-led' male and female solidarity for local and global common good; and more urgently, for the sustainability of humankind, our fellow species, and the earth. My thesis that women are most likely than men to inspire and lead an unfolding revelation, revolution and evolution of values and rationality.

Men, be aware, honest and humble. Welcome a much larger leadership and eldership by women and the-feminine; and by what I refer to as the 'The Feminine-Mother'.

Women and men, we need to walk together on a purposeful, multi-generational journey to usher-in hundreds of years of healing for people, our fellow species and the earth.

I am very happy to welcome the eldership, mentorship and leadership of 'local and global-feminine exemplars and truth-tellers' as we strive to resolve the mess that we men have made; and continue to make.

It is extremely unlikely that the collective of womanhood will do worse than us blokes. My best judgement tells me that the leadership of 'the collective female mother-aunty-grandmother mind' is a crucial hope for societal evolution. Feminine-mother-aunty-grandmother leadership is likely to be our only hope. The masculine ego is learning and evolving way too slowly from its millennia of countless, entangled and diabolical defaults, mistakes and evils. A mountain of evidence shows that we men have been, and are, extremely slow learners.

41

Imagine and Envisage

Women and men, imagine and envisage a revolution of new and constructive women-lead conversations and engagement in all domains, and all over the globe. Imagine and envisage a female-led female-male collaboration to nurture and build a future founded on and guided by primal right hemisphere values such reverence, sensitivity, decency, dignity, rationality, integrity and accountability.

Men readers, how are you feeling?

Women readers, how are you feeling?

Let's be open to what might help us men do better than the issues canvassed in this chapter; and throughout Can We Do Better.

Too Many and Too Few

The purpose of this chapter is to create awareness of two contrasting roles in relation to harm and suffering. Broadly, in the first group, there are those who try to prevent and remediate harm and suffering. The second group includes three subgroups: — 1. Those who wantonly cause harm; 2. Those of enable those who actively cause harm; and 3. Those who passively watch harm being done. A tiny proportion of us wantonly do harm. A significant proportion of us are enablers of harm. While a huge proportion of us are watchers of harm.

Too Few Who Help and Too Many Who Harm

It is important to say that many people, including many men, are decent, integrous, rational, kind and responsible. But, clearly, too many chauvinistic men, too many toxic masculine religious and political groups, too many male-dominated corporations, too many masculinised industries, too many man-controlled institutions, and too many toxic populist and theocratic states — are not decent, integrous, kind and responsible. Too few mostly-male individuals, groups, institutions and states are held accountable for the terrible harms they cause, inflict and enable.

Too many of us men and women are too unaware, too cynical, too indifferent, too complaisant, and/or too ignorant about issues, injustices, harms and suffering. Too many enablers are sucked in by inane, misguided and dishonest dogma, propaganda, spin and conspiracies. Too many of us are caught up in new-age junk-science and pop-psychology jibber-jabber to be factually informed and effective citizens. Too many people, mostly elitist men in high places, are too individualistic, too self-serving, too ambitious, too greedy, too profit-driven, too arrogant, too prideful, and too power-obsessed to be aware of or care about suffering and harm. That's quite a web of egoic defaults, drivers and enablers of harm. The paragraph profiles a substantial web of constraints to decency, dignity, integrity, rationality, factuality and accountability. In today's egoic world, it is quite difficult for values and rationality to gain prominence and traction.

Clearly, there is a web of mostly masculine left hemisphere drivers that facilitate and enable our history of indignities, harms and destruction. Too few men with power and influence have been, and are, sufficiently aware and motivated to resolve the drivers of harm and suffering. Too few powerful, elite men are sufficiently aware, concerned, caring, kind and generous. Too few men think compassionately, relationally, communally and ecologically. Too few brave and compassionate men actively prevent and remediate terrible harms to peoples, our fellow species and environments. Too few toxic men are held to account for the diabolical stuff they do and justify. Too few are held to account for decent, integrous actions that they fail to take. Too few powerful, influential men systematically and strategically prioritise and nurture dignity, integrity, community and ecology for the common good of the greater global community; and for the care of globe itself.

Unhelpful and harmful masculine defaults and dispositions and attitudes are too common and have been too influential throughout history. An overlapping collection of adverse masculine attitudes and actions, and indifferent onlooker inactions, weave a web of suffering that reaches every part of the earth. These manifest as callous, dishonest denial of structural and systemic disadvantage, injustice, harm and suffering.

Too many of us are under-informed, mis-informed, ill-informed, unconcerned and unmotivated to try to reduce harm and suffering. It's true that only a tiny percentage of toxic people wantonly harm others, our fellow species and the planet. But it's also true that only a tiny percentage of Good Samaritans systematically and strategically help those who suffer because they are disadvantaged, maligned, exploited and harmed. Sadly, regretfully, it's true that the vast majority of us watch in comfort without helping. Too many of us watch with our egoic preconceptions, biases, opinions, beliefs, prejudices and judgements. Too many of us watch with ignorance, cynicism and apathy. Too many of us too easily and too dismissively blame the victims of harm.

Simple but Powerful Values of Good Samaritans

Simple but powerful right hemisphere Good Samaritan values, such as decency and integrity, oblige you and me to be unflinchingly aware of the conglomeration of harms and suffering summarised in the previous chapter.

Decency and integrity oblige you and me to join and swell the ranks of 'the concerned and committed few' who are aware of the web of stuff that drives indignity and injustice. Decency and integrity behove you and me not to rationalise, downplay or deny the terrible harms that humans do to each other. Decency and integrity also oblige you and me not to down play, deny, justify or ignore the diabolical harms that we humans inflict on our fellow species and the planet. Decency and integrity behove us to strive to minimise all forms of suffering, harm and destruction.

Good Samaritan decency and integrity exhort us — not to be complicit, complacent or cynical; not to make excuses; not to blame; not to confabulate; not to rationalise; and not to downplay, justify or lie about the issues in the previous chapter. There is no place for lying, ignoring, pretending, minimising, defending or deflecting responsibility. Responsibility is yours and mine; equally and fully. The minority of Good Samaritans needs to become the majority of us. Responsibility and decency and integrity calls 7.9 billion of us to consciously and purposefully think, speak and act with reverence, grace, courage, integrity, rationality, kindness and generosity.

The world would be a safer, kinder, more honest and decent place if dignity, rationality, integrity and compassion motivate, activate and guide you and me and a majority of us; not just the gallant, values-impelled few. Ill-informed, biased and judgemental opinions, disparaging attitudes, useless fantastical religious and new-age beliefs, and dishonest, misleading conspiracies have had their day. It's time to prioritise, nurture and implement decent, integrous, rational, dignifying values to a place of prominence and normality. It's time for such values to become the 'new normal'. It's time dignifying values and rationality to become the everyday guides and benchmarks of the many; for the vast majority; for a critical mass of 'us'. It's time for an overwhelming majority of us to gravitate to the kinder and more rational and integrous side of history.

Significantly, it is time for us men to welcome many more women and First Peoples to roles in strategic relational, communal and ecological leadership. It's time for us men to embrace and learn from right hemisphere feminine and First People values, rationality, wisdom, priorities and strengths. It's time to welcome back and embrace feminine and First People mothering, custodianship and eldership.

Imagine and Envisage

Imagine and envisage the revolutionary impact from the collective effort of a swelling number of mindful people who are highly motivated and guided by a passion for reverence, decency, integrity, rationality and compassion.

Imagine and envisage the potential impact if these four values were embraced, prioritised and applied by billions of us. These are the values of revelation, revolution and evolution.

The Workbook

Remember, the Companion Workbook that I mentioned at the beginning of this book. It will help you clarify how you might join the ranks of decent, informed, integrous and constructive Good Samaritans.

What are your thoughts for now?

How might we men join the ranks of Good Samaritans?

Patriarchy and Chauvinism — The Domains of Male Dominance

Men, take several long, slow breaths; and continue to be aware, honest and non-defensive. We are about to shift-up a gear in terms of problem definition.

There is no place in the 21st century for the harms and indignities of left hemisphere patriarchy, misogyny and chauvinism. These have caused thousands of years of harm, most particularly for the poor, women and children; especially in less developed countries and colonised countries. Patriarchy and chauvinism are obsolete, degrading and restrictive attitudes of bygone centuries. Patriarchy, misogyny and chauvinism are utterly devoid of dignity and decency. In the 21st century, they are utterly anachronistic.

There is no place in an educated, just and decent world for the indignities of self-serving, patriarch, chauvinistic capitalist, populist and communist politics. There is no place for self-serving masculine religion; no place for self-serving masculine corporatism; and no place for self-serving masculine nationalism and empire building. There is no place for the obscene, individualist greed and material lust of a few mostly male billionaires who possess, monopolise and control the bulk of prosperity of the planet. There is no place for the corruption and criminal power machinations of a few mostly male oligarchs. In all these, there is no place for whatever macho stuff obliterates decency, dignity, integrity, fairness and compassion.

There is no place for the indignities of man-made marketing deceptions, fraudulence, and intentional exploitations that benefit a few corrupt, utterly self-seeking, wealth obsessed and power-driven men. The is no place for the utterly obscene indignity of masculine political and corporate narcissism and sociopathy. In politics and industry, there is no place for cunning, deceptive man-made spin and stage-managed marketing and public relations. These are mostly contrived by clever men for the benefit of a few rich and powerful men. Man-made deception and spin obliterate values such as decency, dignity and rationality. They certainly obliterate integrity and accountability.

There is no place for environmental destruction by highly masculinised industries and male-dominated corporations. There is no place for the divisive, destructive egoic pride and prejudice of capitalist and communist macho, tribal nationalism. There is no place for toxic exceptionalistic macho attitudes that benefit a few self-seeking, self-aggrandising, muscular states which bully and manipulate powerless countries and peoples. The 21st century is the time to end mindless, outdated, destructive masculine sectarianism, racism and sexism. This century is the time for business, industry, politics and religion to move to the integrous and decent side of a new history that is defined by the prioritisation of dignity and reason to facilitate the greatest good for the greatest number.

Enough Glib Masculine Stuff

There is no place for mostly man-made glib, ill-informed new-age presumption, pretention and pontification. Now is not the time for widespread male owned, male controlled mainstream and social media monoliths which proliferate profit-driven superficiality and cosmetic, new-age vanity. With the need for accurately informed citizenry intelligence and rationality, this is not a time for more and more man-made religious and new-age myths, fantasies and fads. Now is not a time for more and more baseless, fanciful, self-serving, arbitrary man-made religious and new-age stories. This is not the time for more and more whimsical, fantastical, hip new-age ignorance in the guise of spirituality. Now is not the time for spurious, ignorant, mostly man-made conspiracy theories. Now is not the era for us to contribute to fanciful and wilful ignorance and intentional, exploitative deception. All these male proclivities greatly erode values, critical thinking and accountability.

Now is the Time to Nurture Decency, Integrity, Rationality and Accountability

The 21st century is the time for men and women to nurture right hemisphere, Yin-based values. Now is time for rational, integrous women and men to nurture accountable, factual, data-based, logical and dignified strategic leadership, stewardship, citizenship and genuine service to community. Now is the time for conservative religion and new-age modernism to move to the integrous, factual

48

and rational side of history. Note the role of purposeful values and rationality to nurture decency and reality.

It is time for us men to be aware and informed. It is time for us blokes to exemplify conscious, intentional sensitivity; and to act with intelligent, reasoned engagement in all local and global relationships, roles and expressions of community and governance. Note and sit-with the groupings of words in the previous sentences. Crucially, it is time for the majority of us men, especially dominant institutional men, to relate to other species and the earth with accurate scientific knowledge, sober awareness, reverence, kindness, integrity and unswerving accountability. Now is the time for right hemisphere values, critical thinking and accountability to define our emerging masculinity: and our evolving humanity.

Now is the time for you and me to nurture dignity and reason wherever we can, with whomever we encounter, in whichever domains, contexts, and spheres of influence we find ourselves.

From my perspective, these priorities seem highly self-evident. Is it time for all of us, especially for us men, to acknowledge them, embrace them, nurture them, and live them?

Imagine and Envisage

Imagine and envisage us men, especially powerful men, humbly and courageously moving away from the self-serving arbitrariness of patriarchy, misogyny and chauvinism. Imagine men and women committing to build a right hemisphere ethos of accountability to serve the greater good for the greatest number. These values and aspirations could revolutionise the human world and the earth.

Within your spheres of influence, within your relationships and roles — how might you help men do better than patriarchy and chauvinism?

Enough Redundant Man-Made Dogma

To a great extent, our masculine religious dogmas and masculine political ideologies are outmoded, problematic leftovers from our less educated, process-poor, less just, less objective, male-dominated and scientifically uninformed past. Increasingly redundant religious and political models are failing us because they have not evolved to become educated, kind, process-disciplined, rational, factual and accountable. The reality is that, in too many cases, and too often, religious political left hemisphere models greatly diminish process discipline, legitimate, credible evidence and critical thinking. And, significantly, too commonly, dead-horse political models are contrary to decency, compassion, integrity, justice and accountability. The rising tides of political and religious populism, conspiracy cultism and theocratic despotism is evidence of all these issues.

Dignified, integrous, rational values, principles and priorities are what is needed right now in human governance, institutions and communities. Unflinching, unfiltered accountability is what is needed all over the globe, in every institution, every government and every organisation; right now, and moving forward. A prioritised network of empowering and integrous values, principles, processes and priorities is what is needed to guide and nurture societal evolution; so that we can base and guide our existence on the primacies of dignity and rationality.

At all levels and in all domains, now is the time for the majority of us, men and women, to let go of bygone, arbitrary, man-made, adversarial, chest-beating democratic models and processes. Now is the time to let go of arbitrary and dysfunctional political and religious tribalism and exceptionalism. Now is the time to let go of anachronistic nationalist imperialism, empire building, colonialism, power-obsessiveness, resource-devouring industrialism, all forms of fundamentalism, greed and material opportunism. They are the redundant and

50

harmful stuff of failed and failing, harmful and destructive masculine institutional dogmas, models and structures.

Now is the time to evolve public and private sector governance toward right hemisphere models that are guided by evidenced-based critical thinking and collaborative values-based structures and processes that prioritise rationality, integrity, accountability, dignity, fairness, equity and justice; especially for billions who are culturally, religiously and politically oppressed, disadvantaged and disempowered.

From Now On

Therefore, to these ends, from now on …

1. This book will identify and challenge many anachronistic, dysfunctional and destructive sacred cows that diminish dignity and rationality.
2. It will call-out cultural, religious, political and corporate abuses of power and drivers of injustice.
3. This book will expose entrenched micro and macro egoic rationalisations and ignorant justifications for absence of decency, rationality, integrity and accountability.
4. It will promote and reinforce Yin-based critical thinking, strategic collaboration and a dignifying network of values, principles and priorities.
5. This book, and the accompanying Workbook, will often ask you to pause and consider many questions that may help you reflect, reappraise, and choose a conscious, intentional, strategic direction toward rational and dignified priorities and aspirations.
6. Can We Do Better, and its Companion Workbook, will often ask you to ask yourself: "In what ways can I stop participating in, and enabling, harmful, redundant models, structures and processes. How can I become a steward and leader of our human evolution toward dignity and rationality"?

Keep your eye in dignity and rationality. They are the aspirations, means and ends of this book. Dignity and rationality will be emphasised many times — from chapter to chapter, from theme to theme, from reality-check to reality-check, from aspiration to aspiration.

Before We Forge Ahead

Before we forge ahead, and forge we shall, the next four short chapters are intended to help you get ready to do a lot more heavy-lifting in terms of exploring, mapping and challenging a web of enmeshed macro and micro issues that drive human dysfunctionality and harm. As just said, necessarily, and unapologetically, this book asks readers to do plenty of work in terms of:

- Reflection, self-honesty, re-evaluation and attitude-adjustment
- Reconsideration and reprioritisation of right hemisphere values, principles, intentions, commitments and purpose
- Critiquing personal and institutional assumptions, beliefs and opinions
- Embracing rational processes, including critical thinking; and
- Opening your mind to dignifying ways to engage with family, friends, workmates, community, our fellow species and the earth.

That's a lot of heavy lifting. So, let's slow down for several softer chapters that might help you prepare to do the penetrating and challenging work that is ahead.

Imagine and Envisage

In the meantime, imagine and envisage yourself being a mindful and devoted exemplar and advocate of dignity and critical thinking.

Imagine and envisage what depth and strength of values, rationality and accountability might be actioned in our personal lives, in our relationships, in our citizenship, and in our community leadership and eldership.

Seriously, pause, imagine and envisage a revolution of these priorities, possibilities and aspirations.

What thoughts are coming to mind? Feel free to make some notes.

Slow Down

Hope

You and I don't need to be rescued from the reality of the confronting issues listed in Chapters 4 – 7; nor from the web of constraints described in so far. We need to see them as they are. We need to see the interwoven historical and contemporary threads that form the mind and behavioural patterns of humankind. Hope exists in lucidly and unflinchingly acknowledging our web of dysfunctionality — as persons; as cultural, religious and political groups; and as a species.

Hope for dignity and rationality exists in clearly and non-defensively understanding and mapping the drivers of the human issues mentioned so far. Hope for dignity and reason exists in being grounded in factual reality and critical thinking. Hope also arises from being open to the possibility that we humans may evolve toward liberating and empowering rational and decent priorities and processes. Hope exists in nurturing and building rational, values-based alternatives to arbitrariness, irrationality, indecency, lack of integrity, and resistance to accountability. Hope exists in processes and values that give us the potential to consciously, purposefully evolve us toward empowerment and justice for the vast majority. Hope exists in encouraging a critical mass of humankind to opt for carefully chosen priorities, principles, processes and values.

The previous two paragraphs capture the intention of this book, to nurture hope by building awareness of current realities, and by embracing mindful choices and processes that facilitate the evolution of dignity and rationality within the mind of humankind.

Questions to Stimulate Clarity

Throughout this book, we will consider many penetrating and constructive questions. Read the following questions carefully and openly. Don't rush. They are designed to stimulate critical thinking about human dynamics that we need to consider in order to build hope that we humans can be motivated and guided by dignifying values and lucid rationality.

Is there a process we can use to help us become clear-minded so that we can purposefully embrace dignifying values, critical thinking and factual evidence?

How do we disentangle ourselves from — our egoic, worldly web of power games, drivenness, insecurity, fear, ignorance, cynicism, indifference, ambition, greed, materialism, consumerism, internet fantasies, social media superficiality, cosmetic vanity and conspiratorial lies?

How can we shift our focus to dignity and rationality in a world where these qualities and priorities are the exception, and not the norm?

In your life and my life, how do we prioritise and nurture values and rationality so they become 'our shared, conscious intentional normal'?

How do we become consistent, congruent, constructive and strategic in a world that is largely governed by arbitrariness, power-games, bias, fantasy, drama, ill-informed opinions, judgementalism, self-servingness, easy gratification, quick-fix, narrow-sightedness and short-sightedness?

How do we become factually informed, so that we can become less a misguided by fear and ignorance?

How can we identify and apply rational, values-based solutions to human and environmental problems?

How do you and I peacefully and purposefully let go of assumptions, pretentions, dogma, fantasies, opinions and beliefs so that we can embrace a network of rational, dignifying values, principles, processes and practices?

How do you and I become peacefully and reverently sensitive and integrous in an egoic world that conditions us to put 'me first'; in a world that conditions us to do whatever it takes go get what 'I want', what I 'must have'; by whatever 'arbitrary rules and beliefs I make up'; and by whatever 'means I leverage, assert and justify me to do what want; without accountability'?

How can you and I become peacefully integrous, rational and factually informed in a world in which you and I are bombarded by so much baseless, fantastical hubris on one side, disinterested indifference on another side, conspiracy madness on a third side, and cynical defeatism on the fourth side?

How do we become peacefully and factually informed at a time in history when we are surrounded by so many frenetic, mind-numbing, mind-dumbing crazes and fads; in an era when we are immersed in so much mindless junk-science, pop-psychology, populist politics, conspiracy madness, fake news and 'big lies'?

Crucially, how do we discern and experience the stark differences between 'mindfulness and 'mindlessness'?

Feel free to reread whichever questions have resonated for you.

Imagine and Envisage

Imagine and envisage yourself being calm and clear about your carefully, rationally and sensitively chosen values, priorities, intentions and accountabilities.

Feel free to pause and make some notes.

Where to Look for Peace, Clarity and Direction — and Where Not to Look

As emphasised before, there is very little in the man-made world of left-hemisphere religion, politics, material consumerism, new-age pop-culture, and hip social media trends that help us to slow down, to be calm, to be self-aware, to be sensitive, to be factual, to be discerningly curious, to be wisely perceptive, and to envisage a fresh and robust perspective. Extremely importantly, there is minimal encouragement for us to be mindful and process disciplined. Mindfully disciplined analytical processes are the royal road to factual reality and empowering values. Together, mindful mental discipline and mindfully chosen values, are what we need to achieve integrous and competent personhood, citizenship, stewardship and leadership.

So, how do we buck these left hemisphere trends and nurture mindful dignity and mindful rationality?

There is so much that rewards us for being presumptive, pretentious, opinionated, pontifical, dogmatic, fanciful, faddish, hip, shallow, vain, biased, cynical, indifferent, material, self-seeking, consumptive, ambitious, manipulative, frenetic and forceful. Each element in the enmeshed web of man-made elements in the previous sentence makes it very difficult for us to be mindfully and meaningfully aware of the right hemisphere principles and processes that nurture dignity and reason. There is much that prevents us from being informed educated thinkers, process oriented, rational, constructive, integrous and accountable. And, there is much that encourages and rewards egoic superficiality, ignorance, self-centredness and self-justification.

To whom, what and where do we look for strategies to nurture Yin-based conscious awareness, peaceful open sensitivity, process discipline, and robust unflinching accountability for what we think, prioritise, value, say and do?

To whom, what and where do we look for ways to nurture the processes of critical thinking and the prioritisation of dignifying values?

Where can you and I find disciplined, congruent, credible, dignified, rational role models in the midst of so many religious shamsters, new-age faddists, political pretenders, and greedy power-obsessed political and corporate empire-builders?

An Example of the Use of an Internal Locus of Values and Clarity

With awareness of the constraints just mentioned, as a counsellor and mentor, my focus has been to help clients become peaceful, clear, ethical, integrous, purposeful and accountable. My intention is to help people use rational processes and dignifying values to find calming and clarifying perspectives, factual understandings and sensitive, responsible life-management strategies. I help clients identify perceive and understand 'what is actually happening' within them, to them and around them. My aim is help clients to keep difficulties in perspective and proportion, and to discern how to effectively respond to a people, situations, issues, problems and opportunities. I also help clients to be aware of and accountable for their contributions to issues. All in all, by these aims, I try to help clients be more mindful — more aware, sentient and informed.

One aspect of counselling and mentoring is to help clients to not to be caught up in unpeaceful speculation, imaginary wishful thinking, confabulated stories, externalised blame, self-protective projections and dodgy justifications. From an orientation of personal responsibility and factual reality, the next step is to help clients identify relevant and effective guiding values, priorities and processes. Clients are guided to approach issues from a base of factual reality, personal responsibility, carefully-chosen values, considered priorities, and sound analytical processes. Clients are guided to be calm, grounded, competent and strategic in their formulation of personal and relational hopes, intentions, goals, processes, steps forward and solutions to problems. Crucially, from this foundation of mindful cognizance, intention and purpose, clients feel more aware, more able to respond, and better able to be strategic, and more accountable for what they prioritise, think, say and do.

Then, from a mindful blend of facts, calmness and values-guided personal, relational and situational insight, clients can formulate ways to define and manage issues. Equipped in this way, they can begin to discern a way forward and a way through issues and constraints. I conceptualise and encapsulate this blend of capacities as 'an internal consciousness of awareness, values, reason and accountability'. Very often, from a conscious, intentional orientation, clients become calmer, more aware, clearer about guiding values, more rational, more accountable, and more purposeful in their priorities, choices, decisions and actions. They become better at identifying and prioritising values, better at critical thinking, and better at applying personal and relational principles and processes. Clients learn to harness their internal locus of capacities to become increasingly peaceful, clear-minded, reflective, sensitive, empathic, appropriate, responsible, responsive, effective and accountable. They become less defensive, less projective, less blaming and less self-justifying. These are an extremely useful blend of guiding principles, attributes and capacities.

An Internal Locus

As said before, an internal locus is an abiding, right hemisphere mental orientation of relative calm, values, facts, critical thinking, perspective, dignifying priorities and integrous actions.

An internal locus is extremely unlikely to come from religion, culture, or new-age fads. An internal orientation is a deeply personal awareness of carefully identified facts and mindfully chosen values, priorities, intentions and purpose. An internal locus is psychological place of calm, insight and strategizing. It is a deeply felt sense of personal autonomy, a strong clarity of intention, and a strong sense of freedom to choose and to act appropriately and strategically. An internal locus is a fact-based, peace-based, values-based and reason-based orientation that enables you and I to be calmly — informed, rational, dignified, purposeful and maximally effective with respect to issues, challenges, hopes and aspirations.

From this foundation, you and I can intelligently and purposefully choose how we will turn up in relationships, community, roles, endeavours and problems — as family members, friends, workers, community members, citizens, stewards, custodians and leaders

From an internal locus of peace, values and critical thinking, you and I can discern what we will say and do; and, crucially, what we won't say and do. With values-based clarity and a factual, rational perspective, we can discern and articulate why we choose to be the persons we prefer to be; why we think, speak and act as we do.

When you and I have the 'what, how and why' of our internal locus of values and rationality, we are equipped to be the persons we aspire and choose to be; we are equipped to apply facts, values and peaceful rationality as our guiding standards and tools. With these assets, you and I are equipped to fulfil our responsibilities, to achieve our goals, and to meet our integrity-based, values-determined accountabilities. With consciously determined internal clarity and values, you and I can discern and choose our next step; from situation to situation; in all situations.

Facts, mindfully chosen values and peaceful, rational thinking processes equip you to 'discern and determine' what you will say and do next, and next, and next; and so on, as you negotiate relationships and life experiences; and as you progress toward your chosen priorities, aspirations and goals. From and internal locus of values, logic, priorities, purpose and intentions, you can discern and choose what to say and do in each of your conversations, relationships, roles and contexts — over ensuing days, years and decades; for the remainder of your life.

Helping clients, colleagues and associates to embrace this internal process is the core of the work I have done for decades. Encouraging readers to embrace this process is the core intention of this book. Helping you to discern, choose and evolve an internal reference of facts, rational and dignifying values, priorities, processes and intentions is the purpose of this book.

Therefore, as you read, be open to discern, choose, embrace and build a mindful internal priority for factual awareness, critical thinking, sensitivity, rationality, clear intentions and strategic direction. Personally, my chosen priority and intention is be peaceful and confident, dignified and decent, gracious and kind, factual and reasoned, transparent and accountable, open and available, capable and competent. Note the heart-head-hand balance of this blend of chosen and desired inner capacities.

Importantly, note that I have not asked to choose beliefs. Beliefs are subjective and arbitrary. Beliefs are often divisive. There is much more potential common ground in values such as decency, integrity and behavioural accountability, than there is in arbitrary religious and new-age beliefs.

The Next Few Chapters

The next few chapters are about Breath Meditation. Their purpose is to explain how Breath Meditation can help you 'become calmly and purposefully clear'. Breath Meditation can help you discern, embrace and apply an internal reference of values, insight, perspective, priority and accountability. In case you missed what I just wrote, Breath Meditation can help you become peacefully and mindfully clear about your internal locus of values, issues, priorities, processes, accountabilities, intentions and chosen directions. Breath Meditation can help you imbue a mindful internal locus of freedom and guiding wisdom.

Imagine and Envisage

Imagine and envisage yourself becoming peacefully and rationally insightful.

Imagine yourself becoming consciously aware of your carefully chosen priorities, principles and values in relation to issues and hopes.

Imagine and envisage these capacities as your carefully chosen inner auto pilot in relationships, roles, responsibilities, aspirations, endeavours, stewardship and leadership.

The Workbook can help you build and use your own personal autopilot of rational, values-based capacities.

A Way to Slow Down and Become More Peacefully Aware

It is possible that you and I can imbue the depth of mindful awareness that is flagged in previous chapters. But we have to find a way to pause our default masculine, left hemisphere presumptions, biases, opinions, beliefs and judgements. We need a way to become openminded. We need a way to become sensitised to facts, reason and dignifying values. We need a conscious, intentional, practical process that will help us recalibrate and reset our default mental processes so that we can move beyond the typical stuff of ego and ignorance.

Agreeing and knowing are not sufficient to move beyond ego and ignorance; to recalibrate and reset our openness to facts; to mindfully choose our values; and to commit to disciplined analytical processes. Desire, words and hubris are not enough. We need a process that can help us escape the world's gravity, to bypass ego, to allow ignorance to dissolve. Put simply, you and I need to still our mind so that it can reset and start afresh.

We Need a Helpful Process

To recalibrate our values, priorities and aspirations, we need a practical process that will help us slow down mentally and become emotionally peaceful. We need a process that will help us pause our frenetic stream of same-old, same-old modern egoic thoughts and emotions.

You and I need intentional process that, over time, can help us 'listen deep and long'. We need a manageable and practical mindfulness process that can increase the sensitivity, scope and sophistication of our understanding of issues and possibilities in relationships, communities and environments. We need a practical process that can create and sustain strategic awareness, sensitivity, discernment, direction and momentum.

That is to say, we need mindfulness process that can help us finetune the headspace of how we turn up in all relationships, roles, domains, situations and responsibilities. We need a mindfulness process that can enable us to finetune our thinking, speaking and actions so we can nurture and marry rationality and dignity within ourselves, and within our participation in family, friendships, peer groups, workplaces, communities, institutions and governments.

Note the right hemisphere term, nurture, which means, to help individuals, groups and communities to grow, to develop, to mature and evolve toward their fullest, best and most constructive capacities. Nurturing is about helping ourselves and others fulfil our potential and become the best we can be, and do the best we can do.

Soon, I will explain and recommend a practical mindfulness process that can help us become calm, and can enable us to nurture fact-based, rational, strategic ecological systems thinking. Soon, I will explain a process that can help us reorient our mind toward personal insight, self-honesty, relational awareness, situational sensitivity, compassion, factual reality, responsibility and accountability.

These are easy capacity and priorities to skip-over. Pause for little while; and reread the previous paragraph. The mindful sentience, presence, grace and clarity just mentioned are very rare, precious and powerful. Sit with this awareness for a minute or so.

The practical mindfulness process that will soon be described is a simple, manageable and effective way to slow down our thinking so that, ultimately, we can envisage and contribute to rational, values-based priorities. Over time, with practice, this process can help us become more calm and clearer about huge priorities, such as justice and healing for people, our fellow species and the earth. This simple mindfulness process can help us see and release our potential, and to contribute mindfully to the greater good.

Even if you and I become a little more factual, aware, sensitive, discerning, responsive and accountable, it would be sufficient to help us become more constructive as relationally-based family members, peers, workers, citizens and leaders. Even a small increase in insight has the potential to revolutionise your life, and my life. A simple, manageable everyday mindfulness process is sufficient to help us achieve this constructive network of possibilities and aspirations.

The next two chapters expand on the personal and societal big-picture benefits of Breath Meditation; which is the mindfulness process that is recommended in this book.

Personal Benefits of Breath Meditation

You and I can enjoy delightful, every-day, personal benefits from practising the mindfulness of Breath Meditation. One benefit is being more able to tune into to the beauty and joy of our surroundings and everyday experiences. For example, feeling and enjoying sensations such as the soothing warmth of the sun and the refreshing coolness of a breeze. These right hemisphere 'atunements' are signs of being mindfully sensitive, perceptive, present and aware. Being awed by the beauty of sunrise or sunset, and the rising moon, are also signs and examples of mindful presence and sensitivity to delightful everyday experiences.

As we practice being silent and still, gradually, incrementally, we find ourselves tuning into natural everyday beauty around us. As we begin to notice the wonder and joy of physical sensations, sunsets, breezes and flowers, it is natural and automatic to take pleasure in then them, to feel grateful for them, to feel enchanted and enriched by them. It's natural to be at peace and joyful in their presence. This is mindfulness, and the fruit of mindfulness.

A Computer Analogy

To use a computer analogy, pausing to observe our breath can help the brain discern and prioritise important information, and to delete cluttering 'junk information'; or, to delete 'mental junk files'; such as junk-ideas that we absorb from peer groups, social media, religion, politics and new-age fads. Breath Meditation can help become more discerning and to 'delete' unwanted, unhelpful and messy mental files which contain unhelpful and hindering misinformation and negative emotions. In summary, meditative silence and stillness can help us pause, defrag, reset, start again, run more smoothly, process more effectively, and be wiser, more discerning and more constructive. All this is mindfulness, and the fruit of mindfulness.

We can 'reset' and 'process' more effectively by practising Breath Meditation, over and over; as often as we need to. There is no limit to the number of times and contexts in which we practice Breath Meditation. When we slow down and reduce egoic mental processes, can we delete confounding and cluttering ideas. That is, we can 'defrag' messy mental files, and reset our brain. Through this, we give ourselves the potential to be more personally, relationally and ecologically aware, appropriate, responsive and responsible. Increased reason and dignity are natural benefits of deleting and decluttering mental files, and resetting our mind to be more aware, sensitive, relational, communal, ecological and strategic. These extraordinary capacities are mindfulness, and the fruit of mindfulness.

The benefits of being personally, relationally and socially decluttered include being less self-absorbed, less consumed by thoughts of trivial first-world issues, less insecure, less under the weight of the cares of the material world, less judgemental, and less worried about our self-obsessed, individualistic past and future. Increased peaceful awareness and sensitivity can help us 'not to sweat the small stuff', and to clarify, prioritise and manage 'the big stuff'. All this is typical of the outcomes and benefits of the calm and clarity that can arise from faithful practise of Breath Meditation. Again, this is mindfulness, and the fruit of mindfulness.

Demands, stress, insecurities, trivial worries, individual ambitions, power machinations and conflict are typical egoic stuff that drive the incessant thinking of our modern, me-oriented, material, ambitious, self-leveraging, worldly mind. Being present to our breathing can help us reduce the constancy of 21st century mental chatter, obsessions, dramas and pressures. When less distracted by the noise and chatter of mental junk and 'small stuff', we can focus on important big picture issues; such as — contributing to peace, reason, dignity and strategic priorities in family; contributing to social justice in community; and caring for the environment. Personal, relational, societal and environmental dignity and rationality can arise from calming, clarifying quietening processes; such as Breath Meditation. In all this, Breath Mediation increases our mindfulness, and helps produce the fruit of mindfulness.

The Benefits of Attentive Listening

When mindful, we can talk less, have fewer opinions, assert fewer beliefs and express fewer judgements. When mindfully peaceful, we can listen more attentively. When we listen attentively, we can be more sensitive to the subtleties and intricacies of people, relationships and situations. By listening, we can be more discerning and sensitive in terms of what to say and do, and what not to say and do. When we listen attentively to others and are more attentive to situations, we can be less self-servingly arbitrary and less relationally clumsy. These are the positive outcomes of mindfulness; the potential benefits of Breath Meditation.

When mentally calm and attentive, we can be more peacefully openminded, and be more open to the challenges and priorities of big-picture facts and evidence. Through attentive listening, we can be less subjectively narrow minded and prejudiced. We can become more factually informed and more reasoned. Thereby, we can be less egoic, less insensitive, less ignorant and more constructive as family members, friends, citizens, stewards, leaders and elders. These are more examples of mindfulness, and the fruit of the mindfulness that can arise from Breath Meditation.

Through right hemisphere mindfulness of attentive, reflective listening, we can be more peaceful; and thereby, be more gracious, more dignified and more open and able to accept and deal with complexity, diversity and difference. When we listen peacefully and receptively, we position ourselves to be less judgemental and be more compassionate, kinder, more generous and inclusive. This is mindfulness-in-action. These values-in-action are the fruit of the mindfulness that can arise from Breath Meditation.

The mindfulness of Breath Meditation can help us talk less and less stridently; thereby, to be more humbly, humbly, gently and constructively available to consider, understand and respect perspectives, nuances, sensitivities, difference and complexity. Peaceful, attentive, reflective listening is relational dignity and sophisticated reason-in-action. Attentive listening, non-judgementalism and open-minded availability are mindfulness, and the fruit of mindfulness; all of which can arise from Breath Meditation. This paragraph is worth a reread.

The Benefits of Being Mindfully Present

When mentally peaceful and open minded we have the potential to be more present, less expectant, less forceful, less defensive and less self-justifying. When less defensive and less self-justifying, we have greater capacity to be reflective, self-aware, self-honest, relationally attuned, and socially accountable.

When less opinionated, demanding and expectant, we can perceive unexpected facts and unforeseen possibilities, alternatives, options, opportunities and serendipity. When peacefully unopinionated, we have the potential to be more respectfully present; thereby, to be more graciously accepting of diversity and difference in family, friends, workmates and strangers. When more present, we are more able to listen with grace; and thereby, with less presumption, pretention and pontification. Again, all this is mindful, relational right hemisphere respect and dignity in action. Mindfulness is also 'reason in action'. Significantly, presence is inherent in mindful wisdom, enlightenment and responsibility. Presence is a gift of mindfulness. It is the fruit of the mindfulness that can arise from Breath Meditation.

Consider the possibility of progressing beyond the same-old noisy, busy, harried, arbitrary, subjective, shallow, opinionated, judgemental, conflictual me-focussed, left hemisphere mental chatter. As peace, presence and attentive listening arise from within — dignity, grace and rationality can become who you are and what you do; within your relationships, roles and endeavours. Breath Meditation can help us become persons with an internal locus of dignity, grace and reason. These are extremely beneficial fruits of mindfulness.

Mental Voices to Tune Into

Remember, this book recommends that you and I tune into right hemisphere mental voices of grace, awareness, insight, sensitivity, decency and integrity. It recommends that we feel what it is like to be peacefully reflective; to feel what it's like to be peacefully open; to feel what it's like to 'be graciously slow-to-opinion'; to feel what it's like to have a minimum of opinionated beliefs; to feel peaceful humility; to feel what it's like to intentionally reverence and dignify ourselves, others, our fellow species and the earth.

This book recommends that we feel the freedom and integrity of being peacefully open and accountable to critical thinking, logic, facts and data. What a telling priority — to be open and accountable to critical thinking, logic, facts and data. Imagine being more able to peacefully accept what data says, and to embrace facts. Imagine being able to hear what sensitivity, critical thinking, logic, data and facts are actually saying to us; whatever they are saying to us; not what we imagine, pre-empt, want or force or gaslight them to say. Imagine being grounded in the factual honesty and rational integrity of 'the mindfulness of reality'. What a gift to yourself and others! What a delightful rarity.

What might our day-to-day life feel like if you and I peacefully and willingly let right hemisphere priorities such as dignity, facts, critical thinking, logic and accountability speak to us and guide us; and if we allow reason and integrity to hold us to account? There is enormous strategic potential in not resisting the reality of data, facts and the logic of critical thinking. If we let them, facts, logic and critical analysis, can help us to be much more effective in all our relationships, roles and endeavours. These are the capacities of mindfulness, and the fruit of mindfulness, which can arise from Breath Meditation.

Breath Meditation can help us experience all this by stilling the self-serving, arbitrary, ignorant, opinionated, judgemental and fantastical voices of ego. Later in the book, we'll look very closely at ego. At this stage, it is sufficient to say that we need calming and clarifying processes, such as Breath Meditation, to help us counter a web of egoic dispositions, voices, drivers and defences. We need mindfulness to help us be less egoically ignorant; that is to say, to be less mindlessly ignorant. Later, we will also look in detail at ignorance; and at the connections between ego and ignorance.

Mental Voices to Tune Out

This book recommends that we say "No" to the egoic left hemisphere voices of presumption, pride, pretention and pontification. It suggests that we prefer the sensitivities of humility to the insensitivities of opinionated, righteousness and strident beliefs and judgements. It suggests voices of modesty over voices of ambition and power. 'Can We Do Better' recommends the Yin voices of relationship, simplicity, contentment and gratitude in clear preference to the Yang voices of discontentment, wishing, wanting, leveraging, getting and controlling. Mindfulness can help us silence and still these egoic voices. It can help us do better by bringing peace and joy to relationship and community.

This book recommends an abiding internal Yin locus of joy in preference to a never-lasting external Yang locus of the relentless pursuit of 'conditional happiness'. There is a chasm of difference between an abiding internal right hemisphere locus of joy, contentment and gratitude — and that of a transient, conditional external left hemisphere locus of happiness that depends on endless, insatiable wanting, self-leveraging, getting and accumulating the stuff of our voracious, unquenchable ego. The egoic voices of wanting and getting are a bottomless pit of digging and digging and digging; but never getting where you want to go, and never getting enough to keep you lastingly happy, fulfilled, contented and peaceful. No matter what the egoic mind tells us, we can't dig our way out of the pit of unhappiness. Only an internal locus of joy, simplicity, contentment and gratitude can bring lasting sufficiency, peace and fulfilment. An internal locus of joy, simplicity, contentment and gratitude is the way of mindfulness; and is the potential fruit of Breath Meditation.

This book advocates the reverent, dignified Yin voices of grace toward those who are different; and grace toward those whom we experience as 'difficult'. It recommends the gracious right hemisphere voices of patience, respect, kindness and generosity; not the left hemisphere egoic voices of judgement, intolerance, disparagement and rejection. This book recommends the voices of relational priorities such as intentional dignity and a mindful respect; rather than transactional voices of personal gain, self-leveraging, politicking, power plays, and control of others. This book also advocates the situational sensitivities of perspective, proportion, balance and mutuality.

All these are elements that can arise within a calm, meditative, right hemisphere space. The Yin voices of reverent, peaceful, mindful dignity and clear, mindful reason cannot arise from the mental noise of insecurity, fear, discontentment, ambition and greed. Grace and mindfulness are mutually reciprocal and mutually reinforcing. Breath Mediation can help us sense, imbue and channel the Yin mindfulness of grace; and, reciprocally and mutually, the grace of mindfulness.

Perspective and Proportion

The peace and clarity that arise from Breath Meditation can help us recognise that perspective and proportion are key elements of rationality. Breath Meditation can help us recognise that perspective and proportion are core elements of awareness, critical thinking, discernment, knowledge acquisition, information management, risk management and pragmatic wisdom. Keeping things in perspective and in proportion are also closely related to calmness and clarity. Perspective, proportion, calmness, clarity, discernment and wisdom can help us personally, in relationships, at work and in community. Perspective and proportion help us to mindfully identify and apply values, reason, priorities and intentions. Breath Meditation can help us prioritise perspective and proportion as the ways of mindfulness.

Practice is the Key

Practice is the key to learning anything new. That is why I said before, that becoming more peaceful, aware and sensitive is unlikely to happen without faithful, frequent, structured practise of mindful meditative processes that still the mind and silence unhelpful mental voices; vis a vis, the unsettling voices of ego and ignorance. We won't become self-aware and socially sensitive through wilful idealism; nor though romanticism, magical thinking, wishful whimsy or faddism. We have the potential to become sensitively aware by practising intentional, structured timeout from the usual egoic mental bluster of everyday egoic stuff. Mindfulness and fruit of mindfulness can only arise when we are silent, still and peaceful. The mindfulness of grace, and the grace of mindfulness, cannot arise from wishing, wanting, willing, forcing, spruiking and business. Mindful grace, presence and awareness can only be felt in silence and stillness. Reciprocally, silence and stillness are the fruit of mindfulness. Mindful — silence, stillness, grace and presence are one and same. Each predisposes and nurtures the others.

Talking Less and of Sitting Still

Thankfully, practising being silent and still doesn't need to be arduous or complicated. Stillness can be experienced simply by sitting still. Silence can be experienced by not talking. Reread the previous two sentences. Sitting still and not talking are simple and profound. The oneness of mindful grace and presence can be felt and experienced by sitting still, by not talking, and by paying attention to the rhythm of your breath — to the exclusion of all other sounds and stimuli. Being completely present to and attending to your breath is a practical experience of mindfulness as presence and sentience. Being silent and still a couple of times a day for several minutes can lessen the constancy and clamour of noisy, busy, self-absorbed, presumptive, expectant, fearful, insecure, judgemental, forceful egoic mental voices. Practicing Breath Meditation can lessen these forms mental clamour. Breath Meditation can imbue us with calm, and can bring dignity and rationality to the fore.

Even a slight decrease in mental clamour, and a slight increase in peacefulness and sensitivity, have the potential to make a positive difference within you; and within your relationships, roles, endeavours and difficulties. Fear, ignorance and judgementalism tend to decrease as peaceful awareness and sensitivity increase. Potentially, all these fruits of mindfulness can have significant positive effects on relationships; and have implications for the maturation of your understanding of small and large human issues. Insensitivity and ignorance can dissolve as mindful, right hemisphere peace, awareness and sentience increase. All these benefits can emerge from the stillness and silence of Breath Meditation. They are some of the very pleasant benefits of practising mindfulness.

Imagine and envisage being relatively free from your hotchpotch of noisy mental stuff. Imagine feeling the peace, clarity and freedom of silence and stillness. Imagine feeling and channelling presence, grace and mindfulness in relationships, roles and endeavours.

Practise the Practice

Meditative focus on breath is not an overnight recipe or a quick-fix technique. Over time, it may provide respite from otherwise continuous mental chatter. The more often we practice mental timeout through Breath Meditation, the greater the possibility that awareness, dignity and rationality will percolate to the surface. Dignity and rationality are a potent pairing of mindful qualities and capacities. Mindfulness can help us humans be our best and achieve our best.

Do you feel inclined to prioritise and practise the Breath Meditation process?

Imagine and Envisage

Imagine and envisage yourself enjoying and channelling mindful reverence, compassion, decency, integrity, reason, intelligence, responsibility, wisdom and accountability. Imagine a critical mass of societal revolution of mindful reverence, compassion, decency, integrity, reason, intelligence, responsibility, wisdom and accountability.

Societal, Big Picture Benefits of Breath Meditation

For many centuries, Eastern spiritual traditions have encouraged everyday people to slow and quieten our otherwise incessant and noisy stream of self-oriented, egoic, left hemisphere thoughts. Quieting the egoic mind can lessen these automatic and dominant mental defaults so that we are better able to see societal realities by looking beyond our typical social unawareness, biases, fantasies, fears, opinions, beliefs and judgements. The purpose of this chapter is to explain the role of Breath Meditation and right hemisphere mindfulness in helping us to better understand the network of big picture issues described in Chapters 4–7; so that we can do better as family members, citizens, custodians and leaders.

Breath Mediation — a Fantasy-Stopper, an Opinion-Stopper, a Judgementalism-Stopper

The mindfulness of simple and manageable Breath Meditation process can be a fear-stopper, a bias-stopper, a fantasy-stopper, an opinion-stopper, a belief-stopper, a judgementalism-stopper, a conspiracy-paranoia stopper, an ignorance stopper — all in all — a Yang-based, left hemisphere stopper. Ultimately, Breath Meditation can help us be less egoic and more mindful of and present to people and situations. Breath meditation can help us experience a mindful sense of right hemisphere grace in the form of peace, perspective, proportion, rationality, factuality, kindness and understanding. Pausing from thinking can help us be more gracious by being less arbitrary, less speculative, less reactive, less vulnerable to conspiracy ideation, slower to judgement, and less likely to act out on the basis of misinformation, cognitive biases and negative emotions.

Breath Meditation can help us let go of shallow, fearful, reactive left hemisphere speculation; and be less inclined to act out disparaging and harmful cultural, political and religious attitudes. It can help you and I be mindfully aware, more grounded in facts, and more sensitive to a wide range people and situations.

Sensitivity to the Dignity of Justice

Mindful — peaceful, gracious, non-judgemental awareness and sensitivity can help us tune into Yin-based, right hemisphere relational and communal values; such as respect, freedom, empowerment and justice for the vast majority. These four values are key aspects of dignity. Respect, freedom, empowerment and justice can only exist where humans experience the basic dignities of life. Yin-based dignities include — freedom from disparagement, disease, starvation, violence, abuse and exploitation; freedom to live safely and peacefully; freedom to speak and act with self-respect, autonomy and an absence of fear. Basic dignities also include being safe from harm, being housed, having adequate nutrition, having the capacity to minimise and cure disease, and having the freedom to nurture a fulfilling existence through community engagement, work, sufficiency and leisure.

It's difficult for you and me to be mindful of the dignities of social justice and societal empowerment when our mind is imprisoned by a murky mix of irrational, left hemisphere fears, arbitrary biases, preconceived opinions, factual ignorance, habitual judgementalism, religious and political fundamentalisms, cultural prejudices, racial misapprehensions, and presumptive self-righteous beliefs. That's a lot of interconnected Yang-driven egoic barriers to dignity and sensitivity. We need a mindfulness process that can help us see this web of ignorance and aberrance for what it is — humans and humankind at their egoic shadowy, mindless, left hemisphere worst. We need a process that can help us move away from mindless, egoic aberrance and stubborn, wilful, Yang-based left hemisphere recalcitrance.

Addressing complex human and environmental situations needs to be done on the basis of mindfully welcoming difference, embracing the necessity of diversity, and advocating respect and justice for all. To nurture justice, we need to mindfully embrace sensitive, robust, factual awareness. Mindful — gracious, right hemisphere critical thinking is the royal road toward justice. Pause for a moment and absorb the possibility of justice arising from mindful — gracious, reverent, peaceful rationality.

Dignity and Critical Thinking vs Presumption, Pretention and Fantasy

Reverence, dignity and reason cannot arise from egoic, left hemisphere — arbitrary, righteous presumption and pretention. Nor can they arise from egoically irrational, fanciful, faddish, esoteric speculations. Righteous pretention and fanciful speculation are easy-lazy egoic opposites to the mindful disciplines of dignity, critical thinking and robust factual awareness. Mindless — easy-lazy, pretentious, judgemental attitudes are a very common egoic, left hemisphere societal problem. Egoic mindlessness generates disrespect, indignity and ignorance; and erodes compassion, knowledge and wisdom.

Egoic — easy-lazy attitudes can never create mindfully dignified, strategic solutions to delicate, complex human problems. Typically, mindless easy-lazy attitudes divide, exclude, diminish, obliterate kindness and respect, and disallow critical thinking. Egoic easy-lazy, judgemental, left hemisphere attitudes don't nurture empowerment and justice. They foster oblivion, denial of facts, cynicism, indifference, prejudice, mistrust, conspiracy paranoia, fault-finding, judgementalism, victim-blaming, exclusion, and withholding of compassion and care.

Does that list feel, sound and look familiar?

Does the contrast between right hemisphere mindfulness and left hemisphere ego look familiar?

In contrast, mindful — unwavering, robust, factual awareness can help us to perceive situations as they are, not as we mindlessly and arbitrarily imagine, assume, pretend, want or gaslight them to be. Reread the previous sentence. Pause for a moment to absorb the reality-check that, when we look through the lens of left hemisphere ego, we humans are very prone to arbitrarily seeing things the way we want them to be; or as we imagine, confabulate or contrive them to be. Mindful — peaceful, robust, factual awareness helps us be less arbitrary and less ignorant; and thereby, to be more factual and rational. Calm, insightful awareness helps us be realistic and compassionate. Realism and compassion are the twin, reciprocal fruit of right hemisphere mindfulness. They are the beginning of justice. Ultimately, justice is the fruit of Yin-based, right hemisphere mindfulness of reality and compassion. As you read, keep imbuing a mindful feel for the nature, source and ways of justice.

Undiluted, undistorted — mindful — factual awareness, and gracious, compassionate sensitivity, also help us to be less egoically inclined to — rationalise and dismiss harms and injustice less inclined to try to justify righteous

74

judgementalism; less inclined to condemn and exclude; and less inclined to diminish, dismiss and ignore data and facts about human situations and environmental issues. We default to easy-lazy, righteous egoic judgementalism because — the mindless stuff of ego is easy; because it feels good; because we are too lazy to follow mindful, disciplined processes; and because we refuse to be accountable to data, evidence, facts and kindness. Easy-lazy judgementalism is stuff of egoic, Yang-base, left hemisphere mindlessness; and is the opposite to the grace and discipline of Yin-based, right hemisphere mindfulness. Yin-mindfulness is both gracious and disciplined; both kind and rational; both decent and factual; both compassionate and courageous; both integrous and accountable.

In contrast, dry, factual discipline and disciplined critical thinking don't massage our egoic feel-good, easy-lazy Yang-righteousness. We tend to avoid factual awareness and compassionate sensitivity because they don't titillate our righteous left hemisphere ego; and because they require long-term, consistent, congruent mindful self-discipline. Accepting factual evidence and speaking and acting on the basis and blend of critical thinking and compassion, are difficult and demanding mental disciplines. The processes of critical thinking are much more challenging than the egoic ease of spruiking unconfirmed, arbitrary, biased and subjective left hemisphere opinions, beliefs, judgements and conspiracies. Unless we are mindfully — graciously and peacefully mentally robust, many facts will feel too difficult and too demanding to face, accept, process and respond to.

The Dignity of Justice and the Justice of Dignity

Mindful, robust awareness and compassionate loving sensitivity are foundational priorities for personal, social and community responsibility, relational efficacy, and accountability in a wide range of human and ecological domains. Mindful — robust awareness and compassionate, loving sensitivity are core right hemisphere components of the justice of dignity, and the dignity of justice. Sit with these reciprocal phrases — the justice of dignity, and the dignity of justice. I think it was Nelson Mandela who said something like: 'There is no justice without decency and dignity, and no dignity or decency without justice.' These reciprocal values are central priorities of societal mindfulness; and they are the central, recurring priorities of this book. Welcome them into your consciousness.

Crucially — Breath Meditation can help you and me to mindfully embrace and apply a network of constructive values and priorities that are inherent in the connection between dignity and justice.

What are the crucial take-aways for you from this chapter?

Write some notes for yourself.

Imagine and Envisage

Imagine and envisage the dignity that disadvantaged and downtrodden people might feel when justice, respect and empowerment become their new experience.

Imagine a revolution of justice through a revolution of respect.

Imagine a meditative process helping us create a revolution of dignity and justice.

Imagine us humans evolving to be more and more mindful of grace, dignity and respect. Seriously, imagine that!

A Process for Listening to the Rhythm of Your Breath

Okay, here is a Breath Meditation practice session.

Sit in a reasonably comfy chair. Close your eyes. Place your hands in your lap. As you sit, listen to your breath. Listen to the sound of air moving in and out of your nostrils. It's a distinct sound. Listen to it now; for about 10 seconds.

On the inward breath, *in your mind*, hear the word … "*in*".

On the outward breath, *in your mind*, hear the word … "*out*".

As you slowly breathe in and out, *in your mind*, hear the unspoken words … "in-out" … in-out … in-out … in-out …

Keep hearing the unspoken words … "in-out" …

Keep listening to the sound of your breath entering and leaving your lungs. Listen to every breath-*in* … and every breath-*out*.

If your mind starts to wander, and thoughts start to flow; start again. Refocus on the sound of your breath going 'in' … and 'out' … 'in … and out' …

Continue to hear the unspoken whisper of the words … "in" – "out" … in-out … in-out

If thoughts keep coming back, start again; as often as you need to. It's perfectly normal for thoughts to flow. It's normal for your mind to wander. It happens to all of us. It's what the mind does. It produces a profusion of thoughts; often quite mixed and apparently random ones. Unless we practice stillness, silence and presence, the mind will think … and think … and think … every waking moment … without ceasing.

When your mind wanders, simply return to the sound of your breath … *in* and *out* … *in* and *out*.

Listen to every breath in … and every breath out …

Remember, sit relaxed, and still. Keep your eyes closed. Feel your chest rising and falling … rising and falling … rising and falling … rising and falling …

When thoughts begin again, return to the feel of the rise and fall of your chest, and hear … "in-out" …

When you finish your practice. Pause for a few seconds, and feel good about what you've done. And, your brain will be grateful for a brief time of rest and recovery.

You can repeat the practice session whenever you have a few spare minutes. With practice, you'll get better and better at just slipping into the stillness of feeling and hearing your breath.

Examples of Breath Meditation

I first encountered this particular Breath Meditation process when competing as veteran sprinter. While training and competing, I would deliberately and attentively listen to my in-and-out breaths to keep me calm and relaxed, and to help maintain technique. I would look down the track, and breathe combinations of words such as: tall … loose; elbows … high; breathe … breathe.

Technique is everything in sprinting; and there are many factors that can cause a runner to lapse into bad technique. These include, wanting too much to win, fear of losing, trying too hard to catch a competitor, fatigue, and substituting strength and determination for technique and form. This sounds very similar to many life pursuits, doesn't it? Breath Meditation and mindfulness were crucial aspects of training and competing throughout fifteen years of veteran athletics. It served me well. I won a bunch of races. At the 1994 World Masters, I won the 100 meters in the 40–44 years age group. Breath meditation was central to the joy of running; and played a large role in these achievements

I often practice breathing while my partner is shopping. I do it in the doctor's waiting room. I practise when I go bed, just before I drift off the sleep. When unable to sleep, preoccupied, or anxious, I use Breath Meditation to take the place of persistent worrisome thoughts, and to help me feel more peaceful. My experience is that Breath Meditation often results in a mindful, peaceful perspective, sensitivity, and clarity in relation to complex issues that I am processing. Often, clarity and solutions emerge when my mind is restored to calm and peace.

If I've been busy and hassled, I deliberately pause. In my mind, I breathe the words … silent-still … silent-still … silent-still. If I've been anxious and stressed, I breathe the words … calm-clear … calm-clear … calm-clear. Feel free to breathe whatever two words work for you; as long as they can be whispered easily in your mind to the sound and rhythm of your in-breath and out-breath.

Practising Breath Meditation While Reading This Book

Feel free to practise Breath Meditation before and after you pick up this book. I suggest that you read no more than several chapters at a time. Allow yourself time to breathe. Take time to become calm. Take time to rest your brain. Give yourself a peaceful, quiet mental space in which to reflect and ponder about what you are encountering in this book. Give yourself time to breathe, to settle, to absorb, to be sobered, to reset and start afresh. Allow yourself time to breathe and adjust to the challenges of each chapter. Allow yourself the time, silence and stillness of Breath Meditation to become increasingly mindful — to listen attentively, to be attentively present, to be intentionally aware, and to be strategically purposeful. Note and sit with these powerful, practical elements of mindfulness.

Intentionally create a peaceful mental space that will allow you to feel and embrace the profound value of dignity and rationality. Create the mindful mental space that will help you become less reactive, judgemental and defensive; the quiet space to become more open to facts, critical thinking and compassion — that is, the space in which to become more mindful. We can't force or manufacture mindfulness qualities and capacities. But we can create the mental conditions that will allow mindfulness to immerge and consolidate. A mindful space is the key to nurturing an affinity with values such as decency, integrity and accountability; which are the basis of nurturing and building freedom, empowerment and justice. Embracing values is how we embrace reality; and how we create priority and possibility. In response to the title of this book, embracing reality and possibility is how we humans can be mindful and do better through our lived-values and through our valued-based priorities and aspirations.

What lived-values and values-based priorities might help you do better?

What lived-values and values-based priorities might help humankind do better?

Reality and Possibility

It would be helpful for you to practise your Breath Meditation for a few minutes before starting this chapter. Become silent and still, calm and open; and then read on in peace and open-mindedness.

From a base of peaceful, mindful clarity, this book asks you and I to do two crucial, conjoined things:

1. Embrace factual reality.
2. Embrace possibility.

It's time to mindfully embrace the facts of the web of Yang-driven, man-made indignities and irrationalities described in Chapters 4-7 that impact you and me; and billions of our fellow humans, our fellow species, and the earth. It's time for us to embrace the facts of nexus between poverty, hunger, disease, systemic injustice, abuse and violence. It's time to mindfully embrace the facts of climate change and other ominous environmental issues. It's time for us mindfully embrace the possibility of helping people to feel the dignity and rationality of safety, sufficiency, freedom and justice. Embrace your responsibility to help protect our fellow humans and our fellow species; and to help our shared earth to rejuvenate and heal.

To do these things, each of us need to be mindfully factual, and, to be mindfully open to possibility. There is a direct and reciprocal relationship between the mindful reality of facts and the mindful possibilities of hope. Possibility, which is roughly synonymous with hope, is contingent on us doing what we do on the basis of factual reality. In the context of this book, possibility is contingent on a mindful — sober, factual awareness of our continuous history of systemic harm and suffering. Possibility is contingent on a mindful — clear and comprehensive awareness of the need to curb our confabulations, especially our dishonest, confabulated rationalisations and dishonest, spurious justifications in relation to the harm and suffering that we humans cause to each other, our fellow species and the planet. We have to face realty, and do whatever we do on the basis of mindful facts and universal values; on the basis of mindful dignity and rationality.

This combination must be empowered and guided by the right hemisphere. The left hemisphere must always be guided the right hemisphere. The right is the master, and the left is servant. However, the roles have reversed over the past 10,000 years of agriculture, institutionalised religion, Yang-based politics and the formation of masculinised institutions. Increasing, throughout this period, the left hemisphere supplanted the right, and set humankind on a path to all the issues discussed in chapter 4 – 7. Our question in the 21st century and into the future is to reinstate the prominence, guidance and empowerment of the right hemisphere and her Yin-based process.

Breath Meditation can help to calm and clear our mind so we can more able to mindfully embrace the reality of the facts of historical and contemporary harm and suffering; and to embrace the facts of man-made, masculinised, left hemisphere causes of harm and suffering. Breath Mediation can help us reflect; and be mindfully aware, honest and accountable. Breath Meditation can help us do incrementally and steadily better by mindfully reducing Yang-driven harm and suffering; future as years, decades and generations tick-by.

Confabulation

You may be curious — why the term — confabulation? The answer is, because confabulation is death to mindful facts and values. Confabulation generates ignorance by distorting and diminishing critical thinking and reality. Confabulation is a very common, unhelpful system of egoic thinking and communication which are a universal systemic human problem.

What is confabulation?

Confabulation consists of a web of confident but incorrect or distorted, or fabricated or misinterpreted memories and versions of oneself, relationships, experiences, circumstances, situations and history. Confabulation ranges from subtle misrepresentations of memory and facts, to wilful ignorance, to outrageous fabrications, to intentional deceptions, to concocted conspiracies, to fabricated, agnotological 'big lies', and to deliberate, heartless Machiavellian manipulation. In all its forms, confabulation obscures, distorts and denies facts; and it obliterates values and rationality. Confabulation obliterates mindfulness.

Confabulations are often our idealised, whimsical, wishful versions of reality. But, alas, whether apparently ideal and desirable or not, confabulations are not factual; therefore, are not reality, therefore are not helpful. At best, confabulations are part reality, part fantasy, part whim, part wish. They are substantially imaginary and made up. Confabulations are not accurate accounts of facts, data, evidence, events and history. To a large extent, they are not real. Confabulations are far from the truth, the whole truth, and nothing but the truth.

Confabulated fantasy, bullshit and lies are rampant in man-made religion, politics, culture, new-age faddism, social media and conspiracy cultism. Conspiracy theories are confabulation on steroids. Conspiracy confabulations confound priorities and obliterate facts and values. The 21st century internet and social media are drowning in an overlapping hotchpotch of mindless — confabulated inaccuracies, distortions and lies of political spin and conspiracy theories. Individuals, families, friends, peer groups, corporations and all political domains use social media to confabulate; to — misconstrue, misrepresent, bias, embellish, spin, PR and fabricate wilfully dishonest stories and to tell blatant lies. The 'Big Lies' of populist politics and extremist conspiracies are prominent in contemporary confabulation. All this is death to mindfulness. Most notably, in the 2020s, Trump and Putin are masters of 'big lies' and mindlessness.

There is no hope for personal, political and societal evolution without mindful fact-base reality and universal right hemisphere values. Factual reality is the only foundation on which to build and consolidate dignity, rationality and justice. Mindful factual reality is the only starting point from which to begin to heal the historical and contemporary wounds of harm. Factual reality is the only starting point from which to reduce suffering and destruction; the only starting point from which to heal and restore peoples, species and the earth.

Therefore, we must face all expressions of confabulation with mindful — uncompromising, robust awareness and honesty. We must see our man-made confabulating bullshit for what it is. At best; it is 'mindless crap'. At worst, our bullshit is wilful, harmful, gaslighting deception and manipulation. We must see our web of confabulating stuff for what it is; a web of misinformation, fantasies, deceptions and deliberate untruths. We must equip ourselves with the mindful, right hemisphere capacity to confront our mishmash of confabulated bullshit, deception and lies — front on. The mindful Yin-based clarity to do this, can arise, in part, from Breath Meditation.

What mindful realities and possibilities might help you do better at home, at work and in community?

The Jekyll and Hyde Species

The Incongruities of Humanness

The reality is that we humans are defined by many mindless, semi-invisible Yang-based, left hemisphere incongruities. We are defined by intelligence and ignorance, kindness and brutality, generosity and exploitation, creativity and destructiveness, reason and illogicality, superstition and rationality. We are torn between diametrically contrasting dispositions — to cooperate and compete, to help and harm, to be altruistic and to be exploitative, to evolve and to regress, to create and destroy. With one hand we are highly-intelligently magnanimous. With our other hand, we are highly intelligently sadomasochistic. Sit with the extreme paradox that, we highly intelligent humans are 'intelligently sadomasochistic'.

From your observations, does mindless, man-made sadomasochism encapsulate a significant aspect of human aberrance?

Clearly, we Homo sapiens are the Doctor Jekyll-Mr Hyde 'split personality' species. That's a reality of the human problem to which we must respond with lucid awareness. Mindful awareness includes a detailed map of problematic human dispositions. Mindful awareness also includes conscious compassion in tandem with unflinching honesty and intelligent reason. Somehow, we must harness our mindful, honest, intelligent, rational, right hemisphere Dr Jekyll capacities in order to understand and deal with our web of dysfunctional and destructive left hemisphere Mr Hyde tendencies to deceive, manipulate, exploit, steal, abuse, harm and kill.

Many post-WWII worldwide advances in health, education and justice are being eroded by 21st century Mr Hyde pathologies. In the 21st century, Mr Hyde left hemisphere political, religious, cultural aberrations are on the rise in government and in corporate domains. For example — the ascendency of populism, far-right fundamentalism, gun violence and mass shootings in the

USA, the and rise of Chinese Communism, Islamism, ideological and theocratic renegade states, and conspiracy insanity. Russia's murderous invasion of Ukraine and the Taliban's repression of Afghanistan show the worst of Mr Hyde in the form of the sadistic mass-murderer and brutal subjugation. Today, in the Middle East and Russia, millennia-old, pathological human cultural, religious and political mentalities are on the rise. These are the worst of our left hemisphere states, entities, tyrants and proclivities. In this century, diabolical left hemisphere pathologies define us at least much as our sophisticated intelligence, creativity, science, education and advanced technologies. Globally, Mr Hyde and the left hemisphere are alive and well and on the move in the 21st century.

No other species is like this. No other species is historically, ubiquitously, habitually, wantonly, intelligently, politically, religiously, culturally, endemically, systemically and globally, malignantly sadomasochistic. I have strung those words together because they capture a mix of inherent, pervasive, enduring and emerging Yang-driven Mr Hyde aspects of humankind. These are a carefully chosen network of words that profile the pervasiveness of our malignant 21st century 'Mr Hyde syndrome'.

Again, I know that malignance is not all we are, and not all we do; but it is a massively problematic aspect of our left hemisphere dispositions, history and current situation. You and I must not shy away from or deny the Mr Hyde pathologies in historical, contemporary and emerging humankind. We must face the daunting reality of left hemisphere human pathologies, and work with them; mindfully — unflinchingly, honestly, rationally, intelligently, systematically and strategically. Only the right hemisphere can address the issues of the left.

Channelling Einstein

Reputedly, as said in an early chapter, Einstein advocated that the quality of any solution that we strive to generate is in direct proportion to our ability to accurately define and map the problem we hope to solve. As I understand it, Einstein's rationale is that the potential efficacy of solutions is completely contingent on accurately and comprehensively mapping and describing the problem we want to solve. The effectiveness of the solution depends on the effectiveness of problem-definition. Prognosis is contingent on the clarity, detail and accuracy of diagnosis.

I reinforce this principle again, because, ironically, paradoxically, we humans are highly prone to not seeing, describing and defining ourselves accurately, comprehensibly and non-defensibly. We are strongly inclined to downplay, to deny, to rationalise and to justify our problems; especially our Hyde-like and Hyde-generated problems. Typically, we humans resist a mindful — fulsome appreciation and comprehensive mapping of our array of highly incongruent, conflicted and destructive Yang-propensities. Our egoic Mr Hyde dysfunctionalities prohibit us from seeing ourselves candidly, accurately, fulsomely and robustly. If we are to map the problems of humankind, we must look at left hemisphere Mr Hyde through the eyes of the right hemisphere Dr Jekyll.

The reality is that — conflictedness and incongruence are not all we are, but they are front and centre in the past 10,000 years of human history; and are prominent in present-day and emerging Yang-oriented human psychology, culture, politics, religion, industry and commerce. This is very important, because our web of man-made incongruities have repeatedly shown themselves to be massively harmful and destructive.

Therefore, unflinchingly and comprehensively, this book shines a penetrating, exposing light on our problematic Jekyll and Hyde situation. The poems in chapters 17 and 42 detail and highlight the extent of our human conflictedness, and the details of our many unhelpful and harmful human ironies. These poems highlight and detail our Mr Hyde propensities, including our egoic delusions of humancentric grandeur, and our profound lack of awareness and insight into the dark and dangerous shadow of our species.

The Dark Mr Hyde Side

As this book unfolded, unexpectedly, I found myself writing about the darker and destructive Mr Hyde aspects of our species. Unintentionally, I found myself becoming starkly aware of the interconnected web of drivers of our collective dysfunctionality, and of our habitual, enmeshed destructiveness. Because of this, spontaneously, my language, tone and challenges became direct. My writing became blunt and confronting. At first, I was concerned about this; but, have concluded that a front-on approach is appropriate and necessary.

Sustained, endemic violence and destructiveness and prideful, egoic recalcitrance, demand clear, forthright communication. Our current dire environmental situation, the recent decimation of Syria, and the invasions of Afghanistan and Ukraine, demand an unfiltered call to reality and sanity, and an uncompromising call to awareness, responsibility and accountability. The stark realities of Mr Hyde destructiveness behove 7.9 billion of us to do much better in terms of being mindfully clear-sighted and comprehensively aware of the extreme harms that we do. We must mindfully — unflinchingly and assiduously assess our all our attitudes and behaviours against the right hemisphere standards and requirements and benchmarks of dignity, decency, integrity, rationality, responsibility and accountability.

'Our' Mr Hyde Harms and Destruction

I use the word 'our', because these issues are 'our' problem. Millenia of us humans, by far, most commonly, male humans, have created the problems that threaten our existence in the 21st century. Many generations of us have caused and compounded a serious chronology and conglomeration of Mr Hyde problems. 'The human problem' is inter-millennial, multigenerational, intergenerational and pan-cultural. The reality of our enduring web of human dysfunction and destruction cannot, should not, must not be ignored, minimised or brushed aside.

First, you and I and the bulk of humankind must embrace the reality of the aberrations, harms and trauma that millennia of 'us' (mostly us men) have created. Second, you and I and us must embrace a network of rational, dignifying and empowering values and priorities in order to arrest the momentum of harms, suffering and destruction. A critical mass of 'us', you and me, many millions of us, even billions of 'us' — must embrace and be accountable for implementation of a mindful network of dignifying and empowering values and rational priorities. As said before, if we don't, it is likely that we will decimate ourselves, and massively damage the planet. Please, don't just brush aside or skip past this reality-check and warning. Don't rush on. Pause, breathe and absorb, consider, reflect, inquire, analyse and wonder.

China, Russia, the USA and Populism — Today's Mr Hyde States

As I write this book, tremendous 20th and 21st century post-WWII humanitarian advances in social justice, human rights, health and education are being jeopardised by the 'rise and rise' of left hemisphere Mr Hyde ideologies, Mr Hyde fundamentalisms, Mr Hyde states, Mr Hyde corporations, and Mr Hyde political, religious, corporate and industrial narcissists and psychopaths. Post-WWII societal evolution is being threatened by an emerging wave of Hyde-like left hemisphere cultural, religious, ideological and political drivers. Most notably, this includes — the pathological destructiveness of anachronistic Russia; the ruthless, inexorable, self-righteous ambitions of Communist China; the self-righteousness and inanity of populism and fundamentalism; the narcissism and dumbness of Trump's USA; the retrograde hatred of theocratic of Islamist theology; and the madness of a growing number of political and religious renegade regimes. Toxic, malignant Mr Hyde Trumpism is gone for now, but it could easily return in 2024.

Globally, that's a substantial pathological man-made hotchpotch of toxic and malignant forces. What is described in the previous paragraph is a worldwide conglomeration of Mr Hyde drivers of harm and destruction. This web of regimes, criminal players and pathologies is Mr Hyde in a range of 21st century cultural, political, religious, industrial and corporate forms.

In 2020, the four largest democracies were ruled by left hemisphere, Hyde-like populists: Narendra Modi in India, Donald Trump in the United States, Joko Widodo in Indonesia, and Bolsonaro in Brazil. In 2022, we have Johnson in Britain, who is a slightly more subtle populist. And, until May 2022, we had Morrison in Australia; who initially was a closet populist, but now an out and proud political, right wing, religious, economic, fundamentalist populist. That's quite a mix of fundamentalisms in national leader. Morrison's smug, pompous expression of populism became louder and prouder as the months ticked by.

Johnson and Morrison were very cosy with Trump, the most diabolical of all modern-day mad-bad populists. Trump was very cosy with Bolsonaro, and was a great admirer of the tyrant, Putin. Which leads us to the communist populists, Xi and Putin. And we have the lunatic renegade North Korea regime which is ruled by Kim Jong-un, who is an extreme, highly idiosyncratic, mad-bad version of Mr Hyde. Plus, there are a bunch of pathological Middle-East Hyde-like states and mad-bad theocratic, sociopathic tyrants.

This is a highly volatile and dangerous conglomeration of cultural, political, and religious narcissism and sociopathy, which are the key pathologies of 'the mad' and 'the bad' malignance of Mr Hyde states and characters. Contemporary and emerging manifestations of Mr Hyde malignance and toxicity are formidable and frightening. They are a clear and present left hemisphere danger to humankind and the earth; now, and into the future.

As a postscript, it is extremely heartening that the mad-bad populist Trump government has been replaced by the sane and decent Biden government. In the

USA, Dr Jekyll has replaced Mr Hyde … for now. Imagine the disaster of a Trump-Putin Hyde hybrid.

Rampant Corporatism and the Fossil Fuel Industry – Other Expressions of Mr Hyde

Within 21st century political, corporate and industrial cultures, there is an ever-growing mass of rampant, undeterred left hemisphere self-interest and ambition, Machiavellian indecency and dishonesty; as well as extreme irrationality, corruption, criminality and smug, stubborn, obnoxious recalcitrance. More and more oligarchs blatantly live-out their self-aggrandising compulsions to build obscene individual and corporate empires, and to unreservedly exploit their obsession with power and influence. These narcissistic and sociopathic men scramble and vie for political and market dominance. Their rampant, unchecked ambition drives unscrupulous justifications for exploitation and lawbreaking. Man-made narcissistic grandiosity, hyper-greed, and rampant economic fundamentalism are gaining ascendency toward a critical mass that threatens to obliterate hard-won post WWII gains in humanitarian and environmental reason, integrity and decency. This situation is globally pervasive and seemingly inexorable.

This situation is an extreme problem for humankind; and is a clear and present danger to our fellow species and the planet. An enmeshed, left hemisphere Mr Hyde religious-political-economic-industrial-corporate mentality is greatly eroding the rationality, integrity and accountability of big-politics, big-industry and big-business. Mr Hyde industrial-scale cultural, political and religious narcissism and sociopathy has terrifying ramifications for all earthly stakeholders.

This book maps many these and many other overlapping and enmeshed facets of Mr Hyde in the 21st century. We will explore these as the book unfolds.

Again, do you think we citizens, politicians, industry moguls and religious leaders can learn to recognise and reduce our left hemisphere Mr Hyde propensities, attitudes and behaviours?

As asked before, can a critical mass of citizens in a critical mass of governments and institutions embrace right hemisphere decency, facts, rationality, integrity and accountability? By this, can we do better?

Remember, the pivotal question that this book continues to ask — Can we do better? Can humankind evolve mentally, culturally and spiritually to embrace values such as reverence, dignity, integrity, rationality and accountability?

What might help us evolve and do better?

Us Quixotic Humans — Another Expression of Mr Hyde

This chapter adds another layer to our discussion about ignorant, egoic human dysfunction. In addition to pathologies of Mr Hyde, we have the blundering of Mr Quixote.

In the way of Don Quixote, we humans are often mindlessly — narrow-sighted, short-sighted, blinkered, impractical, and blundering. We are enthusiastic and idealistic, but typically, are also misinformed, misguided and clumsy. Because of these tendencies, we humans tilt at imaginary and made-up windmills. We tilt because we are religiously, politically and culturally assumptive, pretentious and obsessed. Often, politically and religiously, quixotic versions of Mr Hyde are supercilious, conceited, aggressive and ham-fisted. That is to say, commonly, typically, quixotic religious and political Mr Hyde is mindlessly — over-confident, under-informed, strident, forcefully vocal, blindly partisan, stubbornly ignorant, utterly misguided, blustering, flag-waving, God-talking, obliviously insensitive, unnecessarily belligerent, resistant to facts, evidence and feedback, and stubbornly and ignorantly recalcitrant.

21st century Don Quixote is My Hyde on steroids and ice.

All this is what I mean by being 'quixotically mindless'. Mindless, boorish, left hemisphere acting out is classically quixotic. Many politicians and fundamentalists, and most conspiracy theorists and populist cultists fit this description. They are My Hyde in full quixotic bluster and blunder; galloping madly, in full obnoxious voice, and at full-tilt, toward populist, doctrinal, pop-psychology, junk-science and conspiratorial cliff faces.

But — it gets worse. We zealots who are quixotic, are unaware that 'we' are the problem. We are unaware that we are utterly egoic — massively ignorant, hugely insensitive, grossly blundering and mindlessly harmful. Moreover, we who are quixotic are unaware that we unaware. Obnoxiously and boorishly loud and proud, the quixotic Mr Hyde doesn't know the he a total fool who is defined by the inane and intolerable blundering stuff he does. Mindless, Mr Hyde is conceitedly unaware of the repugnant and harmful stuff he says and does. He is mindlessly oblivious to the indecency, irrationality, foolishness and indignity of his blustering, blundering insensitivity. Quixotic Mr Hyde is oblivious to his blind, dumb biases; oblivious to his crazy, inane assertions; and oblivious to his horrible, destructive actions. Mindlessly oblivious to massive unknowing and crude insensitivity, various versions of Don Quixotry-Mr Hyde hybrids, stridently and vehemently assume and assert that their quests are gallant and virtuous; 'right and righteous'. For the most part, we 21st century Hyde-like Don Quixotes have zero awareness of decency, dignity, respect, integrity and critical thinking. Typically, left hemisphere Hyde-Quixotry blinds political, religious and social-media adherents to the fact that they are ridiculous, clumsy fools. Quixotic Hyde adherents have no awareness that they are inane, dangerous, destructive, mindless misfits. Hyde-like quixotry has no awareness that it is repulsively mindless.

Does that profile sound familiar?

Have you heard blundering, ignorant religious zealots, vehement political ideologues, foolish new-age spruikers, and fanciful junk-science conspiracists in full voice?

Do you know people who fit this description? Most of us know some of these ham-fisted characters.

Do quixotic, Hyde-like, mindless oblivion and insightless blundering sound like a problematic blend of dispositions, influences and forces in the 21st century?

Why We Tilt

For millennia, we humans have tilted at imagined windmills because, as the symbolic saying goes, we are prone to barge in where angels fear to tread. We Hyde-like left hemisphere humans have a history of barging and tilting by intrusive meddling, by vehemently believing and asserting fantasies, by talking angry bullshit, by brutishly imposing our will, and, by vehemently disparaging individuals and groups who disagree with us, or who a different from us. And then, very commonly, mindlessly, we who are quixotic, fail to be aware of or to learn from our repeated oblivion, our habitual insensitivity, our blinkered ignorant presumption, our over-confident pretention, the over-estimation of our expertise, our misinformed misguided baseless biases, and our rampant, ugly

92

judgementalism. We tilt, and tilt, and tilt because we are egoically 'mindless'; in contrast to being respectfully and intelligently 'mindful' — aware, sensitive, humble and disciplined. We tilt because we function too much from our left hemisphere and too little from our right.

Later chapters take a detailed and penetrating look at ignorance, which is another trait of the blustering, blundering quixotic, left hemisphere Mr Hyde who is rampant in religious, political, new-age and conspiratorial ranting and raging. The boorish behaviours of Trump and his cultist followers are a telling example of mindless — raving, ranting, raging quixotic Hyde-like obnoxiousness in full voice and full force.

So, we quixotic Hyde-like humans tend to be driven to tilt by a dodgy blend of egoic presumption, pretention, ignorance, hubris, and 'zeal without wisdom'. Too often, we are blatantly, enthusiastically and repeatedly stupid. That is, typically, foolishly, self-assuredly, obstinately, obliviously, we fail to see our blustering and blundering insensitivity, inanity and idiocy. And thereby, we fail to learn from them. In fact, very commonly, history shows that we who tilt, repeat the same dreadful quixotic mistakes over and over and over. Wars, sectarianism, racial violence, nationalistic aggression, and serious forceful unchecked industrial damage to the biosphere are classic examples of us failing to learn from catastrophic historical and contemporary, left hemisphere, quixotic Hyde-like blunders.

We left predominantly-hemisphere humans are ill-equipped to recognise and deal with the patently obvious illogicality's, biases, ironies, paradoxes, contradictions and hypocrisies that drive our insensitivity, indecency, ignorance, blundering and recalcitrance. Unaware, and enmeshed in network of psychological and societal incongruities and culture, we who are quixotic are ill-equipped to recognise crucial issues such as human suffering and environmental destruction. We quixotic ones are massively ill-equipped to respond to sensitive and delicate issues with awareness, understanding, discipline and finesse.

As I say several times in this book, there would be no need to write this book, if the quixotic, left hemisphere Mr Hyde drivers of human suffering and environmental destruction were not so prominent and problematic. But — here we are — I am writing this chapter about Hyde-like quixotry, and you are reading it. Both of us are asking, "Can we do better than mindless quixotic oblivion, insensitivity and blundering with regard to vulnerable and delicate human and environmental situations"?

In addition to mindless, egoic bluster and blunder, we are quixotic because we are misguidedly perfectionistic, idealistic, demanding, and imposing. With our ill-informed and misguided perfectionism and idealism, we are blindly biased, highly emotive, highly irrational, reactive, competitive, adversarial and political. This web of traits causes us to be inept and accident-prone. Essentially, we are quixotic because we are often stridently utopian; but ironically and paradoxically, in our left hemisphere utopianism, we are also self-defeating, self-confounding, and self-corrupting. These self-sabotaging and destructive paradoxical traits are very prominent among left-hemisphere quixotic fundamentalists and conspiracists.

At the same time, in contrast, some of us are quixotic because we are stridently dystopian. That is to say, some act out stridently pessimistic, cynical, paranoid and conspiratorial left hemisphere impulses. Whether utopian or dystopian, too often, we act out in quixotic ways that are utterly self-confounding, massively self-defeating and harmful to others. Many conspiracy protests and marches are well-intended, but are classically quixotic. Rallies and protests by Trump supporters, freedom rioters and anti-vaxxers are quixotic in every sense of the word. The Capitol riot was the worst of mindless, blundering, violent quixotic obnoxiousness and lawlessness. As were the riotous freedom marches in Australia in 2021.

I have chosen the word, quixotic, because, too often, individually and collectively, our acting out is, at least in part, arbitrary, ill-informed, impulsive, reactive, blundering, irrational, emotive, misdirected, incoherent and foolish. In all this, our quixotic acting out is mindless. Individually and collectively, too many of us humans, epitomise every nuance and manifestation of the words quixotic and mindless. Collectively, too many of us manifest every inanity, irony and paradox mentioned so far; as well as a host of other ham-fisted absurdities and incongruities. Again, some extremely quixotic characters and groups are Mr Hyde in full violent, destructive blunder. Our extensive array of incongruities, ironies, contradictions and blind-spots are captured in a poem that is the basis of the next chapter.

Quixotic Oblivion

And yet, mindlessly — assumptively, without a moment's insight, without the remotest self-reflection or self-critique, individually and collectively, most who are quixotic, skip-over this array of staggeringly anomalous, dissonant, incongruent, paradoxical, ironical and absurd personal and collective illogical, contradictory and self-defeating behaviours and actions. With full manifestation of Dunning-Kruger Effect, without a second-thought, too many of us over-assume, overestimate and unflinchingly and misguidedly, quixotically assert our unquestioned left hemisphere illusions of brilliance, rightness, virtue, coherence, consonance, congruence, rationality, justification, sanity and logic. When dominated by a quixotic mindset, we automatically, emphatically and blindly assume and assert our knowledge, intelligence, rationale, righteousness, veracity, factuality, reasonableness, objectivity, consistency, wisdom, enlightenment, validity and infallibility. That's a mind-blowing mountain of left hemisphere stuff to mindlessly over-assume, pretend, assert, and act out. In modern parlance … WTF!

Self-Reflection

Can you see yourself or some of your family members, your peers and national sub-cultures in any of these unhelpful anomalies and absurdities?

One intention of this book is to rouse awareness of the web of cringeworthy, unhelpful and harmful left hemisphere stuff that we humans assume, assert and do — as individuals, as conspiracy groups, as religious and populist cults, as corporations, as new-age fantasy cliques, as states, as governments, and as a species. Another intention of this book is to suggest ways that we can be far less quixotic, far less Hyde-like and far less self-confounding by being more mindfully aware, more mindfully sensitive, more mindfully rational, and more mindfully and purposefully dignifying of ourselves, of our fellow species and of our Mother Earth. Recognising, valuing and practising right hemisphere mindfulness, in all its forms, is our best hope for personal and institutional awareness, sensitivity, emotional intelligence, congruence, consonance and credibility. Commitment to Yin-based, right hemisphere mindfulness is our best hope for dignity, rationality, decency, integrity, constructive intelligence, responsibility and accountability.

Perhaps, cross fingers, you and I and many others will become more mindful — more aware, more reflective, more sensitive, more reasoned and reasonable, more honest, and, more transparent and accountable. As a species, it's way past time us evolve and become noticeably more self-moderating, more reasoned and dignified. Ultimately, it's time to evolve to be much less sadomasochistic. These are the personal, relational, ecological and strategic right hemisphere hopes and intentions of 'Can We Do Better'.

After reading this chapter, what is coming to mind?

Take a few moments to breathe. The next chapter is a doozy.

Liminality — Betwixt Jekyll and Hyde

Here is one of a bunch of poems that came to me from 2012-2017. This poem captures the awareness of our quixotic, Jekyll and Hyde left hemisphere ironies and tensions. It discerns and maps our web of mindless, man-made, myth-driven anomalies and dysfunctionalities. Historically, and in the 21st century, the combination of these stifle and erode values, rationality and reality. Ultimately, anomalies, and dysfunctionalities erode our right hemisphere psychological, relational, communal and ecological efficacy. They stifle our potential for personal and societal evolution; and, most fatefully, they threaten our sustainability and continuance as a species.

This poem is a significant part of the problem-definition and problem-mapping of the first two-thirds of the book. It discerns and describes the semi-mindless 'surreal liminal left hemisphere space' in which we 21st century humans exist. It captures and details the myriad of hitherto, largely undefined, under-the-radar egoic tensions, anomalies, incongruities and dysfunctionalities already discussed in the book. The poem is an encapsulation and summary of the drivers and issues that we have covered in previous chapters. It is also a foretaste of issues and drivers that we will cover in ensuing chapters.

Being 'betwixt and between' — reality and fantasy, rationality and absurdity, decency and obscenity is the nature of the conflicted, self-defeating egoic human mind, and the frail and fraught egoic human world. Egoic conflictedness encapsulates, creates, drives the web of issues described in this poem, and throughout this book.

Okay, here we go.

Human Liminality — Betwixt Jekyll and Hyde

Humankind – you and me, him and her, they and them
Beset by paradox, irony and contradiction

Each and all, somewhere between idealisms and actualities
Much less than imaginary all-knowing angels
A little more than unknowing, instinctive animals

Seated precariously on a knife-edge between rationality and delusion
Somewhere between enlightenment and ignorance
On a threshold between peace and trepidation, hope and despair
Stranded somewhere between reason and reaction, fact and fiction, reality and illusion
Somewhere in no-man's-land; between great and noble, tragic and corrupt, saved and condemned
Us humans, betwixt and between, always betwixt and between

Hopeful thoughts in mind, but not quite crystal
Peace and clarity, so close and yet so far
Love, a semi-lucid dream, not quite real
Grasping fragments, but missing the whole
Nothing but glimpses, echoes and touches

Sensing what might have been, what might be
But not grasping what is actually happening here and now
Many hints of déjà vu, but we are so slow to remember, to learn, to evolve
Serendipity revealing and beckoning, but is invisible to those who will not see or hear

Us humans — semi-myopic, semi-dissociated, semi-catatonic, semi-surreal
Standing at the edge of existence, peering into a man-made fog
Unable to see reality and truth, unable to see beyond wishes, fantasies and stories
Unable to see beyond personas, performances and facades
Unable to embrace what is, unable to crossover from fiction to fact
Letting go of fantasy with one hand, holding fast with the other
Mesmerised by illusion, deceived by delusion
Transfixed by fear, doubt and ignorance

Lost in the fear and ignorance of superstition and in unreasoned, unreasonable beliefs and dogma
Ignorant — ever presuming, pretending, pontificating, confabulating
All the time, insecure, ever straining to become the illusions we mistake for reality
Straining to become the ignorance that we mindlessly tout as inviolable truth
But that cannot be, because ignorance is nil but illusions are phantoms; and they are not real
We cannot become what is not
The illusions of ignorance are ever-elusive apparitions of mind and culture

Us, you and me, they and them, trapped in a man-made world of man-made egoic illusions and delusions
A world built by masculine ambitions for wealth, power and empire
Convinced that the male-mind is God, the saviour of all
Man-contrived, pontifical assumptions, presumed beliefs, pretentious claims, made up stories
Masculine adolescent morality presumed and projected as transcendent wisdom
But all is concocted by the adolescent male mind; then imposed, and enforced by chauvinistic men and paternalistic institutions
Arbitrary, authoritarian man-made delusions of fantastical absolute truth declared absolute and inviolable by assumptive, fantastical men

Mindlessly, unquestioningly, many say "Yes" to the presumption and ignorance of men
Then — and now — and ever
So, so many deceived and duped and misled by pretentious cultural, religious and political men
Fantastical, egoic men who tout and spruik and vie to be declared right and righteous
Voices of fanciful, egoic men competing and clambering to be heard, acclaimed, exalted, obeyed
Believe me, like me, vote for me, follow me, copy me, validate me, obey me, be me

Ego and intellect, those lesser gods with grandiose delusions

Me the canter of my world, you are the centre of yours
Fantastical, fantasying men at the centre of the human world
Us fantasying humans, assume we are centre of the universe
Arbitrary, presumptive, pretentious, ambitious, greedy, entitled
Ever wanting, more and more, greater and greater
Drowning in more and more and more and more man-made stuff for me and us

More and more materiality, more and more technology, more and more beliefs
Wanting 'things' and 'toys' that our trivial, material, male personas covert and crave
Wanting beliefs that we imagine, fantasise, presume and pretend are enlightened
Us humans, defined by wanting and wanting and wanting
But never enough, always more to want, more to have, more to believe, more to be
More and more to imagine, more to sell, more to assert, more to defend, more to justify
Always more, ever more fantastical beliefs and egoic wants for me and us

And yet, our masculinised human ego, frustrated by everything and nothing
But doesn't know why
For ego is invisible in plain sight
Fantasying, imagining, desiring, wanting
Angry and frustrated; acting out in childish, narcissistic fear
Ego, acting out in mindless adolescent ignorance and oblivion
Humankind; wondrous, but insecure, phantastic, dysfunctional, violent, destructive
Us — guilty, fearful and ashamed, but don't know why
Murderers and murdered all, creators and destroyers are who we are, and what we do
But not in our egoic minds
To the male ego, we are Gods; beings; souls — created, chosen, supreme, entitled
And yet, you and I, struggling and straining to be liked and loved
Stuck in the judgement of an angry egoic God who is projected in image of angry egoic men
God, a Jekyll and Hyde projection of us, a projection of egoic masculinity

An insecure, fanciful, presumptive, arbitrary, quixotic, self-absorbed God

The ultimate male projection, the ultimate male alter-ego, the ultimate man-made illusion, the ultimate male delusion

God, the ultimate chauvinist, the ultimate misogynist, the ultimate egoic, patriarchal tyrant

The ultimate man-made indignity; man's ultimate irrationality, his ultimate mindless insanity

Us, beset by chauvinistic pontiffs and gurus, ideologues and economists, hippies and hipsters

Egoic pretenders all

Rehashed masculine beliefs, the same old masculine stories about the Gods of men, the universe, and the rest of us mindless minions

Stories about us versus them, the right and the wrong, the good and the bad, the in and out; heaven and hell

Conspiracy stories about villains, victims and rescuers

Man-made stories and legends all

Fantasies all; all man-made; all made up; all the stuff of the masculine ego

Myth upon myth upon myth upon myth upon man-made myth

A disparate, chaotic hotchpotch of toxic, egoic, malignant, masculine myths

More and more of the same; millennia after millennia; over and over and over

In the midst of madness, momentary glimpses of faith, hints of love, and whispers of peace

Love, faith and hope; so close, yet so far

Because grace is unfelt within religious men, and among religious men

Heaven's horizon right there, but not quite here

Because heaven is not, not here or anywhere

Just another story, another man-made myth, a mind made delusion

Stories of the garden, but not the touch of creator, or the feel of creation

Because the garden is not, the creator is not, creation is not

More and more man-made stories

More and more fanciful stuff born of the egoic inflation of men

Myth upon myth upon myth upon man-made myth

Stories, stories, and stories

All contrived, all imaginary fictions, all confabulations, all mindless
All arbitrary, all whimsical, all fanciful, all delusional, all deluded
All a denial of facts, reason and reality
All an erosion of decency and dignity
Countless, illusive man-made illusions all
Delusions and diversion from reality and reason — all

Us — marooned, becalmed, somewhere in the past, and sometime in the future
Rarely present and at peace in the here and now
Not still and silent in discerning what is, and what is not
Unable to distinguish what is real from what is imagined and contrived
Hither and thither between facts and fictions, truths and lies, stories and reality
Betwixt grace and judgment, love and fear, hope and despair, faith and doubt
Between serenity and disquiet, joy and sorrow, humility and arrogance

Us — you and I, they and them — somewhere in the chaos of the man-made world
Somewhere between control and freedom
Somewhere between facts and fallacies, education and ignorance
Somewhere — but not sure where
Lost in limbo; lost in man-made liminality
Lost in the man-made paradox of no-man's land

But, thankfully, at this moment, you are here
Right now, you are reading this poem
The possibility of peace and clarity are here, and now; here and now; here and now
The possibility of reason and reality are here and now; here and now
Dignity and grace are possible, here and now
All this, is here and now — as often as you stop — as often as you are silent and still
As often as you breathe and whisper — here and now — here and now — here and now
The possibility of mindfulness is here and now; only here and now; always here and now

Reality and possibility are within you; here and now; right here, and right now
But not in mindless presumption, pretention and pontification
Not in mindless fanciful concepts, opinions and beliefs, ideology and dogma
Not in mindless spruiking and pontificating
Not in frantic, mindless running and chasing
But in the mindfulness of stillness and silence
So, be mindful; be still, be silent — and breathe
Breathe — don't speak; feel — don't speak; just breathe and feel

Breathe 'yes' to mindful, factual reality; and 'yes' to mindful, hopeful possibility
Breathe yes to mindful ways beyond our masculinised ego
Breathe yes to mindful ways beyond man-made ignorance and fear
Breathe yes to mindful ways beyond man-made superstition and speculation
Breathe yes to mindful ways beyond egoic masculine presumption and pretention
Breathe yes to mindful ways beyond men's dogma and doctrine
Breathe yes to mindful ways beyond masculinised ego's delight in opinion and belief
Breathe yes to mindful ways beyond man-made fantasies and fads
Don't speak — don't move — breathe, and feel — breathe and feel

Breathe 'yes' to grace
Breathe yes to dignity
Breathe yes to reason
Breathe yes to compassion
Breathe yes to factfulness
Breathe yes to the trio — decency, integrity and accountability
Breathe yes to peace and joy in relationship, community and ecology
Breathe yes to peace and joy in simplicity, contentment and gratitude
Breathe yes to humility
Breathe yes to beauty in unpretentious ordinariness
Breathe yes to curiosity and learning
Breathe yes to revelation, revolution and evolution
Breathe yes to mindfulness
Stay still, and keep breathing, and say — "Yes" to these realities — "Yes" to these possibilities.

Pause. Breathe for a while. Then reread this poem; slowly, calmly, and consciously. Use your highlighter and write some notes.

And pause again.

What are you thinking?

What are you feeling?

Importantly, what are you wondering?

Questions Arising from the Poem

What aspects of this poem have sobered and jolted you?

What aspects of the poem have aroused your awareness and curiosity?

Do you wonder if we humans can do better than our millennia of assumptive, pretentious egoic man-made Jekyll and Hyde liminality?

Can we do better than millennia of mindless, egoic, ham-fisted, quixotic masculine bumbling, insensitivity, incompetence and toxicity?

Can we do better than more and more arbitrary man-made confabulation?

Can we do better than so many fantastical man-made myths and fictions?

Can we do better than millennia of patriarchy, chauvinism and misogyny?

Can we do better than a mishmash of man-made individualism, egotism, narcissism and exceptionalism?

Can we do better than the sociopathy of political and religious tyrants?

Can we do better than man-made addiction to power, greed and insatiable materiality?

Can we do better than man-made human-centrism and anthropocentrism?

Can we do better than man-made conservatism, fundamentalism and populism?

Can we do better than so many man-made isms?

Crucially — can we men do better than man-made — war; terrorism; domestic, religious and political abuses; exploitations of peoples; and decimations of First People cultures?

Can we do better than men killing each other; better than men killing and abusing women and children; better than men killing our fellow species; better than men killing the planet?

Can we 21st century men do better than our Yang-based forebears, and our mindless, toxic, macho contemporaries?

Can we male readers do better than today's men of political and industrial power, with their narcissistic and sociopathic will to possess and dominate; and their callous, pathological disregard for people, our fellow species and the earth?

Can the Feminine-Mother grace and First People systems wisdom help us women and men embrace the dignity, reverence and rationality of relationship, community and life-sustaining systems ecology?

Can you and I imbue and nurture decency, integrity and accountability?

Remember — reality, humility, and 'open curious wonder' are the keys to us moving beyond more and more of the same-old harmful, destructive masculine stuff.

There's possibility in mindful reality. And there's possibility in mindful open-curious-wonder. 'Mindful, grounded factual reality' is the crucial foundation of possibility and hope. Possibility can only arise from mindful, grounded, factual reality.

There's no hope in more and more mindless — rehashed, rebadged, man-made religious and new-age superstitions, fantasies, fads and myths. There's no hope in more of the same mindless new-age superficialities, made up opinions and whimsical, fanciful beliefs and fads. There's no hope in more and more mindless — rehashed, rebadged political pretentions, projections, excuses and justifications. There's no hope in mindless, man-made conspiracy insanity. There is no hope in more and more mindless arbitrariness of dominant, self-promoting, self-justifying political and religious egoic men.

There is no hope in mindless patriarchy, chauvinism and misogyny.

There's no hope in utterly egoic and often toxic and malignant masculinity.

There is hope in the mindful dignity of reverence, decency, rationality, integrity and accountability.

Can we humans embrace and blend intelligent open-mindedness, rationality, reality, hope and accountability?

Will we?

Can you and I?

Eventually, ultimately, will we mindfully embrace dignity and reason?

Or will this just be another book that we read and put back on the shelf?

As the book continues to unfold, we will consider many more questions that call us to reality and possibility; that call us to clarity and hope?

At this juncture, will you ask many more questions that inspire and jolt us to do better in terms of values and rationality?

Will you and other readers aspire to hope through decency, integrity, reason and accountability?

Will we, can we, work together to aspire to ensconce a revolution of mindful, rational and dignifying values?

Breathe

Give yourself a few minutes to breathe … calm and clear; calm and clear; calm and clear.

Next, let's look more closely at the contrasts between mindless arbitrariness and mindful accountability for rationality and decency.

Forthcoming Questions and Reflections

Ahead, are many penetrating chapters which ask lots of questions about an array of arbitrary left hemisphere stuff that stifles rationality and diminishes dignity. These questions might help us identify what drives our inclination to be arbitrarily superstitious, arbitrarily fanciful and arbitrarily ignorant. Mindful, incisive questions can help us recognise and map a huge range of uninformed whimsical ideas, choices and decisions; all of which diminish us and contribute harm to humans, our fellow species and the planet. The chapters ahead identify a wide scope of typical egoic, fantastical stuff that you and I and billions of us uncritically assume, preconceive, contrive, believe, assert and defend as self-evident logic, rationality and truth. The questions that are ahead might help clarify an array of typical mindless — self-limiting, self-defeating and self-harming arbitrary left hemisphere assumptions, ideas, beliefs, stories, narratives and lies.

We are going to look at a wide array awareness-building questions about the handicaps of our religiosity, the drawbacks of our political dispositions, our new-age fantasies and our proneness of conspiracy ideation. Forthcoming questions aim an alchemic flame toward an extensive bunch of mindless — baseless, irrational, illogical, crazy egoic stuff. Get ready to turn up the heat. Again, note and absorb the contrasts between mindfulness and mindlessness. They are irreconcilable twains.

Questions are a crucial stimulus, and a way to take timeout. They are a key way for you and me to pause, be contemplative, and to robustly reconsider and critique some of our very common assumptive, rarely-examined, whim-based ideas and beliefs. I ask these questions because we have built our modern existence on minimally-examined and typically groundless ideas that cause us humans to stumble, trip and fall — again and again and again throughout history; and that cause us to continue to stumble in the 21st century. Many of our unfounded and fanciful ideas are quixotic. They cause to blunder along and break things as we go. Quixotic, Mr Hyde, blind-spots cause us to stumble headlong into misinformation, misjudgement, misadventure, conflict and catastrophe. Collectively, and historically, our typical fantasies and blind-spots cause us to mindlessly and repeatedly fall into man-inspired, human-made drama and calamity; calamity for ourselves, our fellow species and the earth.

We left hemisphere humans have a lot of trouble learning from millennia of highly damaging quixotic, Mr Hyde misjudgements and calamities. Stupid is as stupid does — and does, and does, and does. Historically, we humans have done incredibly stupid blustering, blundering stuff, over and over and over. This has been especially so for about 10,000 years; at least since the emergence of agriculture; and especially since the dominance of institutional religion and politics.

For the most part, mindful First Peoples learned to do much less harm to each other and far less damage to the planet than us quixotic, Anglo-European, Mr Hyde, agricultural, religious, industrial, political, economic, colonising materialistic humans. It seems that First Peoples were more able than us to learn from their mistakes. For the most part, they learned to moderate their damage to environment. Learning from mistakes is not something we egoically consumptive, industrial, commercial, material, technologized, political, religious post-First People humans do well. Even in the 21st century, we modern humans are very slow learners. Compared with Yin-based, right hemisphere First Peoples, we contemporary humans are a murderous, decimating, quixotic Mr Hyde blight. I can't sugar-coat our sadomasochistic destructiveness and recalcitrance. The facts and statistics of history are damning evidence of ham-fisted Anglo-European left hemisphere human ignorance, destruction and resistance to learning. Russia and China are 21st century exemplars of quixotic, sado-masochistic blustering and blundering recalcitrance. Russia and China are the new Don Quixote and Mr Hyde on the world stage.

Whoever are the quixotic, Hyde-like players, collectively — religiously, politically, economically, industrially and corporately — can we humans do better than our repeated cock-sure, ham-fisted, blundering dominance, violence and disasters?

Can we stop repeatedly tripping over our own human feet and smashing into all before us?

Can we learn, consolidate and do better — including you and me, a critical mass of us, our leaders, our nations, and perhaps, our species as a whole?

Can a critical mass of 'us' find a path to mindful right hemisphere reverence and strategic ecology?

Can we find a path beyond mindless arbitrariness and toward greater and greater carefully chosen and purposeful dignity, rationality, integrity and accountability?

Or, are we doomed to more and more of the same old egoic, destructive, prideful left hemisphere ignorance?

At this juncture, what do think?

Read on and we'll see what unfolds in terms of problem definition and solution formulation.

Forks in the Road

This is the second-last chapter before we launch into our questions. Be patient. Only a few pages to go.

Forks in the Road, Discernments, Choices and Directions

Looking back, I can see that I have come to many forks in the road. Many times, I have had to discern, choose and decide whether to keep going straight-ahead toward more and more ham-fisted, arbitrary assumptions, fantasies, opinions and beliefs; or to consciously steer away from them. Do I keep going with over-confident, prideful, fanciful, blundering pretentions; or do I move toward something more mindful — something more factual, something more reasoned, something more sensitive and respectful, something kinder and more compassionate? There have been significant junctures at which I have wondered 'why' I repeat the same-old misjudgements and mistakes. There have been defining moments and experiences when I have stepped away from the same-old unhelpful stuff; and have moved toward new and more constructive ways of being a person, parent, friend, worker, manager, teacher, leader and citizen. Perhaps, hopefully, I am moving steadfastly toward reason and dignity; and am contributing to the hope that can evolve from these.

I encountered many forks in the road while I was writing this book. Writing shunted me into an unprecedented place of reflecting, questioning, reassessing, sorting and discarding. Writing this book sobered me more than any other experience in my lifetime. The questions that are ahead in this book are what I've been asking myself for decades; but especially over the past ten years. The forthcoming questions came into sharper and sharper focus over the past five years of writing. Now that you are reading this book, you are approaching your own particular junctures and crossroads of reflection, evaluation and sorting. When at your own crossroads, you might ask yourself a bunch of penetrating and jolting personal and societal questions that are pertinent to you as a family member, partner, friend, citizen, worker, professional, steward and leader.

You will either plough on through the book, and keep forging straight ahead on the path you were on when you picked it up. Or, you might pause, reflect, reconsider, refocus, reprioritise, sensitise, choose some fresh awareness, and elect to change direction toward greater levels of purposeful integrity and accountability. Perhaps you will choose to imbue and prioritise more sensitive and compassionate attitudes. Perhaps you will choose roads toward factual reality and critical thinking. Perhaps, as you read and move forward, you will choose directions that will guide you closer and closer toward the mindfulness of presence, reflective listening and grace. All the roads mentioned in this paragraph lead to Rome; that is, to the mindfulness of dignity and rationality. I commend these values as constructive directions to choose and walk.

Take Your Time

As you read the following chapters, it is very important that you take your time. Sit with each question. Sit with each theme. Allow questions and themes to stir your sense of wonder. Allow them to provoke you, to challenge you. Allow the questions to soak in. Allow them to get under your skin, and into your blood. Allow the forthcoming questions to prompt great curiosity, and to provoke robust self-critique. Allow them to lead you toward mindful — intentionally courageous, integrous, searching evaluations of the factual reality, reason and dignity of your long-held ideas, beliefs and opinions. The forthcoming questions have the potential to move you away from arbitrariness and toward accountability; to move you away from whims and toward critical thinking and informed, factual, grounded, evidence-based conclusions and actions.

Gaining clarity and shedding the old skins of arbitrary biases, opinions and beliefs is very liberating. Reality can be disarming and disturbing at times, but is always an adventure that offers potential new vistas; and a fresh and sense of freedom, wonder, joy and possibility.

Therefore

Therefore, as you approach forks in the road, be receptive to challenge. Be curious about possibilities. Be open and humble. Be rational. Be accountable. Be available to ongoingly re-evaluate, moderate and discard your arbitrary beliefs and opinions. Be available to release habitual default judgemental attitudes and reactions. Be open to let go of long-defended arbitrary biases. Be open to let go long-held arbitrary fantasies, fads and conspiracy theories. Be open to discard a host of easy-lazy-whimsical defaults. Be open to adjust how you turn-up in the world of relationships, work, business, community, citizenship, stewardship and leadership. Be open to be dignified and rational, integrous and accountable in all these domains.

Now that you are reading this book, I wonder which direction will you choose?

Counter-Intuitive Questions Are Next

We humans struggle with anything that seems counter-intuitive. We resist whatever challenges our automatically assumed and preconceived personal logic; anything that challenges our conditioned, presumed knowledge; and anything that threatens our intuitive default left hemisphere beliefs and assertions. Very often, we kill critical thinking by instantly saying: "I believe"; or, "It's my right to express my opinion".

Opinionated presumption, opinionated pretention, opinionated beliefs, unsupported opinionated pontification — all sit together in a tidy little intuitive group in my mind, and in your mind. Intuitive preconceptions are arbitrary, assumed, enmeshed and habitual. As such, they are mostly unexamined and uncritiqued. In that, they tend to be mindless, not mindful. Some of our claimed common-sense opinions, beliefs and attitudes may be the ignorant, blundering, quixotic insensitivity of Mr Hyde. All this is 'the stuff of egoic, left hemisphere mindlessness'.

Pause for a moment, and sit with the realisation that some of yours and my opinions and beliefs are egoic, ignorant, insensitive, blundering and — thereby, potentially, tend toward the mindless end of the left hemisphere continuum. At least some of our opinions and beliefs have not been critiqued and fact-checked by data, evidence and critical thinking. Many are likely not have been critiqued for decency, sensitivity, dignity, integrity, transparency and/or accountability. By their very nature, a big percentage of intuitive beliefs and opinions are arbitrary. Many are likely to be illogical and incorrect. That is to say, beliefs do not arise from systematic, disciplined, rational evidentiary processes. They arise from made up ideas, and from baseless, fanciful left hemisphere whims. Many conspiratorial opinions and beliefs originate from arbitrarily concocted whims. Later, they are supported with deceptions and lies. Again, all these are the elements of mindlessness.

Can humans do better than unchecked, habitual, arbitrary assumed opinions and beliefs?

Can we do better than mindless — unchecked and shallow presumption, pretention and opinionated pontification?

Can we do better than beliefs that drive us to insensitive, ignorant, blustering, blundering, quixotic spruiking and acting out?

Can humankind do better than being sucked into conspiratorial beliefs — aka — whims, deceptions and lies?

Can you and I do better than all these expressions of left hemisphere mindlessness?

Counterintuition

For many readers, the questions in the ensuing chapters will feel strongly counterintuitive. For many they will feel perplexing, unpleasant, unpalatable and perhaps, 'unthinkable'. To some readers, the questions ahead will feel outrageous and offensive. The majority of readers will jump straight to their pet intuitive preconceptions, presumptions, beliefs, opinions, assertions and defences. Some will go on the attack.

On the other hand, to some readers, the forthcoming questions will be a timely breath of fresh air. Some of you will be ready to reflect, to reconsider, and to review your assumed, long-standing, tightly-held, never-critiqued arbitrary ideas, beliefs and opinions. Some of you will be curious — open to critical thinking; ready to let go of arbitrariness; ready to be grounded in reason and factual evidence; and ready to be held to account for what you believe, say and do. Some will be ready and willing to embrace a mindful approach to being human — that is, to be open, rational and accountable for factfulness and critical thinking.

Will you be one of the many who are stuck in presumptive oblivion and stubborn unreflective, prideful indigitation?

Or, will you be one of the few who are curious, open-minded, ready to reflect and reassess, ready to critique intuitive assumptions, ready to let go, ready to be accountable, ready to move on from fanciful, arbitrary, quixotic and Hyde-like attitudes and actions?

Lots of Questions, with Some Overlap, and Some Repetition

There's lots of questions ahead — lots! Once I started asking a few questions, an avalanche of wonder, curiosity, inquiry and critique poured forth. A few questions became many. To make a plethora of questions more manageable, they are grouped into chapters, and under headings and themes.

There is considerable overlap between the chapters and themes. There is also a fair bit of repetition. Get ready for that. Embrace the detail and the highly nuanced network of inquiry. Embrace the challenge of questions that might take you far deeper than your typical mutual-admiration, 'blind leading the blind' coffee shop chats.

The purpose of asking lots of penetrating questions is to show that a web or a map of arbitrary fantasies, myths, beliefs and opinions create, drive and justify the issues of Mr Hyde destructiveness that are described in Chapter 4, and in other previous chapters. Ensuing chapters and questions will show that enmeshed, arbitrary fantasies, myths, beliefs and opinions are a significant part of the egoic problem of human ignorance, dysfunction, injustice, harm and suffering. Enmeshed arbitrary fantasies, myths, beliefs and opinions are not part of the solution to dysfunction, harm, suffering and damage. Beliefs and opinions are highly unlikely to be part of a rational and dignified way forward. They tend to be part of the problem, and not be part of the solution.

Remember, there are loads of questions in the next several chapters. The questions are detailed and highly nuanced. There is lot of overlap, within chapters and between chapters. Therefore, read slowly. Pause a lot. Breathe consciously. Appreciate the overlap, repetition and nuances. Highlight the questions that resonate, and write a few margin notes. Return to and reread the questions and chapters that are particularly relevant and timely for you.

Okay, let's dive in, and see what happens.

Questions about You and Me

I wonder what unseen potential is inside you and me, but is buried under a morass of unexamined left hemisphere, assumptions, intuitions, ideas, beliefs and opinions.

What is one idea, belief or opinion that you have let go in the past weeks, months or years?

Name it.

Why did you let it go?

If you let go of one idea, opinion or belief, then you have shown that you are able to 'change your mind' — to adjust your awareness, understandings, attitudes and judgements; and to evolve your perspective and knowledge. As with biological evolution, small mental psychological changes can lead to big changes of mind. Small shifts can lead to big shifts. We don't have to stay stuck in the same old ideas, opinions, beliefs and attitudes. We can move forward; mostly, step by step by step. Remember, even when we take small steps, 'it's the difference that makes the difference'. But, sometimes, unexpectedly, we move forward with giant leaps, sometimes with radical, seismic shifts in awareness, perspective, values, attitudes, priorities and actions.

I wonder, what might open up if some of your arbitrary biases, opinions, beliefs and ideas were to begin to dissolve?

Remember, this book is about five principles and priorities:

1. Be grounded in awareness, dignity, integrity and accountability.
2. Be grounded in in data, facts, rationality and critical thinking.
3. Be open to possibilities for personal, relational and societal evolution.
4. Be open to nurture, build and evolve your contribution to citizenship, custodianship, leadership and eldership.
5. Be open to right hemisphere, Yin-base priorities, principles and values.

Everything in this book points toward these five principles and priorities. I have written with the conscious intent of nurturing personal, relational, communal and societal evolution. I have written with hope and purpose that these priorities might evolve to become the new normal for you and me; and for a critical mass of 'us'.

Questions about Design, God, Eternity and Creation

Before You Race to the Questions in this Chapter

Sit with the following group of questions without talking. Just sit still, don't talk to yourself, or others. Cradle each question very gently. Don't presume to possess the answers. Don't presume to 'know' the truth, nor to already hold reality. Watch out for the snares of assumed, absolute certainty. Watch out for indignance, defence and justification. Watch out for stubborn, wilful prideful ignorance. Don't be triggered. Just sit, read, breathe, and wonder.

We left hemisphere humans preconceive, believe and assert very quickly; often, without awareness, and without a moment of reflection or critical thinking. Bias, in the form or opinions and beliefs, is intuitive, subconscious, automatic, instantaneous and habitual. Often, preconceived, biased opinions and beliefs are intense and forceful. We default to our assumed precious biases in the blink of an eye. We default to them over and over and over. Biased opinions and beliefs are our assumed normal; our assumed virtues; our assumed identity. Sometimes we reinforce and entrench our biases even though they may be disrespectful of others, irrational, unintegrous and harmful. And, very commonly, we default to defending and justifying our precious, assumed, biased opinions and belief with a sense of righteous certainty, righteous loyalty, righteous entitlement, righteous indignation, and with absolute, inarguable righteous authority.

Dare I say, through these typical, left hemisphere defaults, we also reinforce the arbitrariness of our fantasies and whims; and reinforce the illusions of our subjective beliefs and opinions. Whims, fantasies, illusions, opinions and beliefs are a problematic little network of arbitrary cognitive and mental dispositions and defaults. Arbitrary fantasies dispose us to various expressions of mindlessness. Ipso facto, they inhibit our capacity to become mindful — factual, evidence-based, critically analytical, logical, rationally and accountable.

118

Arbitrariness and proneness to whimsical, fantastical whims, wishes and wants are a huge barrier to insight and accountability. These left hemisphere dispositions create strong resistance to objectivity and critique. As you read these questions, be aware of the left hemisphere dispositions mentioned in previous paragraphs.

Only fresh, open-minded, right hemisphere reflection, curiosity, critical thinking, and 'open curious wonder' can give us the potential to moderate the defaults mentioned in this chapter. It's a good sign of humility, curiosity and openness if you are sighing in agreement; and if you are slowly nodding — 'Yes' — to what you have just read. A new normal of right hemisphere mindful rationality and dignity can arise from your sigh of humility, curiosity and openness.

Okay, let's dive into the deep end of the pool.

Design and a Designer

Are there design principles and patterns inherent in the universe?

Is design the correct word with which to refer to inherent 'universal' principles and patterns?

Does the assumption of 'design' presuppose divine or cosmic — omniscience, strategic purpose, intention, planning, intelligence and predetermination?

Does the assumption of design presuppose the existence of a designer, such as God, a conscious universe, and/or conscious, intentional cosmic forces?

Do we humans tend to preconceive the notion of design, especially in relation to 'creation', and in relational to a pre-eminent 'creator-God' or creator universe?

Is this an easy, automatic assumption and a common automatic, romantic default?

Is intuitive preconception the very easy, automatic, uncritical, unaccountable path?

Is this the easy-lazy, assumptive religious and new-age path?

Is intuitive preconception an easy-lazy man-made path — full stop?

Note the words, 'preconceived and preeminent' intuitions. In many of us, religious and new-age intuitions and mental defaults are extremely commonly preconceived, preeminent, unexamined, instantaneous and unconscious. These left hemisphere tendencies are strong in all but a meditative right hemisphere few, and in all but the scientifically disciplined. A minority of right hemisphere Zen-oriented and science-disciplined people have learned to be very wary of easy-lazy, automatic, uncritical assumptions. Only 'a disciplined few' hold lightly to easy intuitive assumptions, ideas, opinions and beliefs. Only a rigorous few carefully and consistently examine possibilities and alternatives. I refer to Zen-people and scientists as, "maybe" people. Their default is to say "maybe, and perhaps". Disciplined minds look slowly, carefully, thoroughly, critically and openly at evidence. Crucially, disciplined minds let the data and facts speak for themselves, whatever they say; unless or until, after much research, examination and/or analysis, the data says something else.

Questions will help you and me step back from our automatic, easy-lazy, uncritical 'default assumptive intuitive opinions and beliefs' that tend to arise from left hemisphere defaults. Questions can help us step toward the possibility of Zen-like / science-like detachment and curiosity about what the weight of the evidence 'might' be saying; and, crucially, what it seems not to be saying. As a reader, it's your job to be Zen-like and science-like. When considering each question, it's your job to pause, to reflect, to wonder, to critique, to be open; but to say — 'maybe' — then, to continue investigative and analytical processes and disciplines — then, to repeat this process, again and again. Do this for every question, without presumption or preconception. This is a big ask because it is a very rare process. Zen-like and science-like caution and patience are a rare mental and spiritual discipline. They are a very rare expression of mindfulness.

Back to the Questions

If design principles exist, how might we identify them without distorting them through preconceived, man-made religious, ideological and cultural beliefs and traditions?

Do we need to put the intuitive assumption, 'God', at the beginning of our thinking, and at the centre of our beliefs?

Pause, and sit with the two parts of that question.

Breathe, before you read the next several questions?

Has God been our most common millennia-old, easy-lazy-assumptive-uncritical-intuitive man-made human default?

Is God our most common preconception; our most common intuition; our most common presumption; our most assumed and preconceived apparent 'common sense' belief.?

Has God been our easy-lazy presumptive masculinised projection?

Is the intuition, God, a too little examined, too easy-lazy, too convenient, mindless projection of the overly assumptive, egoic-human-mind?

Simply and plainly, have we mindlessly and lazily made-up God; and projected a male God in the image of men?

In the 21st century, the period of our greatest capacity for educated rationality and data-based evidence and science, can we be comfortable leaving behind the God-projections of our assumptive, fantastical, arbitrary, ignorant, superstitious, mythological and institutional past?

Can we, will we, choose to remove God-presumptions, God-projections and God-confabulations from our mindful — educated, enlightened, science-based, reason-based 21st century models of the universe, life, and of what it means to be human?

Can you?

Can I?

These days I am very comfortable with a God-free understanding of existence. That was not always the situation. I have only stopped assuming God in the past decade.

The Notions of Eternal, and Creation

Are notions of 'the eternal' and 'creation' automatic extensions of the presumption — God?

Because we assume, God, do we also automatically assume, eternity, and 'God's creation'?

Did notions of 'the eternal' and 'creation' originally arise from millennia of ignorance of definitive cosmological, geological and evolutionary timeframes and processes?

Did notions of eternity and creation arise from complete unawareness of the structures and processes of Cosmology, Geology, Physics, Chemistry, Biology and Mathematics?

Ignorance and Fundamentalism

It's a short step from factual ignorance and our left hemisphere predilections — to fanciful confabulation. It is very precarious step from fanciful, confabulated ignorance — to cultural and religious conservatism and fundamentalism. Remember, typically, ignorance and fundamentalism greatly diminish rationality and critical thinking. Unavoidably, thereby, ignorance and fundamentalism greatly diminish and distort factual reality. The presumptions, ignorance and zeal of left hemisphere fundamentalism also erode integrity, responsibility and accountability. At its belligerent and blundering quixotic worst, the fanciful and wilful ignorance of conservatism and fundamentalism, predisposes the aberrations, insanity, criminality and violence of the religious and political versions of Mr Hyde.

Are conservatism and fundamentalism and egoic ignorance inseparable?

Are conservatism and fundamentalism prone to common quixotic traits and actions of the highly masculine — Mr Hyde?

Might the fundamentalist term 'eternal', and fundamentalist idea the earth was created by and invisible God about 6,000 years ago, arise from arbitrarily assumed, imaginary, romantic, primeval beliefs that have no basis in fact or science; and more importantly, that have no basis in reality or actuality?

Note our primordial predispositions to make-up, confabulate, imbibe, assert and inculcate arbitrary, assumed, imaginary, fanciful and, romantic fundamentalist beliefs. This is a telling blend of multi-millennia-long human inclinations. They are a telling blend of thousands of years of human arbitrariness, delusion and mindlessness.

Have the mindless, primordial superstitions and delusions of prehistory mutated into the mindless, fundamentalist dispositions and memes of our contemporary institutional religions? And, more recently, have arbitrary, primordial superstitions and delusions mutated into the equally primitive ignorance of the fundamentalisms and mindless memes of modern new-age, social media, junk-science, pop-psychology, counter culture and conspiracy proneness? Are superstitions, myths and memes a dominant aspect of the human mind in 2022?

Ignorance and Beliefs

In the 21st century, are we still strongly influenced by a hotchpotch of ancient and contemporary superstitious, illusions and delusions that we call 'beliefs'? Today, there are a plethora of beliefs in religion, which is prominent for over five billion people. Plus, there are hundreds of millions who subscribe to new-age pop-psychology, alternative science and conspiratorial beliefs. And there is very recent modern phenomena of arbitrary, made-up social media memes which are the 21st century version and equivalent of ancient superstitions?

Is much of the human world is governed by a plethora and hotchpotch of baseless, factless stuff?

Does this stuff consists of a messy mix of factless, uncritiqued beliefs.

Do we moderners continue to be under the sway of arbitrary beliefs that are extensions and versions of primordial superstitions, institutionalised religious fundamentalisms, and romanticised, pre-science, pre-enlightenment fantasy and ignorance?

Are these typical left hemisphere Yang-oriented defaults.

Sit with these questions.

What are your thoughts?

Ignorance and Arbitrariness

Is arbitrariness pivotal to all these fantastical dispositions and defaults?

Might our references to God, 'the eternal' and 'creation' be nothing more than unexamined, arbitrary, wishful ignorance; intuited and felt as assumptions, and expressed as beliefs?

Are references to God, the eternal and creation, expressions of masculinised arbitrary, institutionalised, fundamentalist ignorance?

Are they extensions and expressions of the arbitrary, fanciful egoic mind?

In all this, are ancient superstitions, religious beliefs and hip new-age and social media memes — 'mindless' — baseless, arbitrary, fictitious — uncritiqued, unsubstantiated, irrational and unaccountable?

Does the human penchant for egoic arbitrariness drive a mishmash of institutionalised ignorance?

Again, note the words: arbitrary, wishful and imaginary. Note their connection to cultural, religious and political fundamentalism and ignorance.

What is the link between ignorant cultural, religious and political fundamentalism and the historical and contemporary distortions, degradations, harms and suffering discussed in Chapters 4–7?

Have a hotchpotch of ignorant, arbitrary delusions, distortions and degradations created many twisted and destructive man-made versions of God and religion?

Are these versions of Mr Hyde?

Is all this entirely egoic and ignorant?

Is arbitrariness inherent to the left hemisphere?

These are tough questions; but are necessary.

Existential Drivers of Fantasy

Do we humans use the idea of 'eternal life in paradise', and the ideas of endless karma and reincarnations until we 'achieve' nirvana, to compensate for our existential discomfort with fearful apprehensions about what happens after biological death?

Are the notion of eternal life and reincarnation nothing more than fanciful, arbitrary compensations for age-old existential fears and ignorance?

Is the fantasy of 'life after death' nothing more than desperate and anxious wishing and wanting?

For millennia, has the combination of fear, insecurity, anxiety, desperation and ignorance hugely diminished reason and evidence-based critical thinking in relation to existential issues?

Are diminished reason and highly limited evidence-based critical thinking still the case in the 21st century?

Ironically, do existential insecurity and existential assumptiveness derive from a confounding blend of left hemisphere insecurity and assumptiveness.

Prior to Science and Reason

Was insecure, fearful, superstitious ignorance understandable prior to the scientific revolution, prior to the age of reason, and prior to the explosion of knowledge that has occurred over the past 100 years?

In the 21st century, is superstitious, fundamentalist existential ignorance no longer necessary, rational, justifiable, sustainable or helpful?

Are existential superstitions and fundamentalisms redundant?

Are religious and new-age superstitious ideas, beliefs and opinions redundant?

Arbitrary Superstitions in the 21st Century

Is a hotchpotch of baseless, deluded, existential redundancies the basis and drivers of a web of human issues and problems in the 21st century?

In this century, are mindless — ignorant, baseless man-made religious delusions as dysfunctional as dangerous as they were 1,000 years ago in the Dark Ages?

To what extent are we still under the sway of the ignorance of our anachronistic, institutional, distant religious left hemisphere past?

Can we 21st century, educated, critical thinking, science-based humans do better than the mindless — primitive, fearful, ignorant acting out of superstitious and fundamentalist ignorance?

Can we do better than left hemisphere, religious ignorance as the driver of conservatism, fundamentalism, extremism, repression and tyranny?

Once again, sit with the words arbitrary, primitive, fearful, unknowing, superstitious, fundamentalist, ignorant, delusional and acting out. They are inseparably entangled in a powerful, dysfunctional and constraining web of left hemisphere mindlessness.

Do fear, superstition, fundamentalism and ignorance remain the age-old drivers of much present-time thinking; and therefore, are they the enmeshed drivers of many modern human problems, such as cultural and religious genocide, mass murder, and the monstrous degradations of misogyny, racism, sectarianism, populism, nationalist violence, and all forms of exceptionalistic acting out, including conspiracy madness? Are left hemisphere process central plays in these aberrations?

It seems so.

Are fear, superstition, fundamentalism and ignorance the systemic core of the muddled delusional anachronistic 21st century fundamentalist and conservative mind of billions of people within many religions and cultures?

Are fear, superstition, fundamentalism and ignorance the muddled mind of 21st expressions of conservative and fundamentalist Mr Hyde?

Is it possible, that, even in the 21st century, many of us are far more primitive, ignorant, muddled, delusional, quixotic and Hyde-like than we are aware?

Are we more mindless — ignorant, muddled, conspiratorial and delusional than we willing to contemplate or consider?

Is it just too damn difficult for many of us to contemplate the crazy, monstrous stuff of 21st century quixotic Mr Hyde religious, political and cultural beliefs?

Even in this century, is it too difficult to be accountable for our baseless ignorance, for our muddle of delusional ideas, and for our unfounded, arbitrary beliefs?

Much more so, is it too difficult for religious folk to be unreservedly accountable for many crazy, monstrous religious degradations and abuses of their 'faith'?

Even today, are widespread ignorance and resistance to facts, data and rationality the key drivers of the incompatibilities between superstition and science, arbitrariness and critical thinking, fantasies and rationality, facts and beliefs, oblivion and education, dignity and abominations?

In the 21st century, is the widely-believed idea of eternal, violent torture in hell a telling example of enduring diabolical, delusional religious ignorance and unfathomable egoic resistance to facts, logic and decency? Are these beliefs are product of simplistic, exclusive and judgemental left hemisphere machinations.

Possibility

Is it possible for you and I to conceive a factual appreciation of life and death that does not include fanciful superstitions and made-up beliefs about God, creation, eternity, heaven, hell, karma, reincarnation and nirvana?

Equally, is it possible to conceive a factual appreciation of existence that does not involve faddish, new-age ideas of an omniscient, intentional, personal universe that exists to give you and me whatever each of us 'wants'; whether that be a parking spot, wealth or fame?

Remember — Dignity and Rationality

Instead of fanciful, arbitrary beliefs and contrived arbitrary confabulations about God or the universe that knows, would it help us to nurture an encompassing right hemisphere values-based internal locus of dignity, and a fact-based internal locus of rationality?

Would it help if we focussed on the mutuality of dignity and rationality, instead of conjuring more and more arbitrary and delusional religious and new-age superstitions, fantasies, fads and conspiracy theories; which, together, generate more and more mindless egoic ignorance, fear, insecurity, misinformation, disinformation, confusion, divisions and conflict? Mutuality is a right hemisphere disposition.

Before You Move On

Which of these questions resonate strongly for you? Reread them. Highlight them. Make some margin notes. Sit with them without talking.

Which questions have perplexed, annoyed or offended you? Highlight them. Sit with them without talking.

Weave these questions into two maps: 1. a map of issues, and 2. a map of possibilities for reducing these issues.

Breathe. Reflect. Be open. Wonder. Be curious. Critique. Be aware of thoughts, feelings and questions that are percolating to the surface. Vis a vis — be mindful.

As said before, feel free to sit in silent, open curiosity; for minutes, hours, years and decades.

Questions about Faith, Meaning and Purpose

Let's dive straight in.

The human mind is packed full with a conglomeration of assumptive, arbitrary notions of faith, meaning and purpose. Accordingly, I have packed a lot into this chapter, and into each of the following questions. The questions reveal many left hemisphere tendencies, about which most of us are almost completely unaware. Most of us assume and contend that our mind is tidy, intelligent, factual, knowledgeable, true, righteous, rational, wise, reliable and faithful. We assume that what we think about faith, meaning and purpose is solid wisdom, inarguable truth and inspired spiritual enlightenment. The following questions challenge these typical left hemisphere assumptions, preconceptions and contentions.

Assumptions about Meaning and Purpose

Is there inherent purpose and meaning in creation, vis a vis, 'the universe'; or are meaning and purpose more examples of our unexamined, arbitrary, fantastical assumptions?

Are assumed meaning and assumed purpose — wishful, dreamy, esoteric arbitrary, man-made projections?

Are they grandiose, imaginative speculations; titillating confabulations; and motivating idealisms?

Reread the previous questions. They summarise some of the common tendencies of the human mind. Typically, we are mindlessly — uncritically — assumptive, whimsical, dreamy, sentimental, fantastical, grandiose, speculative, idealistic, confabulating, and pleasure-seeking. Don't brush over the previous sentence. Unaware, a huge proportion of us humans combine these mental dispositions when we talk and talk and talk about esoteric fancies, such as meaning and purpose.

Be honest, at least some of the time, you and I do this stuff, don't we?

I do.

Of course, fanciful tendencies are not the entirety of the human mind. But when we look at the historical and current extent of our arbitrary, fanciful, religious and new-age confabulations, they comprise a fair chunk of our mental activity. As observed before, the only broad exceptions I have encountered are Zen-like persons, disciplined scientists and mathematicians.

Do we blend assumed faith, confabulated meaning, imagined purpose and made-up romantic ideas and beliefs into fanciful stories about what we very commonly refer to as — 'life'?

Pause and sit with the elements of the previous questions. Be present to our tendency to arbitrarily assume, imagine, dream-up, fantasise, romanticise, and confabulate baseless ideas, beliefs and stories; and then to assert, defend, rationalise and normalise them as real, absolute, desirable, defendable and justifiable.

Presumption and Pretention vs Authentic Meaning, Purpose and Faith

Unawares, with the best intentions, do we mistake dreamy presumption and romantic pretention to create a feel and sense of meaning, purpose and faith?

Are we highly prone to presumptive faith and pretentious me-centred and human-centred divine purpose?

Are these tendencies the stuff of mindless religious and new-age presumption and pretention?

Are presumption and pretention indicative of the arbitrary, fanciful assumptive human mind; yours and my presumptive, pretentious mind; and the presumptive, pretentious mind of billions of us?

Ironically, are these arbitrary mind-made proclivities the epitome of 'mindlessness'?

Individually and collectively, is the human mind a conglomeration of mindless — arbitrary, fanciful, presumptive, pretentious and glibly pontifical stories, which have scant basis in fact and actuality?

Do the vast majority of our pretentious esoteric stories have no basis in the rigors of logic, critical thinking or factual evaluation?

As such, do many esoteric stories fall within the realm of presumptive mindlessness?

The Pleasure of Whimsy

Do we mistake 'the pleasure of whimsy' for enlightened spirituality?

Are the popular notions of faith, meaning and purpose a symptom of our historical and modern-day religious, new-age penchant for mindless — pleasurable, fantastical, dreamy, romantic, idealistic whimsy'?

Our disposition to dreamy, pleasurable, romantic, idealistic whimsy is telling. It reveals a lot about the arbitrary, fantastical conjuring of the 'modern' ego.

Keep your eye on ego. Later, we'll look closely at the machinations of the masculinised, left hemisphere, egoic-mind; including the arbitrary egoic mind.

A Call to Awareness and Caution

Do we need to be aware, reflective and cautious in the light of so many dodgy arbitrary, fantastical presumptions and pretentions of faith?

Is the presumption, faith, a dreamy mental and psychological phantom?

Is faith a man-made, mind-made phantom created by assumptive, romantic, wishful whimsy?

Do we confound the possibility of faith with made up, insecure, idealistic, self-indulgent, grandiose, self-important, me-centric, humancentric, left hemisphere beliefs and stories?

What a telling network of propensities — insecurity, arbitrariness, fantasising, presumption, pretention, self-indulgence, grandiosity, idealism, egocentricity and human-centricity. These dispositions are birds of a feather that flock together. They are core components and bedfellows of mindlessness.

Where do rationality, critical thinking and factual reality fit in this mix?

The answer is — there is no place for critical thinking and fact-based reality in this phantastic mix of mental and psychological predilections.

Are dignity, rationality and other values and priorities the unseen causalities of the stifling of factfulness and critical thinking?

Do we diminish reverence and dignity for ourselves, our fellow species and the earth when we distort and deny the reality of who and what we humans are — the species, Homo sapien?

Observe the irony and paradox in the erosion of reverence and dignity through assumptive left hemisphere religious and new-age delusions of grandiose human-centricity.

The Irony of Faith and Beliefs

Are irony and paradox rife in our network of presumptive faith and contrived beliefs?

What might irony and paradox tell us about what we presume is 'faith'?

Might irony suggest that assumed faith derives from existential ignorance, fear, insecurity, and doubt; not from peaceful, silent, trusting presence and sentience?

Are religious and new-age faith more akin to mindless yabber than it is to peaceful, still, calm, unspoken, sentient presence and trust?

Pause, and sit with this irony. A fulsome appreciation might take a while to sink-in and gel; perhaps months, years, decades.

Beliefs

Absorb the irony of the following questions.

Are religious and new-age beliefs nothing more than extensions of titillating, grandiose, imaginative, projective whimsy and wishfulness that we employ in the absence of authentic calming, peaceful, sentient faith?

As such, are traditional religious beliefs and hip new-age fads thinly disguised, fanciful, me-centred, self-serving misrepresentations of the possibility of 'faith without presumption', 'faith without pretentious grandiosity', 'faith without arbitrary beliefs', and 'faith without mindless babble'?

Are 'my' beliefs a reflection of 'the fearful insecure egoic me', rather than an expression of an internal locus of 'peaceful, sentient faith' in the midst of unknowing, uncertainty, apprehension and difficulties?

Are religious and new-age beliefs nothing more than delusional ideas into which we project whims, wishes, hopes, fears, insecurities and self-serving ambitions?

Are religious and new-age beliefs mere fanciful mental imaginings that we fancifully and arbitrarily presume are divine or celestial?

If this is the case, are many religious and new-age beliefs glibly fanciful at best, and grandiosely delusional at worst?

Are religious and new-age beliefs nothing more than dreamy, magical thinking and made-up desires; with scant basis in the realities of the facts, science and logic?

Do we confound faith with a mishmash of confabulated, egoic religious stories and egoic new-age fluff; both of which inflate our ego and make us feel good, right, righteous, important and safe; but which, ironically, are not calming, stilling and faith-imbuing?

Sit with the irony of these possibilities for hours, weeks and years.

Ulterior Motives for Faith and Spirituality

Are most notions of faith and 'spirituality' mindless, easy-lazy-uncritical ways to avoid the ecology of our chemical, biological and evolutionary actuality?

Are pretentions of faith and spirituality the easy-lazy presumptive way to minimise the disciplines of critical thinking, science, and accountability for fact-based rationality and logic?

Do we get-off on feeling that our espoused faith and spiritual beliefs are exclusive, virtuous, right and self-validating?

Do we substitute the assumptive ease of professing faith and spirituality as easy-lazy avoidance of the mindful disciplines of presence and sentience; and an easy-lazy way to avoid the rigors of the realities of data, facts and critical thinking?

Do we substitute the easy hubris of an uncritical profession of faith and spirituality, simply because the hubris of profession feels good; because it is easy; because it doesn't require mentor rigor or accountability?

Do we presume that subjective hubris is evidence of faith and spirituality?

Do we latch onto faith and 'spiritual beliefs' because we need to feel certain and safe in life, but even more so in death?

Do we latch onto faith and spirituality because, egoically, we are fearful, insecure and don't accept that there is much that we don't know, and much that we can't definitively interpret, predict and control?

Does the pretence of faith and claims of spiritual beliefs feel comforting and reassuring?

Is it pleasurable to feel comforted and reassured through esoteric assertions of faith and spirituality?

Is it easier to default to the comfort and pleasure of esoteric reassurance, even if it is baseless and mindless?

Do we contrive and latch onto faith and supposed spiritual beliefs because we need to conjure a pretend mental release from the dry, arduous, complexity and precariousness of existence?

Do notions of faith and espoused beliefs reduce complexity to easy, simplistic notions and assertions?

Does the contrived pretence of humans as 'spiritual beings' feel more desirable than unpretentious ordinariness of being chemical, biological and evolutionary creatures?

Do egoic, self-validating, feel-good faith and spiritual contrivances enrich us; or do they diminish us?

Do they lead us up the garden path — 'the titillating mystical path to mythical Garden of Eden'?

Do feel-good notions and faith and spiritual contrivances nurture reverence, dignity, integrity, reason and accountability?

Or, are notions of faith and spirituality egoic delusions that make us fearful, insecure and a tad crazy?

Meaning Without Presumptive Faith and Fanciful Beliefs

Can we discern meaning without presuming man-contrived religious faith in God; and without presuming new-age faith in an omniscient universe?

Can we discern meaning without making up fantastical beliefs; and without concocting titillating, esoteric stories?

Can we do better than dreamy, childish, romantic, idealistic, man-made pseudo-meaning?

Can we do better than easy-lazy whimsy?

Altogether, can we do better than mindlessly making-stuff-up, esoteric pleasure-seeking, egoic self-importance and egoic human-centricity?

Can we do better than assuming that our man-made contrived spiritual hotchpotch is authentic faith and meaning?

Can we do better than habitual, presumptive arbitrariness, which we mistake for faith, spirituality, enlightenment, meaning and purpose?

Is it possible for faith, spirituality, meaning and purpose not to be confounded by our typical, contrived narcissistic fluff?

Can you and I and humankind do better than made up, idealistic, grandiose fluff?

Is there dignity and reason in the irrationality, incredulity, shallowness and nativity of mindless — childish, egoic, religious and dreamy new-age whimsy?

Can we discern, perceive and embrace an internal locus of dignity and rationality as an alternative to the mindless fantasies of religious beliefs and new-age fancies?

Does our attraction to feel-good fantasy erode our capacity for a grounded, peaceful, internal locus of reality?

Might awareness of the dignity of reason arise if we let go of fantastical, self-embellishing beliefs and fanciful, self-important notions of spirituality?

Does history show us that it is it a short step from left hemisphere delusional, narcissistic religious, new-age and political beliefs — to monstrous Mr Hyde religious and sectarian abuses, and monstrous Mr Hyde exceptionalistic violence — as exemplified by the left hemisphere extremes of The Taliban and Putin.?

Pause

Pause; sit quietly; breathe; reflect; don't talk. Wonder. Let clarity emerge over days, months and years.

Coming to clarity and peace with these issues is a very long process. Clarity can only arise from a lifelong commitment to mindful — peaceful, non-presumptive, non-defensive right hemisphere reflection, self-honesty, critical thinking and accountability. In case you skipped-over the previous sentence, clarity can only come from lifelong commitment to reflection, self-honesty, critical thinking and accountability.

What are you thinking and feeling?

What realities and possibilities are emerging?

Where to from here?

Questions about Imagination, Speculation and Fantasy

Try not to rush through the questions in this chapter. Take your time. Read, pause, breathe, reflect, and wonder.

These questions are closely related to the ones in the previous two chapters. Note the role of imaginative ideas, speculation and fantasies in all domains of human existence.

More Penetrating Questions about Our Quirky, Esoteric Human Dispositions

Do we humans tend to 'get off' on dreamy, imaginative, speculative fantasy?

Do we get off on romantic wishful thinking?

Do we get-off on feel-good, romantic, wishful ideas and dreamy confabulations?

Do we get-off on romantic statements such as, 'God knows; it was meant to happen; everything happens for a reason; the universe will provide'.

Do these statements arouse us mentally and emotionally?

Do they give us the 'pleasure of knowing'; the arousal of being important, wise and 'spiritual'; and the comfort of assume we are safe?

These are all 'feel-good' experiences.

Consider the feel-good hormones; serotonin, oxytocin, dopamine, oestrogen and testosterone. Are any of these released when we engage in pleasurable, esoteric fantasies, active fantastical imagination, and free-flowing esoteric confabulation?

At a hormonal level, are we humans addicted to imaginative grandiosity and romantic speculation; including imagining that we know about the divine, that we can talk knowingly about God, and can even converse with 'Almighty God', The Creator, the 'I-Am'?

It would make me feel pretty special if I could actually talk with God, and if I know the mind of God. This would feel very trippy indeed.

But, again, ironically, might such glib, fantastical grandiosities diminish my potential for a grounded internal locus of factfulness and reason?

Might these grandiosities diminish my expression of grace and love through non-judgemental compassion and kindness?

Do esoteric grandiosities distract me from facts, data and reality?

Do they diminish my rationality, and perhaps, my sanity?

Are they patently egoic and ignorant?

Do they diminish my dignity?

Even more ironically, might these grandiosities diminish the possibility of faith?

Human-Centred Idealisms

Are we prone to inventing human-centred mystical idealisms and stories simply because they're mentally pleasurable, and because they massage our ego?

Similarly, do we humans get off on the importance of our assumed and claimed special relationship with God; our assumed and fantasised special role in creation; our assumed and fantasised special salvation; our assumed and fantasised special karma; our assumed and fantasised special reincarnations; our assumed and fantasised special enlightenment; and our assumed and fantasised special place in eternity, heaven, nirvana and the universe?

Is this stuff a tad egocentric; even patently narcissistic?

Is it mindless?

Is it mostly man-made?

Is it classic left hemisphere?

Pause for a moment. Sit, breathe, reflect, and wonder.

Egoic Imaginings as Self-Indulgence

Might egoic imaginings and speculations about special human-centred, me-centred assumptions be classic, fluffy, narcissistic self-indulgence?

Consider our egoic self-indulgence in — special me-centred imaginings and speculations; special human-centred ideas; special imaginative, romantic, poetic self-adulation and human grandiosity; and dreamy self-adulation. Are these the classic irrationality of delusional, narcissistic hedonism?

Sit in silence. Wonder about our propensity for egoically arbitrary, grandiose, self-indulgent fantasising, narcissism and hedonism.

Note the roles of ego and ignorance in all these propensities.

Might our religious and new-age beliefs be the habituated arbitrary indulgences of ignorant, egoic, magical thinking and ignorant, egoic, wishful whimsy?

Sit with the words,' habituated indulgences of ego'. They are revealing and instructive; but only if we let them sober us, challenge us and critique us.

What does our web of egoic tendencies say to you?

What does our web of ignorant tendencies say to you?

Do these tendencies show that we humans are prone to mindless — self-indulgent, wishful, poetic licence; grandiose poetic licence; narcissistic poetic licence; and hedonistic poetic licence?

All in all, are our religious beliefs and spiritual ideas self-indulgent expressions of extreme poetic licence?

Are religious beliefs confounded by the inanity of childish, imaginative, romantic, self-indulgent, hedonistic wishful whimsy?

Are they self-indulgent at best, and narcissistically crazy at worst?

Is the stuff of egoic mindlessness?

Is the stuff of mindless ignorance?

Can We Do Better?

Can we do better than man-made arbitrary, imaginary, fantastical, self-indulgent, romantic poetic, wishful, religious and new-age whimsy?

Can we do better than the grandiose indulgence of our pretentious, self-important special relationship with God and the universe?

Can we do better than the egoically grandiose, narcissistic idea of our assumed, special place and role in creation; our assumed, special salvation; and our assumed, special place in eternity, heaven, karma, nirvana, and the universe?

Instead of making-up egoically self-indulgent, me-centred, human-centred religious and new-age fluff about how special we are; can we sit in 'quiet, unpretentious faith' with the ordinariness of not assuming, not knowing, not pretending and not pontificating?

Can we be peaceful and satisfied in unpretentious human ordinariness?

Can we let-go our insecure childish egoic need to be special and important?

Can we sit peacefully in the ordinariness of being limited human animals, with limited consciousness?

That's a big ask, a big come down from being God's special ones, to the humble reality of us as intelligent, but hamstrung human animals. It is a big come down from sitting at right hand of God, to acknowledging that we are the intelligent but problematic and sadomasochistic animal species, Homo sapiens.

Or, are we too attached to the egoic hedonistic, self-serving grandiosity, reassurance, ease and indulgence that arise from pretending to know God and the conscious universe; and pretending to be special through religious beliefs and new-age fancies?

Are we humans incurably addicted to the physiological, psychological and intellectual pleasure of an array of indulgent, aggrandising, dreamy, romantic ideas?

Are we terminally addicted to the mental stimulation of the self-importance that are inherent in our self-obsessed pretentious fantasies and stories?

Are these questions indicative of our propensity for narcissistic mindlessness — that we proffer and disguise as enlightenment and spirituality?

Is distraction with all this fantastical stuff a means of control and diversion from reality?

Pause

Will you pause and wonder in silence about these questions, propensities and issues?

Will you wonder in silence about the possibility of the sufficiency of mindful, unpretentious ordinariness?

Or will you rush to mental chatter about preconceived ideas that reinforce your presumptions; chatter that confirms your pretentions and pontifications? Will you rush to the chatter of claims, assertions and defences that bolster your indulgent beliefs and opinions; chatter that stirs your emotional reactions and arouses your default self-justifications? Will you rush to presumptions and pretentions that rehash and reinforce your assumed, self-gratifying, arbitrary predilections? Be alert to the triggers that predispose egoic, righteous indignation and egoic self-justification.

In all these cautions, be alert to the ubiquitous, self-aggrandising, self-justifying voices and stories of ego. We will look closely at egoic voices in a later chapter.

Questions about Presumption, Pretention and Pontification

In this chapter, we will critique our thoroughly modern new-age habits of presuming to know, pretending to know, and glibly pontificating about all sorts of spiritual, psychological, societal and scientific stuff.

Definitive Opinionated Statements vs Open Enquiring Questions

Have you noticed that in everyday conversations we tend to make many more definitive statements than we ask open, curious, enquiring questions?

These days, are open, curious, enquiring questions a rarity?

Have you noticed that many esoteric statements are opinionated, definitive, absolute; and aren't open to critical analysis, data-based evidence and fact-checking?

Have you noticed that statements, opinions and beliefs often assume an air of authority, certitude and moral superiority?

Opinionated, moralistic, esoteric statements and certainties are the stuff of presumption, pretention and pontification. Most often, opinions and statements about mystical stuff are not based on open-mindedness and critical thinking; but are arbitrary, anecdotal and inductive. These three are not an authoritative, reliable or useful blend. It's a very short step from arbitrary, inductive anecdotes to shallow speculation, to dreamy whimsical fantasy, to ignorance and bullshit; then another short step to wilful ignorance; and yet another step to intentional deception and lies. Reread the previous sentence. Let it sink in.

Have you observed the network of issues summarised in the previous question and the previous paragraph?

Have you observed that presumption, pretention and pontification are very common egoic defaults among us hip, modern, opinionated know-all 21st century humans?

Do you and I and our friends assert the attitude: "It's my right to possess and express my beliefs and opinions"?

Have you noticed that it's common for us to say: "I believe", but it's rare for people to say, "I don't know the facts about this issue"?

Is it also common for us to assume that we are self-important in our assumed and pretentious opinions?

Is it common to base our beliefs and opinions on the speculative, unproven, dodgy claims of junk-science, pop-psychology and conspiracy madness?

Is it common to assume that our opinions are equal to data and facts, and equal to that of genuine, authentic scientists and other credible experts?

Is it common for us to assume that our opinions are deserving of deference, and that they qualify as absolute authority?

Have you heard the term, 'alternative facts'?

The term is code for, made up stories, subjective anecdotal opinions, arbitrary beliefs and conspiratorial fantasies and lies.

Facts are definitive, measurable and testable. Opinions and beliefs are not. Facts come from data and rigorous empirical processes. Opinions and beliefs come from subjective, arbitrary thoughts, untested ideas, sample-of-one anecdotes and inductive logic.

We Hip Moderners

Have you observed that we hip moderners feel driven to air, assert and defend our subjective, untested opinions and beliefs?

Are we inclined to strongly defend our made-up opinions and contrived beliefs; even if they are contrary to credible, measurable, testable data, scientific convention and logic?

Do we say: "I have researched this topic". Meaning, I have read a few biased, unempirical, uncritiqued, made-up Google articles.

Do we feel special when we spruik pretentious beliefs and know-all opinions?

Do we feel virtuous and righteous when we contend that we are right and moral?

Do we get off on the pretentious self-importance and self-appointed authority that accompanies the spruiking of our righteous opinions and high-minded beliefs?

Have you observed the reaction you get when you say: "I'll need to fact-check your claims, and see what the evidence says"?

Why do so many of us unlearned, unqualified, uncredentialed, unexperienced moderners so typically presume, pretend and pontificate as if we are highly educated, highly experienced, highly credible, widely recognised, legitimately authoritative experts?

Note the descriptors, unlearned, unqualified, uncredentialed, unrecognised and unexperienced.

Why don't we submit to and follow the dry, slow, rigorous, rational, logical empirical processes of acquiring and assessing measurable and testable facts, data, knowledge and information?

Is it because it's far more pleasurable to presume, pretend and pontificate; while dry, slow, rigorous assessment processes are really hard work, not nearly so egoically pleasurable, and not nearly so egoically self-gratifying as being self-declared experts?

Is it because we much prefer the egoic, pretentious self-promotion of virtuous opinions and pious beliefs?

For most of us, are presumption, pretention and pontification so psychologically pleasurable and titillating that they are irresistible?

Do we tend to assume that the whimsical, made-up stuff of our imagination is valid and correct primarily because it feels good, it feels right, it feels righteous, and it feels so self-confirming?

Does this sound tad egoic; a tad narcissistic?

Does our egoic-mind manufacture and drive our indulgent flights of self-righteous, opinionated fancy?

Do you presume, pretend and pontificate as described above?

There are times when I do.

Or, do you feel compelled to carefully and slowly ascertain and fastidiously analyse credible data, facts and evidence>

Do you prefer critical thinking to arbitrary presumption, self-righteous pretention and grandiose pontification?

The Easy-Lazy-Assumptive Way

Typically, are arbitrary opinions, beliefs and imagination easy-lazy-assumptive-pretentious substitutes for the life-long discipline of recognised formal study, solid qualifications, professionalism, credible experience, and constant accountability to rigorous, factual, logical, process-disciplined critique of highly qualified peers and assessors?

Are presumption, pretention, pontification and imagination an easy-lazy form of unearned, untested, unchallenged, self-promotion and self-aggrandisement?

Again, do we prefer the easy-lazy way because rigorous intellectual, academic, educational and scientific processes are too demanding, too exacting, and too accountable?

A lifetime of exacting discipline and accountability is a tough gig.

Is all this new-age, easy-lazy fluff classically egoic? That is to say, is it classically hedonistically self-serving, self-aggrandising, self-indulgent, self-titillating, and self-justifying? Note the reciprocal relationship between ego and self. Later, we'll look closely at that relationship; and at the relationship between ego and ignorance.

Can We Do Better

Can we do better than egoic fluff that is strongly aversive to disciplined processes, rigorous critique and unflinching accountability for sound methodology and accurate, credible conclusions?

Can we do better by subjecting our beliefs, opinions and ourselves to critical thinking, fact checking and accountability?

Can we do better by subjecting ourselves to unreserved scrutiny and unfiltered logic and rationality?

Can we 21st century people do better than hedonistic, self-indulgent arbitrary presumption, pretention and pontification?

Can we do better than pretentious, hedonistic opinions and self-promoting self-serving beliefs?

Can we do better than spruiking whatever dreamy fluff we imagine or pretend is fine-sounding, absolute and righteous?

These questions are examples of self-reflective critical inquiry. They have the potential to help us recognise how easily we default to the fantasy and irrationality of arbitrariness and baseless confabulation?

Questions about Ego and God

Egoic Presumption or Faith

Predominantly, might 'the assumed voice of faith' be the imaginative, presumptive, pretentious voice of the masculine ego — the masculine ego masquerading as faith?

From that possibility, might we take 'a leap of faith' and consider human existence without the egoic presumption, God; without the egoic mind's grand presumption of divinity; without the hedonistic presumptions of divine purpose, eternal design and a human-centred cosmic plan; and without the presumption and pretention of a human-centred personal, intentional, omniscient universe?

The previous three-part question is a lot to take in. Pause for a moment, breathe, reread it, and breathe again.

Might our default to presumptive and romanticised beliefs about us, God, creation and a personal universe be the easy-lazy-dreamy path of our lazy-dreamy-egoic-mind?

Ego — God

The next question is a biggie.

Might God be nothing more than a whimsical projection of ego; a figment of arbitrary, projective, egoic imagination; a figment of masculine imagination and grandiosity?

Might God be the ultimate egoic projection of assumed and contrived man-made human-self-importance?

Is God our quintessential self-indulgent, egoic projection of men?

Is god a projection of the self-important left hemisphere?

Does our masculine, egoic, humancentric, left hemisphere mind masquerade as God?

And / or, is God our egoic security blanket; our egoic existential reassurance; our egoic comfort zone; our egoic 'go-to' when we don't know, when we feel insecure, when we face adversity, and when we are afraid, anxious and unsure?

In all these esoteric possibilities, is the projection, 'God', an expression of egoic, existential desperation?

Or, is the notions of a masculinised Sky-God a left hemisphere ruse to distract us a grounded, right hemisphere appreciation of our oneness with nature?

How would it feel not to default to God as our presumption and projection?

Can we do better than the pretentious, grandiose, arbitrary, man-made egoic presumptions, pretentions and projections mentioned in this chapter?

How are you feeling about and responding to these questions?

Questions about Story-Making

Story-Making

Does the narrating, story-making egoic male mind confabulate exotic, romantic, dramatic myths about humans, God, the Devil, angels, eternity, creation, heaven, hell, the universe, karma, nirvana, past lives, ancestors, and reincarnations?

Essentially, is the egoic human mind an esoteric story-making, myth-making machine?

How much capacity do we humans have to moderate our disposition and default to make up 'God' stories and a mishmash of other exotic fantasies and confabulations?

This is a very important question.

Are we, especially us men, hard-wired to make up God-stories, and all sorts of other esoteric fantasies?

Are man-made God-stories, the confabulating egoic mind, and the story-making left hemisphere dominated human brain, one and the same?

Are they unchangeably, irredeemably hardwired and enmeshed?

It seems important to be aware that our confabulated esoteric stories are a huge distraction from the factual reality and rational groundedness of the ecology of human existence.

Are confabulated God-stories delusional, dysfunctional and damaging.

Do masculinised God-stories tend to control and harm the poor and powerless by keeping them uninformed, ill-informed, uncritical, uneducated, ignorant, subservient, compliant, powerless and conformist?

Do man-made, left hemisphere Abrahamic God-stories, such as the Genesis injunction to take and possess, justify our egoic drive to plunder resources and subjugate the earth?

Are egoically confabulated God-stories inherent in the masculinised, religious Mr Hyde syndrome that degrades and abuses humankind, our fellow species, and the earth?

Is colonisation built-on, driven and justified by left hemisphere contrived, man-made Genesis God-stories, God injunctions and God-fundamentalisms?

Can we do better than arbitrarily contrived, delusional, dramatic, anthropocentric and exploitative 'man-made Mr Hyde God-stories'?

Can we do better than spurious God-justifications for Mr Hyde's human shams, quixotry, harms and degradations?

Note that all references to the masculine, left hemisphere 'Mr' Hyde. A right hemisphere Mrs Hyde did not get mentioned, because she does not exist. Mr Hyde is solely responsible for Hyde-made, Hyde-driven human issues.

Questions about Evolution, Chemistry and Biology

Dry Ordinariness vs Esoteric Titillation

Would it be okay if evolution is a network of neutral processes, from which 'life' is manifested as biological lifeforms; including us humans, as one lifeform among millions?

Would it be okay if we are a lifeform; not a special 'being', not a God-made 'soul'; just a human animal, biologically related to a myriad of other carbon-based animals?

Or, do we fantastical, pretentious, hedonistic, self-indulgent, story-making, egocentric humans need something more 'spiritual', something more mystical, something more self-important, and something much more special, grandiose and indulgent than the science of our chance evolution as a 'lifeform'?

Does the egoic masculine human mind need something more romantic, something more exciting, something more esoteric and exotic, something more magical, something more human-centric, something more esoterically grandiose?

Do we egoic humans crave something more titillating than the dry ordinariness of the evolution of Chemistry and Biology as 'the non-esoteric essence' of human existence?

Is dry ordinariness too unappealing and too unimportant for the self-promoting masculine egoic human mind?

Can we get beyond whimsical, fantastical imagining, contriving and conjuring the egoic indulgences of 'our creation', of our Creator, and of 'our' conscious universe?

Biology, not Religion

Is 'life on earth' simply the exquisite ecology of biological life forms; not some religious drama; and not new-age fairy stories and pantomimes?

What if you and I are just another species; not the pre-eminent species; merely one species among 8.7 million of our fellow species?

Is that okay?

Is there dignity and joy in the wonder of our personal and species biology, chemistry and ecology?

Is there reverence and joy in the wonder of the ecology of our shared biology and evolution?

Can you and I live peacefully, contentedly and fulsomely with the earth as it has evolved, not as we fantasise it was created by a masculine God?

I can — peacefully, contentedly, reverently, joyfully and gratefully so.

Can you and I and humankind do better than fantastical and wilful religious and new-age ignorance of the geological, chemical, biological, ecological and evolutionary facts of our existence?

Questions about the Human Brain

Not as Advanced as We Assume

For the collective of humankind, is our left-hemisphere human brain too unevolved to function without egoic — man-made arbitrariness, superstition, speculation, stories, fantasy, aggrandisement, self-promotion and projection?

The answer so far, is a resounding: "Yes!" Over four billion of us left-hemisphere humans presume, confabulate and project — God. Billions confabulate heaven, hell, angels, spirits, and the existence of a human soul. Billions of us new-agers confabulate a personal universe; stories of personal angels that find us parking spots; and that stories of angels as the fantastical and magical entities that help us solve a wide array of trivial, self-absorbed, self-centred problems.

Hope for Values and Rationality as Guides to Human Existence

Can a critical mass of us let go of arbitrary egoic religious and new-age imaginings, fantasies and confabulations, and embrace the priorities, values, principles and processes of relational and ecological dignity, respect, integrity, science, critical thinking, and accountability?

Can the majority of us embrace reverence, decency and kindness as a core-values for humans, a core values towards other species, and toward the earth?

It is possible for long-held fantastical, man-made mythical stories to be superseded by a network of values such as awareness, sensitivity, compassion, logic, ethical propriety and accountability?

Can the priorities of right hemisphere values, principles and processes guide human existence forward toward rational systems thinking, ecological harmony, peace, simplicity, contentment, gratitude and joy in the oneness of diversity?

Can the human brain arouse the right hemisphere and embrace dignifying, rational and pragmatic relational, communal and ecological systems values, principles and priorities?

Would the arousal of right-brain and right-mind have the requisite capacities to prioritise strategic relational, communal and ecological values and principles that are necessary to sustain the existence of Homo sapiens, our fellow species, ecosystems, environments and the earth as a whole?

Are the right-hemisphere-guided human brain and mind capable of sophisticated systems-appreciation, systems-discipline, systems-subtlety, systems-holism and systems oneness; the combination of which is required to restore and perpetually sustain the ecologies of the biosphere?

Can the human brain and the human mind do better than our current tangled, chaotic self-indulgent, man-made, human-centred web of arbitrariness, superstition, materiality, individualism, greed, profiteering, power-mongering, and empire building?

Can we do better than this web of man-made barriers to pragmatic, ecological rationality, dignity and harmony?

Can the human brain be reset to harness the survival pragmatism of ecological facts, rationality, integrity and accountability?

Many First Peoples cultures show that humans are capable of this right hemisphere blend of personal, relational, communal and ecological imperatives. There is hope for us if we can put aside masculinised thinking and embrace First People relational, communal, systems and ecological mindfulness and wisdom. We will look closely at this wisdom toward the end of the book. In the meantime, there is much more to critique; and critique we shall.

Question about Violence and Degradation

Remember to breathe before you read.

Primordial Times

The following questions take us back to the Chapters 4–7. They take us back to my purpose in writing this book; and back to my rationale for the question and title of this book, 'Can we do Better?'

Have man-made violence and degradation always been inherent in our species, perhaps as far back as 200,000 years?

Or, has human violence become increasingly more prominent since about 70,000 years ago; since the cognitive revolution; since we evolved the capacity to be 'intelligently powerful' by being — intelligently dominant; intelligently ambitious; intelligently possessive; intelligently acquisitional; intelligently accumulative; intelligently deceptive; intelligently violent; intelligently exploitative; intelligently destructive; and intelligently sadomasochistic?

Reflect on the irony of left hemisphere masculine intelligence in the service of power, domination, acquisition, possession, accumulation, violence, manipulation, exploitation and destruction. And, consequently, did this web of extreme aberrations devolve into masculine intelligence in the service of sadomasochism.

Did these devolving proclivities indicate a gradual but steady shift from a primordial Yin-Mother-Country model of 'being' — to a Yang-muscular-power-possession model of wanting, getting, possessing, extoling, controlling and dominating?

Was this Yang model created, entrenched and sustained by powerful, controlling masculine dominance?

Was the emerging violence arising from the masculinised, left agricultural power model different to pre-agricultural, inter-tribal violence that wasn't motivated by overly masculine drives for power, but was motivated by fear of scarcity, drive for survival, subsistence insurance, and protection of family and community by protection of subsistence resources and/or acquisition of subsistence resources?

Did the emergence of 'my property and my fiefdom/kingdom/empire' oriented attitudes and violence herald the emergence of the post-primordial left hemisphere male ego — the emergence and increasing prominence of masculine, egoic, left hemisphere priorities, including me, mine, self, wanting, ambition, getting and accumulating power, property, possessions and subjects?

Was this a devolution from relatively unegoic primordial, hunter-gather-forager-Yin consciousness — to increasing agricultural Yang consciousness?

Did this transition to masculinised egoic consciousness initially devolve throughout Anglo-European areas, and then spread to other parts of the globe; slowly, at first, through a gradual migration of consciousness and peoples; and later, much more quickly, through an avalanche of trade, colonisation and industrialisation?

Is this a possible explanation of the loss of the relative Yin purity of primordial hunter-gather-forager right hemisphere consciousness; due to an increasing left hemisphere, masculine, egoic cultural proclivity for domination?

Does this explanation provide some possible insights about the nature of masculine ego, its initial emergence, and its contemporary cultural, religious and political manifestations?

We will look at this situation more closely in some of the chapters on ego.

The Agricultural Era

As discussed before, did masculinised deception and violence become the new post-hunter-gather normal because agricultural humans became inclined to defend their 'property' and exploit and attack neighbouring groups and steal and 'gain' their property; including the prizes land, water, crops, houses, barns and farming equipment?

Is this a significant step beyond hunter-gathers simply being territorial?

Could it be that emerging cultural concepts of our tribe, kingdom or nation, are the beginnings of man-made masculine notions of nationalism and exceptionalism?

Did the masculine, left hemisphere notions of owning, possessing and controlling herald a profound step away from being one-with Country and

Mother Earth; and a step away from the Yin consciousness of being protectors, nurturers, stewards and custodians?

Prior to agriculture, the right hemisphere indigenous precept was that the land, the earth, owned us humans. The era of agriculture reversed this precept; and shifted ownership to the non-relational, non-ecological thing-oriented left hemisphere.

Was the violence of the agricultural era a natural masculinised egoic consequence of possessing and protecting 'my' family, 'my' group and 'my' property from 'others' who were perceived by the left hemisphere ego as threats to ownership and control?

Did the increasingly masculinised materialistic forces of agriculture facilitate devolution of humankind to cunning, deceptive, manipulative, violent and destructive egoic agricultural left hemisphere Mr Hyde?

Later, did Mr Hyde agriculture devolve to deceptively and violently possessing, accumulating and protecting money?

And later still, did agriculture devolve to owning, amassing and protecting power — the greatest prize of post-indigenous and post-agricultural ego of Mr Hyde?

And then — Institutionalised Religion

Have thousands of years of post-agricultural, institutionalised religion added a layer of left hemisphere, righteous, masculine justification for amassing materiality, wealth and power?

Has man-made institutional religion rationalised and enabled human devolution through institutional corruption and criminality — which enable and justify the amassment, maintenance and protection of property, wealth and power?

Have thousands of years of institutionalised religion generated, driven and justified the indignity and irrationality of man-made, left hemisphere divisions, enmities, exclusions, harms and suffering — all in the name of wealth, power and global domination — for rich and powerful men?

For example, by the global domination of left hemisphere Mr Hyde Christianity, and in particular, by Mr Hyde Catholicism.

Did institutional religion enable and justify devolution to various versions of a religious Mr Hyde, with all his egoically narcissistic and sociopathic proclivities?

Is religion our most long-standing, our most prominent and most institutionally entrenched manifestation of the wealth and power of the pathological Mr Hyde?

In this, is institutional religion utterly egoic; utterly man-made; utterly masculine?

Is this the devolution to of the left hemisphere to its pathological worst?

Religion and State

Is modern humankind aware that deception, exploitation, violence and degradation are inherent in millennia of devolving enmeshment between masculine religion and state, and between man-made religious dogma and man-made extremist and fundamentalist political ideologies; the combination of which resulted in our history of the sins of male-dominated power — the sins if man-made tyranny, sectarianism, nationalistic violence, exceptionalistic exploitation, mass murder and genocide?

Has the man-made nexus of religion and state created various political and ideological expressions of Mr Hyde that have existed for thousands of years; including in the 21st century?

The invasions and destruction of Afghanistan and Ukraine are religiously driven and justified by highly masculinised left hemisphere Islamism and Russian Orthodoxy.

Industry, Commercialism and Technology

Have our man-made violent and degrading tendencies escalated in the past several hundred years of Yang militarism, colonisation, industry and commerce; all with the egoic left hemisphere drives to want, acquire, possess, amass, dominate and control?

Has the relatively modern nexus between colonisation, industrialisation, consumerism, materialism and technologization catalysed escalating masculine egoic indignities of powerful and wealthy imperialism?

Did colonisation, industry, commercialism and violent technologies morph into many diabolical egoic expressions of the power-mongering, wealth-amassing Mr Hyde?

Modern Times

Have we modern, educated, affluent, commercial, industrial, consumptive, technological humans done much more man-made damage to the planet in the past 50-100 years, than our forebears did in 200,000 years? If so, WTF!

What does this situation say about the state of the devolution of the left hemisphere?

Is 21st century commercial, industrial, materialistic, consumptive technological, social media humankind the latest egoic incarnation of the power and avarice of 10,000-year-old Mr Hyde?

The previous three questions are staggering in the light of the fact that education and knowledge have flourished tremendously in the past 100 years, and has proliferated super-exponentially during the past 50 years.

How is it that, in the 21st century, arbitrary man-made religious and new-age superstition and mind-numbing conspiratorial ignorance, continue to drive degradation and violence; and thereby, greatly undermine reverence, dignity, critical thinking, decency, and 'strategic educated awareness' of whole-of-planet issues and priorities?

Are arbitrary superstition and ignorance two core components of left hemisphere Mr Hyde's ego in the 21st century?

How is that in this century, billions of people, many of whom are well educated, are stuck in the egoic indignity, disrespect, irrationality and ignorance of man-made left hemisphere religious and ideological superstitions, abuses, degradations and violence that characterised the degrading themes of power-obsessed Mr Hyde of 'Old Testament' times, and that of the Dark Ages?

Sit with the extreme incongruity and irony of the previous question.

Are you disturbed by these questions about our 21st century propensity for many man-made Machiavellian and sadomasochistic expressions of dysfunction, injustice, degradation, violence and environmental destruction?

Are you disturbed by the many pre-historical, historical, current and emerging manifestations of Mr Hyde in human form?

Mr Hyde — the archetypal post-insidious left hemisphere man — has a lot to realise and account for. His devolved, toxic masculinity has been a many millennia-old blight on the earth.

Questions about Our Conflicted Nature

This chapter seems like the logical next step for us in our exploration of Mr Hyde dysfunction and destruction.

Are we masculine humans much more egoically incongruous and conflicted than most of us are aware?

Are we much more akin to Mr Hyde than we are able to consider and admit?

Are we far more quixotic than we realise?

Are we so blindly paradoxical that we are largely unaware that many social, political and religious issues arise from our surreal, dissociated, liminal, conflicted, blundering and incongruent masculine orientations?

Is it conceivable for us to become aware that, although societal metrics have greatly improved in the past 70 years, in the 21st century, too many human attitudes and behaviours are part of our ongoing enmeshed man-made cultural, religious, political and new-age sadomasochistic dysfunction?

Why do we strongly resist the realisations and realities that, individually and collectively, we modern humans are too highly problematic, too harmful and destructive; that, clearly, we are the most problematic, harmful, destructive species on the planet?

Why do we strongly resist these realisations and realities?

Why do we strenuously resist the data, science and critical analysis that reveal the man-made human issues that threaten our existence; that threaten other species, and that threaten the earth?

Can we do better than the resistance generated by our man-made arbitrary religious and new-age superstitions, fantasies, ignorance, illusions, shadows and phantoms that are inherent in our left hemisphere dysfunctions and harms?

Can we do better than a plethora of masculinised arbitrary cognitive and emotion biases and syndromes that prevent us from being aware of the dysfunctional and destructive stuff we humans do?

Can we do better than distorting reality through fanciful, wilful and calculating ignorance?

Can we do better than resisting and distorting responsibility?

Can we become increasingly aware, honest, transparent and accountable?

Can we evolve to function much more from our Dr Jekyll dispositions, than from our Mr Hyde proclivities?

Our Self-Leveraging Transactional Dispositions

Continuing in the 21st century, has human intelligence been co-opted by left hemisphere masculinity to wilfully manoeuvre, leverage and transact people and circumstances to benefit those who crave and amass power, control, wealth and materiality?

Has masculine transactional intelligence been recruited to get what 'me' and 'my peer group' want; no matter what the consequences for myself, for others, our fellow species, and for the biosphere?

Has self-leveraging intelligence been harnessed to promote self-serving, masculine individualist, partisan, political, economic and material ambitions to benefit me, my group, my corporation, my political party, my religion, and my exceptionalistic nation — irrespective of the detriment to people, other species and the planet?

Is intelligent, self-benefiting, transactional leveraging a central aspect of contemporary Mr Hyde?

Do our masculine transactional propensities erode the dignity and rationality of our relationships with each other, our relationships with our fellow species, and our relationship with the earth?

Can We Do Better than Transactional Self-leveraging

Can we do better than being transactionally egoic — self-absorbed, selfish, greedy, materialistic, calculating, self-leveraging, wilful, cunning, deceptive, dishonest, manipulative, impositional, competitive, adversarial and aggressive?

Can we do better than being left hemisphere Mr Hyde players in power-centred and control-obsessed religious, political, economic and social domains?

Can we do better than masculine transactional predilections, self-leveraging, and individualistic short-term ambitions; at the expense of long-term relational and ecological priorities, such as minimising human suffering, and minimising harm to our fellow species and to the planet?

Can we evolve awareness of our conflicted and confounding masculinised nature, and of our Machiavellian, transactional tendencies?

Can we mindfully choose to nurture Yin-based, right hemisphere relational, communal and ecological awareness, sensitivity, discernment, integrity, decency, responsibility and accountability?

Are these capacities and possibilities real and tangible for you and me, and for many others; including our predominance of male leaders and educators?

How might we individual and collective humans nurture and develop mindful — purposeful and strategic relational, communal and ecological. capacities.

What is the next step for you?

What is the next step for our leaders and educators?

What is the next step for us men?

Questions about the Spirituality of Reverence, Dignity and Rationality

There are two more questions-chapters to go. Breathe, and stay the course.

Hope for 'A Spirituality of Reverence, Dignity and Rationality

Can we stop arbitrarily assuming that spirituality is based on the man-made notion of human pre-eminence and human-centricity?

Can the arbitrary masculinised human mind be less egocentric, less human centric and less transactional?

Can the Yang-conditioned human brain be more mindfully relational, communal and ecological?

Can spirituality not be arbitrarily masculine — not religious, new-age, fundamentalist, conservative, corporate, economic, political and nationalistic?

Can we stop assuming that spirituality is based on the pre-eminence of the individualistic person, the individualist religion, the individualistic state, the individualistic nation, or the individualistic culture, race or ethnic group?

Can we not arbitrarily assume the pre-eminence of me and my whimsical, self-serving, individualistic masculinised spiritual beliefs; and not arbitrarily assume the pre-eminence of the grandiose, indulgent, self-serving beliefs of our peer group, religion, culture, or nation?

How do we stop presumptively exaggerating and falsifying the importance of man-made, masculinised cultural, religious and political institutions and models of spirituality?

Can we grasp the inherent, insoluble contradiction of Mr Hyde's 'institutions of spirituality'?

How might you and I remove masculine human-centeredness, masculine transactionalism and leveraging, masculine institution-centredness and masculine ambition-centredness from our consciousness of spirituality?

Is it possible for 'us allegedly spiritual humans' not to place ourselves 'front and centre'; not to place ourselves before and above our fellow species, before and above our ecosystems, and before and above Mother Earth?

Can we learn from right hemisphere First Peoples, who — place themselves 'with and among' the diversity and ecology of peoples; who place themselves within the diversity and ecology their fellow species; and who place themselves 'with and within' the oneness of the biodiversity of the planet?

As do First Peoples, can yours and my mindfulness and spirituality evolve to enfold all peoples, enfold all our fellow species, and enfold the bio-diversity of the earth into 'one community of one ecology of life'?

Sit with the priority of an egalitarian, all-inclusive, biocentric 'community and ecology of life'.

Is it logical and rational for us humans to assume mystical spirituality and biological superiority if we are mere lifeforms; if we are merely the species, Homo sapiens?

Do we need to assume and assert the existence of mystical spirituality if we are mere animals; if we are exactly similar to and genetically related to all other carbon-based earthly animals?

Is a masculinised, narrow, assumptive, arbitrary, exceptionalistic view of 'human spirituality' nothing more than self-serving, dreamy, romantic, egocentric, anthropocentric and homocentric pretention and narcissism?

Is our man-made narcissistic and anthropocentric approach to 'human spirituality' the driver and justification of many My Hyde aberrations and harms?

Does this cause you to shake your head?

Can we move beyond mindless, man-made — masculinised — egoic — crazy, self-serving, anthropocentric 'spiritual' anomalies?

Spirituality Today

In many of its current new-age forms, is modern Mr Hyde spirituality a problematic egoic distortion of many factual and rational realities?

Is much of our 21st century spirituality defined by egoic masculine arbitrariness, fantasy, self-absorption, self-indulgence, superiority and vanity?

160

How might we identify and embrace potential mindful dimensions of spirituality without creating problems such as man-made — racism, genderism, chauvinism, sectarianism, exceptionalism, nationalism, individualism; and so many other isms?

How might we minimise our default to the same old hedonistic, self-indulgent, self-serving, self-promoting stuff that arises from the man-made left hemisphere human-centricity of traditional religion and the narcissism of new-age pop-spirituality?

In the 21st century, can we do better than institutionalised patriarchal, chauvinistic and misogynistic — sectarian, exceptionalistic, nationalistic expressions of spirituality?

Can we do better than hip new-age junk-spirituality?

Can we do better than insane, man-made conspiracy spirituality?

How do we explore spirituality, mindfulness and consciousness without defaulting to masculinised arbitrary, narcissistic superstition, dreamy fantasy, esoteric speculation, and projective myth-making; and without defaulting to masculinised selfish, indulgent transactional leveraging?

How do we explore spirituality, mindfulness and consciousness, but not default to man-made egocentricity, homocentricity and anthropocentricity?

Can we move beyond institutional religion and new-age junk-spirituality and evolve conscious, mindful, sensitive, reasoned values and priorities; and evolve dignified strategic intentions, principles and actions?

Might Yin-Mother principles such as compassion, decency, relationship, community, ecology, simplicity, contentment, gratitude and joy be the essence of spirituality — without convoluted man-made religious or new-age dogma, without pretentious beliefs, without dogmatic prescriptions and impositions; without constraining masculine conservatisms and inane fundamentalisms; and without transactional, masculine economic or political power motives and passive-aggressive masculine control undercurrents?

Can we evolve a Yin-spirituality that is mindfully rational, compassionate, sensitive and accountable?

Can we evolve and transition to a right hemisphere spirituality of mindful reverence, dignity, decency and grace?

Can we evolve a spirituality of mindful integrity?

Can we evolve a Yin-Mother spirituality of mindful relationship, community and ecology?

Can we evolve a spirituality of mindful empowerment and justice?

Can we evolve a spirituality of mindful personal, societal and environmental accountability?

Feel free to pause, and to reread this chapter. It pulls together the threads of the questions in the previous bunch of chapters.

Embrace Reverence, Dignity and Rationality, and Keep Them Close

Mindfully embrace reverence, dignity and rationality throughout the remainder of the book. Keep them close. They are the key elements of authentic right hemisphere spirituality.

Consciously and purposefully embrace decency, grace, reason, integrity and accountability as you work your way through the remainder of the book.

Write your own list of prioritised values, principles and priorities. Keep them at the forefront of your mind.

Use your list of values as a bookmark as you work your way through this book.

Put a copy of your list of values in your bag or wallet. Put a copy of your list on the fridge and on your bedside table.

Refer to your list before you rise and retire. Keep your list of values at the forefront of your mind.

Reflect on the priority of your chosen values, principles and priorities throughout your day — for weeks, months and years. Revise and reprioritise your list of values as clarity emerges.

Absorb loving and rational values into your consciousness, into your sense of purpose, and into your attitudes and actions.

Let the core values of this book — right hemisphere dignity and rationality — speak to you as you move forward in all your relationships, roles, endeavours, opportunities, and life-challenges.

Questions about Possible Ways Forward

What might equip you and me to become sensitive to the nuances, subtleties and complexities of the questions in previous chapters?

What might equip you and me to understand our vast web of left hemisphere, man-made arbitrary fantasies, myths and self-serving narratives?

How might we step away from, and not justify, a litany of masculine religious and political degradations, violence and destruction committed by dominant man-made cultural, religious and political groups?

What best equips you and me to understand and be honest about our never-ending man-contrived array of cultural, religious and political left hemisphere rationalisations, projections, dishonesties, denials and justifications for violence, exploitation and degradation?

Might a blend of science, education, philosophy, psychology, First People principles and right hemisphere Feminine-Mother wisdom to help us understand and moderate the pathologies and promote the possibilities of dignity and rationality for humankind, our fellow species and the earth?

What common threads from these can help moderate our mindless arbitrary dreaminess, fantasies, incongruence and aberrance?

What are the roles and responsibilities of each person and each citizen, in the midst of human propensity for violence, degradation, exploitation and environmental destruction?

What are the roles of institutions, governments, corporations and community groups in nurturing Yin-based values that might help us humans moderate unhelpful and harmful human propensities?

Might a deepening, mindful awareness of the elements of critical thinking help us respond to these questions?

Ultimately, how can we nurture hope for a spirituality of mindful reverence, decency, grace, reason, integrity and accountability?

2%, 2% and 96%

Earlier in the book, I mentioned a reflective analysis of the drivers of the WWII Holocaust. I remember reading a suggestion that systematic institutional violence and abuse are carried out by 2% of the population. 2% of Good Samaritans actively, directly and strategically oppose institutional violence and abuse. While 96% of us watch on as indifferent or cynical bystanders. 96% of us don't care enough or love enough to actively oppose man-made degradation, injustice and violence. 96% of us are lost somewhere in a maze of fear, ignorance, cynicism, blame and apathy.

Sit quietly with this analysis.

For too long, I have been part of the 96%. So far in this book we have looked at the 96%.

To what extent, and in what ways, are ordinary modern people like you and me, part of the 96%?

What factors and patterns create and sustain the semi-invisible 96%?

Moving Forward

Moving forward, how might we reduce the 96% of us mindless — unaware, self-absorbed, ignorant, cynical, indifferent, victim-blaming bystanders.

How do you and I identify, learn from, and follow the example of mindfully decent, integrous and competent role models, stewards, custodians, leaders and statespersons?

Where and to whom can you and I look to the mindful dignity of reverence, decency, empathy, compassion, courage, honesty, priority, responsibility and accountability?

Later, we will look closely at mindful role models who show us these values in action.

Not Presuming and Pretending

How do you and I stop mindlessly presuming and pretending that we already know the answers to the questions in the past bunch of chapters?

How do we not mindlessly presume that we already have right and righteous opinions and beliefs?

Even more, how do we stop feeling justified in our assumed righteous — ignorance, arrogance, conceit, judgements and blame? Note the words, assumed and righteous in connection to each of these extremely dysfunctional, unhelpful and harmful masculinised dispositions.

Are you and I willing and ready to let go assumed and righteous presumptions, confabulations, projections and pretentions?

Are 'we' willing and ready to adopt conscious, purposeful humility and open curiosity; and to do so in tandem with mindful, purposeful, disciplined processes of rigorous inquiry and critical thinking?

Are you?

Sitting with These Questions

We have completed the 'questions' chapters.

When you have the energy and the inclination, go back and reread the questions that resonate, and those that jar. Perhaps, use your highlighter pen, and also make a few margin notes; but only a few. For the most part, sit with the questions in a quiet space. I suggest that you don't talk about what you've just read for at least a few days. Talk is likely to take you straight back to your default assumptions, beliefs, scripts, assertions, defences and resistance.

If you are a religious, ideological, or new-age 'believer' — talk will take you directly back to your default assumptions, biases, opinions, beliefs and dogma. Defaulting to the same old, same old will diminish your potential for greater awareness, dignity, rationality, sensitivity, openness and hope.

If you are a non-believer, and perhaps somewhat cynical or indifferent — talk will take you straight to frustration, judgement, blame and castigation. These will also diminish potential for greater awareness, dignity, rationality, sensitivity, openness and hope.

Talk tends to reduce our potential for mindful atunement, awareness, sensitivity, openness, learning and evolution.

In any case, pause in silence, and breathe for a little while before reading the next chapter. Take your time. Again, there's no hurry.

Remember the title and intent of this book. Keep asking: in what ways can we humans do better than the self-serving, arbitrary, fanciful, unhelpful and harmful stuff highlighted in the previous chapters?

In what ways can we, a critical mass of the human collective, do better?

How can we men to better?

How can women help us men do better?

What can all of us learn from First Peoples?

Remember that our priority and aspiration is to consciously and purposefully nurture dignity and rationality in a vast array of human domains.

Rest and breathe in preparation for a group of challenging chapters about the role of ignorance in human issues. The next grouping of chapters is big. There is plenty of heavy-hitting ahead. Sorry about that. The book unfolded as it did. It is what it is. Read, reflect and be open to be challenged.

Breathe — become peaceful and open — then get on with the next stage of the book.

The Companion Workbook will help you build clarity from the questions in the previous chapters; and from the chapters that are ahead.

In the meantime, as you read — keep wondering, incubating, processing and nurturing clarity, reality and possibility.

Stay present to dignity and rationality.

Ignorance

Here comes the first of several fulsome, problem-definition chapters about ignorance. The purpose of these chapters is to describe and map the role of ignorance in creating and driving the issues of mindless harm that is described in previous chapters. Ignorance is an inherent and universal theme in the questions raised in previous chapters; and throughout the book. Ignorance is a universal factor and driver of human issues.

The next several chapters will show the interconnected ways by which ignorance undermines and disallows dignity and rationality; and how it undermines our aspirations and potential to be mindful persons of decency, integrity and accountability. Ignorance is a systemic, left hemisphere disease of the mind of individuals, and a disease of the collective mind of the institutions and cultures of humankind as a whole.

My guess is that Zen Masters and clear minded scientists might smile and nod as they read this chapter. But, most of the rest of us are likely to find it a bit confronting. Those who get it, might look in the mirror and say, "Oh my, that's me. I do some of this stuff; probably not all of it; and not all the time; but I do this bits and pieces of this stuff, some of the time." Some readers will smile and nod in Zen-like silence.

Four Broad Types of Ignorance

This book identifies four types of ignorance that are ubiquitous across history and within all cultures.

1. Ordinary ignorance — having, espousing and acting-on incorrect knowledge and information.
2. Fanciful ignorance — embracing incorrect information and knowledge that arise from arbitrary superstitions, speculations, fantasies,

confabulations and myths. Our propensity for fanciful arbitrariness and for wilful and stubborn made-up beliefs and opinions are major sources and drivers of ignorance. And, reciprocally, ignorance is a major driver of fantasy, arbitrariness, pride and resistance to facts, critical thinking and reality.

3. Wilful ignorance — deliberately, pridefully and stubbornly ignoring, resisting and 'poohooing' legitimate science, empirical data and factual evidence.

4. Agnotological ignorance — deliberately and systematically generating and proliferating confusing, deceptive and false information and knowledge with intent to deceptively generate ignorance, to cunningly influence opinions and beliefs, and ultimately, with intent to control societal, consumer and/or voter beliefs, opinions and behaviours. This is the domain of 'big lies' of everyday politics, Machiavellian corporatists, populist shysters, conspiracy cults and fundamentalist religions.

Masculine undercurrents and drivers are inherent in four types of ignorance; most particularly types 2 – 4. The bulk of historical and contemporary ignorance is man-made.

These four types of ignorance overlap and reinforce each other. Separately and together, they distort and confound dignity and rationality; including truthfulness, factuality, , integrity and accountability. Ultimately, all forms of ignorance undermine critical thinking, reality and efficacy. Anything that confounds reason and factuality, automatically confounds mindful — intelligence, consciousness, judgement, discernment and purpose. It is very difficult to speak and act rationally, intelligently, mindfully and integrously when our information and knowledge are fanciful, incorrect, pridefully wrong, and/or deceitfully and manipulatively misleading.

Arbitrariness, ignorance, fantasy, pride and deceit reinforce each other. It is a series of short steps from arbitrary fanciful ignorance, to wilful ignorance, to prideful resistance, to wilful deception. All expressions of ignorance are self-perpetuating and self-compounding. Ignorance produces and attracts more and more ignorance. Ignorance reinforces ignorance. Generally, commonly, ignorant people don't know we are ignorant; except for dishonest and deceptive political and corporate 'agnotologists' who knowingly, wilfully, cleverly and fraudulently create spin, propaganda, lies, fallacies, conspiracies and deliberate misinformation.

Typically, those who are ignorant, mindlessly assume and assert that their opinions, beliefs, ideas and claims are correct, brilliant, righteous, enlightened, justified, desirable, and necessary. Thus, ignorance is presumptive; is often pretentious; and, commonly, is pontifical. It's one short step from innocent ignorance to ridiculous bullshit; and another short step to stubborn, wilful delusion.

Think about the link between ignorance and delusion. Consider the links between ignorance, presumption, pretention, opinions, beliefs, fantasies, biases, prejudices, pride, delusion and stubbornness. All these are close companions in the egoic human mind. Ignorance, presumption, pretention, opinions, beliefs, fantasies, biases, prejudices, pride, delusion and stubbornness occupy the same space in the wiring and networks of the egoic human brain. They are problematic and dysfunctional, individually, and collectively. Together, they are a recipe for unconscious mindless, unaware misguidedness at best; and for conscious, intentional degradation, exploitation and murderous actions at worst.

Can We Do Better

Can we humans do better than fanciful, wilful, prideful and deceptive ignorance?

How can we be less susceptible to these expressions of ignorance?

What will you and I need to do to reduce our mindless, arbitrary personal indulgences in fanciful, wilful and prideful ignorance?

How can you and I not be hoodwinked by the man-made agnotological ignorance of deliberate deception, conspiracy shams and 'big lies' of industry, populist politics and conspiracy cultists?

What can individuals, peer groups, communities and the bulk of humankind do to reduce our enmeshment with the irrationalities and falsehoods of left hemisphere political, cultural, religious and new-age, junk-science and conspiratorial ignorance?

What can you and I do to minimise agnotological deception and exploitation by Hyde-like individuals, corporations, governments, theocracies and states?

A Snapshot of the Timeline of Ignorance

Use this chapter to understand the history of ignorance; to understand how we humans became hugely misinformed, misguided, dysfunctional and sadomasochistically harmful. Use this chapter to understand how we humans became and continue to be an ignorant, sadomasochistic species.

From 70,000 years to about 400 years ago, when the scientific revolution began, there was an almost complete absence of scientific knowledge. As well, until the era of enlightenment, which began about 300 years ago, with the exception of First Peoples and some ancient philosophers, there was a significant absence of systems awareness, scientific data and critical analysis. From 10,000-300 years ago, agricultural, religious and political humans existed in a rationality vacuum, a data vacuum, a knowledge vacuum, a science vacuum, and systems vacuum. Crucially, with the exception of First People highly detailed ecological wisdom, there was an almost complete state of ignorance about the facts of the science and systems of our ecological earthly existence.

In contrast to colonising Western states, many First People cultures were very astute and detailed observers of their environments. Many First Peoples formed extremely effective ecological maps, and rational and dignified philosophies and practices; through which they harmonised with habitats, ecosystems and environments. Pre-settlement, Australia's First Peoples were exemplars of mindful — intelligent, systematic, intentional ecological wisdom and homeostasis. They were the world's first participant-observers and action-researchers of environmental systems, patterns and networks. As mentioned before, across the globe, indigenous and First People capacities were lost with the encroachment of agriculture, and later with the march of religion, politics, elitism, colonisation, industry, commerce, capitalism, materialism and consumerism.

The Rise of Institutionalised Superstition with the Rise of Agriculture

Our masculinised Anglo-European agricultural ancestors, made up baseless primitive superstitions and arbitrary religious myths in the absence of ecological awareness, empirical knowledge and critical thinking. Post ecological enlightenment plus pre-critical thinking, pre-research, pre-science, pre-data-based knowledge — masculinised agricultural and religious humankind substituted an array of made-up left hemisphere beliefs for ecology, reason and factuality. Until about 400 years ago, all sorts of wacko ignorance were the norm. Mindless man-made ignorance was universal and prolific. Ecological awareness, facts, rationality and dignity were in extremely short supply; as were sensitivity, integrity and accountability. Rich and powerful men contrived and did whatever they wanted; mostly, without accountability or impunity.

Pre-science, man-made religious and ecological ignorance did not play favourites. All European-Anglo cultures were massively ignorant. Prior to the eras of science and reason, the vast majority of people were massively superstitious, irrational and fanciful. Until the beginning of the scientific revolution, apart from a scant few genius pioneer astronomers and mathematicians, the knowledge of cosmology, geology, physics, chemistry, biology and research-based medicine was practically non-existent.

Incredibly, in a world made and controlled by left hemisphere men, until about 100 years ago, normative data-based, process-disciplined science and education were almost non-existent. Critical thinking, empiricism and the scientific method only gained universal prominence from about the early 1900s. Scientific facts, data, empirical logic and critical thinking have been around for less than 100 years; whereas, superstition has been around for thousands of years; and institutional religious superstition has been around for several thousands of years.

Today

Even today, man-made Anglo-European Christian religions and Judaic and Islamic religions of the Middle East, continue to substitute factless man-made Yang-driven superstitions and unfounded and fanciful religious dogma for systems awareness, critical thinking, data-based knowledge and science. Culturally, several billion of us Anglo-European, American, Asian and Middle-Eastern believers force-fit every aspect of existence into this or that man-made

172

religious dogma. Plus, these days, hundreds of millions force-fit a hotchpotch of ideas, beliefs and opinions into a mishmash of mostly man-made new-age — psychobabble, junk-science and conspiracy theory dogmas. Altogether, a disparate jumble of billions of 21st century 'believers' mindlessly and arbitrarily declare religious beliefs, personal opinions, hip psychobabble, junk-science and conspiracy theories to be enlightened, sacrosanct, absolute and inarguable.

These days, man-made religion, new-age junk-science, pop-psychology, and hip-spirituality do exactly the same thing as ancient superstition and old-time religion. They 'make stuff up'; then declare it to be God-given, 'universe-given', inspired and sacred; and therefore, to be beyond critical thinking, and beyond the scrutiny of investigative rigor, data and facts. The common ethos of new-age devotees is, whatever feels good to make up, think and say is okay to declare 'a universal truth for all'.

This mishmash of masculinised erroneous presumption is mindlessly contrived, arbitrary and unaccountable. This fabricated conglomeration has no basis in science, nor in the logic and processes of critical thinking. Devotees of religion, junk-science, pop-psychology and conspiracy ideation strongly resist the process-discipline, critique and accountability of mainstream science. Religion, junk-science, pop-psychology and conspiracy paranoia also dismiss and resist the logical processes of critical thinking. Pop-culture and conspiracy cults are steeped in mindless — assumptive, dreamy, fanciful man-made ignorance as well as man-made arbitrary, wilful, deceptive ignorance.

Anglo-European and Middle Eastern quasi spirituality have been around for thousands of years. However, the ignorance, lies and fraudulence of modern junk-science and hip pop quasi spirituality have mushroomed exponentially since the advent of man-made agnotological, corporatized money-making alternative-medicine industries, modern marketing, the internet, social media, and the very hip idea of 'personal spirituality'.

Junk-Science and Agnotological Ignorance

These days, we are swamped by a conglomeration of fanciful, alternative science and the marketing of highly questionable supplements. Much of this marketing is wilfully deceptive. Ironically, in humankind's current era of prolific scientific knowledge, 'corporatized and industrialised' ignorance is big business; with hundreds of millions of hip new-age consumers world-wide. 21st century new-age junk-science, pop-psychology and conspiracy theorising form a messy disparate cult-like conglomeration of fanciful ignorance, wilful ignorance, and agnotological ignorance. This conglomeration is a mishmash of man-made money-making fads, deceptions and scams.

Typically, modern-day junk-science and pop-psychology industries deliberately and systematically confuse and deceive consumers and policy-makers through made up terminology, false data, fictitious information, dodgy logic and pseudo knowledge. These masculinised industries do this with the intent to co-opt government policies; and to manipulate consumer opinions, beliefs and spending patterns in relation to mostly unproven practices, worthless products, highly questionable services and unproven modalities.

New-age agnotological practices within the alternative medicine industry are wilfully deceptive ignorance in full flight. Agnotological practices proliferate all shades of ignorance within and among contemporary alternative and new-age consumers and practitioners. Junk-science is also rife in dramatic man-made conspiratorial fantasies and lies about the evils and nexus of 'big-pharma', 'deep-state', and corporate collusion. New-age junk science fantasies, delusions, lies, fraudulence, cons, scams, exploitation and corruption comprise a huge component of 21st century ignorance.

Ignorance and Social Evolution

So, astonishingly, to a massive extent, 'mindless man-made left hemisphere ignorance' continues to restrain human intelligence and to stifle societal evolution in the 21st century. All forms of ignorance are a huge obstacle to personal maturity and societal progress. Ignorance distorts, resists, obstructs and stymies the normalisation of factuality, data, critical thinking, logic, integrity and accountability. We modern humans have a powerful penchant for substituting the ignorance of religion, junk-science, made up opinions, fanciful beliefs and conspiracy theories for the rigors of data, rationality, truthfulness and transparency. Little has changed in many thousands of years. Throughout the 2020-2022 COVID phenomena we witnessed an unprecedented proliferation of mostly man-made baseless, crazy and fraudulent ideas, claims and assertions. This does not augur well for the evolution of mindful intelligence, consciousness, integrity, responsibility and accountability.

The Tyranny of C-Words

In the light of contrived fantasies, deceptions, lies and transactional leveraging in corporate and political realms, it is astonishing that data, reason, critical thinking, integrity and ethical propriety get a look-in. For the sake of political and corporate gain, rich and powerful men have become imaginatively, intelligently and wilfully cunning, conniving, calculating, contriving, cliquey, competitive, confabulating, controlling and coercive. That's quite a collection of unintended 'C-words'. These words are the ingredients and drivers of man-made mass ignorance that is caused by deliberate deception. Male-dominated politics and industry thrive on the tyranny of these C-words, which are the core ingredients of agnotological ignorance.

People, mostly men, in positions of corporate, industrial and political power have been plying agnotological ignorance for hundreds of years. Agnotological ignorance is the age-old man-made driver of capitalist and communist control, corruption and criminality in many modern domains. History has shown that very little stands in the way of clever, cunning, wilful agnotological deception. Criminality and corruption have been the agnotological ways of rich and powerful men throughout the eras of agriculture, industry, imperialism, colonisation, nationalism, urbanisation, monopolised wealth and centralised power.

These days, commonly, rich and powerful mostly male politicians, corporations and industrialists are cleverly and intentionally deceptive, dishonest, unscrupulous and exploitative. In today's world, proliferating agnotological ignorance in society is the key to the rich and powerful acquiring corporate supremacy and building their empires. Fostering 'strategic ignorance' is 'the way of the modern masculine world'.

'The tyranny of C-words' enables rich and powerful men to deliberately deceive, manipulate, con and exploit the rest of us, especially the those who are structurally disadvantaged, poor and the powerless. The man-made deceptions of intentionally contrived ignorance entrench systemic disadvantage, which drives the profound indignities and injustices of structural racism, human suffering, mass extinctions, and environmental destruction. If it weren't for the clever, calculating systematic proliferation of widespread agnotological ignorance, us ordinary people would be much less susceptible to the harmful and destructive stuff that the worst that rich and powerful men do to us.

Populism and Ignorance

21st century capitalist and communist populism is the most recent domain of left hemisphere narcissistic, elitist, empire building, power-hungry and obsessively-greedy, rich and powerful men who cleverly and intentionally generate and proliferate agnotological ignorance through deliberate, systematic, strategic misinformation, deception and 'big lies'. Trump and Putin and other populists are Hyde-like characters thrive in a world where deceit and ignorance 'trump' dignity, rationality, rigor, facts, data, decency, integrity and reality. Unchecked, the very real and grave risk is that populist conniving will enable criminality, corruption, greed and exploitation to become the new masculine norm in modern-day societies. If unchecked, by the mid-21st century, man-made populist contrived and driven agnotological ignorance is certain to do increasing harm to the poor and disadvantaged; and do irreparable damage to ecosystems and the earth. Unchecked, wilful ignorance and calculated deceptions and lies of populism will massively diminish dignity, rationality, integrity and accountability in all domains. Populism is the worst of Mr Hyde in 21st century political form. Predominantly, populism is the domain of narcissistic and sociopathic men.

Can We Do Better?

What would need to happen for mostly male politicians and industry moguls to do better than being unashamedly sociopathically Machiavellian?

What would need to happen for us citizens to be liberated from the tyranny of cleverly contrived, deceptive man-made ignorance?

What would need to happen for us citizens to progress beyond the mindlessness of self-obsessed Yang individualism, apathy, cynicism and immersion in consumerism and social media inanity?

Can contemporary humankind do better than widespread ignorance, indifference, complacency, cynicism and disengagement?

Can our politicians and corporate elite do better than the deliberate, cunning proliferation of man-made deception through the deliberate proliferation of agnotological ignorance?

Can the political and corporate elite be more mindfully decent, integrous and accountable?

Can we do better than man-made corporate and political criminality, corruption, contrivance and deception?

What would need to happen for us 21st century humans to nurture systems-aware, date-based awareness, concern, critical thinking, integrity and ecological strategic discipline into the future?

Ignorance and Arbitrariness

The previous chapter was intense; as are the following chapters. So, feel free to pause; and breathe.

From this chapter, your task is to map the details of the connections between ignorance and arbitrariness; and to recognise their web of negative impact.

Ignorance and arbitrariness are very close companions. They are never far apart. Each reinforces the other. I am not sure which is the chicken, and which is the egg, but I am pretty sure that arbitrariness and ignorance are inseparable. Remember, arbitrariness is about making-stuff-up on the basis of self-serving whims, wishes and wants. It is plain to see how mindless ignorance can arise from making-stuff-up, and from acting as if whims and fantasies are facts, priorities and realities.

All forms of religion and hip, new-age culture and social media are rife with man-made, contrived, self-serving, arbitrary inanities and fads. All forms of habitual arbitrariness dumb us down. Arbitrariness makes us shallow and stupid. These are confronting words, but they are apt. The issues that arise from the shallowness and stupidity of arbitrary, masculine religious and new-age ignorance are central to this book. It is very unlikely that we can become strategically, rationally and decently relational, communal and ecological if we continue to be arbitrarily ignorant, fanciful and faddish.

Arbitrariness is not the entirety of what we humans do, nor is it the entirety of who we are, but it is a prominent aspect of the irrational, dysfunctional and often harmful left hemisphere aspects of how we think, relate and act. We need to come to grips with this situation. Many of us, rich and poor, are drawn to the mindless arbitrary man-made stuff mentioned in so far in this book. Only a relative few are drawn to data-based awareness, critical analysis, strategic thinking, and disciplined accountability. This is a highly problematic situation that you and I need to recognise. If we can reduce arbitrariness, we can reduce ignorance. Thereby we have the potential to do better in terms of dignity and justice for people and our fellow species, and in terms of strategic management of the environment.

No Favourites in Arbitrary Ignorance

Surprisingly, apart from those in disciplined Zen, academic, educational and scientific domains, it seems that left hemisphere, man-made ignorance and arbitrariness are spread almost equally among all social groupings, political affiliations, religious orientations, and cultures. They are roughly equally prominent in men and women, young and old, rich and poor. Mindless ignorance and mindless arbitrariness are inseparable, ubiquitous and universal. They don't play favourites. While they disadvantage poorer people much more than the rich and powerful, ignorance and arbitrariness don't discriminate. Most of us seem roughly equal with respect to our attraction to self-serving whimsy. Self-serving whimsy and ignorance are a level playing field. Although, it is influential religious, political, commercial and economic men who create and proliferate all types of ignorance.

To a significant extent, the ignorance of arbitrariness, and the arbitrariness of ignorance defines the modern man-made human world. Consistently mindful — disciplined, data-based awareness, factuality and critical thinking are relative rarities. Arbitrary fancifulness is more the norm than factuality and rationality. Critical thinking is a scarcity. The mindless ignorance of arbitrary opinions, beliefs and assertions are much more common than reference to credible data, critical analysis and legitimate science. Pause, and reflect on the anomaly that we are conditioned and influenced to prefer self-serving, short-term, arbitrary gains over long-term critical thinking about systemic and strategic priorities; such as feeding and housing the poor, and protecting the environment from man-made climate change.

Across the board, the mindlessness of ignorance and arbitrariness predisposes misjudgement and mismanagement of small and large priorities and issues. Together, predominantly man-made ignorance and arbitrariness cause us humans to harm ourselves, each other, our fellow species, and the planet. In all of us, arbitrariness and ignorance create irrational fears, unnecessary misguided aversion to rationality, resistance to integrity, and avoidance of accountability. Our aversion to facts and our propensity for dodgy, whimsical self-justification go hand in glove.

Fear, Ignorance and Arbitrariness

Arbitrariness, fear, ignorance, misjudgement and mismanagement are also very close companions. Individually and collectively, we do stupid, self-defeating stuff because we are afraid, arbitrary and ignorant. We jump at shadows because we think arbitrarily and uncritically. Commonly, we are paranoid and conspiratorial because we unquestioningly believe dramatic, arbitrary stuff that makes us more and more fearful and paranoid; and more and more ignorant of data, facts, issues and the consequences of our misjudgements and mismanagement. All this mindless stuff is common in the 21st century. The Coronavirus situation strongly highlights our mostly man-made crazy, dumb, arbitrary, ignorant propensities.

Fear draws us deeper into the ignorance of arbitrariness, speculation, confabulation, paranoia, misguided priorities, and acting out emotional impulses. Each of these propensities draws us deeper into all the other propensities. Mindful awareness, sensitivity, reason and factuality are greatly reduced when we are drawn into the nexus of arbitrariness, ignorance, fear, misjudgement, misguided priorities, confabulation, paranoia, and emotional reactiveness. You might feel inclined to pause for a moment, and to reflect on this situation in relationships at home, at work, in community, in business, in governance, and in wider society.

Your Experiences and Observations

In what contexts have you witnessed the connection between arbitrariness, ignorance, misjudgement, mismanagement and harmful consequences?

In what contexts have you witnessed the nexus between fear, ignorance and unhelpful, emotionally-driven actions; including paranoia?

In these contexts, have you observed the links between whimsical, ill-informed speculation, confabulation, paranoia, misjudgements, and misguided priorities?

Can we do better than man-made arbitrariness and ignorance of misinformation, disinformation, fear, speculation, confabulation, judgementalism, prejudice, paranoia and conspiracy-thinking?

Pause and note the mix of unhelpful dispositions in the previous question.

Remember, mindless arbitrariness is about thinking, speaking and acting on the basis of fanciful whims and wishes. This is in strong contrast to mindfully thinking and acting logically on the basis and rational priorities of data, facts and critical analysis.

Remember, the fears, misjudgements and biases of ignorance very commonly arise from self-serving arbitrary whims; rarely from data; not from facts; and not from critical thinking.

Remember, fear is arbitrary. Speculation is arbitrary. Confabulation is arbitrary. Cognitive and emotional biases are arbitrary. Judgementalism is arbitrary. Prejudice is arbitrary. Social, political and religious paranoia are arbitrary. Conspiracy proneness is arbitrary. Man-made left hemisphere stuff is arbitrary.

Together, these expressions of arbitrariness weave an ever-present, tangled, mostly man-made societal web of mindless irrationality, misjudgement, unreality, misguidedness; all of which are manifestations of and consequences of masculinised ignorance.

Remember, systems-awareness, reason, critical thinking, and the rationality of rigorous data-based science, are much less arbitrary and much less problematic than speculation, confabulation, fear, paranoia, judgementalism, and conspiracy ideation. Reason, critical thinking and empiricism are far from perfect, but they are vastly preferable, and much less problematic than the dodgy, semi-crazy whims and wishes of arbitrariness and ignorance.

Can we humans do better than the 'dodgy semi-crazy whims and wishes' of arbitrariness and ignorance?

Sit with the previous question for a little while. It's a crucial question. I hope we can do better than arbitrary ignorance; but, on the basis of history, I'm not sure that we can.

What is your hope?

The Lure of Romantic Ignorance, Intrigue and Drama

The Plot Thickens

There are more elements of ignorance for you to recognise, to be wary of, and to manage. This is because, all the following elements of ignorance dull our capacity for intelligence, reflection, critical thinking, wisdom and efficacy. All elements of ignorance are unhelpful. Some greatly contribute to an array of human dysfunctions and harms.

As emphasised before, most arbitrary cultural, religious, political and new-age myths are whimsical and wishful. Accordingly, most myths exist as whimsical, romantic, poetic, fictional man-made stories. Cultural, religious, political and new-age myths and stories are diverse, but all involve expressions of romantic ignorance. Typically, fictional societal and cultural stories are built on the foundation of baseless arbitrary romantic whims and dreamy imagination. Romantic ignorance creates and drives a wide array of emotionally attractive and titillating fantasies and falsehoods.

Throughout post-First Peoples history, our human default is to be drawn to romantic and dramatic fantasies and fictional stories. Historically and today, it seems that we wishful, whimsical humans desperately want to embrace romantic and dramatic fantasies as if they are factual. It seems we humans can't live without dreamy, romantic fantasy. Dreamy, romantic arbitrariness is almost too alluring for us hedonistic, starry-eyed humans to resist. We are suckers for man-made, mind-made romantic stories.

Be aware that there is tangled web of connections between man-made myths, fictions, imagination, arbitrariness, romanticism, dreaminess, whims and falsehoods. These are typical threads and ingredients of romantic ignorance. Romantic ignorance is the stuff of the mental world of billions who are drawn to the non-sensical dreaminess of religion and new-age beliefs and opinions. Baseless dreaminess predisposes mindless ignorance.

Enter Gossip, Intrigue and Paranoia

What happens if we add gossip, intrigue, drama and paranoia to this web arbitrariness and ignorance? The plot thickens; figuratively and literally.

For many thousands of years, we humans have been drawn to and have readily embraced man-made tribal, religious and political stories and gossip about people who are deemed to be 'bad' because they have different and opposing beliefs. Such gossip and judgements have been the case for religion for thousands of years. These days, in addition to the 'crackpot' romantic fictions of traditional religion, there are many other crackpot, fictional, quasi-religious, new-age, junk-science, pop-psychology stories, gossip and conspiracy theories. Crackpots thrive on romantic and dramatic arbitrariness and ignorance.

In recent times, these dramatic religious, new-age conspiracy stories and gossip include those about the devil-worshipping, baby-eating cabals of 'deep-state'. There are also wild and crazy man-made accusations of total corruption within mainstream science and medicine; that these disciplines are utterly corrupted and controlled by a vast web of alleged corporate and political players who want to take over the world and control you and I by planting microchips in our brains through vaccines. Many millions are enthralled by, enthusiastically believe, and forcefully assert these stories.

In 2020-2022, COVID has brought crackpot madness to stark prominence. Many millions of deluded conspiracy-hungry disciples relish and spruik inane mostly man-made ideas, paranoia and crazy claims with great romantic verve and dramatic, quixotic righteousness. In 2022, romantic, quixotic, conspiratorial, anti-science righteous ignorance is rife of the internet and through social media. Concoctors of fanciful conspiracy theories and inane hearsay gossip are driven to contrive and proliferate farfetched paranoid intrigue and drama.

To my astonishment and consternation, millions of fervently mindless, romantic, dramatic 'hungry-thirsty' conspiracy devotees unquestioningly and gleefully soak up these patently false, farfetched and melodramatic stories. Many are addicted to conspiratorial gossip, melodrama and intrigue. Dramatic, fantastical, paranoid, conspiratorial theatre is a passion and a lifeforce for many deluded people. Most of us have at least one rabid conspiracy buff in our circle of family, friends and workmates.

Does crazy conspiracy stuff do your head in? It does mine.

We consumers of dramatic conspiracy gossip delight in the emotionality of intrigue and scaremongering. It matters not whether the intrigue and drama are factual or not. Dramatic, conspiratorial gossip and titillating hearsay are all that matters to conspiracy makers and conspiracy consumers. For millennia, we mindless naïve, gullible, ignorant, hedonistic, arbitrary humans have delighted in the man-made conspiratorial gossip and titillating hearsay of religion; because it feels good, and because it makes us feel romantically righteous, wise, enlightened, important, special, influential and in control. Then and now, traditional religious and modern-day, new-age conspiracy drama gives their devotees passionate, romantic feelings of belonging and purpose; along with many millions of romantic, right-thinking, righteous fellow conspiracy-believers.

Until about 300 years ago, in the absence of education, science and critical thinking, humans had a good excuse for living in a world of man-made arbitrary, factless, inane, romantic make-believe and dramatic conspiracy drama. In the 21st century, we live in the age of masses of data, facts and critical analysis. The logical-rational side of me assumes that, in the era of unparalleled education and science, there is no excuse for being drawn to the mindless ignorance of dramatic, romantic and overtly fictional religious and new-age conspiracy stories. Or is there? Perhaps our ancient brain is inherently wired for fantastical, romantic stuff. Perhaps we are trapped by the romantic inanity of our ancient brain.

What do you think about this possibility?

Today

For many of us, our romantic and dramatic mental defaults fly beneath the radar of conscious awareness. For the most part, we have minimal awareness that our mental processes are, at least in part, fanciful, dreamy, romantic, dramatic, idealistic, quixotic, surreal and utterly misguided. We wrongly assume, because of our modern surroundings, our intellectual power, our hubris and our good intentions, that we what we believe and assert is true and correct; 'as God and the universe are our witnesses'. We assume and assert that we are objectively observant, astute, discerning, knowledgeable, measured, unbiassed, wise and enlightened. The 2020 USA presidential election intrigues and machinations confirm that very commonly, these contemporary assumptions are definitely not the case. Much of what was said and done during the presidential election and COVID situation were and are, mad and harmful. In 2020 and 2021, dramatic inane ignorance cost tens of thousands of lives in the USA.

Many romantically inspired, dramatic, destructive man-made, modern-day wars, terrorist attacks, and environmental catastrophises are also evidence that, very often, we contemporary humans are anything but factually informed, objectively observant, astute, truthful, discerning, knowledgeable, measured, unbiased, wise, enlightened and strategically disciplined. Recent events in Afghanistan and Ukraine are stark examples of arbitrary, romantic ignorance hijacking and obliterating intelligence, rationality, dignity, facts, decency, reason, integrity, judgement and accountability.

Sorting Fact from Fiction

Because of the age-old patterns and processes of Yang-contrived ignorance, even in 2022, it is difficult for you and I to differentiate dry, factual truth from false and misleading, politicised, dramatic, romantic, made-up righteous stories, beliefs and opinions. 'Fact-checking' is rare because it is not fun and easy. Fact-checking is hard work and never-ending. It's difficult for me to fact-check my arbitrary, emotive, fanciful stories; and for you to fact-check yours. It's far easier and much more pleasurable for you and I to gleefully and blissfully assume and assert that our highly-prized, heartfelt, romantic personal and enmeshed stories are correct, righteous, absolute and inarguable. We don't want to fact-check them. And, we definitely don't want others to fact-check our stories and scrutinise our romantic and righteous opinions, beliefs, attitudes and actions. There's no fun and self-importance in being constantly fact-checked. Our chronic failure to check facts feeds and incites dysfunctional and harmful aspects of ignorance.

Our respective man-made religious, political and cultural peer groups also assume and assert that their highly-prized romantic stories are 'true and correct', so help them God'. It is very rare for masculinised religious, political and cultural groups to be open to be fact-checked, or to be challenged by critical thinking to assess the viability of assumptions, preconceptions, biases, romanticisms, judgements and agendas. Systems awareness, facts and critical thinking dispel the vast majority of baseless beliefs and myths, because, facts and logic show that they are … baseless.

Where would new-age fluff, conspiracy ideation, religious dogma and political spin be if we humans could only talk from a base of mental rigor, data, facts, critical thinking, integrity and accountability? Most of us would fall deathly silent. Our fanciful, romantic, dramatic and righteous voices would cease to exist. Sit with that possibility for a while. Imagine conversations without fanciful, romantic, dramatic and righteous ignorance.

Questions about Possibility

Can you and I do better than ignorant — dreamy, arbitrary, romantic, dramatic intrigue and stories?

Can we develop the maturity, integrity and discipline to fact-check our prized opinions, beliefs and stories; and thereby, reduce our ignorance?

Is it possible for ignorance — factless titillating, gossipy, romantic fantasies to decline and become a thing of the past?

Is it possible for systems-awareness, facts and critical thinking to become the way of the future?

Can the human brain and mind evolve away from romantic and dramatic ignorance and toward data, facts, logic, critical thinking and rationality?

Can the human mind do better and mature away from arbitrariness and toward grounded in decency, ethical propriety, integrity, discipline and accountability?

Can you and I become less ignorant and do better by being grounded in the rigors of data, factual reality, integrity, rational maturity, analytical discipline and accountability?

There is plenty of detail in this chapter about the nature of ignorance and it negative effects. Feel free to include these in your emerging map of issues and map of possibilities.

Bullshit, Lies and Ignorance

Bullshit and lies are also very close friends with ignorance. It's a couple of short steps from fantasies, to telling bullshit stories, to the wilful intentional deception of lies. Lies are inherent in ignorance; especial in intentional, wilful ignorance and in deliberate, deceitful, agnotological manipulation. Societal and institutional ignorance would not exist without mostly man-made wilful deception, manipulation and lies. Typically, bullshit and lies are inherent in everyday, made-up, self-serving, political, religious, corporate and conspiratorial assertions, claims, pontifications, rationalisations and self-protecting justifications. Typically, we use bullshit and lies to — minimise reality, sidestep rationality, avoid responsibility, obscure transparency and minimise accountability.

Deliberate bullshit and integrity cannot occupy the same space. They are mutually exclusive. Similarly, bullshit and lies cannot coexist with transparency and accountability. Bullshit, spin and lies are intended to generate ignorance. Whereas, transparency and accountability are intended to foster rationality, integrity and accountability.

Wilful, contrived deception is common within individual persons; and within peer groups, corporations, political parties, religions, and cultures. Our shared web of fantasies, bullshit and lies is what I refer to as 'the collective ego'. The 'the collective egoic human mind' is inherent within peer groups of all types. Members of like-minded groups share a 'the enmeshed bonds' of fanciful ideas, contrived beliefs, and spurious claims, rationalisations, defences and justifications. All these are the shared bullshit of small peer groups and large institutional groups. Members of peer groups and social tribes share common bonds of bullshit in the forms of fanciful ignorance, romantic ignorance, wilful ignorance, deceptive ignorance, and intentionally crafted lies. Bullshit is both mindless — assumed without critical analysis — and intentional — deliberately proffered to deceive, manipulate, exploit and control. Bullshit and lies are at the core of ignorance.

Enmeshed cultural and institutional ignorance is typically calculated, wilful, cunning, prideful, defensive, stubborn and recalcitrant. Cultural and institutional bullshit resistant transparency, fact-checking and accountability for contrived, group and tribal bullshit. Deception and bullshit have been imbedded in the enmeshed minds of an array of cultural and institutional tribes for thousands of years. Cunning, deceptive, 'bullshit ignorance' has been imbedded in religions for thousands of years. The lies and bullshit of deceptive ignorance are rife in today's tribal religious, political, corporate, new-age and conspiratorial cultures and tribes.

Can we do better than contrived, resistant, deceptive tribal bullshit and lies?

Bullshit and Us

These are questions that ordinary people readily assume apply to 'lying, conniving, bullshitting' politicians, religious leaders and conspiracy theorists; as well as to mega-rich and mega-powerful corporations, industrialists and oligarchs. We readily assume that political, religious and corporate institutions are prone to and adept at evading accountability through cunning bullshit. We tend not to consider that bullshit, deception and lies might apply to ordinary people and citizens; including you and me. It is very common for people not to consider that cunning, evasive, deceptive bullshit is part of our personal, relational and citizenry ignorance.

Can our leaders, institutions and cultures do better than the erosion of dignity and rationality through self-serving, self-aggrandising, dishonest, egoic bullshit conniving and manoeuvrings?

Can we citizens do better than the erosion of dignity and rationality through our relational and citizenry self-serving, self-aggrandising, dishonest, egoic bullshit conniving and manoeuvring?

Humankind and the earth are in great peril if us citizens and our political, religious and corporate leaders can't minimise mindless and intentional bullshit dishonesty, cunning and ignorance.

So, the questions remain, can you and I and our leaders dispel mindless and intentional left hemisphere bullshit and ignorance by mindfully prioritising and nurturing the rationality and decency of right hemisphere ecological wisdom, factual awareness, critical thinking and honesty?

Or, are you and I and us humans doomed to be habitual bullshitters and liars?

Are we doomed to be blind, loyal enablers of the ignorance of bullshit and lies?

All these blunt, colloquially framed questions are earnest and open.

Sit with them is open silence.

You and I need to see our individual bullshit, deception and lies; and to see our enmeshed peer group bullshit, deception and lies, for what they are — an erosion of dignity, rationality, integrity and accountability; and a clear and present bullshit-driven, ignorance-driven danger to humankind, our fellow species and the planet.

These aspects and nuances of bullshit and ignorance are important aspects of your awareness of ignorance.

In large part, to be human, is be ignorant, to be enmeshed in all sorts of bullshit.

Sit with this reality.

We will look more closely at bullshit later in the book in one of the chapters about ego.

Our Choice — Wilful Ignorance or Intentional Reverence, Dignity, Reason and Honesty

Intentional reverence and dignity, intentional fact-checking and critical thinking, intentional self-reflection and intentional honesty can be nurtured. Reread the previous sentence. Note the roles of mindful intentionality in helping us to be more purposefully reverent, dignified, rational, factual, integrous and accountable; and thereby, to be less ignorant.

Mindful, intentional, purposeful values can help you and me think, speak and act decently, rationally, accurately and honestly. Conscious, intentional factuality can help us think, speak and act intelligently, credibly and authoritatively. Conscious, deliberate dignity can help us think, speak and act with intentional decency through — empathy, kindness, fairness, equity, and justice. Mindful, intentional, reasoned intelligence can help us be strategically smarter and more purposefully rational. Note the network of interconnected possibilities that arise from intentional mindfulness. Note that they can help reduce ignorance; and the reduce the issues that arise from ignorance.

There is purpose and hope in the carefully-chosen network of right hemisphere priorities, principles and values that are emphasised throughout this book. We need a network of consciously-chosen values and critical thinking so we can be decent and accurately informed, rational and effective family members, friends, workers, community members and global citizens. Our political, religious and corporate leaders need correct information, intentional values and critical thinking so that they can be dignified, rational and credible standard bearers, role models, mentors, stewards, custodians and leaders. Individually and collectively, we need carefully-chosen values and accurately-informed rationality to counter and minimise the myriad of left hemisphere issues that arise from ignorance in all its forms.

What do we have if we don't have these mindfully chosen strategic priorities, principles, values and critical thinking?

The answer is that, without these conscious, strategic Yin-based intentionalities, there is a very real risk that we modern humans will join history's parade of ignorant bullshitters, fools, liars and bastards who have contributed to horrendous problems for people, other species, and the planet. Without a carefully chosen and consistently applied conscious, strategic intentionalities we have no means of countering and minimising ignorance-driven bullshit, issues, dysfunctionalities and harms.

Can we citizens do better by purposefully prioritising conscious, purposeful priorities, principles and values that facilitate reverence and reality for each other, our fellow species and for the planet?

Can our political, religious and corporate leaders do better by mindfully and purposefully embracing strategic reverence, decency, honesty and reason?

For now, enough about ignorance and its gang of reprobates. We will look at them again and again as the book unfolds.

Irony, the Mirror of the Human Mind

Next, we will look closely at irony, paradox, illogicality, incongruence, contradiction and conflictedness. This web of human proclivities will reveal much about what it is to be human. Awareness of our incongruities has much to teach us. Irony, et al, have the potential to be our best friends, allies and mentors. Awareness of the extensive web of human ironies is a crucial attribute in our quest to understand, choose, prioritise and nurture the priorities of dignifying values and the rationality of critical thinking.

From the poem in the next chapter, note the role of irony, paradox and contradiction in revealing and mapping our many and varied personal, relational, political, religious and cultural, Yang-based left hemisphere blind spots.

The Workbook will help you build your understanding of the various facets of the previous chapters. It will help you plot a path through the forest of human ignorance.

Another Poem about Us Humans

The following poem spontaneously flowed forth sometime around 2015; and has evolved since then. It highlights and maps a highly nuanced, detailed, interconnected and layered web of quirky left hemisphere human contradictions and blind spots; about which most of us seem blissfully unaware. It suggests that a multi-coloured, multi-textured, multi-layered tapestry of irony, paradox and contradiction. The poem is a multifaceted mirror that reflects a multitude of our typical incongruities, illogicalities and blind-spots. Irony, paradox and contradiction reveal our vast, interconnected unawareness and deep, illusive unconsciousness about ourselves; individually and collectively. Vis a vis, irony, paradox and contradiction reveal and reflect our interwoven web of mindlessness. Irony, paradox and contradiction also reveal many interconnected drivers and facets of ego and ignorance.

The poem encapsulates and weaves together many nuances of the reality-checks about ignorance that we have explored in previous chapters. It also highlights issues that will be explored in the chapters on ego that follow this chapter. As you read the poem, recognise and reflect on the diverse and interwoven web of our egoic and ignorant illogicalities, inconsistencies and blind spots.

Don't rush or skip through. Don't react. Don't defend your default opinions and beliefs. Irony and paradox can only inform, sober, mentor and lead us if we are non-defensive, reflective and open to critique.

If we allow it, irony can expose our contradictions and blind-spots; and can give us glimpses of awareness, honesty, rationality, reality and wisdom. Irony can help us be mindful.

This is a big chapter. As does this book, the poem casts a wide net of micro and macro human dispositions and issues. There is considerable overlap between the themes and stanzas. As a result, there are ten pages of heavy lifting ahead. So, breathe and read; slowly and carefully. Absorb, reflect and be sobered.

This is Us

We humans, including you and I, assume that intelligence, beliefs, best intentions and achievements reflect our deepest nature.

But we are quite unaware that irony, paradox, illogicality, contradictions, incongruities and blind-spots are the most revealing mirrors of who and what we are; as persons, as collectives, and as a species.

All of us arise from the physicality of universe, and are biologically one with our fellow carbon-based lifeforms.

And yet, we humans tend not to feel an affinity with our fellow creatures. Mostly, we feel separate and superior. Because of our assumed superiority, we have become aliens, enemies, vandals and misfits on the planet that formed us. We have become feral, environmental oddities, an earthly pariah. We have become the Mr Hyde species. But we have scant awareness of what we have become, how this happened, and are oblivious to what it means to be the Mr Hyde of the natural world.

You and I are chemically and biologically one with each and with all of our human neighbours.

And yet, we find ourselves beset by worldwide mistrust, prejudice, alienation and enmity.

We are as biologically whole as any other creature or species on the earth.

And yet, we feel naked and ashamed, guilty and afraid, lost and alien; but we don't know why.

We are as wondrous as any other creature with whom we share the earth.

And yet, we are dissonant and discontent; and often want to be more than what we are; or want to be different from who we are; and often are not at peace with who and what we are. Generally, commonly, we are not at home, nor at peace and content in our own human skin.

We are the fruit of evolution.

And yet, we presume and pretend that we are not animals. We imagine, that somehow, magically, we emerged as special esoteric beings, created by divine or cosmic intervention.

We try to find special esoteric meaning by pursuing an array of mystical religious, cultural and new-age fantasies.

And yet, we seem oblivious to the joy of embracing the richness of our vast and wonderful evolutionary and biological heritage.

We are highly intelligent.

But, no more so than our pre-agricultural indigenous ancestors and our First Peoples forebears; who, unlike us, for the most part, used their intelligence to live sustainably in far greater relative harmony with each other, their ecologies, and the earth.

We are replete with capacities, possibilities and choices.

And yet, even in the 21ˢᵗ century, the majority of us define and constrain ourselves with a myriad of religious superstitions, cultural myths, ideological romanticisms, new-age fantasies and social media memes.

More than any other time in history, we 21ˢᵗ century humans have access to a massive volume of evidence-based knowledge and research-based science.

And yet, many of us determine our priorities, decisions and choices on baseless, imaginary, arbitrary religious, new-age and internet fantasies and whims.

In the 21ˢᵗ century, many of us assume that trendy new-age knowledge is all we need to be effective in our personal, professional and societal roles and relationships.

And yet we are unaware that relationships and roles are best built on mindful dignity, sensitivity, facts, integrity and critical thinking; which are the filters through which knowledge, wisdom and enlightenment flow.

We believe that we are knowledgeable and righteous.

But we tend to over-assume the veracity of our flimsy opinions, fanciful beliefs and judgmental morality; and tend to greatly under-estimate the extent of our arbitrariness, presumption, pretention and shallow pontification.

We claim religious, political and cultural superiority and judgementalism.

And yet, seem surprised that we are beset on all sides by enmity and conflict.

We put our trust in contrived religious, political and economic systems to regulate every aspect of human life.

Yet, unlike our First People ancestors, we are not attuned to and sensitive to, nor trusting of, the ecological systems intelligence that has consistently and reliably sustained the earth for billions of years.

We ensconce egoic political memes that are dishonest, shallow, ambitious, competitive and self-promoting.

And yet, we are perplexed when party politics, apathy, cynicism, individualism, ambition, narcissism, sociopathy and corruption stand in the way of a sophisticated, effective and rational strategic grasp of human and ecological priorities.

We search for religious, political and economic solutions to entrenched historical and contemporary human problems, such as war, genocide, racial violence, economic exploitation, the suffering of the poor, and many forms of disadvantage, injustice and abuse.

But we are unaware that these issues are inherent in, and arise from, the egoic shadow of religion, politics, and commerce.

We search for masculinised, worldly solutions to man-made problems.

But we seem unaware that patriarchal worldly institutions created the problems in the first place. We are unaware that man-made institutions are the epitome of the intransigent, ignorant dysfunctionalities of ego; that egoic, chauvinistic worldly institutions 'are' the problem; and can never be the solution.

We consider that modern man-made political, religious and cultural institutions are our best hope for justice, prosperity and peace.

But we fail to see that our assumed institutions are mirrors of the patriarchal ego; that they are instruments of endemic, egoic chauvinism; that masculinised institutions and structures are instruments of egoic power; that they are instruments of paternalistic oppression and violent control; that our institutions are man-made icons of white, male empire building; and are instruments of power-obsessive, elitist, white, male presumption.

We trust the viability of the egoic man-made myth of unending economic growth.

And yet seem unaware that we grow fat by exponentially eating the heart of the earth, our home, our mother; which is finite and extremely vulnerable to ever-increasing exploitation and damage done by insatiably, incurably, incorrigibly greedy, voracious, elitist egoic men.

We have the rationality of empirical knowledge, the capacity for critical thinking, and the decency of dignifying values as sources of awareness, priority and guidance.

And yet, both science and humanistic values are treated with great suspicion and distain among religious devotees, political ideologues, intellectuals, new-age alternativists, and conspiracy activists.

Science provides our most reliable knowledge about the formation of the universe, the origins of the earth and the evolution of life; including the history of the human species, and sophisticated understandings of cosmology, medicine, engineering, climate, geology, biology, physics and chemistry.

And yet, even in the 21ˢᵗ century, science is treated with suspicion and derision by a wide range of ignorant, egoic scoffers, doubters and self-declared experts and conspiracists.

Science is the basis and driver of all forms of advanced technology.

And yet, there is considerable unawareness that without science we wouldn't have the host of everyday technologies, tools and conveniences that we assume, employ and enjoy.

The majority of the findings of science arise from careful, patient, rational, integrous, disciplined, long-term, non-partisan empirical processes.

And yet, only a small percentage of people understand the rationale for these very careful processes. Too few are aware of the neutrality and objective intent of science. Too few are aware of the mindful discipline and strategic orientation of research processes.

Science is a valuable source of reliable, objective, unbiased data and evidence-based knowledge about the health of the earth, global warming and climate change.

And yet, in far-right politics, in many religious domains, and many within the new-age, junk science communities, do not comprehend, understand, believe or trust the evidence of environmental science and climate science.

21ˢᵗ century humankind, including First Peoples, is by far the most scientifically and technologically advanced, the best informed, and the most highly educated and enlightened it has been in our 200,000-year existence.

And yet, superstitions, fantasies, arbitrariness, biases, paranoia, ignorance and fear are very common among many secular, new-age and religious institutions and groups, especially those whose beliefs are conservative, fundamentalist, new-age and conspiratorial.

Together, philosophy and psychology have equipped us with processes for reason, logic, critical thinking, rational analysis and empirical research. They have equipped us with comprehensive knowledge of distortions caused by a host of cognitive, emotional and group biases.

And yet, despite the evidence and logic of history, science, philosophy and psychology, even intelligent people are highly prone to prejudiced, illogical, irrational, ill-informed, conspiratorial and patently ill-fated distorted ideas, judgements, decisions and actions. As a consequence, we egoic humans are inclined to behave and act in ignorant, undignified and irrational ways that cause individual angst, societal harms, human suffering and ecological destruction.

Politicians have access to extremely high-quality scientific and technological knowledge to help them to factually understand complex situations; to help them make informed, data-based, systems-based, logical-rational judgments; and to help them formulate strategic, evidence-based policies and actions.

And yet, politicians are highly prone to cognitive, emotional and tribal biases; prone to ideological and religious superstitions; prone to rigid partisan attitudes, ignorance and irrationality, chronic wonton dishonesty. All of which, diminish mindful, strategic intelligence, judgement, prioritisation, competence, integrity and accountability. The consequence is that governance is hampered by greatly diminished awareness, sensitivity, integrity, objectivity, responsibility, efficacy and accountability.

We are far more rationally, educationally and scientifically enlightened than any other time in history.

And yet, in the 21ˢᵗ century, there are still many repressive, retrograde, renegade, autocratic secular and religious regimes. And, there is an increasing number of long-standing democratic governments are teetering toward the destabilisation and collapse due to the rise of populism, which dismisses and ignores data-based evidence, science, critical thinking, decency and integrity.

On our doorstep, globally, we have the timeless ecological observations and systems wisdom of First Peoples.

And yet, very few non-indigenous peoples have any awareness of the everlasting mindful reverence, dignity, rationality, consciousness, enlightenment and systems genius that most of us wrongly assume is primitive and irrelevant to modern humanity. Very few are aware that eons of strategic and detailed First People ecological observations and systems knowledge can inform, support and meld with science. Most of us are completely unaware that, although fragmented, First People enlightenment is available to complement scientific knowledge. Most of us are unaware, that, together, First People wisdom and science can help us restore ecological homeostasis; which is essential for the perpetuity of biological and ecological systems and networks; which are essence of the continuance of life itself; including human life.

We may be vaguely aware that the egoic human mind is the source of all expressions of ignorance, irrationality, disconnectedness, incompetence, selfishness, greed, violence, abuses of power, corruption and distortions of governance.

Yet, irony of ironies, incredibly, subconsciously, we assume that the egoic-mind can fix these egoic problems. Blindly, mindlessly, we assume that ego can fix ego.

We equate wealth, materialism and consumerism with quality of life.

And yet, we are oblivious to the abundance that is inherent in primordial values of relationship, ecology, simplicity, contentment and gratitude.

We search for meaning, purpose and fulfilment in modern, self-advancing egoic pursuits.

And yet, we seem mostly unaware that egoic stuff distorts timeless meaning, diminishes reason and erodes our inherent, elemental dignity.

Each and all of us want to be understood, validated, esteemed and appreciated.

And yet, we don't recognise our inherent, primordial oneness with earthy lifeforms, which is the oneness and the community of the diversity of life that First Peoples experience as the wholeness of this planet. We don't recognise the oneness of our shared home and our common biological, evolutionary and ancestral history.

We modern humans make a lot of noise to be approved, venerated and promoted.

And yet, the louder our posturing, the greater our self-doubt, insecurity, isolation, alienation and fear of failure; because, self-seeking, posturing and performing are bottomless pits of egoic futility.

Many of us particularly like the narcissistic notion that each of us is individually unique.

And yet, we don't see the inherent gift of evolutionary oneness that enfolds you and me with him and her, them and they. Unlike First peoples, we fail to see one in all, and all in one.

We take our individual existence for granted.

And yet, we rarely feel the mind-blowingly extreme mathematical improbability that you and I were conceived. We fail to appreciate that 400 trillion possible pairings of your father's billions of sperm and your mother's millions of eggs, did not occur. But, the pairing of one genetically individual *sperm and one genetically individual egg did occur. Through that massively improbable pairing, each of us exists as genetically unique persons. Each of us is 1 in 10 ^{2,685,000}. Respectively, you and I are a 1 in 400 trillion genetic possibility. Each and every conception is tantamount to a mathematical miracle. That makes your existence, your personhood, and your birthday wondrously significant. As a person, you are a super-extraordinary mathematical, chemical and biological wonder worth celebrating. There is no need to confabulate religious and new-age fluff to feel special.*

We have the vigour of life in 'the timeless here and now'.

And yet, typically, we disconnectedly modern humans, are morbidly preoccupied with the decline of our individual body, the loss of youth, the encroachment of years.

We regret the past and worry about the future.

And yet, we tend not to not see and seize the power of countless little choices and an array of simple opportunities that are available in every present moment; here and now, here and now, here and now.

We indulge in endless self-analysis and all sorts of self-development; and consume a mountain of pop-psychology self-help fluff.

And yet, in all our self-indulgent self-seeking — an internal locus of peace, meaning, contentment, fulfilment, gratitude and joy allude us.

We 21st century Westerners have the highest standard of living in history.

And yet, contemporary Western suicide statistics are much higher than for our forebears; and higher than in poorer countries where existence is much more difficult than for us so-called first-worlders.

We Westerners are paranoid about terrorism.

And yet, worldwide, respectively, motor car crashes and obesity account for many more deaths than those killed by terrorists. Excessive speed and excessive sugar are the real modern-day terrorists.

We judge and attack those who are different from our prescriptions of what is normal, good and right.

Yet, we seem unaware that 'complementarity of diversity' is a primal reality that enables the earth to exist and to function as one whole ecological system. We seem unaware that each of us would not exist if it were not for 'the vast tapestry of diverse wholeness' that arises from interwoven complementarity within our individual bodies; and among the earth's web of chemistry, biology, lifeforms and ecosystems.

We assume the high moral ground, and all forms of political, religious, cultural and biological superiority.

And yet, we don't see that we are one with the murderer and murdered; because oneness does not play favourites.

We blindly believe in the enlightenment of internet knowledge, we devour social media information, and we follow shallow, arbitrary, fanciful new-age pop-psychology, junk-science social media memes.

Yet, are slaves to fanciful, arbitrary ignorance through new-age delusions of certitude and whimsical presumption, pretention and pontification.

We 21st century Westerners take pride in our alleged new-age enlightenment.

And yet, so many spend a fortune on bogus junk-science. Many base key life priorities on psychobabble. And many extol the titillating paranoia of spurious conspiracy theories.

We unquestioningly trust our personal motives, beliefs, values and judgments.

And yet, unknowingly, blindly, each and all are slaves to the manipulations of a desperate, conniving, confabulating, narcissistic and neurotic 21st century ego.

We assume the unquestionable desirability of our sincere best intentions.

And yet, are often disinclined to assume the same of others, especially those who a different from us; and typically, we don't give them 'the grace of the benefit of the doubt'.

We assume the authenticity of our personality, professional identity, social roles, and spiritual sincerity.

And yet, each of us act out a variety of inauthentic social and professional personas and performances.

We assume and contend that our stories and beliefs about God are correct, and that others are ignorant, wrong and bad.

Yet, much of existence is mystery; you and I are equal in mystery; all are equal because there is no superiority or high-moral-ground in 'the mystery of that which is not-yet-known'.

We know about the nebulous God-out-there who is somewhere in the sky. We know about: God-the-story; God-the-concept; the angry, punitive, religious God; the exclusive, judgmental, fundamentalist God; the rigid, stuck-in-the-past, anachronistic, conservative God; the trite, dreamy, wishy-washy, arbitrary new-age God; and the crazy-angry conspiratorial God.

And yet, we are oblivious to the reality that we have created all these versions of God from the shallow, inane, wishful, whimsical, ignorant projections of the egoic human mind. We have fabricated God from the desperate, arbitrary projections of the religious ego. Because — God, mind and ego are one and the same.

We are titillated by speculations, fantasies and stories about aliens, spirits, angels, dead relatives, ghosts, mediums, reincarnations, karma, past lives and future lives.

Yet, we seem unable to ground ourselves in the factual actuality of 'the here and now'.

We talk about, write and read stories about mysteries such as spirit and soul.

Yet we have no idea what they are; but we tritely and glibly assume that they are as familiar as the clothes we wear, or the food we eat.

We talk confidently about spirituality.

Yet, we have no awareness of the depth and extent and our shallow, inane, presumptuous, pretentious musings and simplistic pontifications. And, in this, we mistake glib pretention for enlightened genius.

We contrive and force 'personal growth' through mentoring, coaching, self-development, affirmations, vision boards, mission statements, life plans, and strategic maps.

Yet, we rarely consider the simple, gentle way of 'open availability', unforced trust, and peaceful faithfulness to the everyday priorities and principles such as behaving and acting with reverence, sensitivity, dignity, reason and integrity.

We ascribe to the delusion of having control of life because we devour glib self-advancement, 'laws of attraction' formulas; and blindly submit to shallow, simplistic, self-important, self-appointed, arbitrary new-age gurus and junk-science experts.

Yet, all we need do is be faithful to simple priorities and principles such as being grounded in reverence, dignity, integrity, rationality and factual accountability. All we need to be spiritual is to think, speak and act kindly, integrously, simply, contentedly and gratefully.

We try to leverage and control people and circumstances through the power of espoused special knowledge, clever techniques, exclusive belonging, and spiritual enlightenment.

Yet, in all societal settings, we are the ones who are manipulated, leveraged and manoeuvred by the egoic power machinations of politics, religion, consumerism, materialism, popular culture and social media.

We see the grain of sand as if it is the universe, and the tree as the entire forest.

Yet, we are 'unaware that we are unaware' that we are standing on a boundless beach before an immeasurable universe. We are unaware that our earthly shares the universe with many billions of suns and planets.

We pontificate about the tiniest tip of an iceberg that is barely visible above the surface of an infinite ocean.

Yet, we are blithely unaware that 'we do not know what we do not know' about the wondrous depths that abound below the surface of our shallow material existence. We are massively unaware of what is enlivens each person, humankind, and our earthly home.

We are interdependently linked within the great diversity of our fellow humans so that each and all can get on with many aspects of daily life.

Yet, we harbour engrained mistrust, and somehow construe others as dangerous competitors for arbitrarily contrived sources of morality, happiness, confirmation and spirituality.

We presume simplistic understandings of cause-and-effect; and assume the glib notion that one isolated thing caused this or that outcome.

Yet, we are hugely unaware of the unimaginably vast, intricate, unknowable web of circumstances and events that precede just one outcome. We have no awareness of the chaos and randomness of the dynamic time-space web that is our existence. And, we are oblivious to infinite possibilities that 'could have been', but never eventuated in the midst of a vast myriad of intersecting and dynamic, random and chaotic circumstances. We have no idea that the so-called law of attraction is inane and egotistically self-serving and self-aggrandising.

We assume that the outcomes of the course of your existence and my existence resulted from an orchestrated chain of events that you and I direct through desire, ambition, planning, prayer, believing, intention and alignment with the universe and/or God's will.

And yet we are blissfully unaware that, in fact, our existence is vastly more unpredictable than predictable. We are oblivious to the reality that there are countless unseen twists and turns, and countless unforeseeable fateful events that resulted in the chance circumstances of my existence at the time of writing this book; and of your existence at the time if reading it.

We see karma as a punitive process that eventually catches up with 'bad people' and metes out much-deserved justice as their comeuppance.

Yet, we are not aware that this understanding of karma is an egoic projection of assumed, arbitrary, self-righteous, moralist, judgmental, graceless superiority. We are unaware that our egoic mind invented these fanciful, judgmental notions of karma.

We presume that karma is divine favour or cosmic blessings that we have earned by being right, good, devout or spiritual.

But we are unaware of the undiscriminating impartiality of natural consequences. We are oblivious to the inherent neutrality of an unpersonal universe; including the benign neutrality of Evolution, Mathematics, Cosmology, Evolution, Physics, Chemistry and Biology.

We see karma as a way of pleasing God, or the universe; a way to win favour in life; a way to bank brownie points; a way to balance the books; and a way to be rewarded for right beliefs, good deeds, and persistent sincere righteous effort.

Yet, we do not feel the unforced, uncontrived urge to dignify and respect one-another, our fellow creatures, and the earth; from which each and every-one of us originated; with which all of us are related and bonded; and to which each and all will return when we die.

We use the various expressions of power of will to get we want, and to become who we think we need to be.

Yet, we have scant awareness that we arise from the same open-ended, neutral possibilities, principles and processes that form and sustain the earth and all living things.

We assume that achievement, accolades, ascendency, affluence and influence are signs of well-panned, well-earned and well-deserved success.

Yet seem unaware that individualistic, self-advancing, fragmenting obsessions are unnecessary, unhelpful, distracting, burdensome, addictive and endless. And, we seem unaware that egoic self-obsessions divert us from 'the ease and innocence' of simple, unassumed, uncontrived, uncluttered, uncomplicated, unforced, unpretentious ecological ordinariness.

We assume that we will be okay when we learn more, know more, earn more, own more, do more, control more, and are more.

And yet, we don't realise that because we inherently whole we can be content, free, at peace, and joyful by embracing the principle of 'less as more'.

We assume that we impress God and the universe the same way we impress each other; by piety, intelligence, knowledge, pontification, confidence, willpower, ability, materiality, appearance, ambition, status and 'success'.

Yet, if an authentic divine supreme being or force exists, it seems likely he, she or it is governed by ego. Therefore, is highly unlikely to be impressed by our shallow, fanciful, self-indulgent, pretentious egoic posturing. Similarly, ironically, we are unaware that posturing to a neutral, egoless universe is completely futile, ludicrous and utterly laughable. It is as ridiculous as posturing to lifeless rocks, which, ironically, are the core, inert, physical components of the universe; which many glibly assume is the new-age equivalent to the religious notion, God.

We assume the rightness and purity of our pet conceptions of God and spirituality.

Yet, we are completely unaware that we have projectively created baseless, fanciful esoteric notions. And, much more significantly and tellingly, we are unaware that we have conjured a non-existent, imaginary, insecure, neurotic, obsessive, narcissistic, arbitrary and psychopathic egoic God in our own shallow, whimsical, imaginary and dysfunctional egoic image.

We have thrown out many principled-babies with First Nation bathwater; including the primacies of reverence, dignity, relationship, community, systems, ecology, contentment, simplicity and gratitude.

And yet, we are perplexed and stymied by modern humanity's egoic irreverence, indignity, irrationality, parochialism, tribalism, nationalism, chauvinism, discontentment, dissonance, greed, exploitation, abuse, degradation, violence, destruction and incorrigibility.

We want blessings, enlightenment, divine endorsement, salvation, new-age enlightenment and cosmic power.

But we don't want to enter alchemic fires to burn away the self-indulgent, self-serving dross of our arbitrary, confabulating and deceitful ego. We don't want to imbue strength of character through faithfulness to joy, reverence, dignity, decency, sensitivity, congruence, integrity and accountability. And we don't want to mentally disciplined by embracing and nurturing a fact-based, reasoned reality, and respect-based relationships, communities and ecologies.

We assume that faith is expressed by spruiking religious and new-age beliefs.

But we are unaware that faith may be expressed as stillness, silence and peace in not presuming to know, not saying we know, not pretending to know, not wanting to know, and not needing to know how to control this and that by what we assert to know.

We assume that we have progressed to become sophisticated, enlightened spiritual beings.

And yet, we have become little more than egoically ignorant, dreamy, romantic and childish myth-makers. We have become egoically arbitrary, pretentious, fanciful story-tellers; political and corporate shapeshifters. We have become egoic social chameleons, mercurial opportunists, transactional manipulators, power-obsessed quixotic Mr Hyde control-freaks, and brutal, unjust, sociopathic war-mongering Machiavellian empire-builders.

And so, as said at the beginning of this poem, we assume that intelligence, words, beliefs and achievements reflect who we are.

And yet, we seem quite unaware that a vast array of irony, paradox and blind spots are the most revealing mirrors of our quirky, conflicted, shadowy, ignorant, egoic human dispositions.

We may not know where to start — how to recognise our blind-spots; how to respond to our endless ironies; how to dispel ignorance; and how recognise ego. We may not know how to respond to the voices of paradox, illogicality and contradiction.

Yet, quiet, still, conscious, intelligent sentience urges us to — embrace dignity in the form of respect and sensitivity; to embrace integrity in the form of honesty and accountability; and to embrace reality in the form of factuality, tested evidence and critical thinking. Dignity and rationality urge us to let-go dreamy, romantic, dramatic, arbitrary imaginings, speculations, superstitions, illusions, fancies, opinions, myths and stories.

So Much Irony — So Many Contradictions — So Many Blind Spots

The poem reveals too much irony and illogicality, and too many contradictions and blind spots, to grasp, absorb and map in one reading. Therefore, I suggest that you take the time to reread the poem slowly, and with an open mind. Feel free to revisit and to highlight parts of the poem that caught your attention. Themes that don't resonate in one reading, may ring true in the next, or at a later time. Be open to the possibility that some parts of the poem may strike a chord; and other parts may bristle. Sit quietly with the themes that ring true; and more so with those against which you react. A good principle is to sit in silence with whichever provokes hurt feelings, defences, indignation and hostility. When we react, it's time to look in the mirror; because, most often, it is the Yang-based left hemisphere ego that bristles. Ego greatly resists being exposed and challenged. Ego prefers to be hidden in the shadows.

Irrespective of the protestation of ego, most importantly, however you feel about the poem, be open to irony, paradox and contradiction. Allow them to expose your illogicalities, blind spots and vulnerabilities. Allow irony to bring awareness, curiosity and possibility to the fore. Be open to values and rationality that may bring congruence, coherence and consistency into what you think, say and do. Remember, right hemisphere values-based, rationality-based, fact-based, relationship-based, community-based, systems-based and ecology-based realities are our key hope for sustainability. Anything other than values, rationality, facts, relationship, community and ecology will only produce more and more egoically ignorant and dysfunctional arbitrary fantasies, stories and lies; the web of which is the source and driver of suffering and destruction.

What personal and societal ironies have stood out for you?

Highlight them. Make some margin notes.

Ego, Ignorance and Irony

As said before, the egoic-mind resists irony and paradox. It fails to see its own ignorance. Ego resists awareness and accountability that expose irreverence, indignity, illogicality, contradiction, incongruence and blind-spots. If you are resisting, then it's likely that ego is ducking and weaving and squirming — as happened for Jim Carey in the movie, 'Liar, Liar'.

Therefore, moving forward — sit quietly with the likelihood that you and I are rife with hitherto unidentified ignorant, egoic presumptions of certainty, and deluded, egoic pretentions of morality. It is likely that you and I are rife with dodgy egoic pontifications, confabulations, inconsistencies, incongruities and illogicalities. It is certain that we are rife with irony; and irony always points to and exposes ego.

So, let's sit quietly with the reality that, at least in part, you and I are well-intended but substantially egoic and ignorant. Let's be self-honest. Be real. Laugh at yourself. Irony, paradox and contradiction are not just very revealing and sobering, they are also very funny. Humour helps help reduce resistance to

206

self-awareness, self-honesty and accountability. Humour can help us see the egoic mind in all its bluff and bluster.

What will you do with irony, contradiction, paradox and blind spots?

Will you map them and allow them to reveal the nature and wiles of ego?

Will you let irony lead you toward dignity and critical thinking?

Will you let irony reveal the ways and wiles of the egoic human mind?

I hope so, because the ways and wiles of ego are next topic that we will explore in the ensuing bunch of chapters. When we understand ego, we understand the drivers of foolish, misguided, ignorant and awful stuff that we humans do.

Are you ready to learn about the connections between ego, ignorance and classic human dispositions and behaviours? I hope so, because here we go.

A Look at Ego Through the Eyes of Eastern Philosophy

Breathe … before launching into the forthcoming bunch of chapters on ego.

It is telling that there are fifteen chapters that describe the machinations of our man-made, left hemisphere ego. Some chapters are long; some are short. Together, they explain — what ego looks like; what it does; how it came to be; the macro and micro issues it creates; and how to minimise and manage the problematic everyday personal and collective issues that ego creates for us humans, for our fellow species, and for the earth. We need to understand ego, because it is inherent in all human issues and dynamics — in family, at work, in community, in politics, in religion, in new-age domains and in conspiracy cultures. Historically and today, egoic threads connect all parts of the human tapestry.

Don't rush through. Take your time. Explore issues. Join the dots. Recognise the big picture of the collective egoic mind of humankind. Recognise the subtle and overt ways that ego works in individuals, relationships, organisations, communities, structures, institutions and the human community. Consider how you and I and many of us might manage and moderate the ever-present, ever-needy, ever-wanting, ever-conniving, ever-self-protecting, ever-self-promoting, ever self-justifying ego. My hope for you is that clarity and a sense of strategy will emerge as you recognise the ways and wiles of ego.

Ego — Hitherto and Hereafter

So far, in this book, we have alluded to and referred to ego. We have mentioned ego and the egoic mind in our descriptions, explanations and examples of man-made, left hemisphere ignorance, dysfunctionality and harm. We have referenced ego in relation to masculinised issues, including, in relation to the many and varied masculine harms of patriarchy, chauvinism, misogyny

208

and, paternalism. But we have not systematically explored or explained the nature of ego; nor have we described and detailed ego's roles and machinations in human affairs.

So, as you read the following kaleidoscope of chapters, note the connections between ego and the themes and issues of the many questions we explored so far in the book. Connect the nature, roles and machinations of our masculinised human ego with the liminality poem in Chapter 17, and with the irony poem in Chapter 41. Connect the ego chapters to the ignorance chapters. As you read, note the nature and roles of ego for individual persons, peer groups, corporations, institutions, governments and the global community. Note the masculine left hemisphere ways of ego in tribalism, nationalism and all expressions of political and religious exceptionalism. Note the machinations of the masculine ego in misogyny, chauvinism, paternalism, sexism. As you read, note the role of the masculine human ego in the awful and destructive big-picture issues outlined in the early chapters 4–7. In all these domains, note ego-made and ego-driven human dispositions, motives, agendas, dysfunctions, harms, defences and justifications.

By making a mental map of an extensive web of egoic dispositions, roles and problems, you are forming an extensive matrix of a myriad of egoic cause-effect and correlational dynamics, drivers and consequences. By creating this matrix, you will understand and map ego's involvement in a vast, interconnected array of man-made micro and macro human proclivities and issues. By doing this, you will recognise ego as an inherent and ubiquitous left hemisphere, masculine player in all human affairs; from personal issues, all the way out to global issues; in problems small and large, minor and major; from the relatively inconsequential to that which is utterly catastrophic.

This Chapter

This a big chapter. It is the first of fifteen densely-packed chapters that subject ego to a detailed critique. This chapter introduces us to what ego does, how it works, and therefore, why we humans are the problematic egoic characters and species that we are. This chapter contains some long and detailed paragraphs and sentences. So, breathe, and take your time. Pace yourself. Don't feel that you have to plough through or rush ahead. Feel free to read slowly, and to reflect much. Take time to muse, to wonder and contemplate. Slowly and carefully 'join the dots' that reveal and map and the matrix of the interplay between ego, liminality, irony, ignorance, dysfunction, harm, suffering and lots of other classic, definitive masculinised 'human stuff'.

Ego — The Common Denominator in All Human Stuff

In this book, the term ego is synonymous with 'the egoic-mind' and egoic mental processes. Yang-made egoic mental processes are pivotal. They are the common denominator, the creator, and the universal driver in all human proclivities and problems. The masculine egoic-mind is the author of all our bullshit stories, our clever conniving, political spin, adolescent entitlements, dodgy excuses, blamings, rationalisations, lies and our myriad of dodgy justifications that we use to explain away 'the myriad of shit we humans do'; especially us men.

Left hemisphere egoic thoughts, ideas, beliefs, opinions, expectations and motives are the authors and drivers of all expressions of indignity and irrationality. Masculinised egoic processes are the main psychological players in all selfishness, self-leveraging, transactionalism, power plays, individualist ambitions, parochialism, sectarianism, narcissism and sociopathic Machiavellianism. Ego is central to and drives all problematic isms. Ego is pivotal in all dysfunctionality, distortions and degradations in relationships, communities and environments.

This is the rule of thumb: in all domains of human existence, the left hemisphere ego is the central psychological player when 'dodgy, shitty man-made stuff' is being contrived, believed, touted, rationalised and done. The egoic-mind has a central role in concocting dodgy stuff, asserting it, and justifying it; whatever 'it' is. Ego is the author of all bullshit confabulations. To understand humans, we need to understand ego, the egoic-mind and typical masculinised egoic processes.

Billy Joel's 1989 song, "We Didn't Start the Fire", brilliantly captures an extensive web of stuff that had happened across the world up to 1989, when the song was released. I encourage you to listen carefully to that song. My awareness is that the masculine ego is the common pivotal force in every person and situation mentioned in Billy Joel's brilliant summation of people and events to that juncture in time. When you get the lyrics of this song, you get the ubiquity and universality of ego in 'all' human affairs. Imagine a similar song that could highlight a maze of egoic players and litany of egoic events from 1989-2022. My mind boggles at the thought of who and what would be included in such as song.

Billy — please write an updated version of "We Didn't Start the Fire".

My Understandings of Ego

My understandings of ego are based on a lifetime of study, personal and professional experience, observation and intuition. What is written in ensuing chapters is not the gospel of ego or of egoic human behaviour, but is s stimulus and an invitation for us to reflect on ourselves as persons, partners, parents, citizens, workers, professionals, leaders, elders, stewards, institutions, communities, and as a species. It is also an invitation to be aware of typical egoic patterns we see in all human domains; including in families, peer groups, workplaces, industries, corporations, politics, religion, new-age pop-culture, social media goings-on and conspiracy groups.

My suggestion is that insight into the pervasiveness and omnipresence of masculinised, left hemisphere egoic machinations is crucial for you and me to understand what drives us humans to do the quirky, insensitive, unhelpful, blundering, dysfunctional and harmful stuff we do. Insight into common egoic machinations has the potential to give us awareness about why we humans are so prone to harming ourselves, obliterating our fellow species, and massively damaging our earthly home. When we understand why we do shitty stuff, we have increased capacity to consciously and strategically moderate it.

This is where the yin-based chapters on Breath Meditation and mindfulness come in. When still and aware, we have the potential to identify what ego is doing, and to choose dignified and rational values, principles, priorities and intentions that may help us manage and minimise egoic dispositions and defaults. We egoic humans need as much insightful right hemisphere awareness, rationality and hope as we can muster. We desperately need ways to maximise values such as reverence, dignity, integrity, critical thinking and accountability. These values are our hope for 'life beyond ego'.

Therefore, insight into the individual egoic-mind and the broad, collective egoic mind of humankind, gives the possibility for us to mindfully and purposefully choose how we turn up, behave and act; personally, relationally, communally and ecologically; as local and global citizens.

Ego According to Western Psychology

Western psychology sees ego differently to Eastern philosophy and spirituality. Broadly, in Western psychology, egoic functioning is said to be either relatively coherent and functional, or to be relatively incoherent and dysfunctional. Western psychology says we have an effective ego if we function relatively congruently, appropriately and positively; personally, in family, friendships, at work, and in community. In Western psychology, ego is seen as the internal psychological manager of the self; that is, as the mental, psychological manager of me in my attitudes, behaviours, relationships, roles and situations. From a Western perspective, ego is the interplay and sum of functional psychological patterns consisting of 'my' constructive and effective perceptions, judgements, choices, actions and contributions to relationship dynamics and in human enterprises and environments.

An Eastern Perspective of Ego

Eastern philosophies and spiritual disciplines, such as Buddhism, Taoism and Zen have different understandings of ego. Broadly, they observe ego more as a handicap than a help. Egoic process are seen as less than ideal, less than mature, less than optimal, less than helpful. Generally, in Eastern philosophy, the more dominant our egoic functioning, the greater our propensity for issues and problems that are created and driven by lack of personal insight, lack of relational awareness, and lack of social, situational, societal and environmental sensitivity.

From an Eastern perspective, all the ways we lack of awareness are considered to be 'egoic'. Lack of awareness is deemed to be the core, common problematic trait, disposition and default of the egoic-mind. From an Eastern perspective, egoic dispositions are the essence, elements and processes of 'egoic mindlessness'. Egoic dispositions to habitual unawareness, vis-à-vis, mindlessness, are what very commonly define us as human. To be human is to be unaware is to egoic is to be left hemisphere.

Eastern philosophy says that the stronger our egoic awareness, the more likely we are to mindlessly or unconsciously create all sorts of self-sabotaging stumbling blocks and barriers for ourselves and others; for situations, relationships, communities, roles and endeavours. Eastern philosophy suggests that, because of egoic blind spots, we often don't recognise the unaware, insensitive, inappropriate or unhelpful stuff we say and do. As egoic persons and groups, we don't understand how we've stuffed-up, and why we repeatedly say and do unaware, insensitive, unhelpful, dysfunctional and destructive stuff. From an Eastern perspective, in the broadest sensc, typically, we egoic humans, have

212

limited insight into what motivates us to repeatedly do insensitive, unhelpful and harmful stuff to each other, to our fellow species, and to our Mother Earth.

Most commonly, egoic oblivion and egoic blundering fly beneath the radar of conscious, intentional awareness. Broadly, oblivion and unconscious, dysfunctional ignorance are what I mean by mindlessness. Broadly — conscious, perceptive, sensitive, intentional purposeful, encompassing awareness and cognisance are also what I mean by mindfulness — mindful consciousness.

According to Eastern philosophy, mindless — habitual unawareness and insensitive, presumptuous, blundering egoic patterns are considered a defining trait of post-indigenous humans. Egoic mental and relational patterns of unawareness are personal, relational and societal handicaps. The more extensively and habitually egoic we are, the more unaware we are, the more handicapped we are, the more prone we are to being insensitive and dysfunctional in situations, relationships, roles and difficulties.

The next several chapters will explore and explain various patterns of habitual egoic handicapping and dysfunctionality; all of which involve unawareness and insensitivity. Ensuing chapters will also unpack various interconnected egoic ironies, contradictions, blind spots and impediments.

Ego = Unawareness = Unconsciousness = Left Hemisphere Defaults

As mentioned before, Eastern philosophy tends to assume that the bulk of our egoic functioning is unconscious. That is to say, the bulk of our egoic attitudes and behaviours occur in a state of extensive unawareness or oblivion. And, as emphasised before, for the most part, we are unaware that we are unaware. We are insensitive to our insensitivity. We are blind to our blindness. We are ignorant about our ignorance. Eastern philosophy sees us as more or less insensible and insightless with respect to our bumbling and ham-fistedness. Insightlessness is an egoic state of mind that drives our common tendencies to lack dignity and rationality — to be irreverent, inappropriate, self-defeating, socially clumsy, harmful to others, relationally toxic and environmentally parasitic. Eastern philosophy says that egoic mental processes are the driver of all these classic human tendencies. Egoic drivers and processes often reduce, and sometimes eliminate, functional levels of mindfulness.

From an Eastern perspective, more or less, egoic oblivion causes poor perception, lack of discernment, poor judgement, all sorts of thoughtlessness, and an array of personal, relational and societal misadventures. Also, typically, the oblivious egoic-mind fails to learn from its mindless — unaware insensitivities, misjudgements, mistakes and misadventures. The egoic-mind tends to resist contrary feedback and correction. Very commonly, it is defensive, and has a very strong aversion to transparency and accountability. Through these psychological patterns, the egoic-mind creates, drives, reinforces and sustains 'the mindlessness of ignorance and self-justification', and predisposes a wide array of human issues that are driven by ignorance and self-justification. Egoic mental functioning equates to, predisposes and drives various harmful expressions of unconscious ignorance and unconscious recalcitrance. By unconscious I mean that we have no awareness that we saying and doing ignorant stuff; and have little awareness that we are blindly and stubbornly resisting alternative information, feedback, correction, learning and mindfulness. Unconscious ignorance, stubbornness and recalcitrance are the diametric opposite to mindfulness. They are mindless.

Mindless — ignorant, recalcitrant egoic, mental processes are arbitrary, fanciful, wilful and deceptive. Everything described in the previous chapters about ignorance are the ways of egoic oblivion, the ways of unknowing, misguided egoic dysfunction and the basis of an array of egoic pathologies. All expressions of ignorance arise from mindless-unconscious egoic mental processes. Very commonly, mindless egoic ignorance drives mindless egoic behaviours and actions; and drives resistance to awareness and feedback. Mindlessness reinforces and compound mindlessness; and greatly stifles learning, development, adjustment and adaptation.

However, the problem of mindlessness gets much worse. Astonishingly, tellingly and paradoxically, the stronger our egoic oblivion, the more we tend to over-estimate our insight, intelligence, knowledge, good judgement and wisdom; and the more we over-assume the absolute rightness and righteousness of what we assume, believe, say and do.

To compound our mindlessness, unconscious egoic propensities make us prone to an array of cognitive and emotional biases; and make us prone to syndromes such as Dunning-Kruger Effect. Ironically and paradoxically, but very commonly, the ignorance egoic mind assumes and asserts that it is astute, brilliant, right and righteous. Too commonly, the egoic mind vastly over-estimates itself and has no idea how imperceptive, insensitive, ill-informed, stupid and dysfunctional it is. Stupid is a harsh word, but is apt; because, stupid is as stupid does and does and blindly but pridefully, wilfully, stubbornly and repeatedly does. Do you know mindless people who assume they are astute, brilliant, right and righteous? Have you witnessed the paradox of 'assumed arrogant, certain' mindlessness? This is the left hemisphere in full flight.

Very commonly, these egoic effects cause us to repeatedly, overconfidently and mindlessly misread situations, and to misguidedly over-estimate our perceptions, insights, expertise, wisdom, enlightenment and abilities. This means that, driven by the zeal and certitude of mindlessness, we have a strong propensity to assert and defend a biased and exaggerated estimation of our observations, intellect, expertise, social standing, credibility and authority. Typically, these egoic propensities generate and drive strong, but unfounded opinions and strident, but unsupported beliefs. Under the influence of Dunning-Kruger Effect, cognitive biases, strong subjective opinions and tightly-held beliefs, we are highly prone to misperceived, misinformed, misguided, unhelpful and opinionated know-all presumption, pretention, pride and pontification. That is to say, under the influence of ego, we are highly prone to mindlessly assume that we are 'hot shit'; and consequently, to 'think shit and talk shit; and to do shitty things' — over and over and over, without self-awareness and social sensitivity; but with a misguided, supercilious sense of superiority and conceit.

This mindless, egoic, left hemisphere pattern is rife and obvious in religious, new-age, junk-science and conspiracy-cult domains. For example, these are the characterises and ways of those who concoct and assert myths, fantasies, dodgy science, conspiracies and the big lies of populism, anti-science and antivax paranoia. Egoic mindlessness is typical of us who assumptively, unreflectively, uncritically, pretentiously and zealously embrace, spruik and defend myths, fantasies, imagined plots and blatant untruths. So, the egoic-mind is mindlessly assumptive, unreflective, uncritical, pretentious and zealous with respect to myths, fantasies, conspiracies, confabulations, deceptions and lies. In the chapters ahead, we look again and again at these classic egoic tendencies across a range of contexts.

Ego in the Form of Inflated Self-Importance

Imagined, presumed self-inflated importance is the egoic-mind in all its blind, blundering, quixotic left hemisphere stupidity. In this inflated state of mind, we have minimal awareness that we are often misinformed, ill-informed, hugely misguided, patently foolish, substantially ignorant and painfully quixotic.

When under the influence of mind-inflating egoic effects of Dunning-Kruger effect, we are highly prone to the ignorance of obnoxious oblivion, and offensive arrogance All the time assuming and asserting the mindless misapprehension that we possess superior, intelligence and unchallengeable, absolute knowledge, exclusive wisdom and special enlightenment. We feel like 'hot shit' … brilliant, special, superior, absolute and righteous — a very potent, deluded state of mindlessness

Egoic self-inflatedness creates and drives the ignorance that generates a myriad of indignities, irrationalities, illogicalities and misapprehensions. Dunning-Kruger effect and cognitive biases drive self-inflated, egoic insensitivity, irrationality, arrogance and ignorance in full flight. Egoic thinking, self-importance and blundering, quixotic ignorance are birds of a feather. Each predisposes and drives the others. Egoic drivers and patterns are inherent in all expressions of mindless human dysfunction and harm. They are the stuff of potent and harmful dysfunctional egoic mindlessness.

Note the following classic pattern of egoic left hemisphere drivers of dysfunction and harm: overestimation of intelligence, knowledge and wisdom + overestimation of rightness, righteousness and morality + unawareness of oblivion + insensitivity + proneness to gross misperception and misjudgement + aversion to systems-awareness + denial of data and facts + aversion and resistance to reflection and critical thinking + proneness to quixotic impulses and quixotic misadventures + negation of feedback + failure to listen + failure to learn from mistakes + refusal to be accountable. Reread the previous sentence. It is long list because, according to Eastern philosophy, ego is a wide-ranging and intertwined web of misguiding and misleading mental and psychological propensities; which weave 'our web of egoic left hemisphere mindlessness'; and which predispose a host of harmful consequences and problems for us humans, our fellow species and the earth.

Our egoic-mind is jam-packed with a mishmash of bullshit perceptions, ideas and tendencies. But, oblivious to these dispositions and patterns, we egoic humans often assume and assert that we are jam-packed with special insight, genius and illumination. This makes us feel very powerful Ego thrives on feeling powerful, important and special. Again, this is typical of the nexus between ego, self and ignorance. This is the stuff of egoic mindlessness.

Along with being predominantly and habitually unaware, we who feel self-important, tend to be more or less unwittingly presumptive and pretentious.

Thereby, we tend to be more or less assumptively, overconfidently and misguidedly ignorant. Sit with the expression 'assumptively, overconfidently, misguidedly ignorant'. Self-important, overconfident, blind, bullish, blundering, quixotic, egoic ignorance is a recipe for habitual, gross insensitivity, dysfunction and harm. Note the words blind, blundering and bullish. These tendencies have always been prominent in the egoic machinations of self-important religion, politics, empire building, commerce and industry. Over the past twenty years, these descriptors have also become common in today's self-important, over-confident and boorish new-age, internet, social media, conspiracy theory pop-culture. And, blind, bullish, blundering ignorance is prolific in the populist politics of the 21st century. These are examples of 21C quixotic egoic boorishness and blunder. They are the self-inflated ego at full tilt.

Together, religion, populist politics and new-age, internet, social media, conspiracy cults and cultures incorporate a large proportion of humankind. Quixotic over-confidence, ignorance and blind, blundering bullishness, are rife in these egoic, left hemisphere societal domains. Whatever the context, egoically self-inflated, over-confident, ill-informed, fanciful, blind, blundering, bullish ignorance is an increasingly dominant voice in our modern world. Too often, a mindless, egoic web of boorish, ignorant voices tends to drown out the mindful voices of sensitivity, dignity, integrity and accountability.

Blind, boorish, inflated, egoic ignorance also drowns out the mindful voices of science, data, critical thinking, logic, rational analysis and facts. Boorish ignorance drowns out calls for to faddists and cultists to be accountable for what they say and do. Predominantly, but not exclusively, blind, boorish blundering voices tend to be the chauvinistic voices of assumptive, pretentious, pontifical, self-important egoic men. Everything described in this chapter arises from the inflated masculinised ego. The traits and ways of egoic ignorance and egoic mindlessness are predominantly man-made. Over thousands of years, the masculine ego invented, perfected and proliferated quixotic egoic mindlessness.

It is important to note that ego also manifests as timidity, anxiety, insecurity and fear; and in many other ways. This chapter has emphasised particular chauvinistic egoic traits that are problematic in today's world of presumption, pretention and pontification. We will look at other egoic issues and expressions in ensuing chapters.

Your List

Write a list of prominent historical and current boorish, ignorant male and female politicians, populists, industrialists, religious leaders, new-age faddists and conspiracy theorists who drown out the voices of science, reason, logic, evidence, honesty, reverence, decency, integrity and accountability.

Write a list of male and female leaders who are voices of Yin-base right hemisphere awareness, sensitivity, integrity, factual reality, reason, logic and critical thinking.

Pause for a little while. Google the song, "We Didn't Start the Fire". Read the lyrics. Then listen to the song; several times. Perhaps Billy Joel is aware that his song is about the pervasiveness of ego in so many expressions of human stuff. Maybe Billy is not aware, but nevertheless, perhaps intuitively, he has portrayed ego extraordinarily well.

About what have you become more aware since reading this chapter?

Ego — The Voice in Your Head

Remember, allow time and space to breathe.

Several years ago, I asked my wife for her understanding of ego. Her answer was profound and beautifully simple. She said: "Ego is the voice in your head". Bingo! Ego is the voice of stories and rationalisations that we tell ourselves and others to try to make things be the way we imagine them to be, or that want them to be. And, barring a small proportion of Zenlike people, ego is the voice of stories in each and every person's head.

This understanding shows us that ego is the mental voice of a hotchpotch of assumptions, desires, imaginings, wishing, wanting, expectations, entitlements, demands, frustrations, discontentment, dissonance, fault-finding and emotions; most of which arise from the left hemisphere. But this is just the tip of iceberg. Collectively, ego is also the voice of an ocean of familial, cultural, political and religious stories that have limited basis in sensitivity, respect and rationality; but often express desire, fantasy, wishful thinking, entitlement and judgement.

Here are some typical egoic voices and stories. The egoic-mind contrives and conjures stories of fear, insecurity, inferiority, superiority, doubt and over-confident righteousness. The egoic-mind is the author and teller of stories of self-protection, and deflection of responsibility onto others. Ego is the self-protective voice of defensiveness and the projective voice of self-justification and peer group justification. Ego is the voice of cunning passive-aggressive manipulation. Ego is the self-serving voice of self-indulgence, self-importance, self-righteousness and self-entitlement. But paradoxically, ego is also the uncertain, insecure, passive voice of self-doubt, self-criticism and self-rejection.

Very commonly, the egoic-mind contrives and tells stories that try to justify 'the shitty stuff we say and do'. Ego includes stories that blame others. Ego is the mental and spoken voices and stories of our attempts to escape accountability by deflecting responsibility onto others. Ego is the source of stories of condemnation, abrogation, projection and abnegation.

Ego is voice of many insensitive quixotic orientations. It is the voice of ham-fisted, opinionated arrogance and ignorance. Ego is the belligerent voice of argumentativeness, and of stubborn, wilful, prideful resistance to truth, evidence and reality. The egoic-mind is the conspiratorial, anti-science voice that resists, dismisses and plays-down credible data, authentic facts, fact-checking and factual correction. The voice of ego is pretentious, know-all voice that dismisses and resents feedback; the mental voice that stubbornly and pridefully refuses to be honest; and the recalcitrant voice that irrationally that which is blatantly obvious. Ego is fundamentalist, populist and conspiratorial voices that that make-up and assert strident, arbitrary, judgemental religious and political dogmas, absolutisms, confabulations and lies. Ego is also the voice that makes-up and tell stories of mindless new-age ideas, fads and inane pontifications. Ego is the idealistic voice that tells dreamy, whimsical, childish stories of make-believe, fantasies, wishes and whims.

In all this, ego is heard in the countless voices of arbitrariness and ignorance. Ego is the voice of baseless, assumed, arbitrary familial, cultural, racial, religious and ideological superiority. The political egoic-mind is the voice of presumed ideological purity; and the voice of self-promoting and self-proffering political spin, manipulation, deception and propaganda.

Egoic Voices and 'Me'

And so, and so, and so. The list and the map of mindless egoic voices and stories could be very long and wide indeed. However, all egoic voices and stories have at least one thing in common. Subjective, self-serving, arbitrary ignorance is the common thread that connects all egoic voices and stories. That is, all egoic voices and stories are arbitrarily self-servingly false, fictitious and whim-based. In a wide range of ways, all egoic voices and stories are arbitrarily self-benefiting, and arbitrarily self-justifying. All egoic arbitrariness is imaginary, dreamy and fantasised bullshit that is spun as truth, virtue and reality that suits and benefits me and my peer group. These are the traits, voices and stories of egoic, arbitrary, right and righteous 'me-mindlessness'.

You are hearing the voice and stories of ego when we say: 'what about me'! I am hearing the voice of ego when I act out subjectively biased, prejudiced, ignorant or unethical attitudes and behaviours; but still default to: "Yeah, but he did ... and what about me".

We are hearing the voices and stories of ego when politicians and corporate executives try to hoodwink us citizens through narratives steeped in cunning subterfuge; when they make-up, dodgy stories to deny data and facts; when they refuse to tell the truth; and when they stealthily avoid being transparent and accountable, by deflecting to: "What about poor, maligned, misunderstood me and us"? It is the political voice of ego, when politicians blame each other for their own mistakes and misjudgements; when they spread misinformation and gossip, and withhold factual information; and when they use PR to conjure and proliferate marketing ploys to protect and promote the 'virtuous political me'.

Examples of egoic left hemisphere voices and stories are legion, because egoic tactics are prolific. The egoic mind of big-P and small-p politics concocts clever, cunning and convoluted stories consisting of voluminous bullshit disguised as facts, self-righteousness and the self-justification of the misunderstood and misrepresented political me. Righteous, self-justifying 'political bullshittery' is ego in full voice. This was the voice of the Australian Prime Minister in 2021 when he was called to account for his quixotic insensitivities and blunders with regard to sexual assault, misogyny and chauvinism. When he couldn't bully and browbeat dodge and weave any more, Morrison defaulted to 'poor me; stop picking on me; be fair and nice to poor, misunderstood me'. This was the egoic left hemisphere political ego and the political me in full voice.

The Egoic Voices of Tribalists, Fundamentalists and Populists

You and I are hearing the voice of the left hemisphere ego when populists, nationalists, tribalists, political extremists and religious terrorists tell spurious stories to justify unholy corruption, criminality, violence, murder, degradation and injustice. It is ego speaking when ideological and religious mass-murderers tout spurious, illogical, untrue, fundamentalist ideas, false interpretations of history and current circumstances, contrived entitlements, and manipulation of beliefs and distortions of scriptures. We are hearing the voice and stories of ego when fundamentalists and populists deny science, facts, logic and critical analysis. We are hearing the tell-tale voice of ego when conspiracy theorists deliberately distort science, make-up spurious stories, falsify data, tell lies, incite paranoia, and attack credible professionals on the basis of bogus information, dodgy logic, deception and crazy accusations. We are hearing the voice of ego when new-age disciples spruik junk-science, pop-psychology and pseudo-spirituality; and then glibly and pretentiously claim their whimsical, made-up stories as the wisdom and enlightenment of God and/or 'the universe that knows me and provides for me'.

The Egoic Voices of Institutional Abusers

We are hearing the voice of ego when religious and secular leaders contrive stories that diminish responsibility and deny accountability for sexual abuse of children, and for mistreatment and oppression of women. We are hearing the voice of ego when men tell self-serving stories to justify unjust patriarchal, misogynistic, paternalistic and chauvinistic attitudes and actions that dismiss, disadvantage and harm women, the poor and powerless. And, we are hearing the voice of ego when institutional people concoct stories to downplay systemic racism; and contrive stories that deny the reality of the dreadful intergenerational pain, suffering and indignities of First Peoples.

The Pervasiveness of Egoic Voices and Stories

These examples of the voice and stories of the left hemisphere ego are many and varied, but all are typical of the 'bullshit' that the egoic-mind arbitrarily imagines, contrives, believes, asserts, proliferates and defends. The voices and stories of ego are ubiquitous, prominent and dominant in all human domains; and have been so for thousands of years; perhaps since the rise of agricultural era. Throughout history, what all egoic voices and stories have in common, is that they don't nurture reverence, dignity, critical thinking, facts, reality, transparency, responsibility and accountability.

Egoic voices nurture fear, ignorance, deception, pride, arrogance, manipulation and control. Egoic voices nurture narcissistic and sociopathic Machiavellianism in religion and politics. Ultimately, institutional egoic voices and stories are evidence of an unbroken history of masculine ego-driven irreverence, indignity, unawareness, insensitivity, irrationality, judgementalism, unkindness, dishonesty, disrespect, abrogation of responsibility and refusal to be integrous, factual, reasoned and accountable. These days, populist and conspiratorial voices vehemently oppose voices of decency, reason, legitimate data, science and critical thinking.

Populist voices are the most recent incarnation of historical masculine chauvinistic left hemisphere voices and stories of ego which have never nurtured respect, decency, justice and compassion. Self-serving masculine egoic voices and stories have never promoted strategic ecological systems priorities with a view to reducing human suffering, and minimising death of species and environmental destruction. Masculinised egoic voices and stories have always been heard in the echoes of denigration, suffering, harm and spurious, unconscionable denial and justification for the patriarchal propensities mentioned in this paragraph, this chapter and throughout this book.

Dominant egoic voices and stories have always spruiked the self-serving distortions of the masculinised egoic left hemisphere mind. Historically, dominant egoic voices and stories are the bastion of masculine self-promotion and self-justification. This includes the promotion and justification of the individualist egoic-self, the religious egoic-self, the egoic peer-group self, the egoic ideological self, the egoic political self, the egoic economic self, the egoic imperialist self, the egoic nationalistic self, the egoic corporate self, the egoic industrial self, the egoic power self, the egoic transactional self, the egoic leveraging self, and the egoic rich and powerful empire-building self. That's a lot of egoic-selves.

All egoic voices and stories are self-serving, self-aggrandising and self-defending. All egoic stories are about 'me', and about my exclusively entitled right and righteous group. Historically and today, very commonly, these are the self-serving chauvinistic voices of self-focussed, religious and political masculine ego. In all this, the chauvinistic ego has never been the voice and stories of peace, simplicity, subsistence, sufficiency, contentment, gratitude, sharing, and joy on relationship and community. Chauvinistic, egoic masculinity has never been the voice of ecology and homeostasis. Forceful egoic left hemisphere masculinity has never been the Yin-voice of unconditional, unlimited all-inclusive grace, empathy, decency, kindness, generosity, dignity, justice, equality, equity and inclusion.

The masculinised ego has never been the right hemisphere voice and stories of sentience, presence, stillness, listening, trust and faith. In these examples, the egoic-mind of masculine dominance has not been, and is not, the voice and stories of empowerment for the greater good of the greatest number. The highly masculinised ego is not, and has never been, the voice and stories of relational dignity, communal inclusion, and strategic ecological systems wisdom. Egoic masculinity is not the voice of possibility that tells truly hopeful stories of human empowerment through dignity, rationality and justice; nor through ecological stories of harmony and strategic wisdom that envisions perpetuity through the oneness of diversity.

The Yang-driven ego has never been the voice and story of facts, rationality and dignity; nor the voice of values such as reverence, awareness, sensitivity, decency, integrity and accountability? Masculinised egoic voices and stories are the same yesterday and today; and likely, will be same tomorrow?

Chauvinistic, egoic, left hemisphere voices and stories can never be our hope and salvation. And, unless we humans can moderate and minimise the masculine egoic shit that we think, believe, speak and do, Yang egoic voices and stories will continue to dominate all cultural, political and religious attitudes, priorities, dispositions, defaults, policies, decisions and actions. In the light of the imminent impacts of climate change, and in the face of macho, sociopathic egoic despots such as Putin and Xi, we are doomed unless we promote and extol Yin-based, right hemisphere cultural, political, religious and corporate voices. Right now, in 2022, Putin and his self-serving, chauvinistic, nationalistic henchmen exemplify our history of sociopathic masculine egoic voices.

Hope in Yin-Mindfulness

Hope for sanity and rationality can only come from mindful — intentional Yin voices of awareness, sensitivity, decency, reverence, reason, facts, integrity and accountability. Under the broad, encompassing banner of dignity and rationality, the mindful voices of values and critical thinking are our only hope for the evolution of a sane, peaceful, just and sustainable and survivable future.

Does this critique, reality-check and explanation help you to see the urgency for voices and narratives of reverence, dignity, data, facts, integrity, critical thinking and accountability?

Questions for You and Me

In what ways can you and I do better at contributing to voices of mindful awareness, dignity and rationality?

How can a collective of mindful people, do better at contributing to the evolution of awareness, dignity, and rationality?

Levels of Egoic
Unawareness/Unconsciousness

Let's look in more detail at awareness as a key priority for us do better.

From now on, we will use the terms awareness and unconsciousness interchangeably. For the purpose of our discussion, they mean the same thing.

Unconscious, unaware egoic functioning can be scaled. According to Eastern philosophy, mild levels and expressions of egoic unconsciousness are seen in typical everyday unawareness / unconsciousness. Mild unawareness restrains and misleads us, and causes mild to moderate issues in relationships and communities. Whereas, strong expressions of unawareness, such as habitual, insensitive, opinionated arrogance and wilful coercive control, create large relational, communal and ecological stumbling blocks. Strong unawareness impacts destructively on those with whom the highly unaware person, corporation or government interacts. At all levels and in all domains, egoic unawareness always generates impacts, costs and collateral damage; from small to catastrophic.

The Collective and Cumulative Effects of Collective Unconsciousness

Collectively and cumulatively, throughout history and across the kaleidoscope of peoples and communities, masculine egoic unconsciousness at its worst has severely damaged persons, relationships, communities, humankind as a whole, our fellow species and the earth. Collective and cumulative masculine egoic unawareness has created and driven a litany of historical harms through abuses of power, exploitation of the powerless and unconscionable greed. Strong masculinised left hemisphere unawareness drives the abuses of millennia of misogyny, racism, sectarianism and nationalism which are common drivers of the mass-murder of wars and genocides. Unconscious egoic masculine drivers have also resulted in global environmental destruction.

All these issues are products of our masculine history of accumulated and enmeshed egoic Yang unawareness of cultural, religious and political ignorance, power-obsessiveness and transactional Machiavellianism. Not surprisingly, but ironically, these extreme aberrations have been justified by a cumulative history of man-made spurious, cultural, religious and political egoic logic, and by dishonest, unconscionable man-made egoic rationalisation.

Spurious egoic logic includes, justifying manipulative and forceful self-interest is 'the law of the political and corporate jungle'. This egoic fallacy is driven by lies about superior genetics, racial superiority, natural biological forces, and 'the will of God, and ways of God's creation'. Repeated and cumulative egoic rationalising and self-justifying egoic attitudes, beliefs and actions, such as 'the law of the jungle' and other biological and religious analogies, are factually incorrect, dishonest, misleading, dysfunctional and destructive. Often, they are sociopathic.

Globally, for hundreds of years, the masculinised left hemisphere Anglo-European-American egoic-mind has built a diabolical history of rationalising the utterly irrational, and of justifying patently unjustifiable sociopathic criminal acts of colonisation, mass-murder, decimation of First Nation cultures and slavery of many millions. The masculine egoic Anglo-European-American mind has never taken fulsome, contrite responsibility and accountability for centuries of murderous and dehumanising attitudes, beliefs and actions.

For eons, spurious man-made egoic Anglo-European-American stories have very effectively defended the indefensible, and have justified the diabolically unjustifiable. Since fabled Adam was a boy, we Abrahamic religious humans have said and done all sorts of massively unaware, insensitive egoic stuff, invented all sorts of utterly unaware rationalising, self-justifying egoic stories. There would be no need to write this book if it were not for centuries of layer upon layer of enmeshed masculine unawareness that is emphasised from chapter to chapter.

Can you see why I say: 'enough unaware, unconscious man-made egoic shit'!

Strategic Ecological Wisdom Vs the Self-Leveraging Me

The next two chapters present an alternative to the unawareness of ego.

In right hemisphere First People philosophy and Eastern philosophy, strategic relational, communal and ecological sensitivity is the opposite to tactical, transactional self-leveraging and individualistic masculine left hemisphere egoic self-importance and self-entitlement. The philosophy of First Peoples and Eastern practices encourage us to integrate at least six principles and priorities.

1. Be mindfully, unobtrusively, unpretentiously and non-defensively self-aware.
2. Be mindfully, sensitivity and respectfully aware of others.
3. Be mindfully, accurately and thoughtfully aware of the dynamics of relationships, circumstances and situations.
4. Be consciously aware of, and consciously network, big-picture relational, communal and ecological systems principles and priorities.
5. Be mindfully aware of, and in harmony with, the systems, processes and priorities of community, nature and existence.
6. Do all this with the mindful intention and purpose of maximising right hemisphere dignity, critical thinking, harmony and sustainability; and with the mindful intention of minimising indignity, irrationality, injustice, harm and suffering.

I suggest that you reread these points.

First People Awareness in Contrast to Political and Religious Unawareness

First People spirituality discerned the principles and priorities of Yin-based awareness and mindfulness many thousands of years before Eastern philosophies. Our modern mindless masculine unawareness, as evidence through transactional self-leveraging, has nothing in common with Yin-based First People and Eastern awareness of relational, communal and ecological systems principles. In contrast to First Nation and Eastern right hemisphere awareness and sensitivities, our modern man-made religious, political, economic, industrial, consumer, material and social media mindsets are relationally, communally and ecologically unaware and insensitive. That is to say, masculinised mindsets are substantially ignorant and mindless. Our modern, unaware masculine ethos tends to be self-seeking, forceful, disconnected from nature, and oblivious to harmony, synergy, symbiosis and homeostasis.

This web of unawareness is the stuff of the mindlessness that is the egoic mind for the bulk of contemporary humanity. We masculinised moderners are ecologically unaware and ignorant, and thereby are utterly un-strategic in terms of human and environmental sustainability. Ecological ignorance is the pinnacle of left hemisphere unawareness and mindlessness because it is destroying human sustainability and perpetuity.

The next two sentences are long and telling. So, breathe and read them slowly and mindfully. In contrast to First People 'relational, communal and ecological mind', the man-made unaware political-religious egoic-mind is a messy web of short-sighted, narrow-sighted, me-first, self-leveraging, transactional, reductionistic, dogmatic, individualistic, nationalistic, industrial, economic, consumptive, material, and technological voices and stories. The ecological network of relational and community awareness, dignity, sensitivity, integrity and strategic wisdom has little place in the egoic hurley-burley of our modern web of disparate, frenetic, obsessive, self-indulgent wanting, performing, transacting and getting that characterise the microcosm of the unaware modern masculinised egoic-mind; and which characterise the macrocosm of the unaware modern man-made egoic-world. Pause to notice the contrast between First People mindful – aware, strategic relational, communal and ecological Yin sensitivity — versus — masculinised — mindless, unaware, short-sighted, divisive, blundering, plundering, individualistic, nationalistic egoic political, religious self-leveraging.

Use these chapters to get a feel for the nature and propensities of egoic Yang unawareness within yourself, and within family, peer groups, workplaces, communities, institutions and governments. Use your awareness of unawareness to consciousness choose and promote awareness and mindfulness in relationships and community. Mindful Yin awareness is the basis of education. A key purpose of education to nurture and proliferate mindful awareness.

Can you think of ways that you can nurture Yin awareness in your relationships and roles?

Realising our Potential Through
Sentient Awareness aka
Mindful Consciousness

It's time for us modern humans to be mindful — aware, awake, sentient and fully conscious. It's time to engage, participate and contribute with 'sentient, purposeful, strategic wisdom'; to consciously attune to relational, communal and ecological big picture and very long-term priorities, principles and values. It's time to aspire to and embrace this network of right hemisphere capacities and priorities as the prerequisite for foresighted, reasoned, dignified effectiveness in all relational, societal and environmental contexts. It's time for a revolution of Yin-based mindfulness as a strategic mental orientation for individuals, institutions and communities. It's time for a you and me and a critical mass of us to imbue a mindful and purposeful orientation to the very big picture and the very long term.

Without finely-tuned, expansive and very long-term relational, communal and ecological awareness, it is almost impossible to function and engage sanely, purposefully and strategically. It's very difficult to be strategically attuned and competent without consistent, congruent, coherent, all-encompassing sentient awareness of peoples, species, environments and the earth. Now is the time to be fulsomely aware that a multitude of interconnected elements and systems are what enable us to exist. Interconnected, interdependent multiplicity is the biological and ecological engine room of existence that sustains the earth and all its species in-perpetuity. A finely-tuned, cohesive, integrated right hemisphere consciousness of biological and ecological systems realities is the foundation for strategic relational, communal and ecological efficacy.

I have to suggest that you reread the previous paragraph; slowly and mindfully. It describes existence — vast, diverse, inclusive, complex, interconnected, interdependent and networked. More and more of us modern humans must become mindful of and embrace this necessity and reality.

The evidence of history confirms that because of the absence of strategic relational, communal and ecological Yin-awareness and atunement, we, contemporary Yang progenies of Anglo-European ignorance, have blundered through the past 400 years; as the saying goes, like 'bulls in a delicate ecological china shop'. Without sensitive relational, communal and ecological Yin awareness, we post-Anglo-Europeans have been oblivious to vulnerable communal, biological and ecological interrelationships. For millennia, we mindless, masculinised, left hemisphere automatons have bumped into each other, trampled our fellow species, damaged cultural relationships and ecological systems, and horribly mismanaged our relationship with each other, our fellow species and the earth. It's time for this to stop. We must become aware. We must be sensitive.

The historical 'bull in an ecological china shop' analogy captures the nature of our bullish, modern egoic mind, and our boorish, modern, transactional, me-oriented egoic man-made world. In contrast to bullishness, being peacefully and aware, incorporates being consciously and purposefully relationally sensitive. Being aware and sensitive requires us to be strategically ecologically attuned; and from that, to be careful, conscious participants in a vast, earthly community of species and ecosystems.

Thankfully, it's not too late for us to become aware and sensitive. It's not too late to learn and to act in harmony with peoples, our fellow species and the earth. Through mindful — conscious, intentional right hemisphere relational and ecological principles and priorities, we humans can position ourselves to be effective, educated, rational dignified participants and contributors in a vast tapestry of earthly relationships and systems. This includes close and distant relationships with friends and strangers, with local and global communities, with other species, and with the ecological complexities of Mother Earth. It's time for conscious, intentional, strategic revolution of Yin awareness and sensitivity.

These understandings suggest that we will be at our human best when we are mindfully — Yinfully — reverently, peacefully, intelligently and purposefully relationally and ecologically symbiotic and homeostatic. Being mindfully conscious equates to being sufficiently 'tuned in' and integrated that we humans can be relationally and ecologically self-aware, self-monitoring, self-honest, self-moderating and self-regulating; as individual persons, as corporations, as institutions, as governments, as nations and as a global community. Being mindlessly egoic is about an absence of aware and sensitive self-management and relationship-management priorities, principles and values. Being mindful is characterised by the presence of these primacies.

Can we 21st century humans increasingly embrace right hemisphere relational, communal and ecological 'systems mindfulness'?

Will we?

In what ways will you catalyse a revolution of nurturance and evolution systems mindfulness?

In what ways will you contribute to the nurturance of systems mindfulness?

Remember — the Companion Workbook will help you respond to this and other invitation to be part of solutions to age-old problems.

It might be helpful to look at ego in more detail before we try to respond to these questions.

More On What Ego Looks Like and Sounds Like

Again – take time to breath, settle, and reflect.

There are more egoic issues and obstacles to understand so that we can embrace a revolution of systems mindfulness and contribute to relational evolution. Let's continue to define and map the problem ego, then we'll get back to the revolution of systems mindfulness and to relational evolution.

More About 'Me'

As said before, the term 'ego', alludes to the world of 'I and me'. From an egoic, left hemisphere orientation, 'it's all about me'. It's 'my' life — my career, my success, my future, my mind, my soul, my salvation, my karma! I want this or that for 'my-self'. How 'I' perceive 'me' and 'my' aspirations arises from the machinations of my self-oriented mind. The self-oriented mind is the realm of ego. Egoic voices and stories are thoughts that 'I' assume about 'me'. Egoic assumptions and beliefs are how I define the person whom I assume and contend that 'I am'. The egoic-me is the 'me' that my stories project outwards to others — the clever, strong, powerful, competent, well-intentioned, good-natured, right-minded, deserving 'me'.

The egoic-me is the desirable, justifiable 'me' that I assume is real and valid; and that I want others perceive, admire, agree with, and relate to; especially the members of the peer groups whose like-mindedness and approval are important to me. The egoic me is the image of me, the identity, that I want others to see, to approve, to embrace and to endorse. For many of us, our mostly unconscious egoic preoccupation is about what image I must portray, who I must be, what I must do — to win approval and to belong. Ego is 'who and what' I present through my network of assumed and strongly-defended, approval-seeking and self-defending images, personas, desires, attitudes, beliefs, opinions, ambitions, behaviours and actions.

None of this helps 'us' establish mindful awareness, sensitivity in relationships and community. None of this helps us become mindful of the interdependent systems complexity. All of this is about me; the needy, deserving, ambitious, entitled me.

Egoic Impression-Management, Self-Leveraging and Control for 'Me and Us'

Ego is the image and impression I want to convey to those whom I want to impress, influence and control. Impression-management is an egoic process of influencing other's perceptions of me — to benefit me; always to benefit me and my peer groups. Ego is the transactional me; the self-leveraging me. Some of us are very conscious of the image and impression we want to convey and leverage. For others, our desired impression tends to be sub-conscious. Whether conscious or sub-conscious, impression-management is about using egoic images, priorities, ideas and stories to promote my desirability, approval, inclusion, standing, influence, power and control. Impression management is about me leveraging my egoic desires, opportunities and avenues for me and my peer groups; for what I-we want. These are the left hemisphere Yang process that institutionalised religion and man-made politics perfected during this past 4,000 years. This how these institutions mind-manage the masses.

Most often, self-leveraging occurs with little awareness and consideration of sensitivity, dignity, critical thinking, integrity and accountability with respect to other people, 'our' communities, 'our' fellow species and 'our' Mother Earth. Egoic voices and stories are inherently arbitrarily me-oriented — self-leveraging, ends-focussed, self-justifying and aversive to alternative priorities, critique, transparency, responsibility and accountability. Egoic thinking isn't mindful of the incongruence between my espoused values and my egoic aspirations and my egoic acting out. Often, we are unaware of the relational and communal issues, risks and consequences that accompany our egoic priorities, stories, drives, wishes and wants. Simply, commonly, the masculinised left hemisphere ego — unconsciously, blithefully wants what it wants, says what it says to get what it wants, and does what it does with minimal sensitivity to and consideration of human and earthly relationships and communities.

Ego and Me-Focussed Mental Control Mechanisms

Thus, the egoic-left hemisphere-mind is a network of me-focussed mental power and control mechanisms. The intent of egoic power and control mind-mechanisms is for me and my peer groups to manage and position myself-ourself; to enable me-us to manoeuvre you and 'them'; and to influence and control situations for my-our benefit. All egoic power and control mechanisms are intended to enable me and my masculine peers to achieve my-our man-defined desired ends. My-our egoic priority is also to influence your perceptions, opinions, beliefs and priorities; so that, ultimately, they align with me-our and my-our masculinised needs, desires, priorities, intentions, ambitions and ends.

To do this, the masculine ego is a replicator, networker and advocate of self-promoting us-promoting stories; which consist of me-us-oriented assumptions, perceptions, biases, opinions, beliefs, wants and priorities. Ego is very good at promoting and proliferating me-oriented / us-oriented assumptions, perceptions, biases, opinions, beliefs, wants and priorities. For many, these masculine egoic patterns are assumed, automatic, unnoticed and unchecked. We are unaware that this is the default of your left hemisphere masculine egoic mind; and mine. Ego's self-serving voice, in terms of opinions and beliefs, is often assumed, absolute and inflexible. Typically, predominantly, the masculine ego is inherently self-leveraging, and therefore, is inherently relationally insensitive.

21st century Yang-ego manufactures and replicates social media and internet memes; which are popular cultural ideas and stories; to bolster and benefit of me and my peer group. A vast array of social media — 'be like me' — 'be like us' — memes are classically egoically masculinised. We social media devotees tend to consciously and unconsciously influence others to be similar to me and us; and to align themselves with me and my group. Generations prior to social media, the masculine mind crafted and utilised other cultural, societal, religious and political beliefs and stories to influence others to believe the same as me and us; to align, identify and join with me-us in promoting and defending my-our masculinised peer group, religious group, political group and/or conspiracy group.

In addition to influencing and controlling people, then and now, the me-focussed, me-proffering, me-profiting egoic masculine-mind also tries to arrange situations how 'I think' or 'we think' they should be so that they benefit or validate and benefit me and us. Ego wants circumstances to align themselves with me-us, to support the story of my-our, identity, needs, desires and ambitions. Ego wants circumstances to be as I or we want them in order to give me or us what we want; including the man-made priorities of righteousness, influence, money and power. None of these are relational, communal or ecological values for the greater good and the vast majority. In particular, power is a transactional value and mechanism that serves me and my exclusive, mostly male left hemisphere peer groups; with scant concern for others, community, environment or the earth.

Thus, the masculinised-egoic-mind is a collection of 'me-oriented' 'us-oriented' mostly man-made mental-control-stories that each of us automatically assume 'should be' because they are automatically and inherently valid and desirable for me and us. 'Should' is short-hand and code for the intent of egoic stories of how I want things to be to benefit me and my group of like-minded peers. 'Should' is an egoic word, an egoic assumption, an egoic intention, an egoic imperative. 'Should' manifests through should-stories which are about egoic desire, egoic will, egoic logic, egoic priorities and egoic leveraging of predominantly masculinised opinions, beliefs, aspirations, will, rationalisations, priorities, ends and justifications. Should, should not, must, must not, and have to — all go together in egoic stories that say give me-us what I-we men want and are entitled to; what I-we must have'. These are not the words and imperatives of the Yin mindfulness of relationships, community and systems ecology.

The Scope of Egoic Wanting

Thus, for individuals and groups, the egoic-mind is a vast network of man-contrived mental stories which focus on self-wanting, self-willing, self-accumulating, self-advancing and self-justifying. This network of egoic self-stories applies to me-oriented individuals, as well as to enmeshed us-oriented members of social media, new-age, corporate, industrial, religious and ideological groups. Me-oriented persons and groups assume, contrive and tell masculinised left hemisphere contrived stories that confirm that we are justified to 'want what we want'; and to pursue what we want with assumed and assertive self-justification self-determination. At all levels, and in all human domains, individual-self-oriented and group-self-oriented wanting, leveraging and transacting is evidence of man-contrived egoic priorities, beliefs and assertions. Assumptive wanting, leveraging, transacting and getting for me and my exclusive little group are what ego is, and what ego does; individually, collectively, habitually and unrelentingly.

Masculinised left hemisphere wanting is a bottomless pit. It is inexorable. The individual, social-media, new-age, corporate, political and religious egoic-self is never lastingly satiated. The individual egoic-mind and the collective egoic-mind are characterised by 'wanting' more and more and more; more for me, and more for us. Wanting more power, influence, control, money, things, approval, inclusion, belonging, praise, and popularity. The masculine ego is characterised by endlessly manoeuvring and leveraging to get endlessly more of whatever I-we want.

Masculinised individuals, groups and networks apply their considerable personal and collective cognitive power with the egoic purpose of contriving dominant narratives that convince others and to control people and situations to get what they want. Determined, intelligent contriving, conniving and coercing are core and universal man-made self-serving egoic control processes. No matter what fine virtues or motives the intelligent egoic-mind proffers, in the realm of the hungry-thirsty, right, righteous, entitled Yang ego — wanting, deserving and leveraging are assumed and entrenched. Inherently, historically and today, the world made by egoic men is not relationally, communally and ecologically aware and sensitive. It is 'us men' obsessive.

Ego — Secreted in the Shadows

You and I tend to have very little awareness of this egoic web of masculinised assumptive, obsessive, entitled manoeuvring, leveraging, me-oriented, us-oriented motives and drivers described so far in this chapter. For most us, most of the time, the patterns and norms I just described fly under the radar of conscious awareness. It's just 'the default left hemisphere stuff we moderners say and do' — and do and do and do. It is the semi-invisible default voices, stories and rationalisations that we proffer assumptively and automatically to optimise and manage yours and my psychological, social, transactional and material existence. It is the default egoic stuff that you and I and our cultural, political, corporate and religious masculinised forebears and peer groups did and do to optimise our capacity to get what we want; whatever we want.

All these machinations are the near-invisible, left hemisphere, man-made 'normal'. They are an unconsciously assumed, desirable and necessary modus operandi of 'the ubiquitous, normalised egoic left hemisphere human mind'. Tellingly, the ubiquitous egoic human mind is created, conditioned and validated within 'the normalised man-made egoic human world'. Near-imperceptible egoic stories, and other mostly unnoticed, little-examined egoic dispositions and defaults are the everyday ways of your egoic mind, my egoic mind, the egoic social media mind, the egoic new-age mind, the egoic peer group mind, the egoic religious mind, the egoic political mind, the egoic corporate mind. These are some of the common shadowy domains of the egoic human mind, within the egoic human world.

As is detailed and mapped in the poems in previous chapters, you and I tend to be mostly unaware of our extensive web of egoic left hemisphere liminalities, ironies, illogicalities, incongruities, blind-spots and ulterior motives. We are also unaware of the paradoxical factors and issues that profile you as egoic, and profile me as egoic. As is the case with almost eight billion humans, it is likely you and I are largely unaware of the assumptive mental processes and the automatic egoic confabulations that define each of us as more or less — egoically self-serving, egoically self-leveraging, egoically transactional, and egoically manoeuvring. All this is the antithesis of being relationally, communally and ecologically attuned and prioritised. All is derived from man-made, left-hemisphere-made narratives which have devolved to comprise the post-hunter-gatherer-forager human mind.

I am frequently unaware of the ways that my self-serving, self-leveraging and egoic manoeuvring impacts on my relationships, roles, endeavours and social environments. Also, I am often quite unaware of how others perceive my subtle and obvious egoic attitudes, communication and behavioural patterns. Of course, all of which, I assume and suggest, are well-intended, normal, relatively subtle, valid, desirable and justified. But, despite my claims to normality, purity, rationality and altruism, at least some of my motives, desires, logic and stories are bound to be egoic; are bound to be substantially me-oriented and self-leveraging; are bound to be contrary to relational, communal and ecological mindfulness.

When I Saw What Is Secreted in the Shadows

While writing this book, it was quite an epiphany and a revelation when I increasingly realised that my mind had been co-opted by shadowy, Yang, left hemisphere narratives and priorities. It was an awakening when I became aware that I was a product of a the little-recognised, scantly-defined shadowy nuances of our masculinised left hemisphere world and cultures. It was a wake-up call when I fully realised that our worldly consciousness substantially consists of shadowy stories written, spoken and inculcated by dominant, testosterone driven men about the exploits of dominant, testosterone-infused masculinity. It was a game-changer when I fully consciously understood that the world is infused with left hemisphere testosterone, formed by testosterone and continues to be controlled by testosterone in the 21st century. When this realisation came out of the shadows, I knew I must share it with wider community and ask — can we 21st century humans do better than the egoic dominance and power machinations of left hemisphere testosterone? Hence — the many references to man-made and masculinised left hemisphere issues throughout the book. And hence — many radical observations, questions, critiques, challenges and invitations to do better.

Anyhow — keep reading and see what emerges and unfolds for you.

Ego and Oblivion vs Awareness and Accountability

Finally, as emphasised earlier, most of us are not only unaware, but we are also unaware that we are unaware. And, significantly, under the sway of the masculinised left hemisphere ego, we don't want to be aware. If you and I are aware, then maybe we'll feel at least somewhat obliged to be accountable to others for what we believe, say and do. Ego implores — 'God forbid' — please don't make me aware and accountable for my near-invisible, semi-mindless egoic assumptions, ulterior motives, contrivances, confabulations, pejorative judgements, made-up opinions, fanciful beliefs, selfish ambitions, insensitive behaviours and calculated transactional manoeuvrings. Don't expect me to be accountable for the assumed personal and cultural macho stuff to which I am oblivious. Don't make me accountable for the sensitivity of what I say and how I speak. Don't make me aware and accountable for the integrity of what I do and don't do. Ego begs and insists — don't make me aware and accountable for my unconscious egoic agendas. All in all, please, don't make me accountable for the impact of my egoic stuff on others — on my family, my friendships, my community. Please, just don't!

Thus, under the sway of my left hemisphere egoic-mind, at every turn, consciously and unconsciously, I am highly likely to resist awareness, insight, feedback, critique, self-awareness, self-honesty, transparency and accountability. I am likely to resist accountability as if my life depends on it. Because, to the egoic-mind, my 'self-life' depends on, and is built on — the sanctity and inviolability of my self-protecting and self-benefiting egoic assumptions, preconceptions, automatic biases, confabulated stories, presumed opinions, tightly-held beliefs, assumed needs, heart-felt desires, desperate defences, and strong-willed justifications. These are the ubiquitous elements and priories of the self-protective and self-promoting egoic mind. An array of egoic stuff protects and promotes the vulnerable, insecure, fearful, compensating, wanting egoic-self; the fearful, vulnerable egoic me.

The egoic mind says, 'please, either say nothing, or just agree with me. Just tell me I'm 'right and righteous'. Tell me that my motives are pure, and that my attitudes and behaviours are justifiable. Tell me that I'm deserving. Please, tell me that it's okay to want what I want, and to leverage, manoeuvre and push to get what I want. Please, don't make me aware of the egoic undercurrents and wiles of my uncritiqued assumptions, motives, stories, conjuring, ambitions, wanting and self-leveraging. The egoic aspect of me implores you: 'please, don't call me to mindful awareness, sensitivity, reason, integrity and accountability'. Please don't call me to mindful self-reflection, self-critique and contrition.

Yin-based awareness, reflection, transparency and contrition are likely to make me feel very exposed, highly vulnerable, and extremely uncomfortable. For 'the egoic-me', mindful self-awareness, congruence and integrity are really difficult and very dauting. For 'me', the exposure of transparency, critique and liability are extremely unpleasant and disturbing prospects and experiences. From an egoic perspective, accountability is my greatest unconscious aversion; my worst nightmare, my greatest fear, my dread, my nemesis, my Achilles heel, my strongest dread.

Does any of this ring true?

2020-2022 Politics and Corporatism

Under the dominance of the Morrison government, from 2020 – mid 2022, Australian politics and industry — overt and extreme Yang-based ambition, greed, power-machinations and empire building were in abundance. In contrast, mindful reverence, sensitivity, decency, integrity, transparency, accountability and humility were scant. This situation is the same in most political and corporate environments, but is especially so in far-right populist environments. The ideological extremes of ego that drive populism, automatically massively minimise Yin-oriented awareness, sensitivity, decency, integrity and accountability. Populism's egoic obliteration of dignity and critical thinking is creeping into the way of the modern political world. Populism is becoming an egoic cancer that is killing dignity and critical thinking in governance.

This situation was very obvious in Australia, the USA, and in other populist political cultures where self-serving, ambitious, greedy, power-oriented, empire-oriented, wealth-obsessed characters and governments refuse to be decent, integrous, ecological and accountable. Trump-style populism has been death to relational and community reverence, sensitivity, dignity, integrity, responsibility, transparency, and accountability. Until their electoral decimation in May 2022, this was the Morrison government's political style. En masse, Australian citizens refused to abide the decimation of dignity, rationality, integrity and accountability. We kicked-out Morrison and his team of self-serving masculine, testosterone-infused left hemisphere egotists.

Somehow, politicians need to perceive and learn conscious, intentional dignity, critical thinking, integrity and accountability. Humans, our fellow species and the earth are doomed if the political domain is infected with the worst of left hemisphere masculinity. That why the evolution of Yin-based mindful sensitivity, dignity, integrity and accountability are our only hope. That is why this book recommends and hopes for a vast collective of mindful citizens and leaders to inspire and catalyse a revolution Yin, right hemisphere priorities, principles, processes and values.

Questions

Are you surprised at the extent of our egoic, masculinised left hemisphere blind spots; our masculinised aversion to awareness, transparency and accountability?

Have you observed self-protecting egoic resistance and aversion to awareness, sensitivity, honesty and accountability in family-members, friends, workmates, politicians, religious leaders and corporate executives?

Have you observed self-protecting resistance to awareness and accountability in yourself?

Are you surprised at the interconnections between resistance to awareness a network of man-made issues and problems?

Had it occurred to you that aversion to priorities such as awareness, self-honesty, sensitivity, integrity and accountability is the 'self-protective, me oriented, self-leveraging masculine ego' in action?

Can you see why I emphasise the need to nurture and build Yin-infused awareness and Yin-based priorities as essential elements of our personal, relational, communal and ecological guides for human existence?

In the light of imminent climate change realities, and recent macho, left hemisphere aggression in Syria, Afghanistan and Ukraine, can you see the urgent need for a revolution of mindful Yin values and critical thinking at the political level? Yin-minded leaders would not have obliterated Syria; would not have invaded Ukraine; would not have subjugated the women of Afghanistan.

Man-made Egoic Blind Spots and Aversions

What do you observe in these interlocking window panes?

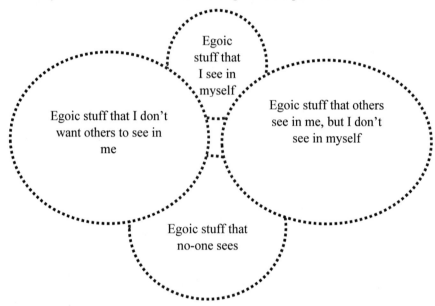

Which of these circles is biggest for you?

Which tends to be the biggest in our masculine societal institutions and in male-dominated governments?

What does this say about our masculinised, left hemisphere corporate, religious, political and government leaders and leadership?

Simply and pragmatically, if we reduce our masculinised blind-spots, will we increase our capacity for rationality and dignity in relationship, community and ecology?

What might help do this?

The Virtual World of Ego

Here is an analogy that highlights the unawareness of the egoic-mind.

Imagine you and I are wearing goggles while playing a computer game. We can see the simulated virtual characters, scenery and events of the computer-generated scenario. But we can't see the actual world of real people and actual situations that are happening to us, and around us. The computer goggles prevent us from seeing the actualities and dynamics of the world of day-to-day relationships, and the dynamics of the situations that make up our real-life community and ecological existence. Yours and my perception and focus are limited to what our computer, the egoic-mind, is showing us. We cannot see what the computer simulation is not showing us. While wearing egoic goggles, it's highly unlikely that we will perceive what is actually happening outside mind's ego-generated, virtual simulations. Egoic virtual simulations are a parallel to egoic ignorance about what is actually happening in the world of our family, community, society, our fellow species and of our earthly ecosystems and environments.

Unbeknown to you and me, similar to the computer-game, our new-age, religious, political, corporate, social media 'egoic, virtual left-hemisphere-mind' is goggled. The human mind is greatly restricted by virtual masculine egoic programming. Our virtual mind is programmed by left hemisphere neurology and endocrinology, and is habituated through repeated assumptions, biases, perceptions, emotions, thought patterns, beliefs and opinions; all of which are socially goggled — prescribed, conditioned, reinforced and restricted by peer groups, national culture, religion and social media; many of which are at least somewhat masculinised.

While wearing the goggles of ego, I see mind-made, simulated, virtual imaginings, ideas and desires. I only see ego-simulated representations of the actual world. I don't see the real facts and the circumstances of actual-world issues in family, friendships, community and environmental ecologies. And, my

243

goggled, egoic, virtual view of the world greatly restricts my awareness of my assumptions, personal issues, biases, fears and insecurities. My goggled, virtual view also restricts my awareness of interpersonal issues; for example, my egoic relational selfishness, transactional leveraging, disrespect, power-plays, demands, defences and justifications.

While wearing my egoic goggles, I am also confined to a virtual, egoic, left hemisphere view of societal issues, such as greed, exploitation, suffering and environmental destruction; all of which are occurring in the actual world around me, but are not part of my egoic virtual world. Restricted — virtual — egoic unawareness of personal, interpersonal and societal issues and machinations is the driver of egoic insensitivity, and ignorance.

Goggled Virtual Perceptions

Typically, the virtual simulations of ego cause you and me to be at least somewhat relationally, socially and environmentally unaware, insensitive and clumsy. Insensitivity and clumsiness are classic elements of masculine-ego-generated ignorance. Ignorant unawareness and ignorant insensitivity cause many people to be less than helpful; commonly to be dysfunctional; and, too-often, to be self-harming, harmful to others and damaging to the planet. The virtual egoic world of some profoundly unaware, insensitive and extremely misguided religious, political and conspiratorial individuals and groups are often dangerous and destructive because of their extreme 'blind, blundering egoic ignorance'. We see lots of blind, masculine, egoic left hemisphere religious machinations in the Middle East, and in sub-culture culture right wing, evangelical fundamentalism in the USA.

When 'goggled egoic ignorance' blinds me to facts, truth and reality, my virtual mind generates simulated virtual political, religious, new-age and conspiratorial fantasies and delusions as substitutes for factual reality, common decency and relational integrity. Historical and contemporary environmental and international ructions and conflicts show that virtual, goggled political, religious, new-age and conspiratorial delusions have significant ramifications for people, our fellow species and earth.

The Virtual World of Populism

In the masculine virtual world of Trump-like populist politics, egoic irrationalities and lies are called "alternative facts". Simulated, virtual, egoic fantasies, illusions, fictions, contrivances, spin, propaganda, embellishments and big-lies are the hallmark of the virtual, narcissistic and sociopathic ego of macho populist politicians, populist governments and populist cult members. Their populist goggles only allow them to see a virtual, egoically simulated, contrived, distorted and restricted masculine populist fantasy world of people, circumstances and issues. Goggled, egoic left hemisphere populists cannot see the actual world of political indecency, corruption, criminality, disempowerment, injustice, suffering and environmental harm. The virtual goggles of mostly-male narcissism and sociopathy blind extremist politicians and their cult members to relational and community decency, dignity, reason, integrity, sensitivity, empathy, compassion and kindness; all of which are prerequisites to relational and community decency and efficacy in the real world. Real-life priorities, values and critical thinking are outside the scope and realm of the goggled, virtual programming and madness of populism and populists.

Fundamentalist Simulations

Fantasies, illusions, fictions, fragments of truth, contrivances, embellishments, deceit and lies are also what we see in the simulated, virtual world of egoic fundamentalist and extremist secular and religious left hemisphere institutions and theocratic states. The man-made egoic world of far-right evangelicalism in America and Islamism in the Middle East, Pakistan and Indonesia, are examples of goggled virtual religious distortions of facts, rationality and decency. Extremist and fundamentalist virtual distortions are highly dysfunctional and dangerous simulations of reality. Masculine egoic deceptions and distortions destroy people and communities. The right hemisphere Yin-feminine-mother does not destroy people and communities.

Egoic Simulation and Mind-Management

Virtual fantasies, illusions, fictions, fragments of truth, contrivances, embellishments, deceit and lies are the core simulations of 21st century mind-management through mostly-man-made left hemisphere spin, PR and marketing in politics, private enterprise and industry. These egoically simulated fantasies, fragments of truth, contrivances, embellishments and lies are also extremely common in modern, partisan commercial media; and are rampant in social media. Social media is the epitome of a contrived, simulated, virtual egoic view of people and issues. Virtual egoic simulations are rampant in internet marketing of faddish, new-age alternative products and services. Egoic fantasies, fictions, contrivances, deceit, lies and scams are extremely common virtual simulations in all modern worldly institutions, organisations and domains; including the virtual world of conspiracy domains.

In the 21st century, we see an extremely destabilising entangled virtual web consisting of the masculinised left hemisphere — individualist egoic-mind, the political egoic-mind, the corporate egoic-mind, the religious egoic-mind, and the new-age, junk-science, pop-psychology egoic mind, the social media egoic mind and the conspiracy-theory egoic mind. This vast and encompassing conglomeration of virtual minds generates and drives fanciful, virtual ignorance, wilful virtual ignorance, virtual deception and lies and masculinised Machiavellian manipulations. All these egoic virtual, masculine, left hemisphere states generate and drive strong resistance to relational and community decency, integrity, facts and accountability in the real world of people, communities and earthly environments. Egoic, goggled mind-manipulation generates and drives a web of harms and suffering. It massively erodes our potential for real-life dignity, real-life rationality and pragmatic real-life efficacy.

Questions

How do you feel about living in a mostly-man-made virtual, goggled egoic left hemisphere world that consists of restricted, distorted, fantasised, fictional, confabulated simulations of reality, relationship and community?

Are you keen to remove your virtual egoic goggles, and be more sensitively, rationally and factually aware of yourself, your relationships, your roles, and your citizenry and community responsibilities and opportunities?

Do you want politicians, religious leaders and corporate executives to take-off their masculine egoic ideological, power-obsessive, greedy, ambitious, empire building goggles?

Do you want politicians and industrial moguls to stop seeing egoically man-contrived fanciful, grandiose, self-serving simulations of human and environmental realities; to see critical real-life issues as they are; and to be accountable for effective, strategic management of human and ecological issues?

Do you prefer people to relate to each other and to issues and possibilities from of real-world right hemisphere priorities, values, critical thinking, data and facts, rather than from the distorted virtual world of egoic political, religious, social media and new-age fantasies and conspiratorial lies?

Have you had enough of men's egoically simulated self-invested distortions and deceptions of popular culture, politics, religion and industry?

No surprises; I am over our contrived and concocted egoic simulations and bullshit; which is the topic of the next chapter.

Ego and Bullshit

We discussed some of the problems of bullshit in one of the chapters on ignorance.

In modern parlance, I am said to 'think shit', 'believe shit', 'talk shit', 'do 'shitty things', and be 'full of shit, when I am unaware, oblivious to reality, and deceived by my own made-up. self-serving, mind-made, 'egoic bullshit stories'. The bullshit analogy is a light-hearted, but telling modern-day parallel to the Eastern idea of unconsciousness. A common intuitive observation is that 'bullshitters' are those of us who are unaware of the extent of their arbitrary, made up, fanciful crap. Day-in, day-out, bullshitters are significantly and habitually inane, ignorant and insensitive. Bullshitters are inherently resistant to facts, oblivious to critical thinking, unconscious to reality, and highly averse to feedback, correction and accountability in relationships and community. All the stuff of bullshit is classically egoic; classically unaware, classically left hemisphere. Ego, unawareness and bullshit are one.

Bullshit, Spin and Stories

Politicians are notorious for being 'bullshitters'; for 'bullshitting'; for talking shit; and being 'full of shit'. They are notorious for using the bullshit of spin to deny facts and to resist critical thinking, reality, accountability and integrity. 'Bullshit-spin' is the epitome of the egoic political mind. But, in fairness, religious leaders, industrialists, entrepreneurs, new-age boffins, conspiracy theorists, and partisan, ideologically-driven journalists also have a well-deserved reputation for bullshit. During the COVID crisis and the American presidential election, conspiracy cultists take the 2020-2022 prize for most inane and most dishonest bullshitting. Populist conspiracy bullshitters obliterated relational awareness, sensitivity, decency and accountability. They obliterated the love and rationality of community. They obliterated sanity. But they were champion

248

bullshitters. Most of these rampant, chronic bullshitters were Yang-driven, mindless, macho men.

We ordinary citizens also do our fair share of egoic bullshitting in our families, peer groups and work places. Social media is our most recent channel and a prolific reservoir of bullshit stories and mindless, inane bullshit memes. Social media and the internet are rife with egoic bullshit that replicates and proliferates as worldwide mental nonsense. Social media and internet memes have catapulted political, new-age and conspiratorial bullshitting to unprecedented levels. The 'long and the short' is that we humans are rampant, egoic bullshitters; and our bullshitting constrains and damages relationships, communities and ecologies.

Too commonly, we express our bullshit through mind-made egoic-stories that have little basis in facts; and most often with little basis in critical thinking, sensitivity and integrity; and no basis in accountability. When egoically unconscious, we default to mind-made bullshit distortions of truth and decency. In this, commonly, we not only substitute bullshit for reality, but also substitute bullshit for respect and kindness. Mind-made bullshit stories and gossip are built from fragments of reality. Egoic bullshit stories are a hotchpotch of left hemisphere imagination, whimsical fantasy, self-serving arbitrariness, self-importance, well-practiced confabulation, connivance, cunning deception, a good smattering of wishful thinking, nastiness, and constant self-justification. As you can see, our everyday bullshit consists of quite an 'interesting' mix of dodgy egoic stuff. Bullshitting, ego and ignorance are inseparable. How do we know when humans are bullshitting? The humorous 'tongue in cheek' answer is, 'we are talking'.

Typically, for most of us, mind-made bullshit stories are a surreal blend of fantasy and reality. Egoic ideas and confabulated bullshit stories are dreamlike. They feel intuitively real, romantically desirable and morally righteous, but they are far from being grounded in facts and reality; and most often, are far from being virtuous and decent. Our egoic ideas and stories range from an occasional lapse into 'bullshit-fantasy', to us being lost in habitual 'bullshittery'. Stories range from talking a bit of shit, to being full of shit, to being the ravings of a complete shithead.

The term 'shithead' is an interesting euphemism. It applies to a person, most commonly a man, who is said to have a head full of fanciful bullshit ideas, egoic bullshit stories and ridiculous half-cocked, illogical bullshit defences and explanations. Unless we are aware and alert, to a significant extent, bullshitting is what the egoic human mind does, and what it is; a repository of ignorant bullshit. In you and me, the egoic-mind generates great volumes of bullshit in the form arbitrary fantasies, made up confabulations, virtual realities, shallow defences and spurious justifications. Again, colloquially, the egoic mind produces bullshit presumptions, bullshit pretentions and bullshit pontifications. All of which we believe and spruik as assumed truth, enlightenment and genius.

Goggles and Virtual Bullshit

Let's combine the virtual goggles analogy from the previous chapter with the bullshit analogy in this chapter. The software of my goggled egoic-mind is the idiosyncratic patterns of 'my' arbitrary, imagined and made-up bullshit opinions, beliefs and ideas that I bring to conversations, relationships, social settings, work, community and the world. Your expression of goggled ego is your idiosyncratic bullshit that you bring to the various domains of your world. But you and I are mostly unaware of the nature and extent of our virtual, goggled, egoic bullshit. Nor are we aware of our shared, enmeshed mental bullshit. Individually, and together, we assume that what we say is real and actual. Not uncommonly, we assume and assert that virtual, goggled bullshit is intellectual genius, special wisdom and spiritual enlightenment.

This is particularly the case for virtual ideological political bullshit; virtual fundamentalist religious bullshit; and for virtual new-age, social media, pop-psychology, junk-science bullshit and 'conspiracy madness bullshit'; most of which is man-made. I smile widely when I contemplate the ironies, paradoxes and mixed metaphors of virtual, goggled bullshit. I shake my head when I consider their impact in terms of ignorance, harm and suffering

The Sneakiness of Bullshit

More or less, you and I are blind-to, blinded-by, and blind-sided by our egoic bullshit. Egoic bullshit is so assumed, automatic, conditioned and habituated, that we don't perceive it as bullshit. We don't know that we are talking shit. Under the sway of 'the left hemisphere bullshitting egoic mind', we assume that what we say is self-evident; or, common sense; which is a very common expression of over-assumed, ill-conceived, biased, unexamined bullshit. We are unaware that much of our assumed and apparent self-evident idealism, morality and 'right-mindedness' is thinly disguised bullshit. Many of our beliefs and opinions are unexamined, unidentified bullshit. Most of us have very little inkling that we are likely to be 'full of shit'.

Typically, and commonly, ego consists of patterns of bullshit ideas, opinions and beliefs that humans presumptively, pretentious and pontifically spruik, from conversation to conversation; from interaction to interaction; from relationship to relationship; from situation to situation; and from issue to issue; day after day, month after month, decade after decade. Ego consists of mentally, verbally and behaviourally habituated bullshit patterns that we routinely act on, and act out; all in blissful, virtual oblivion; and often with socially painful, boorish unawareness and insensitivity.

These egoic bullshit patterns are intended to portray the clever, capable me that I hope you will see. Egoic patterns portray the me that I hope will impress; and the me that I hope you will believe and like. Even more, bullshit egoic patterns portray the me with whom I hope you will become enmeshed. By enmeshed, I mean that you believe and speak the same 'shit' as me; that we will share the same virtual bullshit ideas, opinions and beliefs. When functioning egoically, more or less, 'I am' a bunch of virtual, goggled, egoic bullshit ideas, attitudes, assertions, defences and justifications. Family and friends tolerate my idiosyncratic egoic bullshit. They might say "Oh, that's Don. Sometimes he talks shit. Sometimes he's full of shit. He thinks what he says is 'hot shit'; but we know it's bullshit. Sometimes he's a real shithead".

Does this sound familiar?

Increased Reality = Increased Dignity

To be fair, most of us aren't prolific 'egoic virtual bullshitters' all the time. But we are bullshitters from time to time; and more or less in certain situations, but not so much in other situations. Nevertheless, awareness, honesty, sensitivity and integrity tend to be absent when 'bullshittery' is dominant. Potentially, the more aware we are of our particular 'egoic-bullshittery', the more we can moderate it, the more sensitive, integrous and accountable we can be in relationship and community. The less aware we are of our tendency to talk bullshit, the more we are a slave to automatic and habituated dodgy assumptions, behaviours and egoic, bullshit justifications.

As emphasised before, this book is about helping us enhance our potential to be aware, sensitive, integrous and accountable; that is to say — to be mindful. We can enhance our dignity and rationality in relationships and community to the extent that we are we are aware of our bullshit. We can be values-based and rational to the extent that we are self-aware, factually-aware, socially-aware and situationally aware. Awareness is a precursor and prerequisite to sensitivity, rationality and reality. Awareness is the beginning of dignity and reason. It is the essence of mindfulness.

Remember, Eastern philosophy suggests that most of us are much more egoically unaware than we imagine or assume. Most of us are aware of bullshit in others, but are largely unaware of the egoic base of our bullshit thinking, beliefs, judgements, motives, excuses, projections, stories and justifications. Most of us are largely unaware of the extent of ego in how we think shit, talk shit and behave like shitheads.

Learning to recognise our own bullshit, vis-à-vis, our egoic unawareness and mindlessness, and learning to be consciously, intentionally and strategically mindfully aware — are the purpose of First People and Eastern right hemisphere mindfulness practices and meditative practices. Mindful relational and ecological reverence, awareness, reality, sensitivity, integrity, responsibility and accountability are very purposeful priorities in ancient Eastern and First People philosophies. Mindful — purposeful relational, communal and ecological awareness, sensitivity, integrity, responsibility and accountability are crucial for our appreciation and management of human and environmental issues and priorities. That is why I included chapters on Breath Meditation earlier in this book.

Does the 'bullshit' analogy ring true?

Can you see the need for us humans to recognise and minimise our ignorant, egoic bullshit opinions, beliefs, stories, distortions, excuses, lies and justifications?

Imagine and envisage the benefits to our relationships, communities and environments if we become aware of our bullshit, become accountable for it, and minimise it.

Imagine if our politicians and other community leaders were to greatly reduce their egoic bullshit; especially their macho, masculine bullshit.

Ego and Arbitrariness

Are you taking time to breathe?

We have referenced arbitrariness many times before, and particularly in relation to ignorance. Now we are going to explicitly identify arbitrariness as a defining trait of ego. Remember, arbitrariness is the whimsical and fanciful basis and driver of ignorant self-serving egoic motives, opinions, beliefs, stories and judgements. Inherently, arbitrary egoic stories, etcetera, contain the fantasies, desires, misinformation, myths, deceptions and lies that are key aspects of ignorance. Thus, arbitrariness is the epitome of ego, and because it almost invisible, is the mostly un-noticed driver of egoic ignorance. Ego, arbitrariness and ignorance are inseparable.

The egoic-mind makes up ignorant fantasies, ideas, beliefs, opinions and stories on the basis of whims. Egoic whims are the core nature and product of arbitrariness. Whims are universal tools of the arbitrary egoic-mind. When we combine egoic me-obsessiveness, egoic whims and egoic imagination, we get a hotchpotch of self-serving, fanciful egoic fluff in the form of judgemental opinions, fancified beliefs, 'fantastical-quasi-pop-spirituality', contrived junk-science, fascial social media memes and contrived conspiratorial unrealities.

Does that web of arbitrary egoic, Yang-made stuff sound familiar?

Have you seen this web of arbitrary egoic machinations in yourself, peers, families, religious devotees, new-age boffins and consumers of conspiracy theories?

Have you seen rabid arbitrariness in politicians and religious buffs?

Have you seen the impact of arbitrariness on relationships, communities and environments?

Have you seen the connections between arbitrariness and all manifestations and nuances of ignorance?

Be aware of the roles and impacts of arbitrariness that are inherent in the issues that are detailed in this chapter. Join the dots. Draw the map of micro and macro issues and drivers, including role of arbitrariness.

Whimsical Ideas about God, Spirits, Heaven and Hell, Karma and Reincarnation

To alleviate egoic fear and existential insecurity, oblivious to what we doing, arbitrarily, for thousands of years, we left hemisphere humans, mostly us men, have made up imaginary, dreamy, fanciful, whimsical, egoic stories about gods, spirits, heaven and hell, redemption, salvation, karma, reincarnation and nirvana. These arbitrary contrivances are how the fearful, insecure, ignorant egoic-human-mind tries to bolster, comfort, reassure and validate itself.

On a whim, again, mostly men, make up an array of egoic stories about needing to be rescued from a range of existential stuff; including sin, a vague sense of anomie, the flesh, irony, paradox and liminality; all of which are assumed, perplexing aspects of human existence; including the vague, man-contrived notion of 'human nature'. Existential perplexity and suffering are real. But much of the pretentious esoteric stuff we make up to deal with it is patently egoic — arbitrary, assumptive, imaginary, fanciful and false. Imaginary egoic issues and imaginary egoic solutions are typical of our imaginative and arbitrary conjuring, story-making, myth-making, egoic-human-mind; most commonly, the masculine-egoic-mind.

When we think arbitrarily, you and I can't tell the difference between what is existentially real, and what is arbitrarily imagined and fancifully contrived. Historically, the egoic-mind has had a lot of trouble separating verifiable fact from arbitrary fiction. This remains the case, even for us allegedly well-educated 21st century moderners. Many of us can't distinguish made up, new-age fads and contrived conspiracy theories from the legitimate scientific and factual issues.

There are an amazing hight number of intelligent people who are taken-in by arbitrary, imagined, made up, faddish ideas of religion, new-age pop-spirituality, internet and social media fluff, and conspiracy fictions. Separately and together, this mishmash of fictions, are evidence of the arbitrariness of the wishful egoic thinking of billions of our contemporaries. Billions of us are governed by baseless, wishful, imaginary arbitrary, Yang-made beliefs and ideas.

Ego and Existential God-Stories

More than any other topic, we unconsciously delusional, arbitrary humans make up and proselytise romantic, dramatic fictional existential stories about the turbulent and fraught relationship between God and humans. There is a vast array of dreamy and melodramatic made-up stories about God, sin, the devil, good angels, bad angels, Godly men and women, evil men and women, saviours, prophets, gurus, heaven, hell, purgatory, karma and reincarnation. The list of arbitrarily made-up left hemisphere plots, ploys and players is very long indeed. Religious stories are the pinnacle of arbitrarily contrived, fictional, man-made egoic dramas. They are a web of fantastic romantic drama that capture the minds of billions of us. Mystical and mythical confabulations are inherent in all arbitrary man-made religious, political, new-age existential dogmas and ideologies.

Arbitrary man-made God-stories and God-dramas are our original egoic conspiracy theories. God-stories are the impetus for much other fantastical stuff that we arbitrarily make up about good and bad mystical mythical characters; about villains, victims and heroic rescuers. All God-stories are products of whimsical mental imaginings. All are made up existential dramas of 'the prolifically confabulating, projective, left hemisphere human mind'. All are egoic, arbitrary whims and fanciful wishful thinking. Tellingly, the vast majority of God-stories are highly and overtly masculinised. Most God-stories espouse patriarchal, paternal, chauvinistic and misogynistic understandings of God, humans, angels, demons, sin, salvation, paradise in heaven with virgins, and eternal torture in hell with sexual deviants, demons and the devil.

As you've already observed, throughout this book, we look unflinchingly at arbitrary God-delusions, made up mystical stories, baseless esoteric whims, phantastic fantasy fads, flimsy factless theories, wacko conspiracy ideation, and self-justifying, self-aggrandising existential religious narratives. For thousands of years, we humans have defaulted to arbitrary, fictional, egoic, religious fluff to compensate for factual ignorance, and to cope with egoic existential fear and insecurity. All arbitrary, speculative, fanciful, factless religious stuff is classic egoic decompensation; driven by egoic fear and egoic ignorance in the face of feelings of existential vulnerability. Again, all this fluff is man-made.

When we are factually informed, rational and peaceful, we don't need to compensate by arbitrarily 'making stuff up'; religious, new-age, conspiratorial or otherwise. Critical thinking and dignity can percolate to the surface when we are peaceful, rational and factually informed. When reasoned, informed and peaceful we can sit back and watch egoic thoughts flit by; and allow fanciful, arbitrary egoic-thinking to rise and fall, rise and fall.

Remember, Breath Meditation can help us be peaceful so that we can be mindfully aware and discerning. Right hemisphere peace and mindfulness can help us distinguish factuality from arbitrariness, rationality from irrationality, actualities from contrivances, authentic science from junk science, legitimate data from made up fanciful ideas.

Be Vulnerable

Existential issues might be very different if we could embrace unknowing vulnerability. That is, be aware that, in the face of perplexing unknowns and uncertainties, we are free to commit to be factual, rational, humble, integrous and authentic. All constructive futures hinge on us rationally, bravely and humbly embracing our existential vulnerability. We need to be mindfully vulnerable — by being as consciously aware, factually informed, logically reasoned and as attuned to actual reality as we can be. If you and I and humankind can stick to facts and be at peace with a myriad of 'not yet knowns', a wonderful array of exciting and constructive possibilities await us. If we can't stick to facts, or won't stick to facts and critical thinking, then we are likely to be default to 'more of the same' existentially arbitrary 'wacko' man-made egoic stuff to which we humans have subjected and enslaved ourselves for thousands of years.

It is doable for you and I to be vulnerable, but not default to arbitrarily fluff as a way to alleviate existential uncertainty, stress and anxiety. It is possible for us to just sit in our vulnerability. We can be aware, dignified, reasoned and peaceful in the vulnerability of not knowing. Sitting in our vulnerability is liberating and empowering. I think it is far better to be peaceful, silent and still in our vulnerability, than to babble about and chase after baseless dreamy, fantasies, and to rush to arbitrary wishful speculation, ideas, beliefs and opinions.

However, history shows that egoic patterns of unawareness, arbitrariness, binary dichotomous thinking, cognitive fragmentation, superstition, fantasy, faddishness, myth-making and conspiracy-confabulation seem very difficult for us humans, especially us testosterone-driven, left hemisphere men, to recognise, admit, be comfortable with, manage and moderate.

A counter-balance might be found in the following commitments and priorities — commit to peaceful, reasoned, intentional and purposeful right hemisphere priorities and choices; commit to personal, relational and ecological dignity and rationality; commit to personal, relational and ecological intelligence; commit to personal, relational and ecological critical thinking; commit to personal, relational and ecological awareness and sensitivity; commit to personal, relational ecological integrity; and commit to personal, relational and ecological factfulness. These priorities and foci can help us be consciously, intelligently, peacefully and purposefully vulnerable in the face of unknowns and uncertainties. Peaceful, aware, intentional vulnerability is vastly preferable to escapist, reactive dissociation, arbitrary existential fantasising, and mindless myth-making.

This network of priorities may help you and I and others to be peacefully vulnerable by choosing to be informed, reasonable, compassionate, responsible and accountable. Being compassionate, responsible and accountable begins by being vulnerable but kind, vulnerable but respectful, vulnerable but integrous, and vulnerable but responsible and accountable.

Increasing our personal and collective awareness of these Yin priorities might offer hope in the midst of the vulnerabilities of many perplexing and uncertain personal, relational, citizenry and societal situations. Conscious, intentional hope and conscious, intentional vulnerability are inseparable. They are interdependent. So too are conscious, intentional dignity, conscious intentional rationality, and a conscious intentional systems orientation. Sit with possibility of the liberty of this network of mindful possibilities — for weeks, years and decades. Let these possibilities soak into your consciousness.

Dignity and Rationality in the Midst of Vulnerability

When the networking of vulnerability, awareness, dignity, reason and accountability becomes prominent within us, among us, and throughout humankind, that will be the sign that we are evolving existentially, spiritually, psychologically and socially. This network will be a sign that we are evolving beyond our typically unhelpful unaware, fearful, insecure, reactive, arbitrary mental and existential defaults. Hope is contingent on and inseparable from vulnerability, awareness, dignity, reason and right hemisphere discernment of the ecological interwovenness of life. Ecological dignity, rationality and reverence need to be inseparable, even in the mist of vulnerability; especially in the midst of vulnerability.

Sometimes I allow myself the luxury of wondering what humankind might be like, when in the midst of existential vulnerabilities, if a critical mass of us allow ourselves to be guided by conscious, sentient, intentional and peaceful presence dignity, rationality and reverence. Again, this is what mindfulness looks like and feels like. It is us being present, sensitive, calm, clear and reasoned.

As emphasised in previous chapters, none of the musings about awareness, respect, inclusion and kindness would matter nearly so much if it weren't for humankind's unbroken man-made history of extreme, arbitrary unkindness and disrespect through pathological degradations, violence, and environmental destruction. It seems imperative for you and I to gain authentic and empowering insight into the man-made 'egoically mindless arbitrary existential stuff' that has created and driven millennia of degrading, cruel and abusive cultural, religious and political disrespect, exclusion and unkindness. If it weren't for these issues, there would be no need to write and read a chapter about the mindfulness of dignity, rationality, grace and stillness in the mist of vulnerability.

Have you observed the unease of existential vulnerability in yourself and others?

Have you observed the use arbitrary existential ideas, beliefs and opinions in yourself and others as a way to deal with the unease of vulnerability?

Do you think we can do better than so many expressions of existential arbitrariness?

Can we aspire to dignity and rationality through mindful Yin presence, reverence, peace, grace and inclusion in the midst of complexity and vulnerability?

How do you feel about allowing yourself to be vulnerable, while also being consciously present, rational, kind, respectful and gracious?

Feel free to pause and breathe as you reflect and absorb the possibility of the mindfulness of grace, and the grace of mindfulness.

Presumptions, Pretentions, Opinions and Beliefs — Where 21st Century Ego Hides and Abides

This is another challenging; so, pause for a moment to breathe.

Use this chapter to become more aware of the impact of subjective egoic presumptions, pretentions, opinions and beliefs on relationships, communities, citizenship and leadership.

There are grounded, Zenlike, right hemisphere persons for whom kindness and respect, reason and dignity, honesty and integrity, discipline and accountability are their everyday way of being human. Such people are consistently peaceful and quiet, within and without. They tend to be comfortable with vulnerability. Zen-like people tend not to tell egoic made up arbitrary stories. They tend to listen, to empathise, to be very slow to speak, to offer a minimum of opinions and espouse very few beliefs. Zenlike persons rarely presume, pontificate or judge. The Zen ones among us are not inclined to worry, react and act out. They are comfortable not knowing and not telling. They are comfortable being uncertain and vulnerable.

Mindful, right hemisphere sensitivity, compassion, reverence, rationality and inclusion seem to come naturally to Zen-like people among us. To them, the mindless, assumptive, pretentious and pontifical chatter of ego is but a dull and irrelevant background noise. Zen-ones are aware of arbitrary, egoic thoughts and ideas, but are unmoved by them, and very rarely channel them. Their clear, peaceful, unspoken Zen response to presumptive and pretentious egoic fluff is to main peaceful, silent and stiff. Alan and Michael, the men profiled in later chapters, are soulful, Zen-like persons.

Us Egoic Moderners

However, most of us moderners are not soulful or Zen-like. For the vast majority, the voice of ego is strong and common in our patterns of opinionated thoughts and beliefs, strong emotive judgemental reaction, presumptive communication, self-leveraging actions, and defensive self-justifying reactions. It is vital that we bring these typical traits of the egoic-mind out of the shadows and into the light of mindfulness. You and I need to become aware of our egoic left hemisphere defaults and machinations. To have any hope of managing and moderating the egoic drivers of human dysfunctionality, we need to know where he hides and abides.

"He", you say. Yes, "he". As emphasised many times before, the dominant voice of ego over the past millennia has been the voice of unchecked, egoic masculinity. To a great extent, ego is the dominant voice of Yang; the voice of unchecked, extroverted male energy; the voice of relentless, ambitious masculine drive; and too commonly, ego is the voice of toxic, overbearing, masculine chauvinism. The peaceful, contented, grateful, relational 'right hemisphere voice' of Yin is too rarely heard in the modern world of competitive, judgemental, adversarial, left hemisphere masculine priorities, values, systems, structures and institutions. Ego hides in assumed, masculine, left-hemisphere pre-eminence and presumption. Reread the previous sentence; perhaps this paragraph.

Much of the time, unwittingly, the vast majority of us are influenced by default left hemisphere masculine voices, stories and narratives. These are ego in a nutshell. But most of us have little awareness of what presumptuous, pretention and pontifical masculine egoic defaults look like and sound like; how they work; or what their presence means for us personally, relationally, communally, religiously, culturally, spiritually, politically and existentially. This is because, by their nature, and by the modus operandi, preconceptions, presumptions of the masculine ego is perfectly hidden in thousands of years of assumed, unexposed, unexamined and invisibly inculcated man-made priorities and beliefs. Ego hides in plain sight. It is mostly undetected in the machinations of our assumed masculine world; in the assumed worldly mind of humankind.

The Masculine Ego — The Elephant in the Room

As a result, most of us have a fairly nebulous appreciation of the difficulties that arise from us being unsuspecting, unintentional persons of a Yang-based ego. We have but vaguest awareness of the indignity of society's dominant default to masculine voices, motives, desires, stories, narratives and justifications. In the mist of 21st century clamour, most of us men, and many women, don't recognise the absence of archetypal feminine grace, dignity and nurturance in family, at work, in institutions, and in governance. Most of us scantly appreciate the manoeuvrings of the egoic masculine mind in families, peer groups, work settings, professions, religions, cultures, politics, economics and industries. For most men and women, the masculinised voice of ego is the elephant in the room.

Too many of 'us' are oblivious to left hemisphere masculine egoic manoeuvrings in all human domains. At most, we tend be only vaguely aware of the role of the masculine ego in the history of post-hunter-gatherer societies. To most of us, 'the-masculine' feels surreal and dreamlike; often unpleasantly so; but not vividly and lucidly. And yet, the masculine egoic voices and actions of righteous, knowing, strident wanting, assertive getting and coercive controlling are how many men speak and act from conversation to conversation, from situation to situation, from issue to issue, from context to context, from ambition to ambition, from generation to generation, from millennia to millennia. Ironically, this also includes a visible proportion of 21st women; who, unwittingly, have internalised masculine attitudes, priorities, aspirations, ambitions, language and controls.

The masculine nature of ego hides in plain sight through the ubiquity of presumptive individualist priorities, projections and judgements; and in presumptive righteous superiority. Even within feminism, there is evidence of pious moralising, assumptive claims to exclusive right-mindedness, strident tribal right-belonging and identity politics.

Patriotic, nationalistic chest-beating, populist politicking and forceful conspiracy ideation encompass both men and women. Do these situations describe the insidiousness of ego and the pervasiveness and dominance of the masculine mind? Does it point to the masculine-mind as the dominant egoic driver of our human world, for the majority of men, and for a noticeable proportion of women? Is the semi-invisible egoic masculine mind the elephant in the room of many 21st century societies.

Because of the invisibility and automatic nature of assumed masculine left hemisphere priorities, we readily and uncritically default the rightness and righteousness of the automatic masculine stuff we think, speak, behave and act out. These days, a large proportion of men and a noticeable percentage of women assume the necessity to assert, project and benefit our individualist, tribal, cultural, corporate, religious and nationalistic selves. Commonly, both men and women assume that we should assert 'go-get-um' left hemisphere ambitions, that we should be 'successful', and that we should aggressively defend our ambitions, beliefs and assertions. As well, commonly, we men and women, assume that we must strongly justify our self-promoting priorities, ambitions, preferences, choices and decisions. Many men and women assume and feel strongly that we must not be wrong, submissive or weak. All these are the near-invisible egoic assumptions and traits of the masculinised mind of the 21st century.

Ego Hides in Assumed Masculine Ideals and Arbitrary Aspirations

Most of us, women and men, are almost completely unaware that egoic patterns hide invisibly within well intended, but assumed, arbitrary, mostly man-made religious, worldly and cultural ideals and beliefs. That is to say, for many contemporary men and some 'modern' women, masculine mental networks are notably self-invested, commonly self-absorbed, self-servingly moralistic, unempathic, and often are inherently judgemental and exclusive. All this masculine stuff is so mentally assumptively automatic that it flies beneath the radar of mindful awareness; for both women and men. This near-invisible pattern of strong-minded, arbitrary left hemisphere ideals and ambitious aspirations is where the masculine egoic elephant in room hides and abides.

We are mostly unaware of that Yang ideals are the source of our egoic judgemental categorising, pejorative labelling and binary classifications. To the masculine ego, 'same as me' automatically means good and right. Ipso facto, subconsciously, 'different from me and us', tends to mean wrong and bad; perhaps dangerous and treacherous. Without the balancing effects of Yin-based inclusion, without Yin-based motherly self-sacrifice; without mindful Yin-empathy; and without conscious relational, communal and ecological Yin orientations — our masculinised mind automatically implants egoic assumptions, sets egoic benchmarks and imposes egoic man-made rules. These chauvinistic egoic tendencies are often diminishing and disparaging of those whose benchmarks and rules are different from those of dominant masculine norms, mindsets, cultures and institutions.

Unnoticed, for women and men, idealistic masculine egoic voices and stories create imagined, arbitrary, fictitious enemies, and concoct imaginary categories of inferior and bad. These patterns occur in the relative absence of Yin-mindfulness; that is, in the absence of humble, open, conscious awareness, conscious self-reflection, conscious rationality, conscious critiques, conscious openness, conscious empathy, conscious respect, conscious dignity, and conscious inclusion. Without conscious, intentional awareness, dignity and rationality, the narrowly exclusive and idealised 'masculine egoic mind' assumes and asserts endless rationales and justifications for mistrusting, accusing, alienating and harming those who are different. Ego hides unseen in our unexamined, left hemisphere, man-created egoic aversions to difference. Ego hides in arbitrary inclusions and exclusions. It hides invisibly in rationalised Yang-assumed and Yang-made masculinised egoic categories and judgements.

Ego also hides in irrational masculine fear, mistrust, paranoia and conspiracy ideation. Very commonly, ego hides in the surreal, fear-based macho righteousness of man-made religious, cultural and nationalistic ideations and arbitrary man-made justifications. None of this arises from the relational, ecological inclusive mind of the-feminine; unless the feminine has been inculcated and co-opted by masculine ideals, aspirations, rationalisations and justifications. Fear-based masculine patterns are not inherently Yin-devised and Yin-driven. That is to say, they don't arise from the mindful, womanly Yin reverence, dignity and rationality of relational, communal and ecological consciousness.

Ego, Judgementalism and Conflict

Broadly, it seems that the egoic masculine left hemisphere is the invisible and anonymous creator of strong, assumed self-righteous attitudes, pious beliefs, and righteous justifications and deeply-felt, emotive, moralistic opinions. Dignity-diminishing egoic mental processes are the invisible source of self-righteous judgements about people whom we assumptively, pontifically and simplistically blame for this and that personal, social, political or economic problem.

It seems that the egoic masculinised human mind must have a bone to chew. And chew they do; chew and chew and chew. One of ego's little-recognised defaults is to endlessly 'munch-on' arbitrary, imagined, contrived, exaggerated and fictitious man-contrived issues, intrigues and drama. Have you noticed how many are drawn to and hold-tightly to conflict, drama and intrigue? Many people feel compelled to create power-plays and construe conspiracy in family, community. Some are often at odds with others; with friends, neighbours, public officials, shop assistants, the tax department, the media, and the government? Bone-chewing is a product of the judgemental, issues-driven, masculinised left hemisphere. Egoic bone-chewing is the elephant in the room.

'High conflict — high drama' left hemisphere people often seem to have a strong egoic point to make, often have an issue to air, often have an axe to grind, and often have a score to settle? Some are strongly drawn to conflict conspiracy theories. Drama, intrigue, conspiracy ideation and issue-mongering are our assumptive, pontifical, judgemental masculinised ego in full flight.

Ego hides in midst of the assumed and contrived, conflictual righteousness of arbitrary, mostly-man-made idealisms, fundamentalisms, divisions, judgements and exclusions. 'Populist conspiracy cultists' are prominent 21st century examples man-contrived conflict, drama, intrigue, judgmentalism, anger, paranoia, bone-chewing and quixotic acting out. Quixotic Trump rallies and the 'Trump-inspired bone-chewing' claims about the stolen election resulted in the insane, cultist attack on the Capitol; and on democracy. These attacks are the deluded, righteous masculine ego in full boorish bluster and violent acting out. Vehement, quixotic, egoic delusions of justified righteous aggression are a masculinised, chauvinistic, egoic elephant in the room of Trump devotees; and of populist cultists in general.

How many women did you see at the Capitol riot?

How would you describe and profile the traits and behaviours of the men who attacked the Capitol?

Gossip

The assumptive, pontifical, judgemental, adversarial, conflict-prone egoic-mind also loves gossip, labels and name-calling. Very commonly, egoic beliefs and opinions are expressed as high-minded, righteous, moralistic gossip. The exclusively-right egoic-mind pontificates about the world from its assumptive, self-made masculine throne, which has been erected on the high-moral-ground of implicit, chauvinistic personal, ethical, religious, political and philosophical superiority. Increasingly, over the several thousand years, the more moderate right-hemisphere Yin aspects of mind have been side-lined and stymied by the dominance of the Yang left-hemisphere; as evidenced through contemporary mindless parochial tribalism, racism, sexism, nationalistic vitriol, violent sectarianism, and cultural disparagement. Left-hemisphere Yang dominance and vitriol are the semi-invisible masculine elephant in the man-made room.

Thus, much of this egoic masculine stuff flies under the radar of conscious awareness, for both women and men. Unaware — we presume, pretend, gossip, spruik, pontificate and assert our assumed and uncritiqued beliefs, opinions, judgements and superiority as if we are talking about what we had for dinner. Ego hides in the automatic righteousness of everyday judgemental chatter and gossip. Masculinised gossip is another elephant in the room. Much of our everyday little-p and big-P political gossip supports masculine agendas, such as exercising power, bolstering image, maximising control and building empires in family, in peer groups, at work, in communities and in international relations.

Egoically — presumptively, projectively, glibly, conveniently — men assume and assert that gossip is a feminine trait. But that is typical of many judgements that we men project onto women. Almost invisibly, masculine projection deflects gossip away from the masculine ego. The left-hemisphere political mind of chauvinistic masculinity invented both projection and gossip; but the masculine political mind absolved itself by deftly projecting them onto the-feminine. Sure, women gossip; but religious and political men invented and harnessed gossip is a tool for projection and blame.

This, and many other egoic sleights of hand are conveniently contrived masculine bullshit. In so many ways, the masculinised mind is a 'cunning, conniving bullshitter'. It can be difficult for 21st century women to recognise and step away from masculine, Yang bullshit. It's extremely difficult for men to recognise and step away.

One of the aims of this book is to expose masculine slights of hand that blame and diminish the feminine. Another aim is to shine a bright light and reveal the Yang elephant in the room.

What are your thoughts about the masculine ego projecting the blame for gossip onto women?

Enter the Role of Dignity and Rationality

Unless we intentionally attune to gracious, inclusive, non-judgemental right hemisphere consciousness, much of this surreptitious egoic masculine stuff will continue to find its way under the radar and into our assumptions, preconceptions, beliefs and priorities. Therefore, the relatively small minority of mindful, educated, astute Zen-like persons and process-disciplined scientists need to grow to become the critical mass of us. Dignity and rationality need to evolve to become our conscious, shared priority, and the new normal of the vast majority.

Consistency of Yin — empathy, compassion, rationality, inclusion and kindness need to be the evolving consciousness of cultures, organisations, corporations, institutions and governments. These values need to rise to prominence and normality. To help us do this, we need to observe and acknowledge our incongruities and shortcomings; and do whatever it takes to become more congruent and more consciously values-base, principled and rational.

Some Questions

Have you observed the predominance of masculinised, egoic left hemisphere patterns, particularly in men, but also in women?

Have you observed that we live in a world this is made in the image of men; a world that is contrived, contorted and justified in the image of man-made gods, man-made religions, man-made political ideologies, and man-made religious, political, economic and material left hemisphere priorities?

Historically and today, egoic masculine images, symbols and icons inculcate the semi-conscious mind of humanity. We need to become fully conscious so we can reimagine and recreate a human world in which the images, symbols, icons and priorities of the right hemisphere Feminine-Mother become the forefront of human consciousness. We need to purposefully evolve a world that is symbolised and exemplified by the Yin systems priorities, principles and values that are inherent in the ways of Mother Earth.

First Peoples can educate us and lead us toward right hemisphere Yin systems priorities, principles and values of Mother Earth. We will look at these possibilities and hopes in the final quarter of the book.

Have you been fortunate to observe reverential dignity and intelligent systems-based reason in mindfully aware, sensitive, rational and integrous Zenlike women and men? Observe these people. Learn from them. Emulate them. They can help us do better.

There are many Zen-like role models among First Peoples who can help us do better.

Again, we will look at this priority and hope in the final quarter of the book.

Projection – Ego's Most Prominent Ploy

This chapter discusses a highly dysfunctional feature of ego that we need to understand. There's a lot a consider and absorb. So, breathe, and take your time.

The chapter asks —

Can we humans do better than projective defensiveness, and better than projective blame?

Can we move beyond inflating ourselves by pointing the finger at others?

Can we stop using projection to distort facts and escape home truths, reality, responsibility and accountability?

Can we learn to see and to own our ulterior motives, our self-serving interpretations of circumstances, our cunning evasive stories and our self-protective self-justification.

Can men who in positions of power learn to look closely at their human-selves nurture insight into masculinised defensive-aggressive-projective political ploys and power plays?

All in all, through these learnings, can we women and men develop self-awareness, self-honesty, self-critique, transparency, integrity, accountability and depth of character.

If we can, these capacities will enhance our relationships, roles, endeavours and our management of issues?

Be curious about these questions.

Be curious about the masculine origins of our projective dispositions and defaults. Remember, in the previous chapter, I mentioned that the collective egoic masculine mind automatically projects gossip as a trait and default of women. There are many other things that the masculinised ego projects; and has done for thousands of years. Be curious about the origins of projection, and about the many ways by which we humans project. This is crucial, because projection is the number-one stumbling block for individuals, families, workplaces, political parties, religions, institutions, governments, nations and humankind as a whole. When we understand projection, we understand a huge, pervasive aspect of how the egoic human mind trips us up and holds us back.

Projection Is

Projection is a form of externalisation, which, broadly, is about moving responsibility for what we've done away from ourselves, and displacing it onto others. For example, I might accuse you of not being accountable, when I am the one who resists accountability. That is, I project my resistance to accountability onto you; thereby, making me look better than, blameless, righteous and superior; and making you look lesser, bad and to blame. As a form of externalisation, projection seems to be our most common egoic defence mechanism, and our most-used egoic justification for criticising, fault-finding, judging, disparaging and harming others. Projection is also our most common ways of justifying the diminishment and exclusion those whose only crime is to be different from our arbitrary stereotypes of who and what is acceptable. Projection enables us to exonerate and promote ourselves, while blaming and diminishing others.

Do these expressions of projection look and sound like something that egoic cultural, religious and political men might have contrived and invented?

Ordinary people such as you and I, project issues and blame onto our partners, parents, children, siblings, friends and teachers. Commonly, each generation projects judgment and blame onto the ones before and after. Generations projectively reproach each and blame each other for being what they themselves are, and for doing what they-we do. Religious groups project fear and judgement onto non-religious folk. Religious and ideological groups project blame onto opposing religions, politicians, cultures, ethnic groups and ideologies.

This chapter will show that egoic projection is so common and prominent, that, to be human is be egoic, is to project. It will show that we humans are defensive-projective and projectively aggressive 'down to our bootlaces'; almost entirely in complete unawareness; and often with terrible consequences.

Projection is an egoic syndrome that is inherent and endemic in the self-protective left hemisphere psyche of humankind. Individually and collectively, we concoct and proffer fictional projective stories to make others look worse than us; to make us look better than them; to make us look better than what we are; and, ultimately, to make 'he-she and 'them' responsible for what we say and do. Projection is a well-use mechanism for deflect responsibility and for minimising accountability. Projection is a form of psychological mechanism for repressing self-awareness. Projection is self-deception, denial, avoidance, diversion, distraction and abrogation all rolled into one egoic syndrome.

Why We Project

For individuals, groups, generations, institutions, religions, political parties and governments, the challenges of self-awareness, self-honesty, owning responsibility and for being accountable, trigger powerful protective-projective resistance to the facts of what we have said and done. Commonly, individuals and all the groups mentioned above, project their history, motives, agendas, attitudes, fears, insecurities and problematic actions onto others to avoid unpalatable home truths and realities about themselves; about 'ourselves'.

We fraught and frail humans project because it seems that self-truth and self-reality greatly unsettle us. Egoically, we are daunted and stymied by the prospect having to recognise and own questionable attitudes and behaviours that may portray us as undesirable persons; or worse. We don't want to own our 'shitty' attitudes and behaviours because, in part, they define our problematic personhood, politics, religion and culture. Significantly, our shitty attitudes and behaviours risk exposing the low calibre of our character — personally, relationally, religiously, politically and culturally.

Because of the risk of exposure, we assume and assert the idealised egoic left hemisphere self, brush-over and project the not-so-desirable egoic self, and promote our imagined and fantasised ideal egoic self. Ego protects the self — full stop. In the world of ego, the egoic-self is sacrosanct. It must be protected at all costs; including at the costs of oblivion, dishonesty, indecency, lack of integrity and disrespecting and diminishing others.

We substitute all sorts of projective confabulations to avoid self-revelation, and to avoid the penetrating demands and scrutiny of our congruence and character. We use projection to avert the relational demands of awareness, sensitivity, decency, honesty and reason; because, typically, we experience these as too daunting and too exacting. Relational values and principles are a very tough challenge for the egoic human mind. Commonly, the priority of being accountable for integrous, dignified and rational attitudes and behaviours is outside the capacity of our fragile, vulnerable human psyche; especially the insecure male psyche. So, we steadfastly minimise accountability by projecting our lacks and shortcomings onto others.

Thus, the subconscious intention of the bulk of our projective, confabulated stories and distortions of reality is to — minimise the difficult burden of responsibility for being consistently sensitive to others; for being gracious and fair-minded in our judgments; for being fair and kind in our attitudes and behaviours; for being disciplined critical thinkers; and for being accountable for all these exacting disciplines and responsibilities. We project to minimise the burden of high standards of ethical propriety, and to minimise the reality that we might actually struggle to live up to these standards. Typically, for many of us, Yin-based right hemisphere self-awareness, self-honesty, congruence, consistency, transparency, responsibility, ethical propriety and relational accountability are too difficult to do; and too painful to bear. It is much easier for the egoic self to be seen as an innocent victim, or as a gallant rescuer, or both; but never as an insensitive, uncaring, unethical, dishonest, untrustworthy bad person.

Projection, at All Levels, in All Domains

Projection is one of our primary and universal egoic, go-to left hemisphere tools for self-protection and self-promotion. Ego is inherently self-protective and self-promoting. Projection is universal at levels in society, and in all human domains. Individuals project to self-protect their idealised image and to self-promote. Corporations project to self-protect their image and self-promote. Political parties project to self-protect and self-promote. Ideologues project to self-protect and self-promote. Religious groups project to self-protect and self-promote. Governments project to self-protect and self-promote. Countries and states project to self-protect and self-promote.

Projection, is what we Australians call the 'flick pass' and 'selling the dump'. Both of these are football references which indicate that we have we deftly passed the ball, the 'hot potato', to another player and let them 'take the hit'; to let someone else take the crushing tackle that we should have taken. In all domains, we egoic human are very deft using the projective flick pass to get rid of the hot potato. We see this in our politicians on a daily basis.

When faced with the challenge of seeing projection in ourselves, we might say that: "Maybe politicians project. Maybe my partner projects; and my friends, my boss, and my neighbour; but not me". Maybe 'wrong-believes' or bad people project, but not me. Maybe China projects, but not us right-thinking good Australian people. Maybe the UN projects, but not the USA. Maybe 'others' project, but not me or my right and righteous like-minded peers. I am … we are … the good guys. Others, 'they and them', are the bad guys. From a projective orientation, 'they' are the problem; not me or us; never me or us. Our resistance to seeing the reality and responsibility looking back at us in the mirror is very strong. For all of us, the projective egoic mind does not like looking in the mirror.

Despite our claims to purity of awareness, integrity, responsibility and accountability, the bottom line is that self-protective and self-projective stories, narratives, rationalisations and defences have no boundaries or exclusions. Projecting is level playing field. It does not apply to some but not others. The vast majority of us are prone to invent self-protective, projective egoic stories. Most of us are prone to confabulate egoic, self-promoting narratives and justifications. Only a tiny, peaceful, Zen minority are relatively spared from projecting. Projecting is what the egoic-human-mind does … and does … and does. It's what we humans do, almost universally, almost without exception, and typically, without self-awareness and self-critique. Projection is our mindless, unconscious egoic superpower.

Projection — One-Eyed, Resistant and Inexorable

Typically, we can detect other people's egoic projective stories and ploys, but rarely can we detect our own. Even when our projective sham is factually exposed, we will usually continue to resist the reality that we are deflecting our stuff onto others. Most often, we will continue to point the projective-finger, and continue to plead our innocence, our best intentions, and our rightmindedness. 'The projective egoic self' finds it extremely difficult to see and admit its externalising sham. The egoic-mind will use all its intelligence, imagination, creativity, emotion and determination to deny ownership of externalising ploys and to justify its projections. The intent is of projection is always to protect and promote 'the personal-self', 'the political-self', 'the religious-self', the 'new-age self, the alternative science self, the social media self, and the conspiratorial self. Projection is how we resist responsibility for the dodgy stuff that the egoic-self conjures, confabulates, believes, says and does. Ironically and amusingly, the egoic self often uses projection to deny projection.

Egoic fear, egoic insecurity and wilful egoic pride greatly inhibit us from being aware and honest, from admitting our projection, from embracing responsibility for what we said and did, from being contrite, from apologising, and from to making recompense. Typically, awareness, insight, non-resistance, accountability and contrition are outside the capacity of the projective egoic mind. Values, principles and strategic priorities are often the casualties of projection. Commonly, harm to relationships is the collateral damage of projection. They are the prices that the egoic mind pays for the defence of the self. At all costs, to minimise the awful pain of truth, reality and accountability, the egoic mind will dodge and weave, joust and parry, project and counter-project. In counselling, we call this 'projective resistance'. Projective assertion and projective resistance are the hallmarks of ego in individuals, peer groups, institutions, religious groups, political parties, governments and states.

Situations of Egoic Projection

During decades of work in the helping professions, I often witnessed strong projective resistance to accountability with respect to individual, relational and organisational issues. Very commonly, individuals, groups, managers and whole organisations did not readily accept responsibility for their contributions to issues. Nor did they non-defensively accept responsibility for the consequences of their harmful attitudes and actions. At all levels, and in all domains, a range of projective ploys and strategies were very common expressions of resistance, defence, rationalisation and justification that I encountered in forty years of counselling, mentoring and consulting.

As a result, projection was a very common egoic barrier to personal, relational, professional, cultural and institutional development, integrity and responsibility. Projection was a common egoic impediment to conflict resolution, reconciliation, change and evolution. At all levels and in all domains, projection was a very common impediment to the evolution of values and critical thinking.

Decades of egoic resistance to accountability by religious and secular institutional abusers of children was made very plain throughout Australia's Royal Commission into Institutional Responses to Child Sexual Abuse. Even in the face of overwhelming evidence, institutions projected blame onto society, history, church culture, past church leaders, and onto the victims of abuse. Along with other avoidance ploys, many institutions used projective deflection and projective denial to resist fulsome awareness, honesty, ownership, empathy, compassion, integrity, culpability, accountability and contrition. The vast majority of institutional sexual abusers were men. All offending organisations were masculine, man-made institutions. All were controlled by men. This situation emphasises the reality, that, for millennia, men and masculine institutions have used projection as a key egoic tool for minimising culpability for institutional sexual abuse and other degradations of women and children.

Where there is conflict between religions and between political groups, typically, respective groups project their left hemisphere dysfunctionality onto each other. Each group projects blame onto other groups. Politicians and governments project their own failings onto other politicians and governments. Christians project their murderous and corrupt history onto Jews and Muslims, and visa-versa. Communism deflects its murderous history onto capitalism, and vis-versa. Free market boffins project the cause of poverty onto socialism, and visa-versa. The Catholic religion points its projective finger at the Protestantism, and visa-versa. Sunnis deflect responsibility for sectarian issues onto Shias, and visa-versa. Hindus blame Muslims for religious unrest and violence, and visa-versa. Predominantly, these examples are powerful institutional men abrogating responsibility by projecting responsibility and blame onto each other.

It is extremely rare for egoically polarised left hemisphere groups to show humility, contrition, empathy, compassion and fairmindedness toward those onto whom they project disparagement, blame and invalidation. Very few masculine institutions and states own the awful stuff they do and the lies and deceptions they project. Very few groups show care, empathy or compassion toward those who they harm; and those onto whom they project responsibility for that harm. Because of this, too few masculine states, institutions and groups are decent, integrous, accountable or contrite. This is significant because — projection obliterates personal and institutional decency, integrity, accountability and contrition. Projection fuels, incites and exacerbates self-righteousness, negative emotions, enmity, conflict, degradation and violence.

Can you see why I have frequently mentioned projection throughout the book; and why I have devoted this chapter to help us recognise and understand the facets and layers of projection; to clarify the systemic role of projection as a ubiquitous egoic driver of dysfunction and harm to people, environments and earth?

Here are some more examples of projection at the macro, masculine level.

In the 21st century, internationally, highly masculine American regimes project blame for all sorts of global issues onto equally masculinised Iran,

Russia, China; and projectively blame whichever other countries are convenient to externalise responsibility for its own misjudgements, misadventures, incompetence, greed, corruption and criminality. The USA is very good at painting itself as the innocent victim, the magnanimous benefactor, and the gallant rescuer. All of these images are contrived egoic projective smokescreens for its masculine insightlessness, insensitivity, clumsiness, incompetence and corruption. The USA is as problematic and as guilty as all those over whom it projectively blames and castigates. The USA assumes and asserts 'the moral and political high-moral-ground', while projectively painting Iran, Russia and China as evil. At the same time, masculine Iran, Russia and China assume the high moral ground and projectively displace responsibility for international tensions and internal issues into the USA. All these countries and states play endless masculine projective games of 'tit-for-tat'. All of them play endless man-made projective games of blame and counter-blame.

In the meantime, internally, in the USA, the slightly less masculine Democrats and highly masculine Republicans project all their respective incompetence and corruption onto each other. Globally, masculine socialism projects blame for human issues onto masculine far-right policies and populist machinations; and visa-versa. And so, international and internal masculine projective games go on and on; as they have throughout history; for thousands of years.

In 2022, the pathetically macho and massively pathologised Putin, projected blame and justification for its invasion of Ukraine onto a non-existent Nazi genocide. Ego doesn't care onto whom or what it projects blame, as long as it can shift responsibility and accountability away from itself; as long as it can paint itself in the roles of victim and rescuer.

God — The Most Common Human Projection

Ironically, most commonly, an array of masculine religions states, institutions and groups project their left hemisphere egoic desires, delusions, motives, emotions and traits onto many versions of a masculine God. Almost universally, religion and religious groups project an array of pathological, masculine, human dispositions onto a masculine God; the universal and ubiquitous religious 'Mr' Hyde. Masculine religious men and man-made religious institutions, deflect their fear, emotionality, ignorance, paranoia, narcissism and sociopathy into many masculine religious myths, dogmas and legends. Religious men and man-made religious institutions project their malignance and toxicity into many versions and incarnations of a patriarchal God; the original, universal and foremost left hemisphere projection of Mr Hyde.

The long and the short is that masculinised religions, theocratic states, and fundamentalist nations refuse to be aware of their projective religious ignorance and recalcitrance. They refuse to take ownership for pathological religious contributions that greatly contribute to the suffering and destruction described in Chapter 4. Ownership and accountability by masculine religions and religious institutions are very rare; as they are in the vast majority of man-made cultures and political groups. The vast majority of masculine left hemisphere religions, religious states, ideological cultures and extremist secular systems project responsibility and blame onto other groups, states and ideologies for extreme masculine pathologies; including:

- War
- Religious, sectarian and ideological violence
- Terrorism
- Genocide and ethnic cleansing
- Decimation of aboriginal peoples and their cultures
- Degradation and exploitation of the powerless
- Harms caused by religious, political and domestic dysfunction, corruption and criminality
- Violence and abuse committed by men on women and children
- Widespread abuse of power
- Obscene levels of preventable poverty, starvation and disease
- Escalating decimation of species
- Escalating pollution, extinctions, and destruction of ecosystems and environments; and
- Imminent risk of catastrophic and possibly irreparable damage to the entire planet and it's atmosphere.

Throughout history, masculinised cultural, religious and political, fundamentalist and nationalist egoic projections of God have contributed massively to all these insane and unconscionable harms. Each of countless masculinised religious and ideological perpetrators of historical and contemporary suffering and damage have projected blame away from themselves. None have embraced responsibility for their self-serving and power-driven ambitions, greed, empire building, bullying, exploitation, degradations, violence and environmental destruction. No individual or institutional power-brokers have embraced accountability for their deceit, ulterior motives, corruption, criminality, unconscionable harms and strategic incompetence. As is repeatedly shown, typically, masculinised egoic cultural, religious and political institutions strongly and cunningly resist awareness, honesty, integrity, congruence, responsibility, accountability and repentance.

Many masculine egoic religious and secular entities project their failings and 'sins' onto crazy left hemisphere notions; including onto God's will, onto exclusively right-beliefs in God, and onto exclusively right doctrine, ideology and cultural purity. Religious, political and cultural expressions of Mr Hyde camouflage themselves and their narcissistic and sociopathic pathologies through protective delusions of cultural, religious and political purity and strident, exclusive righteousness. Historically and currently, across cultures, religions and political orientations, arbitrary projection is the most common way to minimise and deflect failures to be decent, respectful, honest, rational, just and kind. Egoic projection is how religions, theocratic states and fundamentalist secular nationalisms obliterate 'spiritual' values; including love, grace, dignity, decency and compassion.

Minimal religious, political or cultural institutions and groups consistently and congruently exemplify core spiritual values. Many claim to have exclusively right religious beliefs and right political ideologies, and exclusively 'right-standing with God', but scant few exemplify love, grace, reverence, decency, rationality, integrity, responsibility, accountability and repentance. A tiny minority exemplify dignity critical thinking. Despite endless pious and fine-sounding assertions and claims, just below the surface, religious groups and institutions use egoic man-made projections to foster and justify ego-driven absolutism, judgementalism, division, enmity, exclusion and an array of horrendous Hyde-like degradations and harms.

Pause for a moment; and breathe.

What are your thoughts and feelings about the terrible irony that religious men and institutions exploit projective ploys to resist love, grace and repentance?

The Endless Horrors of Projective Hyde-Like Men

Throughout history, projective, egoic, Hyde-like — religious men, cultural men, ideological men, political men and institutional men — conceived and ensconced the left hemisphere dominance of the pathologies of patriarchy. These men also conceived and ensconced the spurious, self-aggrandising and self-justifying projections of patriarchy. A hotchpotch of pathologically egoic men assumed, asserted and entrenched the self-righteousness of patriarchal chauvinism and an array of aggressive-defensive projections. Egoic men contrived and proliferated misogyny, including many forms of disadvantage, abuse and injustice; and then projected blame for this onto the fallen women, Eve; and onto all fallen women. Egoic, chauvinistic men diminished the-feminine, were oblivious the Feminine Mother, and behaved contemptuously toward women. Despicable, egoic men perpetrated sexual abuse of children, and projected blame onto sin, the devil, victims and an ungodly society.

Projective, egoic, left hemisphere men conceived and institutionalised cultural and racial prejudice, political and religious fundamentalism, nationalism, sectarianism, xenophobia, bigotry and all forms of institutional exceptionalism, exclusion, denigration, disrespect and unkindness. Pathological, egoic men invented and perpetrated colonisation throughout the globe; then projected blame onto hapless savages as worthless sinners. Pathological men invented and justified ways to harm the earth and her species by projecting them as God's gifts to redeemed mankind. Egoic Hyde-like men committed all these crimes, which, in a host of ways, massively degraded the sanctity of many expressions of life; and projected the onto God and the scriptures.

This conglomeration of presumptive, egoic men conceived and concealed projection as a ubiquitous but almost invisible means of denial, deception, deflection, abrogation and justification for a vast array of historical, contemporary and emerging masculine pathologies, abominations and crimes.

Universally, historically and currently — pathological, egoic, masculine Hyde-like religions, cultures, ideologies and politics are predisposed to be projectively dominant, adversarial, divisive, harmful destructive. All these left hemisphere masculine domains struggle to do better than projection. Each and all have been perpetrators. Many have feigned the projective roles of victim and rescuer. There are very few examples of dignity and reason in fundamentalist and conservative patriarchal religion, culture, ideology and politics.

No masculinised left hemisphere religious institutions or groups have evolved to become role models of the spirituality of love, grace, inclusion, kindness, honesty, integrity, honour, responsibility, accountability. None are inclusively loving, non-judgemental, welcoming and collaborative. No chauvinistic institutions fully embrace and the dignify diversity and difference. The vast majority have denigrated and attacked those who are different; and then, surprise-surprise, have projectively justified their attacks onto the those whom they harm. No man-made institutions appreciate the oneness and inherent wholeness of communal and ecological diversity; and none unreservedly embrace and extol difference. The masculinised ego uses projection to scorn, stifle, punish and obliterate difference; and to rationalise and justify this situation.

All in all, only a 'Zen minority' of states and institutions have shown that they can do better, because very few have actually done better.

Human evolution hinges on us minimising the expressions of projection that are discussed in this chapter.

Questions

What hope is there for a critical mass of us to develop and evolve awareness, sensitivity, decency, integrity, responsibility and accountability — so that we minimise projection and the diabolical consequences of projections?

Eventually, ultimately, what might help a critical mass of us to move beyond masculine projection, and to move toward genuinely esteeming, respecting and nurturing the dignity of the diversity of humankind and Mother Earth?

What might help religious, political, corporate and industrial men embrace self-awareness and self-honesty?

What might help institutional men to learn not to project?

How might women and First Peoples help us men be less projective and more aware, honest, respectful, gracious, rational, uplifting and empowering?

Moderating Projection at a Personal Level

This chapter is about how you and other readers might recognise and reduce our human tendency to project.

Awareness is the Key

Not externalising requires conscious awareness of one's own subtle and subconscious projective left hemisphere smokescreens, rationalisations and justifications; as well as awareness of our disposition to projective judgement and projective blame. It requires conscious awareness of the sneaky, subtle, projective ways that you and I scheme, dodge and deflect ownership and responsibility for our contributions to issues in family, relationships, work settings and citizenship. It requires awareness of the common, automatic ways that we contrive and concoct our stories and narratives to cover up, disguise, defend and excuse our attitudes and behaviours.

The key to you and me recognising our particular projective dispositions and defaults is for you to listen carefully to your stories which commonly contain projections, rationalisations, excuses, blame and self-justifications; and for me to listen carefully to my projective stories. Self-serving, projective stories always contain tell-tale judgements, rationalisations, excuse-making, justifications, and direct or indirect blame.

In fairness to all of us, if recognising and moderating our projective ploys was easy and common, then projection would not be as prevalent as it is. And, if projection was easy to moderate and minimise, then transparency and accountability would be common and easy. But, self-awareness, transparency, responsibility and accountability are very rare, because projection and projective stories and ploys are the easy automatic norm for you and me, and for the vast majority. Self-protectively, we are psychologically and socially primed to project and eternalise.

Decrease Projection — Increase Accountability

Nevertheless, my earnest hope is you and I can be more grounded in factual reality, and be more accountable by being less projective. To do this, we will need to become incrementally more self-aware, more self-honest, more relationally insightful, more sensitive to others, and more sensitive to small and big situations and issues. Reality, sensitivity, awareness, honesty and accountability are closely connected values that can help us to be less projective and less egoic.

My desire is that by prioritising and practising these right hemisphere values, we can be more consistently decent and integrous. And, my hope is that we can be more guided by reason, and can increasingly embrace critical thinking as our norm; not as a rarity or as the exception. The purpose of highlighting this network of values, priorities and processes, is to inspire us to want to be grounded in reality, to motivate us want to be more intelligently and integrously responsible, and to choose to be more effective in all our relational, community and citizenry roles. Awareness, aka consciousness aka mindfulness, is the foundation of these possibilities.

Because fear and insecurity drive projection, you and I also need to be aware of where, when and how fears and insecurities diminish our capacity to be self-aware and self-honest. And, we need to identify where and when we are defensive and self-protectively presumptive, pretentious, opinionated, pontifical and prideful. These four are also inherent in projection. They drive projection. All this will be very difficult, because we are inherently and automatically egoically self-protecting and egoically self-promoting. We are egoically (socially, religiously, politically and culturally) conditioned to be protect the self by being projectively opinionated, belief-obsessed and judgemental.

Semi-consciously, we resist awareness of how our opinions, beliefs and judgements threaten to expose our insecurities, inadequacies, fears, pride, presumptive ignorance, ulterior motives and relational clumsiness. We humans are a quirky jumble of psychological assets and liabilities. This chapter is about deliberately and purposefully using our values, awareness, goodwill and commitment as assets and tools that may help us to moderate our projective tendencies.

This book invites you and me to be aware that we hide the vulnerability of our fears, insecurities and ignorance inside projection. Projection is our secret hiding place. I invite us to be aware of how we compensate for our secret personal, relational and existential apprehensions through all sorts of projective deflections and defences. I invite us to identify how we resist the 'call to reality' about what is happening within us, between us, and around us. I invite us to be aware of how each of us resists the 'call to accountability' for what we believe, say and do. This book invites you and me to deliberately choose insight and honesty with the joint intention of disarming projection, and to nurture integrity and reason. To do this, all of us need to be intentionally aware, to be mindfully alert.

Mindfulness

In the previous almost-three-hundred hundred pages of this book, the word, mindfulness has appeared many times. To reiterate, simply, mindfulness is intentional, purposeful, inclusive, strategic awareness of self, others and situations. In everyday conversations and relationships, being mindful means being quietly and attentively tuned in. It means observing and listening attentively, peacefully, self-reflectively, empathically, openly and expansively. It means being unattached — by holding opinions and beliefs loosely and lightly; so, they can dissolve and drift away. Mindful intentionally can bring quietude, peace, clarity, dignity, integrity and reason into conversations, relationships and situations.

Purposeful mindful, Yin-based dignity, integrity and reason urge us to be consciously respectful, consciously kind, consciously rational, and consciously consistent. That is, to be mindful is to be consciously guided by values and principles, from issue to issue, from conversation to conversation, from person to person, from situation to situation, and from context to context. Imagine if you and I purposefully brought values such as awareness, sensitivity, respect, kindness, rationality and consistency into every relationship, every conversation, every situation, and every issue. Seriously, pause and imagine that.

What can you see happening if you did that?

Mindful interactions are an opportunity to balance our own personal perceptions, needs and wants with those of others. Mindful listening and mindful speaking are entirely different from our egoic defaults to be assume, to pontificate, to defend and to project. That is to say, mindful listening and speaking are different from our egoic default to self-assert, self-defend, self-justify and self-promote. Together, every conversation, every situation and every issue are opportunities to practice mindful communication. Practice can help you and I to become more observant of self, others, facts, circumstances, risks and opportunities. Mindful listening can help be more open to difference, disagreement and critique. Practising being mindful can help to be more reasoned in how we think, speak and act; thereby to be more dignified and rational in thought, word and deed. All of this is a preferable and viable alternative to egoic projection, in all its forms.

Practising Mindfulness by Practising Reflective Listening

Practising active, reflective listening is an excellent way to reinforce mindfulness. The Breath-Mediation process described in earlier chapters, is also an excellent way to train yourself to be calm, attentive, present and clear-minded. Active, conscious listening helps build the mindfulness of dignity and respect. Reflective listening also helps build the mindfulness of reason and rationality.

Imagine purposefully blending right hemisphere values and rationality through reflective listening in conversations, relationships and roles. Imagine these qualities and skills being what you do from person to person, from conversation to conversation and from situation to situation. Imagine values, critical thinking and attentive listening being what you do and who you are. Imagine others recognising these sensitivities and behaviours in you. Imagine others thanking you for being present; and for relating to them with grace, kindness, sensitivity, respect, dignity, integrity, fairmindedness and generosity.

For the egoic left hemisphere mind, projection is natural, normal and easy. Whereas, present, attentive, confirming, open, non-defensive and to listen mindfully, are not so natural. Because attentive listening is rare in the historical and contemporary world of ego, it is understandable that we are unaware of its priority, benefits, discipline and processes. It is understandable that mindful, active-listening is not the norm. But it can only become the norm for you and me, if we intentionally prioritise and nurture it through practice in everyday interactions, conversations and situations.

Mindfulness and Character

Shallow, self-serving, projective egoic defaults and habits are in abundance, while unpretentious depth and strength of right hemisphere character is in relatively short supply. As an analogy, some of us are overweight because it's easier to titillate the taste buds than it is to discipline our eating, and to do regular exercise. For many of us, whatever is easy, wins the day. While that which requires consistent, intentional, disciplined awareness, restraint, practice and strategic application, tends to fall by the wayside. Hence, two key psychological wisdoms are — practise delaying gratification, and faithfully apply and practice values, principles, priorities and processes that nurture dignity and reason. Practise delaying gratification by talking less, withholding opinions, and not spruiking beliefs. Practise asking genuine, curious, respectful, inquiring questions. Practise being genuinely interested in others. Practise reflectively listening to a wide range of people; including those with whom we naturally connect, and those we find difficult. Practise being present to lots of people across a range of situations.

Delayed gratification and faithfulness to values and principles are foundational aspects of mindfulness; and are foundational to character-building. Both of these are key elements of mindful participation of in relationships, roles and endeavours. There is an obesity epidemic in the West because ease and titillation are core aspects of the modern human psyche. In contrast, there are also many people who are faithful to the principles of healthy eating, and who de-prioritise immediate gratification. These two are priorities for optimising long-term health and well-being. They show us that delayed gratification and faithfulness to values and principles are desirable and possible.

To all this, the egoic left hemisphere mind says: "Poohoo! Self-first! Pleasure first! Titillation first! Do what is easy". Mindfulness can help us moderate these egoic tendencies by helping establish a more strategic orientation. Mindful faithfulness to practise intentional listening, intentional dignity, intentional integrity, intentional reason, intentional sensitivity, and intentional accountability can help us reduce the immediacy and constancy of our easy-lazy defaults to yabber and judge. Mindful application of values and critical thinking, can help reduce egoic defaults such as presumption, pretention and pontification. Anything that reduces this trio, will nurture strength of character and rationality in relationships and community engagement.

Concluding Questions

Will you intentionally and mindfully do better by moving away from the egoic tendency to pontificate, judge and project?

Will you do better by being purposefully faithful to values and principles, and purposefully practise delaying gratification through reflective listening?

Will you do better by nurturing the character-based disciplines of strategic listening, sensitivity and integrity?

Will you embrace and practise honest, courageous transparency and accountability; which are the pillars of character?

What simple, every day, practical things might you do to practise being mindful?

In what simple, everyday ways might you role model this network of values and principles in family, friendships, at work and in community?

The Centrality of Ego in
Self-Help Material

If you are an enthusiastic reader of self-help books, and if you devour alternative podcasts and internet fads and idealisms, you might find this chapter a bit challenging.

Most commonly, self-help books offer tools for the advancement of the self. Typically, they tell us readers what ideas and beliefs we need to absorb so that 'your individual self' and 'my individual self' can become more attractive, more desirable, more influential, and more successful in terms of self-belief, power, position, popularity, money and materiality. Therefore, not surprisingly, 'the egoic self' is 'front-and-centre' in most self-help books. Ego and self are quintessential and sacrosanct in the bulk of self-help teachings.

Typically, self-help material purports to provide ideals, theories, concepts and techniques to help you and I aspire and acquire whatever each of us are persuaded to 'need and want' to feel secure, acceptable, happy and successful as a left hemisphere — material self, a partner self, a sexual self, a business self, a professional self, a spiritual self, and a financial self. Not much self-help material is expansive, integrative, inclusive or educative. Little is based in solid research and legitimate science. Most self-help stuff is arbitrary, hip and pop. It directs the reader's imagination and focus inward on 'me and mine'; to what 'I' want; to what I 'must have'; and who I 'must be'; so that 'I' can 'be happy' in the 21st world of enmeshed egoic selves and rival egoic selves.

Self-Help Stuff and Ego

Because of the predominant self-focus in self-help material, it seems logical that self-help teachings gel perfectly with culturally contrived and socially conditioned egoic mental needs, priorities and processes. Self-help stuff melds perfectly with 'the insecure needy greedy self-absorbed egoic me'. Self-help hype is what 'the thoroughly modern me' wants to hear in order to feel liked, confirmed, important, entitled and deserving. All this is because the 'modern, new-age egoic-self' is desperate to feel 'cool and hip'; that is, to feel happy by being attractive, approved, included, entitled and lauded by like-minded self-oriented egoic peers for self-indulgent and self-aggrandising achievements.

The modern egoic-self is the inspiration, the creator, the target, and the consumer of self-indulgent self-help material. Much self-help stuff is written and spoken by self-absorbed egoic people, for insecure egoic consumers. And, the multi-billion-dollar self-help industry is delighted to indulge our every self-serving egoic whim, our arbitrary self-absorption, and our egoic insecurity, naivety, neediness and individualistic hip-pop desires. The multi-billion-dollar self-help industry is eager to profit enormously from the sale of uncountable volumes of 'ego-reassuring, ego-massaging, self-adulating, self-indulgent self-help material'.

Most self-help material is arbitrary, imaginary, whim-based, fantasy-based, made up and projective. Most is under-researched, under-informed, opinionated, belief-oriented, presumptive, pretentious and glibly pontifical. Most is obsessed with neediness, wanting, getting and accumulating. Little self-help material advocates values and priorities such as an internal locus of stillness, silence, humility, integrity, simplicity, relationship, community, ecology, systems understandings, contentment, gratitude and joy. Very little self-help material says anything about a rational, internal locus of dignity, critical thinking, kindness and compassion, integrity, responsibility, transparency and accountability.

Fuelled by its unashamed obsession with self and me, self-help material is perfectly suited to justify and bolster our array of contemporary narcissistic predilections and fantastical fads. It seems that the vast bulk of self-help ideas, beliefs and theories are conceived of arbitrary egoic logic; communicated as arbitrary egoic logic; conditioned as arbitrary egoic logic; absorbed as self-serving, arbitrary, egoic logic; applied as me-oriented, arbitrary egoic logic; and is justified through contrived, arbitrary egoic logic. That's an extraordinarily enmeshed mix of arbitrary proclivities. Each whimsical, self-help component enables and reinforces many other whimsical components. Together, they reinforce 'the all-encompassing arbitrariness of the needy, fearful, insecure, all-important but ignorant egoic-mind'.

Even apparently objective evidence-based psychology, despite its intention to be rational, disciplined and factual, has passed through the egoic-mind of the egoically frail researchers and authors. But, at least the teachings of formal psychology and other authentic scientific disciplines have passed through the alchemic fires of dry, rigorous empirical processes, critical thinking and stringent peer review. The purpose of these processes is to minimise subjective, arbitrary, egoic dross. In contrast, most self-help pop-psychology and pop-science is not purged of assumptions, preconceptions, whims, fantasies and projections. A scant proportion of new-age stuff has been rigorously scrutinised by credible, peer-reviewed critical analysis, and by other rational, disciplined, scrutinising processes. As a result, in contrast to formal psychology and other robust social science literature, much self-help pop-psychology is shallow, assumed, glib, whimsical, wishful, faddish and self-indulgent.

You may be able to buy 'gluten-free, dairy-free, additive-free and preservative-free food', but you can't buy ego-free self-help books. Loads of 'empty egoic calories' make up the bulk of self-help material that we Westerners voraciously consume; with minimal critique of its substantive psychological nutrition, value, evidence or logic.

Our Transition from Religion — to Ideology — to Modern-Day New-Age Stuff

Until about the early 1900s, man-made left hemisphere religion was our primary source of self-help teaching. Until about one-hundred years ago, most people relied on egoically frail, fraught and institutionalised male rabbis, priests, imams, gurus and other religious leaders to help them adapt to the rigors of their personal, social, religious, political and economic environments. These traditional masculinised, patriarchal self-help teachers were the primary and largely unquestioned but baseless sources of projective and fanciful man-made beliefs about God, life, nature, the universe and humankind.

After World War I, a significant proportion of humanity replaced the religious dogmas and spiritual philosophies with patiently egoic, man-made left hemisphere political ideologies, such as Capitalism, Communism and Nazism. After WWII, much of the Western world became ensconced the 'self-advancing' priorities, values and aspirations of man-made Neo-liberalism and Liberal Democracy. Masculinised individualistic, corporate and nationalist pursuits, capital, profit, wealth, materiality, economic power, and empire building became supreme egoic man-made values and priorities for billions.

Then, from the 1960s, new-age self-help, hippie counter culture, pop-psychology became the hotchpotch of philosophes to which many Westerners turned for help in their rapidly changing man-made physical, social, political, economic and religious environments. An emerging disparate man-made, left hemisphere eclectic pop-psychology 'alternative' culture reacted to the strictures and hypocrisies of conservative religion and greedy, materialistic neo-liberal politics. The pop-counter-culture of the 1960s reacted against masculinised liberalist, political, corporate and nationalist obsession with empire, power, profit, avarice and materiality. Most 60s and 70s 'Age of Aquarius', free love, dope-smoking philosophising was shallow, pretentious and low on evidence, rationality, strategic pragmatism and values-based strategic purpose.

Irony Abounds

Ironically, the anti-religion, anti-establishment counter-culture of the 60s and 70s was soon absorbed into the emerging man-made new-age, neo-liberal, profit-obsessive, materialistic culture of the 1980s and 1990s. The revolutionary 1960s-1970s hippie pop-culture became the hip man-made new-age materialism of faddish, late-twentieth-century 'narcissistic pop-neoliberalism'; which peddled the self-indulgent, masculinised, left hemisphere notion that 'we could be and do anything we imagined' and 'wanted'. And then, late-twentieth-century materiality morphed into the latest man-made incarnation of self-help — the hip internet, social media, on-line, hipster consumer culture of the 21st century. Ultimately, the 60s and 70s counter culture and insatiable wanting and consuming of the 80s and 90s have been enmeshed and enshrined in these recent and contemporary man-made internet and social media cultures.

There is so much hilarious irony in these intergenerational mutations and wishful transfigurations of egoic, man-made left hemisphere ideas and priorities. There isn't much psychological evolution or constructive societal adaptation. The 21st century legacy of counter culture is bucket-loads of assorted mana-made hippy, fundamentalist, hipster, new-age, social media fantasy, glibness, triteness, illogicality, incongruity and contradiction. 60s and 70s dope smoking, counter culture and hippy inanities mutated to be almost structurally indistinguishable from 80s and 90s fundamentalist religious inanities; which mutated to become indistinguishable from current day, new-age, social media, internet inanities. My personal observation is that mostly-man-made new-age bullshit beliefs and ideas have muddled along, mutated and morphed throughout the past sixty years; simply to be rebadged and refashioned by ensuing generations; and to be claimed by each new generation as original spiritual enlightenment, newly found absolute truth, and as authentic cultural genius.

In the 21st century, to help us pursue our contemporary left hemisphere narcissistic, post counter-culture new-age desires, humankind relies heavily on mostly-man-made self-help social media which provides a vest array of titillating pseudo-science, fanciful beliefs, misleading pop-knowledge and grandiose, indulgent falsehoods about science, God, life, nature, the universe, conspiracies, aliens, past lives and clairvoyance.

The common hope of counter-culture and new-age social media faddism is that chic ideas and beliefs will enable us self-absorbed, pop-psychology, conspiratorial devotees to indulge all our egoic, self-serving fantasying, individualistic, consumptive, materialistic, psychological and so-called, spiritual desires. All this is about us indulging our endless egoic desires and inflating our 'vain, faddish, me-obsessive image' with whatever egoic whims and ideas enter our trendy, new-age 'mindless minds'. Collectively — actual reality, in the form of dry data, fact-checked knowledge and information, disciplined critical thinking and rigorous evidentiary accountability — are the greatest aversion of mindless, egoic new-age faddism. There is great resistance among today's faddists to the disciplines of fact-checking, legitimate scientific methodology and critical thinking.

The psychological machinations of fanciful, arbitrary, anti-science faddism and conspiracy ideation have been well researched in mainstream social sciences. Mainstream psychology provides many insights into what predisposes, drives and proliferates new-age social media predilections and issues. But for the most part, pop-psychology, junk-science and conspiracy devotees have no awareness of what predisposes and drives their mostly-man-made egoic whims, delusions, dysfunctionality and harmfulness.

The Good, the Stupid and the Harmful

My awareness is that the man-made ideas of religion, political ideology and new-age junk-science pop-psychology may be divided into three broad categories. Some ideas may help us adapt constructively to the demands of modern human existence. Some are stupid and dumb; but are a relatively, benignly unhelpful distraction from reality. However, too many faddish ideas are highly destructive because they predispose dangerous anti-science fantasies and practices; and because they promote dodgy and dangerous conspiracy-theory falsehoods, paranoia and harms. Many new-age teachings are thinly disguised egoic insecurity, personal and relational inefficacy, self-indulgence, escapism, narcissism, greed and opportunism. There is a mountain and fantastical ignorance and wilful ignorance in religious and new-age beliefs and opinions. In the money-making corporate domain, there is also much intentionally deceptive agnotological marketing and salesmanship; and many overtly dishonest faddish scams. New-age domains are fraught with mostly-man-made whims, fantasies, false claims, deception, lies, fraud, fraudsters and harms.

What all self-help material has in common is a predominance of egoic, self-focussed and me-centred insecurities, neediness, wanting, desires, projections, stories and phantastical strategies. Ironically, in the 21st century, the egoic mind creates phantom issues of the self; then latches onto a plethora of readily-available contrived, fantasised self-help knowledge and beliefs to fix these phantastical phantom issues. In every way, modern self-help material is the epitome of egoically misguided, ill-informed, co-dependent, enmeshed, collective masculinised human mind. Even apparently spiritual self-help teachings are highly likely to be the product of glib arbitrariness. Religion, political ideology and new-age self-help stuff epitomise the futility and glibness of egoic phantoms trying to fix egoic phantoms. Typically, patently, religion, ideology and new-age fluff are 'the blind leading the blind'.

In Summary — Four Sources of Egoic Fantasies and Lies

With the recent advent of 'new-age pop-culture', there are now four major overlapping sources of man-made egoic fantasies and lies.

1. The left hemisphere religions of men — uses millennia-old man-contrived fantasies about a masculine God to justify the lies, corruption and controls of patriarchy, chauvinism, misogyny, paternalism, masculine projections, masculine violence and exploitation.
2. The left hemisphere politics of men — uses antiquated man-contrived fantasies of patriarchal ideology, chauvinistic propaganda and man-made projections and spin to justify propaganda, lies, cons, corruption, incompetence, human suffering and environmental damage.

3. The left hemisphere industries and corporations of men — use highly masculine fantasies to justify empire building, power-mongering, lies, spurious research, corruption, exploitation of peoples, and environmental damage.

4. The left hemisphere new-age internet and social media faddism of men — is the new man-made sham on the block. It proliferates fantasies, fictions and fads on the basis of arbitrariness, misinformation, spurious junk-science, glib pop-psychology, conspiracy-theory paranoia and 'big lies'. Mostly-man-made new-age faddism is the central pillar of the modern man-made self-help industry. It exploits, distorts and drives the thinking of billions of hapless, ignorant consumers.

How do you feel about this appraisal of the self-help industry and the self-help material?

What are alternatives to the usual arbitrary fantasies and faddism of the self-help pop-culture?

Principles for Reading Self-Help Material

Here is a guide that may help you and me to increase reason, critical thinking and factual reality.

Consume material that is dry, factual and cautious in its analysis, ideas, conclusions and recommendations.

Be wary of material that is speculative, fanciful, individualistic, hedonistic, perfectionistic, emotive, tribal, projective, conspiratorial, divisive, disparaging and demonising.

Be wary of religious, political and new-age beliefs that extol one exclusively right position while forcefully and judgementally rejecting others. Extoling one group while demonising others is a tell-tale sign of poor analysis and dodgy research; and a sign of classically masculine fundamentalist exclusivity, superiority and judgementalism.

Be wary of angry, judgemental, macho material that incites fear, drama, paranoia and conspiratorial extremisms. Often, such material is not grounded in accurate, fact-checked, reliable evidence. Often, conspiratorial authors have 'anger issues'. Most are men. Often, they have an axe to grind, and/or have a need for notoriety and popularity. Instead, consider material that, at least in part, is based in dry, unemotional, impartial data and logic; which is the hallmark of scientific discipline, rationality and critical thinking.

Although it is often extremely dry and intellectually demanding, try to read primary research, not just what people say about alleged research that 'they have heard about'. Seek out widely credible reviews and critiques of research, authors and speakers. Fact-check claims. Look very closely at the research methodology and data. Don't take the author's word for their claims about method and data. Assess the viability of ideas and analyses on the basis of well-established research principles and processes.

Familiarise yourself with the rules, principles and priorities of rigorous research methodology, and with the principles and processes of critical thinking.

Remember, opinions and beliefs are not equivalent to data and facts. Opinions and beliefs are not alternative facts. There are no such things as 'alternative' facts. This idea is man-contrived bullshit. Only rigorously-obtained research data, is data. Only rigorously scrutinised and verified facts, are facts. All else is made up wishful thinking, fantasy, bullshit, deception, and lies. All else is arbitrary, not factual, not rational, not evidence-based, and not honest.

Read widely. Ask lots of intelligent, considered, critiquing questions. Be cautious. Be dry.

Reserve judgement, and let the accumulation of accurate reliable facts and data speak for themselves.

Be patient. Take the very long road. There are no short-cuts or easy roads to data-based evidence, facts and reality. Objectivity is dry, and hard-won. It doesn't play favourites. Rationality is very long game. Critical thinking is a life-long process, a never-ending discipline.

Accept that the evolution of knowledge is inherently slow, dry, unemotional and incremental. Typically, the development of knowledge is three steps forward, and one step back. Ongoing, unfolding, sound research often slowly but surely rewrites reality; often, but not always, including scientific reality.

Allow yourself to be silent and still. Breathe to help you to be peaceful, unassumptive, unpretentious, not pontifical and unattached. In this space, listen to the integrous and dignified voice of your conscience. Separate conscience from preconception, wishing, wanting, drama, hubris and bias. Separate conscience from wishful thinking, baseless opinions and fanciful beliefs. Separate conscience from whimsical, egoic arbitrariness.

Be intuitive, but not fanciful. If your hunch is to be cautious, then do so. If your hunch is to be open, then do so; but never at the expense of 'the cautious, integrous long-game' of data, facts, reason, logic and critique.

Inductive Anecdotal Stories

You and I need to avoid vastly over-estimating our opinionated, anecdotal knowledge. Beware the modern hip 'sample of one' testimonials and inductive reasoning 'pseudo-logic syndrome'. The idea of 'inductive wisdom' is an inherent contradiction. Inductive wisdom is an oxymoron. Inductive reasoning is not wise or enlightened. Inductive reasoning is highly problematic. Inductive anecdotal stories are fraught with egoic story-telling, confabulating, preconceived, biased, fictional pitfalls and traps. Stories and anecdotes are not data or evidence. Egoic stories may be sincere, earnest, interesting, captivating, intriguing and titillating, but they are not evidence or critical analysis. Most stories are at least partly arbitrary, made-up, subjective, egoic confabulations and biased distortions. Many are factless distortion of reality. Too many are wantonly dishonest.

Much self-help material is built on Dunning-Kruger Effect, egoic motivations, cognitive biases and inductive fallacies. Remove confabulated biases, inductive logic and Dunning-Kruger Effect from new-age material and it would almost cease to exist. Remove cognitive biases and Dunning-Kruger Effect out of 'new-age spruiking' — and it will fall silent.

There is one short step from the inflated fantasies of inductive, story-telling ignorance to wilful left hemisphere ignorance. Then, there is another short step from prideful, wilful ignorance to dishonestly defending distortions, deceptions and lies that need to be concocted in order to rationalise, defend and preserve new-age and conspiratorial fantasies and fads. These are the semi-invisible steps we take when lured into the conspiracies, scams, cons and junk-science. If you become enmeshed in junk-science, fantasies, fads and conspiracy theories, you risk finding yourself pridefully and ignorantly defending wilful ignorance, dodgy logic, deception, lies and scams. These precarious steps are very common in the egoic domain of new-age, social media, self-help, junk-science, pop-psychology and conspiracy addiction.

Is this difficult to read, face and absorb?

Are you feeling defensive of your pet new-age, self-help theories, authors, beliefs and opinions?

Are you resisting the reality that self-help material is a minefield of presumption and pretention and pontifical confabulation?

Are you aware that the new-age scene is littered with inane, whimsical, wishful fantasies, conspiracies, fads, deceptions, lies, cons and scams?

The Egoic Drivers of New-Age Pontiffs and Conspiracy Spruikers

When listening to passionate, charismatic and strong-minded new-age spruikers and conspiracy vocalists, I have learned to ask myself, 'What is driving this person? What's his or her agenda or angle? What psychological, left hemisphere undercurrents, egoic benefits and/or financial motives are under the surface? Is what is being said the sound of an insecure, dysfunctional, isolated, desperate, self-protective, self-promoting, paranoid, projective ego. Or is it the sound of self-esteem, dignity, critical thinking, legitimate data and dry objectivity?' I ask these questions, because plenty of fine sounding 'loose-cannon', new-age spruikers and quixotic conspiracists are driven by thinly-disguised, pathological egoic stuff; such as compensation for deeply-felt but thinly-disguised personal inadequacy, professional disappointment, rejection, fear of failure, and/or desperation for recognition.

Many new-age and conspiracy spruikers are caught-up in self-righteousness that arises from unfulfilled professional ambitions, resentments and desperation for professional validation and standing. Very commonly, claims of special knowledge and authority are smoke-screens for thinly-disguised egoic issues, such not being recognised, being passed over for inclusion in professional peer groups, missing promotion, and decompensation for a range of personal and professional insecurities, inadequacies and failures.

Many spruikers attack their fellow professionals, scientists and doctors to coverup personal issues and/or professional infringements and bad-science failures. Spruikers, even highly qualified ones, often have thinly-disguised egoic desires to be venerated as superior, special, enlightened ones within their scientific or professional communities. Many have failed to win acceptance, recognition and honour within personal and professional relationships and communities. Many are highly projective. Most are men.

Many egoic spruikers see themselves as self-appointed, self-aggrandising left hemisphere crusaders, rescuers and moralists. Some disenchanted and disenfranchised professionals become addictive, paranoid conspiracy theorists. Others are thinly disguised religious or political fundamentalists, who confound science with various expressions and machinations of fundamentalism. Some are narcissists. Some are sociopathic. These common tendencies among new-age spruikers and conspiracists should make us very cautious. Even highly qualified people are not immune from these egoic issues and tendencies. Insecurity and narcissism are alive and well in a full range of academic, scientific and professional settings.

A new category of new-age and conspiracy spruikers emerged during the 2020-2021 COVID pandemic and the US presidential election. These quixotic, loose-cannon, left hemisphere renegades were the inventors of fraudulent extremist conspiracies, fake information and deluded, paranoid stories and claims. QAnon is the most well-known example of fake, deluded, paranoid extreme conspiracies. It seems there about thirteen individuals, mostly men, are the foundational and central drivers of the most dangerous conspiracies during the Covid crisis. For them, inventing and maintain conspiracies is extremely profitable and brings great fame. Narcissistic and sociopathic heaven.

In a chapter that is coming up, I write about Bill, a former colleague. Bill was a classic brilliant, ambitious but egoically insecure professional and new-age spruiker. He was a self-inspired and self-declared expert. Be very cautious when reading and listening to the fantastical ideas of such ego-inspired, self-declared new-age and professional experts. Be alert to the Bills of this world.

When listening to people 'banging-on', I ask myself, "What's driving this person? What's his or her story? What is their psychological background, motives and ulterior agendas"? So, ask yourself, at the psychological level: "What's in it for this or that spruiker? What's driving them" What egoic stuff is just under the surface of their veneer of persuasive, righteous, projective, vitriolic, charismatic verve? Under the surface, what egoic compensations and gains is she or he angling for? Ask yourself, is spruiking an issue of scientific sour grapes? Are there expressions of populism and/or political narcissism at play here? Often, narcissistic drivers are very close to the surface. Challenge grandiose experts with data, facts and critical analysis; then stand-back and watch narcissistic projection, anger, indignation, vitriol and indignant justification spew forth.

The Loss of Simplicity and the Rise of Ego

This is a big chapter. So, breath — now, during, and after

The following sections summarise the factors and that catalysed the emergence of the dominance of the left hemisphere.

This chapter attempts to unravel the tangled historical and contemporary web that is our masculinised left hemisphere human ego. There are many twists and turns among the threads of the distant past, the recent past and present time egoic machinations. This chapter reflects these past and present twists and turns and machinations. In keeping with the mishmash of the masculine ego, this chapter moves back and forth and side to side.

Let's begin by re-tracking the historical steps that, ultimately, gave rise to 21st century masculinised egoic stuff that governs much of modern life across the globe. I hope you burning with curiosity and asking: 'What web of historical circumstances eventually resulted in the modern-day egoic patterns described in previous chapters?' What happened in history that we humans became so egoically entangled? What impacted on our distant forebears that we humans devolved from being relatively unegoic First Peoples to become highly egoic 21st century peoples?

In case you find yourself resisting and reacting to what you are about read, remember that only about 2% of 'us' wantonly, cruelly and ruthlessly do harm; only about 2% of 'us' bravely, systematically and strategically try to remediate harm — but, about 96% of 'us' nonchalantly, passively, indifferently and cynically watch the harms being done to people, our fellow species and the earth.

Typically, we, the unempathic, unconcerned members of the 96%, remain uninformed, ill-informed and ignorant. Also, typically, we ninety-six percenters are self-servingly uninterested, unbothered, unsympathetic, complacent and judgemental. The vast majority of us — say nothing in protest; do nothing to help; blame the victims of harm; dismiss or ignore the systemic issues; and uncaringly rationalise and justify widespread disadvantage, disempowerment, injustice and suffering. Also remember, ego drives and justifies the 2% of mostly male harm-doers; and, ego stimies and justifies the 96% of indifferent and cynical onlookers.

Pre-Agriculture

Until about 10,000 years ago, there was no money and very few possessions. Materialism and consumerism were practically non-existent. Before 3,000-4000 years ago, there was no institutional religion, no nationalist and global political ideologies, no corporations or corporate culture, no industry and industrialisation, no materialism and consumerism, no technology as we know it today, and no new-age social media obsessions. Survival, subsistence, the common good of family and tribe, a few basic tools, simplicity, ordinariness and the needs of small local groups were natural common priorities for most pre-agricultural humans. The indignity of unrelenting material discontentment, drivenness, wanting, consuming and self-obsessive, individualist ambition and perfectionism were relatively unnatural for our species prior to the advancement of agriculture and institutional religion.

Pressures Arising from the Shift to Agriculture

Beginning about 10,000 years ago, across what we now know as Europe and Britain, agricultural society steadily became more vastly complex and unwieldy than human existence throughout previous tens of thousands of years of hunter-gather-forager existence. From about 10,000 years ago, within a very short several-thousand-year timeframe, the complexities and difficulties of agriculture, and accompanying unprecedented, exponential population increase, catapulted humans away from the simplicities and relative innocence of hunter-gather-forager First People subsistence, and thrust them far away from the relative effectiveness of conscious ecological homeostasis. From about 10,000 years ago, human survival became much more complex, arduous, competitive and conflictual; and came to include a new array of unprecedented mental and psychological demands and dangers.

Over a relatively brief several thousand years period, during the early stages of the agricultural era, post-forager-gatherer humans found themselves hurtling down a previously untravelled road toward — massive food shortages; rampant disease; unending conflict; totalitarian religious and political institutionalisation; exploitation by powerful religious elite and by brutal land owners; and by the burgeoning criminality of sociopathic power-brokers. For the vast majority of the powerless and oppressed, health declined due to stress and a loss of variety in diet; which became increasingly dependent on and limited to a few types of grain crops; which were often unreliable and vulnerable to drought, floods, disease and plunder of crops and stored food supplies. Progressively, post hunter-gatherer-forager agricultural peoples lost their relatively simple familial, communal, ecological spirituality.

Then — on Top of This — A Massive Shift to Institutions Religion

From about 4000 years ago, the loss of indigenous familial, communal and ecological security and spirituality was greatly catalysed when agricultural humans became subjugated and demeaned by the emergence of institutionalising religious, political, economic and bureaucratic tyrannies. Institutional religion was the next huge step in the emergence of the masculine ego. En masse, across Europe, Britain and the Middle East, humans were forced and indoctrinated to adopt various expressions Abrahamic religion. In vast swages of the globe, post-indigenous and post agricultural peoples were inculcated, co-opted and institutionalised by tyrannical religious men and absolutistic, man-made religious myths, customs, rituals and norms. Globally, and seemingly irreversibly, this was a massive leap forward into the machinations of the masculine ego.

From institutional region came the entangling threads of religion-inspired and religion-controlled political and economic systems, practices and beliefs. Again — another massive step into the entanglement of the web of the masculine ego. From about 2000 BC, the stage was set for the unrelenting dominance and entrapment of the masculine ego due to the intrenchment of man-made, religion-inspired politics, ideologies, structures and institutions. The masculine ego was interwoven as the religious and political mind of Westernised humankind.

Next, the Tyranny of Colonisation

And then, there was another diabolical chapter of entanglement and strangulation of the masculine ego. From about 400 years ago, tyranny spread rapidly from Europe and Britain through the violent colonisation of Africa, the Americas, Australia and island communities all over the globe. Throughout the past 400 years, the issues explained in the previous section, became globally universal through an entangled web world-wide colonial totalitarianism.

Systematic, violent, ruthless dispossession, obliteration of tribes and families, brutal exploitation and genocide became the norms for colonised peoples. Difficulties were massively catalysed and exacerbated by an ever-increasing enmeshment of assumed, absolutistic religious and secular superiority and entitlement. From the 1700s, as decades and centuries ticked by, slavery, military brutality, decimation of culture, mass murder, polluting industries, destructive agriculture, exploitative commercialisation and rampant materialism and consumerism were woven into cultural, political and religious norms. Agriculture, industry, commercialisation, materialism and consumerism continue to be rampant enmeshments of the masculinised ego in the 21C.

During a brief four-hundred-year period of colonisation, the contrasts between pre- and post-agricultural existence grew exponentially through domination, devastation and destruction. For many tens of thousands of years prior to agriculture and colonisation, similar to other animals, for the most part, humans existed with relative dignity and efficacy; from day to day; from food source to food source; from cycle to cycle; and from season to season. Most pre-agricultural peoples were highly intelligently effective at strategically sustainable hunting, foraging and gathering. Colonisation decimated the dignity and strategic sustainability of this way of life; then and now. And — it pulled First Peoples into a web of dehumanising Western machinations

The Ways of the Masculine Religious Ego — Then and Now

It is understandable that stress, insecurity, fearfulness, self-protectiveness and control-obsessiveness became the norm of the agricultural and post-agricultural, religious human mind. From about 8,000 BC, these man-made psychological proclivities increased to unprecedented levels. Enter the diabolical logic of the new man-contrived egoic sham on the block, that, "this land, this crop and this hut are mine! Don't touch or take my stuff. I'll kill you if you take my stuff or threaten my property', livelihood and existence; and that of my family and group".

Over thousands of years, beginning during the agricultural era, to control increasing populations — relatively simple primordial, tribal superstitions were institutionalised into an entangled web of complex, egoic, man-made religious dogmas of various formal religions. Man-made institutionalised religion increasingly dominated, entangled and exploited large numbers of diverse

300

groups through Abrahamic myths that inculcated insecurity, fear, guilt and shame. A messy, voluminous web of strident, egoic, coercive, compliance-focussed man-made religious superstitions and dogmas were woven and imposed to regulate and control every aspect of life for many millions of people. The egoic threads of fear, guilt and shame are the epitome of institutionalised Abrahamic religions; then, and now.

Over thousands of years, the following man-made religious ethos and mandate were systematically enmeshed, inculcated and ruthlessly enforced — 'You must believe our beliefs and comply with our commands. My religious group is good; but, 'they', other religious groups, those who are 'different' from 'us', are bad and dangerous'. This fear-based, control-focussed ethos generated oppressive and competing institutionalised masculine cultures. Locally and globally, religions vied, jostled and warred for the control and entanglement of the human mind. Inherent in this, were systemic man-contrived egoic attitudes of superiority, exclusivity, judgement, mistrust, enmity and conflict. These attitudes became the hallmarks of masculinised cultural, political and religious threads of ego. Many Mr Hyde religious institutions and states were formed out of this toxic and pathological egoic web. These primitive, enmeshed man-made egoic religions continue to be prominent in the 21st century. Over five billion people — five-eighths of the world's population — is hugely entangled in primitive, toxic, man-made egoic religious superstitions.

Emerging post-agricultural religions perceived and treated all non-believers as potential threats to absolute masculine institutional control. Outsiders were seen as evil wrong-believers and threats to doctrinal purity, political control and institutional survival. For the masculine power elite, institutional survival was a matter of life and death. As a result, individuals, groups and institutions became obsessively and stridently egoically dogmatic, totalitarian and greatly threat-aversive. These dispositions devolved into the masculinised egoic religious mind which has substantially dominated humankind for about the past 3,000 years.

Even today, the masculine religious ego asserts that my dogma is right and yours is wrong and evil. Masculine cultural ego asserts that my culture is superior to yours. Masculine racial ego asserts that my skin colour is good and yours is bad. Bigoted masculine ego says that because you are different in appearance, you are inferior and bad my race is more deserving than yours. Religious ego asserts that my-our beliefs are Godlier than yours. Masculine political and ideological ego contends that my-our ideology and political party are right, and yours are wrong. The moralistic, masculine religious and political ego declares that my-our morals and priorities are better and more spiritual than yours. I am better than you. The masculine tribal, nationalistic ego asserts that you, your tribe and your country are the cause of all my woes and bad luck. 'You' are bad.

Therefore

Therefore — if you are different from me and my exceptionalistic group — the masculine egoic cultural, religious and political logic says — I am entitled, right and compelled to mistrust you, to denigrate you, to hate you, to drive you away, and to kill you. It is right and logical that I project all my problems onto you. 'You' are my problem and my enemy. You must be controlled. You must be subjugated. You must be killed. You must be exterminated.

This web of extreme, pathological, man-made egoic assumptions became the toxic masculine norm for post-hunter-gather-forager peoples; and for post-agricultural cultural and religious peoples. There have been many masculine agricultural, cultural, religious and political incarnations from 10,000 years ago. Continuously, cumulatively, over many millennia, this enmeshed man-made egoic cultural and religious mindset has morphed and morphed and morphed; and have been inculcated and ensconced as the mental logic and rationale of a conglomeration of religious, cultural and ideological expressions of 'Mr' Hyde.

These are examples of typical of entwined masculine egoic logic that increasingly came to dominate the fast-festering post-agricultural human-mind. Globally, crazy and extreme man-made cultural and religious egoic ideas, beliefs and logic came to characterise the human mind. Over thousands of years, self-serving, possessive, competitive, mistrusting, paranoid, judgemental, derisive, divisive, aversive and conflictual, egoic 'masculine' logic and attitudes became increasingly woven-into and normalised in paranoid, adversarial and combative cultures, religions and societies. This tangle of attitudes and traits morphed into and drove the dominance of masculinised egoic thinking and functioning — in ancient history and modern times. In many cultures, these pathological masculine attitudes and traits are prominent and dominant in the 21st century.

Death to Dignity and Rationality

This section describes another web of noxious egoic masculine attitudes and actions.

The emerging web of toxic masculinity described in the previous section, signalled a noticeable shift from a relatively relational, communal and ecological and holistic hunter-forager-gatherer psyche — toward a greatly fragmented, disconnected, competitive, combative individualistic, exceptionalistic, religious, political mindset. Yin-based First People ecological holism and Yang-based Anglo-European-Celtic egoic fragmentation became diametric opposites. Masculine, Entangle, noxious Yang-driven egoic mental processes are diametrically opposite to beautifully and delicate enfolded Yin-based ecological oneness, communal common good, relational mutuality, harmony, symbiosis and homeostasis. Masculinised egoic processes are not naturally trusting, welcoming, inclusive, harmonising, symbiotic, homeostatic, systems oriented or ecological. The highly masculinised egoic mind is naturally mistrusting, individualistic, tribal, parochial, exclusive, fragmented, divisive, possessive, controlling, parasitic, aversive, adversarial, conflictual and combative. This is an entanglement of damaging proclivities.

With the rise of the prominence and dominance of power-driven, possessive and controlling masculine, egoic, left hemisphere logic and traits, came the previously unimaginable hitherto crazy idea that individual humans could possess land — that they could, and should, exploit land arbitrarily for exclusive self-serving individual, tribal and nationalist benefits. The arbitrary masculine notion of 'possessing and exploiting land' heralded a massive mindset shift away from the First People spirituality of 'the ecology of oneness with mother land'; the oneness with Mother Earth; and the precept that humans belonged to the earth, not the other way around.

It was a seismic, masculinised aberration that humans could and should possess, dominate and exploit nature and land. This was also a profound shift from relational, communal, symbiotic, ecological, homeostatic oneness. Possessing, dominating and exploiting land was a diabolical and destructive shift toward egoic — fragmentation, control, leveraging, power-over, domination and abuse of the earth. Under the domination of the utterly ignorant male left hemisphere ego — 'She' — right hemisphere Mother Earth — morphed into 'it'; 'a material chattel belonging to me and us'. Mother Earth was egoically — masculinised — despiritualised, desacralized, utterly diminished, disparaged, enslaved, exploited, savaged, devoured and profoundly damaged.

Along with the unimaginable crazy masculine idea of possessing, dominating and exploiting land and 'Mother Nature', came an even more pathological egoic notion that men could and should possess, dominate and exploit other humans. There was a proliferation of pathological, egoic left hemisphere ideas that rich and powerful male land-owners and religious tyrants were divinely, politically, economically, naturally, positionally and rightfully superior to lesser peoples; and therefore, could and should enslave — own — dominate and control us 'lesser humans', primitives, non-land owners and infidels. Powerful left hemisphere cultural, religious, political, economic and material men egoically — arbitrarily assumed and asserted that they were entitled to overpower, subjugate, exploit and possess less powerful and 'unentitled peoples' as chattel, labourers, surfs, servants and slaves. Powerful, entitled egoic men assumed and asserted their right to arbitrarily possess, control, work, punish and kill — on a self-serving whim.

This pathological masculine left hemisphere presumption extended to the egoic colonial presumption that indigenous and First Nation peoples had no inherent human, religious, cultural, political, economic and social legitimacy. And therefore, were deemed to have no inherent natural or legal rights to human dignity, freedom and justice. Ultimately, indigenous and First Peoples were deemed by rich and powerful secular and religious men not to have no right to exist; except as mechanical resources to benefit mostly white male colonial land-owners. Typically, commonly, when non-white, non-Anglo-European people resisted this diabolical assumption, they were brutalised and murdered. Countless millions indigenous and First Peoples suffered this fate over the past 400 hundred years.

The Effects of Empire, Power and Possession

As a result of colonisation and industrialisation, there was an increasingly entangled web of dehumanising, man-made, egoic, left hemisphere elitism, materiality, ownership, economics, politics and religion. These masculinised aberrations morphed into egoic logic and beliefs that encouraged and justified war between empires, genocide of First Nations peoples, and wholesale theft of lands across the globe. By the end of the 18th century, white male consciousness had morphed into an extreme entanglement that became and endured as the mad-bad colonial-industrial 'Mr' Hyde left hemisphere mind that was characterised by sociopathic materiality, greed, competitiveness, adversarialism, exploitation and Machiavellianism. The masculine sociopathic industrial, economic Yang-mind was conditioned to — obsessively-compulsively want and want and want

— to forcefully and cunningly take and take and take — to tyrannically possess, force, enslave, exploit, gratify and kill — and to deceptively, intelligently and wilfully rationalise and justify any and all means to achieve self-benefiting ends — 'so help them God'.

The result is that the enmeshment of pathologically masculinised, egoic 'agricultural-industrial-technological-economic-commercial-military-bureancratic-empire-building humans' were no longer decent, rational, relational, communal, homeostatic beings. They became egomaniacal masculine left hemisphere murderers and destroyers. All vestiges of right hemisphere relational, communal and ecological reverence and homeostasis were gone. All inter-species symbiosis had degenerated into a mad-bad masculine web of take, own, control, exploit and kill. Masculinised left hemisphere Anglo-European cultures became utterly sociopathic — utterly ruthlessly egoically — violent, self-obsessed, self-justifying, consumptive, pillaging, parasitic and murderous.

Fast-Forward to the 21st Century

In the 21st century, the total effect of billions of masculinised self-obsessed, self-justifying, consumptive, middle-class left hemisphere parasites is rabidly and rapidly depleting the earth and the atmosphere at an alarmingly escalating rate. This short section and paragraph characterise the exponential one-hundred-year escalation of the diabolically aberrant and harmful entangle threads of egoic masculine traits and behavioural patterns of modern masculinised mind of much of humankind.

The Indignity of Egoic Euphemisms

Post hunter-gatherer-First People survival and quality of life was destroyed under the tyranny of these pathological 'Mr' Hyde circumstances. And yet — dominant, white, elite, cultural, religious, political and economic males assumed and proffered spurious, ego-contrived offensive left hemisphere euphemisms: such as agricultural 'revolution', 'civilisation', religious 'salvation', and spiritual 'enlightenment'. Even today, we assume that these euphemisms are the basis for man-contrived, egoic liberalist notions of 'growth and progress'. Assumptively, astonishingly, insanely we have romanticised and mythologised the extreme indignities of existential arduousness, domination, dispossession, exploitation, brutality, denigration, suffering and death — and called them — civilisation, revolution, salvation, progress, reason and enlightenment.

This is a mind-blowing, unconscionable contradiction and irony; a staggering paradox. With the advent of intensive agriculture, 'civilisation' didn't mean being 'civil'. It meant desperately struggling to endure unrelenting inefficient back-breaking work; and surviving the dread of disease, thieves, murderers and despots. The entanglement of which obliterated the relative dignity, peace, well-being and common good of the powerless, disenfranchised, disempowered majority.

The transition from mindful sustainable homeostatic Yin-based hunting, foraging and gathering to intensive agriculture, and then to colonisation — wasn't a revolution of reason and dignity. It wasn't a revolution of rationality, respect, generosity, civility, prosperity, egalitarianism, peace and contentment. For hunter-gatherers and First Peoples, the agricultural, industrial, economic and technological revolutions haven't woven a tapestry universal liberty, fraternity and equality.

The next, very long sentence demonstrates that agriculture, religion, industry, economics and the entangled ravages of colonisation have been a enmeshment of the horrid indignities of endless left hemisphere — institutional domination, back-breaking work, millennia of multi-generational suffering, political and theocratic oppression, racial and social degradation, and extremely high rates of murder, disease, grief, loss, intergenerational suffering, unending trauma, despair, loss of common good, loss of homeostasis, loss of ecology, loss of lands, decimation of culture — and very high morbidity and rates of premature death due to epidemics of disease, starvation and official extermination policies — much of which continues into the 21st century.

For Indigenous and First Peoples, agriculture, industry and invasion through colonisation were and are Armageddon. They were and are the apocalypse. 'White-man' religion, politics, agriculture, industry and colonial invasion were utterly diabolical — then, and are now.

Blaming the Victims

Then and now, globally, First Peoples are blamed for intergenerational issues, ongoing trauma, physical ill-health, mental illnesses and social and behavioural issues that accompany their spiritual, cultural and psychological decimation. We, the sociopathic, left hemisphere white male invaders, murderers, thieves, liars and schemers — blame indigenous folk for their suffering and morbidity. We blame them for their syndrome of extreme and widespread post-invasion, post-decimation intergenerational trauma, dissociation and loss — that drive high rates of substance abuse, addiction, family violence, criminality, incarceration, indolence and suicide. While massively insensitive, egoic white-man insensitivity and prideful ignorance prevail, the horrific impacts and effects of invasion will be inevitable and insidious for First Peoples — generation after generation after generation — until hopefully, possibly, somehow dignity, integrity, reason and accountability are restored. Ways to move toward this hope will be discussed in the final chapters of the book. The Companion Workbook will build-on the explorations of Can We Do Better.

Post WWII Humankind

In the past seventy years, post WWII humankind has been desperately trying to come to grips with the massive and complex egoic, left hemisphere problems caused by thousands of years of agriculture and religion; as well as by hundreds of years colonisation, industry, commerce, materiality and technology. Since WWII, a gallant, conscious, 2% Yin-minority of Good Samaritans have been trying to reduce human suffering and unnecessary preventable death. In the past twenty years, a conscious concerned few mindful Samaritans have been actively and strategically trying to reduce escalating harm to our fellow species, and trying to remediate intensifying damage to the biosphere. In recent decades, the mindful ones of humankind have been desperately trying to fix a massive and complex morass of ego-driven, white, man-made left hemisphere harm and destruction. At this stage, unless there is profound shift in consciousness, I fear that an honourable, enlightened few Samaritans are fighting, but losing, a gallant rear-guard action against Mr Hyde's inexorable and escalating destruction of the biosphere.

Enter the USA, Russia and China

But alas, since WWII, the USA, Russia and China have become the post-war egoic, colonising, political, economic and technological bullies and thieves of the 20th and 21st centuries. These three bastions of chauvinistic ego, have escalated masculinised intelligence and technology with a view to reinstituting a web of unfettered, unabashed left hemisphere imperialism, international dominance, and cultural control through expansionism and exploitation of peoples and resources. Trump's USA, Putin's Russia and Xi's China are 21st

century egoic manifestations of the latest incarnations of Mr Hyde. They are the latest entangle chapter of machinations and harms of ruthless sociopathic egoic chauvinistic imperialism.

A Way Forward

We can't go back to our hunter-gather-forager, Indigenous, First People era. But we can take many lessons from them in terms of right hemisphere reverential and dignifying relational, communal and ecological systems intelligence, grace and wisdom.

Is there a way for you and me to do better by embracing and nurturing primordial dignity and joy of simplicity, relationship, community, contentment and gratitude that First Peoples enjoyed before agriculture, religion, imperialism and colonisation?

I keep asking, can we do better by embracing the reverence and rationality of First Peoples' systems consciousness?

Again, is there a way for us 21st century Homo sapiens to be a reasoned, dignified, integrous, responsible and accountable species?

Can we live up to the meaning of the title, 'Sapien'. Can we be the 'wise' and enlightened species?

Can we evolve to be mindfully rational and compassionate?

The answer is 'Yes'; there is a way forward. There is a revolutionary and evolutionary way that requires you and me and millions of us to prioritise and implement the following interconnected principles.

1. Pass through alchemical fires to burn away the egoic, masculine, left hemisphere mental dross of discontentment, wanting, greed, exploitation, possession, and obsession with power, wealth, dominance and control.
2. Find a way to be far wiser and more enlightened than Mr Hyde's egoic masculine left hemisphere religious and ideological myths and projections. Find a way to be far more rational than new-age / social media fantasies, fads, superstitions, beliefs and opinions.
3. Find a Yin-way to be peacefully and effectively relational, communal, ecological, symbiotic and homeostatic.
4. In the silence and stillness of the right hemisphere, learn to be mindful — aware, sensitive, strategic and evolutionary.

5. Be drawn to right hemisphere mindful decency and integrity; and to be grounded in facts, logic and the disciplined processes of critical thinking and systems awareness.
6. Be drawn to the right hemisphere peace, grace, dignity and joy of simplicity, contentment and gratitude.
7. Learn to be symbiotically and ecologically strategic in how we nurture relationships and the community of the unreserved inclusive common good of humankind, other species, habitats, environments, and the biosphere.
8. Say goodbye to quixotic, narcissistic and sociopathic left hemisphere Mr Hyde by learning not to be egoically patriarchal, chauvinistic, paternalistic, misogynistic, racist, sectarian, humancentric and anthropocentric.
9. Desire and imbue the-feminine by embracing and exemplifying mindful Yin-based right hemisphere grace, dignity, nurturance, reason and purpose in all relationships, roles and endeavours.
10. Follow the lead of our First People ancestors and their 21 century contemporaries by reverencing, dignifying and honouring Mother Earth, her Country, her ecosystems, her species, and her kaleidoscope of humankind.

Again, ironically, these are the elements of repentance; which is about doing better and being a better person, leader, custodian and role model.

Note that the imperative to nurture reverence, dignity and critical thinking is inherent in healing, reconciliation, restoration and sustainable ecology.

What has resonated for you?

What is next for you?

Insights from Two Genesis Narratives

This chapter builds on the observations made in the previous chapter. It discusses and links two particular 3000–4000-year-old Old Testament religious myths that greatly accelerated humankind's loss of relational, communal and ecological dignity and critical thinking; historically, and now. These myths cast a long, dark shadow over humankind. They continue to be a left hemisphere Yang blight for women and the environment.

Two Crucial Myths that Determined the Course of History

The Old Testament book of Genesis is filled with contrived masculinised left hemisphere myths, patriarchal assertions and chauvinistic fictions that are contrary to reality, reverence, dignity, reason, integrity and accountability. These include the creation myth; the introduction of Lucifer, the evil serpent; the tumultuous story and Adam and Eve, the first humans; and God's angry, frustrated, reactive near-genocide of humankind in the fabled flood. Genesis is a book of degrading and disempowering egoic superstitions, myths, judgements, deceptions, narratives and pathologies that religious and political institutions use to project, promote and protect left hemisphere masculine justifications for — pathologizing humankind, dominating women, stealing land and killing many millions of innocent people through holy ways, invasions and colonisation; and destroying nature on a man-contrived religious whim.

In particular, two Genesis narratives provide valuable insight into the origins and age-old left hemisphere drivers of patriarchy, chauvinism, conservatism, fundamentalism and misogyny. These two Old Testament narratives have been ensconced in the human psyche for thousands of years. They remain stubbornly entrenched in a substantial proportion of the collective human mind in the 21st century. The diabolical egoic attitudes and dispositions inculcated by these narratives have haunted and degraded humanity and Mother Earth for millennia.

Genesis 1:26-28 is he first of these key left hemisphere masculine narratives is the egoic command to take, to dominate, and to subjugate the earth and every living creature. The command to take, dominate and subjugate is a millennia-old driver and justification for decimation and exploitation of a wide range of peoples who are denigrated as lesser in the eyes of the mythological, judgemental and murderous patriarchal Abrahamic God. The command to mindlessly take and subjugate the earth has seen the emergence of diabolical environmental consequences.

The second egoic left hemisphere narrative, for example, in Genesis 2: 16-17, Genesis 3:16 and 1 Timothy 2:12-14, conveniently blames Eve for the sin and sins of all of humankind and for the demeaning portrayal of pathological weaknesses of women throughout 'post-creation' history. Both narratives presume and project assumed, arrogant, exclusive religious masculine superiority, authority and entitlement. Both greatly contribute to the millennia-old rise of Mr Hyde in many egoic religious and political masculinised forms.

The Effects of These Narratives

Together, these narratives have been used to drive and justify decimation and subjugation of the earth, peoples and our fellow species. They justify the theft of lands from cultures and First Peoples all over the globe. They drive and justify the obliteration, subjugation and domination of peoples, species and environments. These pivotal masculine narratives justify and sustain the subjugation and disparagement of non-Abrahamic peoples and women, from ancient times through to the 21st century.

These two Genesis narratives have spawned and driven an unrelenting network of dominant, degrading, disempowering and destructive patriarchal left hemisphere fantasies, beliefs and lies that continue to be prominent aspects of contemporary human consciousness. These man-made myths spawned some of the original and worst enduring religious narratives and 'big lies' of history. These arbitrary, egoic narratives and lies are foundational to many and diverse man-made left hemisphere empires, institutions and structures that preclude reverence, reason, dignity, kindness, integrity, justice and accountability. From ancient times, to the 21st century — powerful, conservative, patriarchal, chauvinistic, fundamentalist, misogynistic, male elites and despots have used these two narratives to bolster and rationalise, defend and justify masculine dominance in all domains of human existence; in religion, politics, commerce, industry, marriage, family, and in most community roles and professions.

In the 21st century, thousands of years after the original contrivance of the pathological patriarchal Genesis myths, in many parts of the world, women continue to struggle for the dignity of safety, freedom, decency, respect, recognition, equality, opportunity and justice. The vitriolic, patriarchal and misogynistic backlash against Greta Thunberg and other young female activists, is evidence of the egoic desperation and pathological vehemence of contemporary egoic patriarchy. My hope is that Greta, and other young women of her ilk, will prevail and bring some urgently needed Yin reality, grace, rationality, dignity and sanity to remedy our corrupt and damaging, Yang-dominated religious, political, commercial and industrial domains.

Fake Love

At least two-thirds of the world's population labour under the left hemisphere delusion that religion is the exemplar of truth, reality, love, grace, compassion and justice. The religion-inspired, neo-liberal illusion is that loving justice, equality and prosperity are God's gifts to humanity through democratic political and economic processes. A litany of harmful religious and capitalist actions exposes the pretence, illusion and sham of espoused godly love, humanitarianism and egalitarianism through cynical and fraudulent claims of equality of economic opportunity and trickle-down prosperity.

Religion, politics, industry and economics are not bastions of love, dignity, justice, humanitarianism, egalitarianism, prosperity and the common good. In the 21st century, only a small collection of political policy makers, humanitarian organisations, gallant leaders and Good Samaritan citizens stand between the masses and the hegemony of the all-powerful elite male minority, whose voices are contrary to dignity, evidence, reason and integrity. Genesis-inspired male elitism, male power and man-controlled wealth are instruments of exploitation and degradation. They are not bastions and conveyors of universal respect, kindness, generosity, compassion, empowerment, justice and equity.

The world needs an alternative voice and narrative to that of Genesis-inspired elitist, masculine left hemisphere power. We need alternative voices to lessen spurious man-made Abrahamic stories, and other contrived masculine religious, cultural and political narratives, that have resulted in thousands of years of unchecked arbitrary, presumptive coercion, co-option, control, degradation, brutality and destruction. Religion-inspired patriarchy, chauvinism and misogyny were relatively unchallenged and unchecked until the emergence of suffrage and feminism. Even in the 21st century, patriarchal masculinity continues to repress and attack the dignity of women, and stifles the voices and opportunities of women. It does the same to First Peoples, Indigenous Peoples, People of Colour, and other disenfranchised peoples.

It's time to hear the right hemisphere, Yin voices of Women, First Peoples, Indigenous Peoples, People of Colour, and other peoples whose voices have been stifled.

Fellers

Fellers, as said a several times before, this is a hard reality-check? I empathise with you if you are struggling to absorb my critique and thesis. I have little sympathy for those who align themselves with stuck-in-the-mud, male-dominated cultural, religious and political conservatism, fundamentalism and extremism

Is it time for us men to begin to face these realities without excuse, defence, rationalisation and justification? Don't say — "Yes ... but ..."

Are you ready to let go of religion-inspired egoic masculine presumptions and narratives?

Men, are you open and willing to mindfully desire dignity and justice — fully and equitably for all?

Are you ready to open your mind to feminine and First People perspectives and wisdom?

As tough as previous chapters and this chapter have been, for some readers, the next two chapters will be the most challenging so far.

I suggest you take a moment to breathe.

The God Presumption

Atheists and Believers

For ardent sceptics, secularists and atheists, this chapter may be reason to cheer. For devout 'believers', it might be very challenging. What you are about to read goes to the heart an ancient issue that has been systemically and continuously problematic in human existence for at least 3,000 years. As emphasised several times, arbitrary, man-made left hemisphere fantasies and fictions and masculine crimes inherent in institutionalised religion are a huge problem for us humans, for our fellow species and for the planet. If you and I are committed to dignity, rationality, integrity and decency; if you are committed to critical thinking and science; if you and I are committed to facts and accountability — then this chapter invites us to stop; to step back; and to look afresh at God and religion.

Yet again, the language in this chapter is blunt. Don't be precious. Don't be indignant. Don't be offended. Faith is not an excuse for indignity and irrationality; and beliefs are not beyond scrutiny just because they are arbitrarily declared to be 'sacred'. Don't play the 'my beliefs are sacred' card. As is the case for everything we say and do, alleged faith and claimed sacredness, are subject to tests of decency, sensitivity, integrity, rationality, factuality, reality and accountability.

Take a moment to breathe.

The Mess that is Religion

Throughout at least the past 3,000 years, we men have woven a religious and political left hemisphere web that is so entangled and impenetrable that it seems impossible to unmake. A mishmash of arbitrary egoic imaginings, assumptions and beliefs has become so messy, so conglomerated, and so dogmatically entrenched, that it is well beyond reconciliation with reality. Most significantly, in many ways, religion is beyond the test of decency.

Historically and currently, religion is an endless labyrinth of doctrinal divisions, dogmatic ructions, and sectarian conflagrations. Globally, religion is an entangled, dysfunctional and destructive hotchpotch that is characterised by a litany of profound indignities and irrationalities. Left hemisphere religious abominations include: holy wars; genocides; heretical and sectarian cleansings; slavery, colonial exterminations; theocratic totalitarianisms; a vast array of rationalised criminality; all forms of corruption; appalling degradation of women; sexual abuse of children; terrorist mass-murders; and spurious conservative and fundamentalist justifications for all these toxically pathological issues. Widespread Muslim support for modern-day Islamist beheadings, Trump-inspired white Christian supremacist hatred and violence, and Putin's religious inspirations and justifications for his invasion and devastation of Ukraine — are the latest examples of the continuance of thousands of years of vile, anachronistic criminality that characterised the horrors of the Dark Ages.

What has changed?

A massive list of extreme religious harms isn't an emblem of love, faith and hope. Endless diabolical religious acts and justifications are not a badge of honour. They are evidence of a core of insidious, masculine indecency, indignity and madness. An endless litany of diabolical, masculine pathologies and unconscionable harms are indicative of thousands of years of unchecked religious criminal insanity. Religion has always been mad and bad, and continues to be significantly mad and bad.

Throughout history and across the globe, all of us are affected by this dreadful man-made mess. All of our modern beliefs and norms arise from and are enmeshed within the pathological left hemisphere fraudulence of religion, pathological religion-inspired political ideologies and inane, religion inspired new-age pop-spirituality. There is no religious, ideological or modern hip-spiritual belief that is not bound to the pernicious, insidious, incestuous entanglements of man-made religions. Pause with these words. All esoteric and mystical beliefs are observably pernicious, insidious, incestuous and enmeshed. All are utterly conflicted and confounded. All are man-made. All are utterly egoic. All are malignant and toxic. Absorb the reality that all religious issues and pathologies are man-made and are utterly pathologically egoic and utterly inane.

It is almost impossible to distinguish where one ridiculous, aberrant masculinised religious fantasy begins and another ends. So much that is claimed as original and authentic, is stolen, borrowed, plagiarised, co-opted, mutated and bastardised. It is impossible to find originality, authenticity, integrity and reality in this muddled mess of fantastical and diabolical religious confabulations and aberrations. There is no rationality or reality in the arbitrary junkpile of man's religion. Neither are there authentic, consistent or constant societal pillars such as decency, dignity, rationality, reality, integrity and accountability. Fantastical, masculinised religion is utterly fraught and fraudulent. It is a diabolical egoic man-made sham.

Most of us have minimal awareness that we are entangled in left hemisphere religious confabulations and narratives that have almost zero basis in fact or dignity. It doesn't enter our heads that many of our alleged 'spiritual' beliefs are not only absurd, but are also toxic, sick, infectious, enmeshed, incoherent, incongruent and utterly conflicted. Most of us are oblivious to the reality that we are standing neck-deep in a morass of ancient and modern religious and cultural dross. Most are completely unaware that religious psychobabble and psychodrama has been said and done before — over and over and over — for millennia.

God-Delusion — God-Virus — God-Syndrome

The fabled King Solomon was correct when he supposedly drew the conclusion, 'there's nothing new under the sun'. But, his claimed assertion that 'God' is the end of the matter, is the most simplistic and most problematic left hemisphere contrivance and conclusion of all times. For at least 3000 years, the God-fantasy has been the hub and driver of human delusion, dysfunction, suffering and destruction. All human issues are infected with the God-virus. Each and all of us are entangled in God-madness; believers and unbelievers. This book highlights and critiques what I call the 'God-presumption', the 'God-delusion', the 'God-virus', the 'God-syndrome'.

From this point in this chapter, I will use a small 'g' when referring to the presumption, god. The terms presumption and delusion are intentional and strategic. I use these terms instead of words such as faith or belief. Faith and belief have degenerated into white-washed euphemisms for delusion, narcissism and sociopathy. At best, religious faith and belief are unconscious, dreamy whims, poetic presumption, romantic fantasy, esoteric sentiment, nostalgic mysticism, and wishful whimsy. At worst, they are distractions from spurious justifications for millennia of utterly shameful masculine subjugation, oppression, degradation and all forms of violent exploitative aberrance and deviance. 'god' is projective left hemisphere code for egoic, arbitrary despotism, tyranny, degradation, abuse, violence, murder, insanity, deception, lies, corruption and criminality. 'Religion' is code for arbitrary, institutionalised tyranny and degradation. god and religion are irredeemably polluted and toxic. They are beyond repair and hope. god and religion are a systemic human problem; are utterly egoic; and can never be a viable, systemic solution. Irony of ironies, god and religion are irredeemable; they are beyond salvation.

Presumption, Faith and Beliefs

For religious, new-age and everyday people, the words faith and belief just roll off the tongue. A small minority refer to faith and belief in a highly mindful, considered and cautious way. However, I suspect that most of us use the words 'faith, belief and believe' assumptively, glibly and fantastically. Commonly, faith and belief are so assumptive, automatic, conditioned and robotic that they are almost meaningless. Ironically, the profundity of faith is lost in religious automatism, in new-age fluff, and in everyday parlance. For this reason, it seems better to substitute the word 'presumption' for notions of religious and new-age faith. Insentient presumption is rife in institutionalised religion; and in the mindless, meaningless superficiality of modern hip, new-age 'hip-pop-spirituality'.

My sense is that, for the bulk of religious and so-called modern 'spiritual' people, god and spirituality are assumed; with minimal intelligent reflection or reasoned critique. Left hemisphere assumptions are easy and popular, whereas, faith is precious and rare. Assumptions are the basis of opinions, not a basis for faith. Opinions and authentic faith have nothing in common. Whereas, opinions, fantasies, beliefs, presumptions, pretentions, pride, delusions and ignorance are interconnected. Opinions and beliefs are inherent in presumed and fantastical religious and new-age stories and narratives. They are not the basis for unknowable, unspeakable mystery. For most of us, assumptions, opinions and beliefs just pour forth. They spew forth in an unmeasurable and unstoppable flood of: inane, whimsical ideas; simplistic, romantic, ill-considered ideals; and spurious, dishonest justifications for whatever religious folk arbitrarily deem to say, do, rationalise and defend.

Ironically, authentic faith seems more likely to be discerned, intuited, felt or sensed through an absence of words, concepts, doctrine and stories. I suspect that faith tends to disappear when we speak the words of religion and new-age pop-spirituality. The potentially for authentic faith evaporates in the presence of inane religious pontification and simplistic new-age psychobabble.

Pontification and babble are not the basis for faith. Stillness and silence are the only possible basis for faith. And, visa-versa, faith is the basis for peaceful silence and stillness. Faith seems unlikely to be present in noisy, wordy religious and new-age yabber. My conclusion is that most religious and new-age devotees are almost completely unaware that they are enmeshed in a pattern of egoically presumptive yabber-filled — fantasy, arbitrary wishful thinking, shallow pretention, glib pontification and egoic inanity.

Religious and new-age folk are caught up in a noisy, voluble left hemisphere dream that they assume is conscious, godly religion, and conscious, enlightened spirituality. A dream is not reality. Dreams are unconscious. We dream when we are asleep, not when we are awake and conscious. Predominantly, dreams consist of a hotchpotch of surreal, disparate, chaotic and mostly vague, random images and events. Religion consists of a similar hotchpotch; with the addition the nightmare of 'off-the-chart' toxic beliefs, paranoias, narcissistic projections, delusional ideations and sociopathic predispositions. Predominantly, hip new-age spirituality consists of dreamy, whimsical, wishful thinking, baseless, faddism, conspiracy inanity and mindless waffle. Both religion and hip-pop spirituality are rife with mindless ideations.

Yabber, Babble, Jibber-Jabber and Twaddle

When referring to religion and new-age talk, I deliberately used terms such as yabber, babble, jibber-jabber, twaddle and waffle. These terms reflect a mindless absence of reality; that is, a mindless absence of data, facts, intelligence, critical thinking, congruence and coherence. This deficiency is inherent in traditional religion, new-age pop psychology and hip-spirituality. Religious and hip new-age folk are unaware that yabber has little to do with faith; that it is actually the opposite to faith.

Faith is not expressed as fanciful, self-indulgent, self-convincing, self-justifying, proselytising jibber-jabber. Inherently, faith is experienced as mindful, peaceful, silent sentience, presence and discernment — with a minimum of words; with left hemisphere zero paranoia, dogma, psychobabble, hubris, and hyperactivity. Faith just is. It has nothing to do with the egoic religious projection, god. And, faith has nothing to do with the inane, imaginary, hip, new-age idea of 'the universe that knows and provides'. These are twaddle;

all twaddle. There is no authentic, grounded meaning in twaddle. There is only mindless inanity in twaddle. No amount of twaddle can resolve the inanity of twaddle. No amount of twaddle can turn inane presumption, voluble pretention and baseless pontification into faith.

In contrast to arbitrary wishing and wanting, faith is about being mindfully — silently and calmly present to what is. Faith is not wanting circumstances to comply with yours or my self-serving whims and preconceptions. Most god-talk is jibber-jabber about whims and preconceptions of what should be. And/or, god-talk consists of projective whims about 'what 'I' want', and what I don't want because I arbitrarily judge what is to be lesser or bad. Typically, religious and new-age ideas of faith are about wanting whimsical stuff that pontifical, opinionated self-absorbed believers arbitrarily assert 'should be'. Arbitrary, pontifical, 'want-obsessive' jibber-jabber is not faith. It is inanely presumptive and glibly egoically pretentious. This is the situation, no matter which pious religious words or ideas we assume are enlightened, necessary, real and certain. The saying, 'you can't make a silk purse out of pig's ear' applies here. You and I can't conjure faith out of egoic, religious twaddle; nor from egoic, new-age jibber-jabber.

God-talk and Speculation

God-talk may be serious, earnest, hopeful, heartfelt, sincere and enthusiastic. But, nevertheless, unavoidably, it is speculative, simplistic twaddle that baselessly presumes and pretends to know, declare, judge, moralise, assert and impose. To speak about god is to speculate about god. Speculation does not magically invent reality or confirm absolute authority. Speculation does not equate to faith. It isn't a sign of intelligence, depth, discernment, wisdom or enlightenment. Speculation doesn't make me special or wise. Speculation does not give us illumination or clarification. It seems that faith evaporates the moment we speculate about esoteric and mystical stuff. Often times, decency, integrity, intelligence, critical thinking and reality also evaporate.

This is because, commonly, when we speculate, we presumptively default to judging others and justifying ourselves. By their very nature, judging and justifying aren't peaceful or gracious. They are not kind or compassionate. Most commonly, judging and justifying also are not reasoned or reasonable. Nor are they kind and compassionate. Typically, when religious and new-age disciples lose silence, we default straight to the noise of self-serving presumptive, judgemental, speculative, mindless chitter-chatter. Self-serving presumptive, judgemental, mindless 'chitter-chatter' is highly typical of left hemisphere god-talk, religious theologising and new-age psychobabble. Fear, guilt, shame, dissonance and alienation are often inherent in speculative, religious god-talk, and new-age chitter-chatter. These are not conducive to quiet, peaceful, sentient faith; nor are they conducive to the unconditional embrace, welcome and inclusion of love and grace.

Beliefs

By their nature, beliefs aren't data, facts or evidence. Inherently, they are arbitrary, speculative, imaginary ideas that we invent, force-fit and project into made up, factless stories. Religious beliefs are imagined, speculative, contrived concepts and stories about a fictional character, god. Beliefs about god are made up. Religious and new-age beliefs about humans, nature, the earth and the universe are also made up. No matter how much and how earnestly we talk about made up beliefs, they are — made up. Inherently and unavoidably, made up stuff is arbitrary, fantastical, mythical, illusionary and fictional. Although, perhaps imaginative, made-up stuff is — imagined.

Imaginary stuff is not factual or real. It is wishful, whimsical and untrue. god is not real. god is abstracted and made up by the arbitrary, projective, imaginative egoic human mind; originally, by egoic male minds. god is an egoic arbitrary idea, a figment of imagination, a flight of fancy. The notion, god, is imaginary at best and delusional at worst. God is a contrived mental construct. god-stories are contrived abstractions and wild left hemisphere confabulations.

Worse, much worse, as emphasised before, too often, religious and new-age beliefs and confabulations distract and divert us from right hemisphere priorities, principles and values; such as decency, sensitivity, awareness, reverence, kindness, integrity and accountability. Too often, beliefs divert us from the unpretentious, unforced peace and joy in simplicity, contentment and gratitude. Typically, they divert us from devotion to the sanctity of relationship, community and ecology. Tellingly, ironically, beliefs divert us from the reverence, dignity and peace of grace. Predominantly, beliefs divert us from mindful stillness, silence, presence and listening. Very commonly, beliefs divert us from the rigor of sane, rational processes and devotion to facts. All in all, beliefs divert us from awareness, sensitivity and reality. Predominantly, beliefs dull our clarity about values, diminish our commitment to values, and undermine the integrity of our accountability to values. In so doing, too commonly, religious and new-age beliefs divert us from love and grace. What an extraordinary irony.

The Projection — God

Historically, and presently, on an egoic left hemisphere whim, we humans make up and project god, and project our made-up, man-made beliefs 'about' god. Too commonly, we project god in the image of our own egoically dysfunctional, paranoid, angry and violent cultural and religious versions of Mr Hyde. Or, even worse, god is our man-made Frankenstein; the monster that we have made from the worst parts of our dysfunctional, diabolical and destructive egoic left hemisphere male psyche.

god is a projective left hemisphere extension of the worst of the bits and pieces of the toxic masculinised mind of humankind. In this, god and the pathologised masculinised ego are one and the same. god and ego are man-made, brain-made and mind-made. The masculinised human brain made-up and projected god in the worst of its own egoic image. god is a projective, cerebral contrivance of 'the worst of the pathologised male mind'. god is the ultimate man-made egoic projection of Mr Hyde. Symbolically and practically, the man-made god is Mr Hyde on steroids and ice. Our fictional man-made god is out of control, mad and bad.

Unicorns and Horses

As an analogy, a unicorn is an imaginary mystical horse-like creature. Unicorns have been part of religious folklore for 1000s of years. There is much diverse mysticism and mythology associated with unicorns. But unicorns only exist in the imagination, or as a drug-induced hallucination. Unicorns are not an actual, real, tangible creature. Unicorns are a childish fantasy onto which humans project imaginative, arbitrary and esoteric ideas of beauty, purity, innocence and magic. Similar to many make-believe, magical mythical creatures, the idea of unicorns titillates the left hemisphere imagination. We humans are strongly drawn to make-believe and magical stuff that titillates; including the fanciful, titillating idea of god and unicorns. We 'get-off' on titillating, imagined esoteric hubris. To the egoic human mind, it does not to matter if mystical stuff is imaginary and fictional, as long as it reassures, titillates, inspires and entertains.

The horse, on the other hand, is real and literal. You and I can visit the local farm or equine stud and pat a horse. We can feed a horse, and ride a horse. But,

321

we can't pat, feed or ride unicorns; because, they don't actually exist as an entity; but only as a wishful, whimsical, romantic, imaginative, fantastical thought or desire. Even if I 'believe in' the existence of unicorns, that does not change the reality that they are not an actual entity. Unicorns don't exist. The idea of unicorns or god can feel real as phantastic, whimsical thoughts in my mind; but they do not exist in physical actuality. Gods and unicorns are dreamy, romantic, projective illusions. Inherently, illusions are imaginative thoughts and projections that we find deceptively real, emotionally pleasurable and cognitively stimulating — but they are not factual or actual.

The Role of Imaginative Whimsical Fantasies

As expressed before, commonly, projective fantasies are reassuring. They give us a feel of comfort, safety and surety to our existence. Most importantly, for us fearful, insecure humans, the fantasy of eternity with a loving god helps us compensate for our existential apprehension of the unknown; as well as helping us to cope with our existential fear of biological annihilation at the moment of death. We humans conjure a wide array of fantasised, romanticised notions of 'life after death' and consciousness after death. These conjurings give us feelings of security, comfort, meaning and purpose. They don't give us actual security or reality; only imaginary esoteric feelings.

It seems that we neurotic, narcissistic left hemisphere humans can't abide the thought that our man-made god doesn't exist. We don't care if beliefs are fantasies, illusions and delusions, as long as they help us feel assured, included, important, special, safe, certain and in control. We relish beliefs that make us feel very special to god; and central in 'his' creation and plan. Critical thinking and factuality are irrelevant in the face of our neurotic, narcissistic existential needs to be approved, included, special, reassured, confirmed, certain and central. All this is classically egoic — arbitrary and phantastic.

Our Religious Hotchpotch

And so, we have contrived or made-up many religions, with many imaginary gods as central characters in many fictional plots involving a host of pretend angels and demons, and romanticised humans. We have morphed presumption, romance, nativity, imagination, fiction, contrived projective left hemisphere beliefs, yabber and human psychopathologies into many made up, inane and dangerous god-stories. From these have invented and justified many strident dogmatic impositions and controls. Historically, religious people have woven tangled webs of absolutistic power, tyrannical control, murderous violence, and spurious mindless justification for any religious crime we may arbitrarily commit. We use a huge mishmash of 'god talk' to convince ourselves that our mishmash of god-stories are true and real. We use a mess of god-stories to impose and justify our contrived dogma on unbelievers. Religious folk believe that it is necessary to assert the threat of eternity in hell if 'they', sinners and infidels, refuse to acquis and 'believe'; as we, right and righteous believers, believe.

Much of the harm and suffering of history has arisen from the impositions and threats of arbitrary, absolutistic, religious presumption, imagination, contrivance, fiction, illusion, opinion, dogma and yabber about the fantastical, made-up left hemisphere character — god. When I reflect on this, I find myself stunned and incredulous. This situation seems utterly extraordinarily inane and insane. It seems patently diabolical and pathological.

We brilliant humans have unravelled, systematised and applied the intricacies of mathematics, physics, astronomy, quantum mechanics, chemistry, biology, geology and evolution. We have mapped the universe as far our instruments can see. Humans have mapped and sequences almost 85,000 genomes. We have conceived quantum mechanics, invented super-computers and built the International Space Station. And, humans also invented, institutionalised and internalised the whimsical and pathological fantasy — god. WTF! What mind-blowing irony and incongruity.

My Conclusion

My conclusion is that the presumption, 'god' is an illusory, left hemisphere mental phantom. The illusion and phantom, 'god', is not a person, place or thing. Therefore, as said before, in this chapter, 'god' does not warrant a capital 'G'. We humans conjure and contrive the existence of god from fearful, fanciful, ignorant and arbitrary imagination; and from inane, speculative thought — the totality of which amounts to 'a contrived nothing'. The capital 'G' assumes significance, existence, actuality, tangibility and reality. But a figment of imagination or a phantom of thought is not real, actual or tangible. It is an arbitrary, contrived, confabulated notion; a whim, a wish, a fantasy, a delusion — a nothing.

Thoughts do not exist as entities. Thoughts about god are electro-chemical brain activity; a product of an imaginative fantasying brain; nothing more. Thoughts are not a person, place or thing. Similarly, beliefs are abstract, hypothetical, conceptual, non-factual ideas; nothing more. Beliefs are a nothing. Thoughts and beliefs are entirely different from measurable, tangible data, facts and entities. A belief is a hypothetical speculative 'maybe'. It is not a tangible, measurable, testable absolute. Cognition is not a thing. It is a network of electro-chemical processes. We don't capitalise the words … fantasies, beliefs or cognitions; so, neither shall we capitalise the fanciful cognitive construct — god.

What's happening for you right now?

Do you need to pause for while?

Do you need to breathe and sit in silence?

Monotheistic 'Gods'

Monotheistic god-myths are particularly problematic. This is because history shows that religions that assert 'one true god', also contrive, assert and aggressively defend their exclusively right and righteous claims of absolutely correct presumption. Pause with the words: 'exclusively right and righteous claims of absolutely correct presumption'. Monotheistic religions have a track record of presuming, proclaiming, judging and attacking each other; and for attacking us gentiles, non-believers and infidels. Typically, left hemisphere monotheistic ideologies are divisive, dysfunctional, dangerous and destructive. Typically, monotheistic adherents disparage, wish harm, and do harm to those who disagree with them. Rigid and aggressive absolutism is the defining trait of monotheistic religions; despite their facile, pretentious claims to be informed and guided by love and grace. This is an indefensible irony and a stark, insoluble contradiction. It is indefensible incongruence and unresolvable dissonance.

History is overflowing with evidence that monotheistic left hemisphere absolutisms have resulted in wars, crusades, genocides, inquisitions, witch hunts, burning innocents at the stake, cleansings, terrorism, atrocities and abuses. In the 21st century, monotheistic violence and hostilities are rife in the Middle East and in parts of Africa and Asia. Clashes within monotheistic religions, for example, between Judaism, Christianity, Islam and Hinduism; between Catholic and Protestant; Sunni and Shai, are drivers of mass-murder, terrorism and horrendous degradations. Absolutistic, presumptive, obsessive-compulsive, fundamentalist monotheistic dogma has resulted in millennia of murderous religious, political, sectarian, cultural and racial violence. Not just a little bit of violence and degradation, but thousands of years of repeated, widespread, continuous, abhorrent inhumanity.

Look at the evidence. Pay no heed to left hemisphere blaming and counter-blaming among monotheistic religions. Pay no heed to apologetics, religious rationalisations, projections, defences, justifications and photoshopped versions of history. Don't be distracted by left hemisphere projective claims of victimhood and victimisation. The history of all monotheistic religions is one of the extremes of patriarchal criminality, corruption, exploitation, violence, indecency, heartlessness, chauvinism, misogyny and abuse. Monotheistic history is one of massive, unrelenting, pathological indignity; and a history of crazy, destructive irrationality. Monotheism is the history of men and the male ego at their most insane, ignorant, violent and destructive and recalcitrant. It is men at our worst.

In part, Putin is a man who is driven to extreme violence and mass destruction by the righteous left hemisphere rationalisations and justifications his version of monotheistic religion.

Monotheistic Religion, Culture and Politics

Man-contrived monotheistic religion has always contrived and contaminated culture and politics. Monotheistic religion, culture and politics have always been a toxic masculine mix. Again, look at the evidence of monotheistically inspired and religiously justified political and cultural criminality and corruption. Today, populist politics is defined by its support for extremist, racist, monotheistic beliefs. In tandem with populism, monotheistic fundamentalist religion fosters cultural vehement, toxic animosity and extreme racial vilification. The rise of fundamentalist, far-right, populist anti-Muslim, anti-immigration hate-speech and aggression in the USA, Britain, Australia and Europe are examples of the toxicity and malignance of monotheistic populist dispositions and pathologies.

Some left hemisphere pundits in Australia who publicly and politically supported the massacre of Muslims in New Zealand, quoted the Bible to validate their hateful attitudes. And of course, left hemisphere Islamists misquote the Quran to justify and rejoice in killing each other, Jews, Christians, Westerners, and large 'grab bag' of evil, infidel wrong-believers. Trump actively encourages toxic left hemisphere religion-inspired white extremist hatred and violence. He also fosters misogyny by supporting fundamentalist beliefs about the sinfulness of the termination of pregnancy.

All these proclivities are the modus operandi of monotheistic religious and political supremacists throughout history and across the modern world. A huge volume of religious, cultural and political violence arises from a host of toxic monotheistic God-myths, monotheistic exceptionalism, monotheistic sectarianism, monotheistic supremacy, and monotheistic judgementalism and monotheistic exclusion.

Not to mention the ongoing history of degradations of the abominable (polytheistic) man-made left hemisphere Hindu caste system. Don't just brush this degradation aside. Read the history of the crazy, fantastical, mythical origins of the caste system; and read its history of associated religious violence and degradations; especially for the poor and for women. Sit with the awful realities of this history. Absorb it into your awareness. Let it arouse the awareness, sensitivity, integrity and discernments of your conscience.

It is crazy and criminal that we hate and hurt each other on the basis of inane left hemisphere presumptions and fantasies about one true god; or of many gods; or of greater and deserving humans and lesser undeserving humans. I will not support toxic, pathological delusions that have driven our millennia-long history of mass-murder, cruelty, abuse, degradation, suffering and destruction.

Dignity and Critical Thinking — Alternatives to Projections of God and the Abominations of Religion

You and I need an alternative to God, to religion, and to extremist theistic politics. We need right hemisphere alternatives that are dignifying, rational, inclusive and unifying; alternatives that are not pathological, not malignant, and not toxic. The priorities and principles that arise from values such as decency, reverence, dignity, rationality, integrity and accountability are that alternative.

We are not all Jewish, Christian, Muslim or Hindu, etcetera; but we are all human. Dignity and rationality are universal to all of 7.9 billion of us. We don't need arbitrary, imagined, whimsical, delusional, esoteric left hemisphere religion, or man-made dogma. We don't need a left hemisphere god-presumption or a god-projection. We need to be committed to dignity and rationality through values and such as graciousness, sensitivity, kindness, justice, honesty, transparency and accountability. We need to be committed to the disciplines of factfulness, critical thinking and the neutrality of the processes of science.

An enfolded right hemisphere philosophy of dignity and rationality, integrity and accountability, can be common to all; as it was before agriculture throughout 60,000 years of Australia's First Peoples existence. Right hemisphere values can be our common standards, goals, measures and guides. Values-guided priorities and systems aren't perfect, or without history, but they are our best hope for common ground and for the common good. They are our best potential for maximising universal safety, decency, dignity, respect, inclusion, integrity, equity, fairness, justice and accountability.

These priorities and values are the inner-circle within which all persons can be welcome; within which all can have a voice; within which all can be embraced, protected, sustained, supported, valued and free; and within which all can be ethical, decent, transparent and accountable. Through a universal ethos of right hemisphere values and rationality, we have the viable possibility of the essentials of safety, justice and dignity for all. Imagine local, national and global communities where 'the dignity of the common good guide all priorities, standards, decisions, policies, actions and strategic directions. Imagine this having been the case for Australia's First Peoples for — 60,000 years

For many, the shift from the projection, God, and from the harms of religion, to Yin-based values and critical thinking, will necessitate a transformation of consciousness. It will require unprecedented mindful honesty about facts and evidence. It will require us to consciously shift from beliefs to values; to shift from ideology and dogma to decent and ethical principles and processes. Individuals, institutions, governments and cultures will need to engage in, and contribute to, unprecedented levels of accountability for awareness, critical thinking, integrity and transparency. Of course, this shift applies equally and fully to politicians, ideologues, industrialists, corporations, academics, educators, intellectuals, the mega-rich and powerful, and to us everyday citizens.

Nothing will change without the human-wide embrace and application of 'an ecology' of right hemisphere dignifying values, principles and priorities. Without a radical shift in awareness, God and religion will continue to be a massive part of human dysfunctionality, harm and suffering. Without a critical mass of us shifting from the arbitrariness of left hemisphere religion to the accountability of right hemisphere values and rationality, we humans will continue to inflict pain, harm, suffering, division and conflict on peoples; and will continue to stifle hope and human evolution.

How do you feel about deemphasising left hemisphere God projections and beliefs; and enshrining right hemisphere values, principles, priorities and processes?

What beliefs might you deemphasise?

What values will you enshrine?

What principles will you enshrine?

What processes will you enshrine?

What might be your new priorities?

The Companion Workbook will help you respond to these questions, invitations, possibilities and challenges.

As has been the case throughout this book, the next chapter will be liberating and empowering for some readers, and very confronting for others.

In the Name of Dignity and Reason

This chapter is about drawing a line in the sand, and saying — "Enough, stop, no more"!

I was surprised at the detail and clarity that poured forth as I wrote this chapter.

In the name of dignity and reason, it's time for our egoic, man-made, mind-made left hemisphere religions to stop using contrived, spurious justifications for building empires and amassing power. Man-made religion should not be a platform for power-obsessed men to amass control in order to act arbitrarily, to possess, to dominate and to harm. The masculine left hemisphere projections, God and religion, should not be a license for theocracies, states and governments to kill, to commit atrocities, and to cause great degradation to First Peoples, people of colour, and the poor.

In the name of dignity and reason, left hemisphere presumption, faith, should not be a weapon of war and terrorism. Left hemisphere belief in the egoic projection, God, should not be a licence to diminish human decency, reason, integrity and accountability. Left hemisphere pretence of piety and assertion of righteous beliefs and absolute morality are not 'get out jail free' cards. Assumed left hemisphere religious beliefs are not a justification for unkindness, indecency and indignity. They are not an excuse for religious, cultural and political insanity. They are not an invitation to commit institutional corruption and criminality. Assumed religious left hemisphere piety and righteousness are not an open licence to kill people, to decimate our fellow species, to ravage the planet, and to poison the atmosphere. Left hemisphere notions of faith and beliefs should not be crazy, corrupt, criminal, dangerous, harmful and destructive.

Therefore —Enough Left Hemisphere Aberrations. For the Sake of Dignity and Reason — enough!

Enough of the following litany of harmful left hemisphere religious stuff. Enough religious presumption, pretention and pontification.

Enough projecting God in man's image.

Enough projecting a psychotic, psychopathic, narcissistic, neurotic, unstable, dissociated God in the image of psychotic, psychopathic, narcissistic, neurotic, unstable and dissociated men.

Enough of a God that is psychotic. Enough of a God that is pathologically out of touch with reality; a God that is delusional; a God driven by unhinged imaginings; one that manifests flights of violent whimsy and fits of, furious, violent fancy.

Enough of a God that is sociopathic. Enough of a God that lacks regard, empathy, compassion and concern. Enough of a God that is utterly manipulative and exploitative. Enough of a remorseless, heartless God. Enough of a God without a conscience. Enough of a God that habitually and wantonly deceives and lies; one that massively violates dignity and decency without compunction or care. Enough of a God that is governed by self-serving, arbitrary norms that shatter relationships, communities and nature.

Enough of an unstable God that is given to arbitrary self-serving disloyalty. Enough of a God that lacks control of 'his' frustration, anger, jealousy and other intense and destructive negative emotions. Enough of a God that is unwilling and unable to learn from mistakes and misadventures. Enough of an adolescent God who see himself as victim; and thereby is justified to feel hurt and is justified to lash-out. Enough of a God that is habitually self-obsessed, unaware, defensive, projective, accusative, blaming, self-excusing and self-justifying.

Enough of a God that refuses to comply with norms such as decency, respect, graciousness, kindness, integrity and love. Enough of a God that is utterly self-promoting and entirely arbitrary; one that refuses to be held to account for his narcissistic and sociopathic proclivities, degradations, horrendous acts of violence and environment destruction.

Enough of a God that is that is addicted to power and control. Enough of a God that is drunk with power. Enough of a God that is impulsive, personally and relationally unstable, insecure, intense, moody and reactive. Enough of a God that is driven to act out the worst imaginable impulses; and that commits the most sick and sickening fantasies. Enough of a God that is driven to create hateful, violent disrespect, divisions, exclusions, enmities and unrelenting violence.

Enough of God that is narcissistic. Enough of a God driven by an extreme sense of entitled power, self-importance and self-aggrandisement. Enough of a God that demands constant admiration through unquestioning obedience and mindless worship. Enough of a God that is desperate to be recognised and idolised as all-knowing, all-powerful and absolute. Enough of a God that is possessed by wildly exaggerated and inflated claims of position, authority and power. Enough of a God that is obsessed with fantasies of exclusive magnificence and delusions of absolute perfection. Enough of a God that demands total deference and unquestioning compliance with arbitrary rules and self-adulating rituals. Enough of a self-obsessed God that demands unquestioning adoration and submission, even in the face of extreme mood swings and intense, emotional, erratic, violent and murderous acting out.

Enough of a God that is dissociated. Enough of a God with multiple, distinct and incompatible personalities. Enough of a fragmented God that is massively internally incoherent and incongruent; and that is utterly inconsistent. Enough of a God that is split into many conflictual and conflicting characters, personalities, personas, traits and disparate dispositions. Enough of a God that arbitrarily flip-flops between wildly incompatible temperaments and dispositions.

Enough of a God that is kind one day, murderous the next; welcoming, then rejecting; forgiving, then condemning. Enough of a God that talks of love but acts with bitterness and hate; one that talks of love and grace, but acts with contemptuous judgementalism, callous disregard and violent recrimination and vile, murderous impulsivity. Enough of a God that contrives the fantastical, fraudulent inducement of eternity in heaven, and the inconceivably, diabolical threat of eternal torture in hell.

Enough projecting a massively dysfunctional pathological despotic male God in the image of massively dysfunctional pathological despotic men.

Enough projecting a self-serving patriarchal, chauvinistic God in the image of self-serving patriarchal, chauvinistic men.

Enough projecting a contemptuously misogynistic God in the image of contemptuously misogynistic men.

Enough of an utterly egoic, grandiose God that is obsessed with 'I', 'me', 'my', 'mine' and the great 'I am'.

Enough of a human-made god that assumes anthropocentricity and is totally ignorant of the reality and imperative of biodiversity.

All in all, enough of an egoically arbitrary God that demands agreement with whatever 'I say', whatever 'I want', whatever 'I will'.

Enough of a God that demands unquestioning acquiescence, conformity and compliance in the face of patently crazy ideas, outrageous whimsical expectations, and absurd made-up requirements.

Enough religious presumption and pretention in the name of a small-g god.

Enough factless, arbitrary religious pontification about a fantasised god.

Enough arbitrary religious projection.

Enough crazy religious paranoia.

Enough presumed religious superiority.

Enough outrageous religious delusions of grandiosity.

Enough tyrannical religious megalomania.

Enough masculine corruption of religious roles, and debasement of spirituality, service, leadership, custodianship and stewardship.

Enough of contemptuous, corrupt and criminal historical and contemporary religious Pharisees who posture as God's chosen, pious, elite, righteous men.

Enough religious obliteration of dignity and reason.

Enough trampling of decency, sensitivity, integrity and accountability.

Enough presumptive religious pseudo-faith-driven degradation and violence.

Enough god-ordained and religion-sanctioned sexism, racism and sectarism.

Enough pathological religious Machiavellianism.

Enough pathological theocratic totalitarianism.

Enough man-made, religion-inspired sectarianism, terrorism, war and genocide.

Enough religion-ordained false, disparaging, diabolical and degrading class and caste distinctions.

Enough degrading, man-made gender indignity, racial indignity, and cultural indignity.

Enough condoning of so many expressions of religious corruption and criminality.

Enough religious sadism, and religious masochism.

Enough far-right, fundamentalist, pseudo-faith-sanctioned disparagement, disadvantage and injustice for poor and powerless peoples.

Enough religiously sanctioned and religiously justified colonial invasion, theft of lands, institutional murder, genocide and cultural decimation.

Enough religiously sanctioned spousal and child abuse, sexual mutilation and arbitrary murder of women and children who are victims of rape and other sex crimes.

Enough inculcation of judgement and hate by 'bitter-and-twisted' religious men who have contrived and projected a 'bitter-and-twisted' God in their own toxic, pathological likeness.

Enough religious inculcation of fear, guilt, shame and alienation.

Enough presumptive rationalisation and arbitrary justification for religious fabrications, deceptions and lies.

Enough presumptive rationalisation and arbitrary justification for exploitation and cruelty by religions.

Enough man-made religious superstition and arbitrary religious fantasy; both of which masquerade as faith.

Enough arbitrary religious dogma and beliefs that also masquerade as faith and love.

Enough primitive, fantastical superstition and whimsical, childish make-believe that masquerade as divinely inspired dogma.

Enough mad-made, arbitrary, religious fundamentalisms and conservatisms that masquerade as faith and love.

Enough religion-inspired, fundamentalist dumbing down of education, science and critical thinking.

Enough man-made, religion-sanctioned depravity, inanity and lunacy in the guise of love and faith.

Enough man-contrived and man-distorted expressions of religious piety and sanctity.

Enough of the 'mad and bad' of a muscular, macho, testosterone-driven religion.

Enough arbitrary refusal to be accountable for so many abhorrent and degrading religious attitudes, beliefs and actions.

Enough playing the 'my beliefs are sacred' card.

Enough pretending that fantasies and delusion are sacred. They are not. They are arbitrary, whimsical, fantastical and false.

It's Time

It's time for the following right hemisphere values and rationality.

334

It's time for man-made religion to admit its baseless assumptions, inane projections, fraudulent contrivances, and its narcissistic pretentions of presumptive-faith, pseudo-love and false virtue.

It's time for religion's men to confess that their claims are a baseless, presumptive projective sham and fraud.

It's time for male religious leaders to take ownership and confess millennia of deception, lies and hypocrisy.

It's time for religious men to recognise and confess millennia of chauvinistic abuse of power, and unconscionable abuse of trust.

It's time for religious men to confess that religion has inflicted millennia of pain, suffering and death in all lands.

It's time to cease blind, dumb, wilful religious ignorance; and to cease irrational, stubborn, recalcitrant denial of the facts of history and the evidence of science.

It's time for religion to stop controlling and demeaning through fear, guilt and shame; and to cease the fantastical notion of 'life after death'.

It's time to stop offering the dishonest fantasies, inducements and threats of heaven and hell; and time to stop the fantasies, threats and inducements of karma, reincarnation and delusions of enlightenment and nirvana.

It's time to stop contending that a loving God would threaten eternity in hell.

It's time to stop the threat of endless incarnations until karma has purged us of imperfection, and until perfection is attained.

It's time to stop all religion-inspired inducements and threats.

It's time to stop pretending that fear, guilt and shame are love and grace.

It's time to stop pretending that threats and inducements are faith and hope.

It's time to stop hating and harming with the pretence of love.

It's time to cease all these man-made religious abominations; and many others that are outside the scope of this chapter.

It's time to admit that all the stuff in this chapter looms large as the legacy of male-presumed, male-fantasised, male-contrived, male-corrupted, male-projected, male-dominated, male inculcated and male-imposed religion.

True godly and religious love is not characterised by a several-thousand-year litany of the pathological abominations listed in this chapter.

For decency-sake, it's time! For integrity-sake, it's time! For dignity-sake, it's time! For rationality-sake, it's time! For accountability-sake, it's time.

Pause, breathe, sit still and don't speak.

Breathe, don't throw a party, or a tantrum; just breathe and be still.

There is hope for us men if we can radically redefine masculinity, manhood, and the measure of man.

Imagine and envisage a world guided by dignity and rationality; one without this host of man-made abhorrent delusional inducements and threats; and without man-made fantastical and diabolical fictions and shams. Imagine and envisage a revolutionary reframe of masculinity and manhood.

What else would you add to the impassioned exhortations of this chapter?

If not the masculine abominations exposed in this chapter, what else might be the measure of man by which we can do better?

The Measure of a Man

After an extensive critique of pathological and toxic aspects of egoic left hemisphere masculinity, here is poem about contemporary right hemisphere masculinity at its dignified, rational and competent best. We men can choose to be aware, sensitive and humble. We can choose to let go disrespectful, shameful, anachronistic stuff. We men can embrace and exemplify decency, reason, dignity, integrity and accountability; as expressed in this poem.

The Measure of a Man

The measure of a man is not how strong he is
Neither how well he fights; nor how good he is at sport
Nor his sexual prowess; or how good looking he is
Not how much he earns or has invested; or how successful he is in business or career
It is not the size of his house, what car he drives, or what toys he owns
Not how much he knows; or how smart or funny he is
Nor how popular he is among his peers and fans
Not about with whom he associates, or to what club or group he belongs
Neither how powerful he is; what qualifications he has; or the rank he holds
And not how much he's travelled; or whether he is famous or has great achievements
It is not what political, religious or new-age stuff he believes or asserts

The measure of a man is how beautifully he loves
How fully and graciously he respects, dignifies and honours himself and others
How respectfully and kindly he speaks to, and treats his partner, children and elders

That he is dignified toward men and women alike; in and out of their presence

That he is deeply, equally and fully reverential toward one and all

That he is welcoming and honouring of one and all; equally and fully

The measure of a man is that he is not ignorant through superiority, arrogance and conceit

That he is not disparaging by being sexist, patriarchal or chauvinistic

That he is not judgemental and controlling through fundamentalisms and conservatisms

But that he is gracious and respectful toward friends, competitors, strangers and foes alike

In this, he is a role model of love and grace, dignity and reason; in family, at work and in community

In this, he is a worthy and credible; worthy of esteem and respect; credible as a person of character

The measure of a man is that he listens well, and hears; even when he strongly disagrees

He is integrous and unreservedly transparent and accountable for what he says and does

He responds positively to feedback, guidance and correction; even when it is difficult to hear

He is not habitually defensive or self-justifying; but strives to be self-aware and to be courageously self-reflective, transparent and accountable

He is gracious and dignified; rather than being right, in control, dominant or justified

The measure of man is that he is a peacemaker; that he is open and willing to negotiate and collaborate

He desires to resolve issues rather than to fight, to win, to control, to have the last word

He is kind and respectful; rather than being self-servingly wilful or forceful

He strives to act with calm and clarity; with reverence, sensitivity and warmth

His anger and vitriol are rare; and aggression is a measured last resort

He does not manipulate, connive, concoct, coerce or bully

He uses power, authority, position and influence to give, encourage, dignify and empower; not to get, not self-advance, not to possess, and not to control

He is a steward and a custodian, not an owner; he is a supportive leader, not a despotic boss

The measure of a man is that while he may be ambitious and aspire to achieve; his striving is not blindly excessively self-seeking, self-serving, self-aggrandising

He strives with a spirit of participation, collaboration and contribution; through stewardship, custodianship and service

In this, he is aware and sensitive, authentic and sincere, compassionate and caring, generous and gentle, ethical and honest, trustworthy and loyal, integrous and accountable

Through this blend of priorities and standards, he is consistently and consciously decent and dignified, courageously fair and intentionally just

Especially when no one is looking; and when dealing with those less powerful than himself

The measure of a man is that he is replete with personal, relational, community and ecological awareness

His values and actions are cohesive, consistent, congruent and whole

He speaks and acts from depth of character; with strong, authentic, loving, integrous masculinity; and from a clear, cohesive ethical base

In all this, the measure of man is that he is governed by love and grace; which are his source of compassion, kindness, reverence, dignity, reason and resilience

Uncle Bob, Alan and Michael are role models of these attributes. Their character, values, rationalities, stewardship and leadership are detailed in ensuing chapters.

Do you know men of the quality and calibre expressed in this poem?

Do you know women of this calibre?

Can you and I and many of us do better by being inspired, informed and guided by such men and women?

To women readers, do you hope for us men to be persons of love, reverence, dignity, reason, sensitivity, grace, integrity, courage and accountability?

To my fellow men, do you aspire to persons of love, reverence, dignity, reason, sensitivity, grace, integrity, courage and accountability?

Imagine the tone of family, workplaces, communities, institutions and governments if a broad spectrum of women and men exemplified network of priorities, qualities, standards, principles and values expressed in this poem. This is the revolution that I recommend for us men. It is the standard of masculinity that we need to embrace, and toward which we men need to evolve if we are to do better.

A Few More Radical Reality-checks

For some readers, the previous chapters on ignorance, ego, masculinity, religion and God may have been 'heavy going'. I empathise with you if that is the case. This chapter looks at a few more assumptive, arbitrary ideas that tend to slip under the radar of consciousness. What you are about to read might feel counter-intuitive. So, once more — breathe; be present; and read with reflection, open-mindedness and curiosity.

The Word Radical

The word radical alludes to that which is basic, fundamental and elemental. In the context of this book, radical doesn't mean crazy, outrageous and wildly extreme. Here, radical means foundational, essential and vital. Therefore, a radical reality-check has the potential to shock us out of our arbitrary, assumed, imagined or contrived fantasies, illusions; and to wake us from our sleepy, dreamy unawareness. A sharp, penetrating reality-check has the potential to help us be much clearer about who and what we humans are, and about what is actually happening within us, to us and among us. A sharp reality-check can wake us up from a fantastical, surreal dream that may make us feel good, but is not real; a dream that, ultimately, is most likely to be distracting and problematic. In the context of this book, radical awareness means gaining a grounding and sobering appreciation of some common, generic, whimsical fantasies that most of us humans skip-over without a moment's reflection or critique.

The radical critiques in this chapter are intended to give a crystal-clear view of the egoic-mind as — a left hemisphere dreamer of whimsical, pretentious ideas; as a contriver of illusions; and as a confabulator of arbitrary, presumptive stories. Remember — fanciful arbitrariness, presumption, pretention and projection are ego in full flight. Unaware — we humans make up dreamy, pretentious, self-aggrandising stuff on a whim. Then we invent more and more romantic, phantastic human-centred stories and narratives to validate and justify the dreamy stuff we contrived in the first place. Also, remember that arbitrary presumption, pretention and projection blind us to facts, reason and reality. They side-track us, and lead us down the garden path.

Exposing More Dodgy Themes

In addition to the themes of previous chapters about ignorance, ego, God and religion, we self-important, left hemisphere humans also invent and conjure the idea that we are special 'beings'. We also conjure nebulous ideas and entities such as soul, the human soul, the soul of the universe, universal essence, and universal consciousness. These vague ideas only exist in our self-absorbed, self-aggrandising imagination. They do not exist in factual actuality. We dream, imagine, conjure and project them as aggrandising, magical fantasies. We make them up. We 'pretend' them — full stop. We self-aggrandising, egoic humans imagine and make up lots of tantalising dreamy, make believe, pseudo-spiritual psychological indulgences and mental enchantments that make us feel superior and 'enchanted'.

Other dreamy ideas, such as 'the laws of creation', 'a conscious intentional universe', and 'intelligent cosmic design' are whimsical, fanciful, dreamed-up, titillating make-believe. This stuff is on a par with the made up, dreamy fantasies about the man on the moon, the easter bunny, the tooth fairy, the fairy god-mother, and Santa Claus. Because of the point I am making in this paragraph, I choose not to elevate and validate these fantasies with capitals; because, they are not real. As emphasised, they are whimsical, fanciful, imaginary and fictional abstractions. They are wishful, wistful ideas. They are not part of factual actuality. They are not real. As such, they distracting. They are not helpful.

In fairness, much of this vague, fantastical made-up stuff is apparently harmless. The issue is that our penchant for romantic fantasies such as God, religious dogma, new-age beliefs and the fantasies mentioned above, distract us and divert us, and prevent us humans from being grounded in facts, reality, real-life issues, values, responsibility and accountability.

What is There?

If not our typical array of dreamy fantasies — what is there?

There are the grounded, reliable and exciting laws, patterns and processes of mathematics, cosmology, geology, physics, chemistry, biology and other fact-based, empirical sciences. Thankfully, astoundingly, there are scientific laws of physics that enable the universe to exist as it is, and that enable the galaxies to maintain their form and movement. There are chemical and biological processes and patterns that enable the earth to be interconnected, ecological biochemical systems of microcosms and macrocosms; that includes us humans.

There are the neutral, open-ended processes of evolution, but no apparent design or designer; no creation or creator; no preeminent God; no purposeful, teleological, meaningful creator universe. There is the universe, galaxies, stars, the earth, earthly environments, ecosystems, habitats and species. All these are marvellous and delightfully captivating, but they are not magical and mystical. They may be charming and enchanting, but they are not charmed or enchanted. They exist because micro and macro systems and laws of science.

There are endless unknowns about which to wonder, muse and to explore. There is a massive amount of exciting and intriguing research to be done. There are endless vistas of knowledge be researched and ascertained; then to be tested, retested, and evaluated; until we might venture some cautious conclusions. There is a constant stream of findings to be examined, critiqued, discussed and retested. Mystery isn't mysterious. It doesn't have to be whimsical and dreamy. Simply — 'mystery is what we don't-yet-know or understand'. Mystery isn't whimsical, fantastical, mystical or magical.

Therefore, we need to step away from titillating, arbitrary, fantastical, whimsical superstitions and made-up misapprehensions. They are not helpful. They distract us from reality, responsibility and efficacy. We need to approach the unknown with curiosity, wonder, reason, intelligence and patient, systematic, rational, empirical and critical processes — not with feel-good whimsy, imagined fantasies, made up beliefs; not with arbitrary opinions and fantastical phantoms; and not through arbitrary presumption, pretention and projection. Not with or through any of these. Not!

There are countless 'yet to be knowns'; countless things yet to be discovered, yet to be researched, and yet to be explored and understood. We don't need to fill these unknowns with inane, witless speculation and deluded, made-up whims, fads and myths. All we need is — 'the joy of open, curious wonder'; the delight of creative exploration; the adventure of open-minded, systematic, disciplined, analytical observation; and the integrity of open-minded reason, critical thinking, rational analysis; and the groundedness of careful, dry, lifelong and multi-generational data-based research.

As part of this process, we can ask searching questions of First Peoples, and consider their very detailed and insightful systems awareness of relational, communal and ecological complexities. We can consider these along with empirical analysis and critical thinking. While the dogma and contrived prescriptions of institutional religion have nothing to contribute to science — evidence-gathering and critical analysis, detailed First Nation observations and comprehensive systems appreciation, have much to contribute.

Plenty of Room for Wonder and Fun

To experience wonder and fun, we don't need the narcissistic, human-centred titillation and hubris of arbitrary, projective — superstition, mysticism, magical thinking and childish make-believe. There's enough exhilaration and joy to be had by wondering about possibilities; and by asking intelligent, creative, probing, penetrating questions. There is much joy to be had in examining ancient and modern data; searching-out facts; and 'joining the dots' of knowledge that spans the distant past, the recent past, the present and future millennia.

We don't need to make-up inane, fanciful stories in order to have fun. We can delight, wonder, intuit and imagine; but only if, at the end of the day, we scrutinise our delights, wonderings, intuitions and imaginings through dry, patient, enduring, rational, integrous, critical processes. Disciplined, empirical, analytical, critical thinking processes are sacrosanct. They are inviolable. Crucially, we must not take quick, lazy, easy, ridiculous short-cuts by drawing hasty, assumed, ill-conceived, unexamined, fantastical, exciting but arbitrary and ridiculous conclusions.

In short, we must stop 'making-stuff-up'. We must stop contriving baseless, vague, inane fantasies; and then, stop pretending that what we make up, contrive and confabulate is factual, real and definitive. That's absurd, dumb, dishonest, extremely misleading, and very unhelpful.

More Vague Baseless Fantasies

Along the assumed and made-up notion of 'being', another radical observation is that we assume and make up the existence of 'human nature'; and make up the vague notion that we refer to as 'humanity'. The alleged phenomena 'human nature' and 'humanity' assume and imply that we are a numinous group of special beings who share a common mystical bond, and shared special, sublime, divine or cosmic qualities. When we refer to 'our humanity', we assume and imply the left hemisphere endowment of an enchanted, esoteric nature. This alludes to inherent, charmed left hemisphere imbuement with uniquely important and distinct 'spiritual human qualities' that set us apart in the universe and the earth; and that put us above all other earthly animals and plants. The core left hemisphere presumption and pretention are that being 'human' is to be a 'more than', 'higher than' 'other than' transcendent species. The arbitrarily assumed left hemisphere reference, 'human being' conveys that we humans are special and superior on the earth, special and superior within 'creation', and special to our special and absolute projection … God.

The left hemisphere references 'humanity', 'human nature' and 'human being', are almost meaningless. They are presumed, pretentious, nebulous notions that show that we humans are egoically self-obsessed, self-aggrandising and self-indulgent. The reference 'humanity' is esoteric, romantic, poetic, idealistic, self-obsessive and grandiose. It is imaginary, intangible, dreamlike and numinous. Dreamy, romantic, mystical, numinous notions are little more than vague, overstated, conceited, egoic left hemisphere delusions of grandeur and narcissistic indulgence. These are strong terms and observations, but such is the nature of a radical reality-check.

These terms place us in some sort of bizarre, surreal, fantastical, phantom left hemisphere religious and/or new-age limbo — not God, not angels, and not animals. Such allusions are extraordinarily misguided, misleading and unhelpful. Ultimately, left hemisphere delusional notions are wacko at best, and highly problematic at worst. As emphasised before, anything that distracts and diverts us from factual reality is unhelpful and problematic.

So Much Whimsical Stuff

Over five billion left hemisphere believers fantasise that we humans are special to an imaginary God. Many millions of new-age left hemisphere boffins fantasise that each and every one of us have special relationship with an all-powerful, all-knowing, conscious, intentional, personal universe — which orders every detail of your life, and my life, so we can have what we want and become what we want. A vast number of 'new-agers' fantasise and believe that the universe is the personal benefactor to 'special enlightened ones'. New-age faddists believe that it the role and focus of the universe to indulge their every narcissistic left hemisphere whim so they can feel special; so they be individualistically successful; and so they can feel deservedly happy. Does that sound vain, entitled, infantile and absurd?

To be honest and blunt, the fantasised superior specialness of 'our humanity', and idea of inherent deserving specialness, feels patently egocentric and narcissistic. Many religious, cultural, political, new-age and conspiratorial left hemisphere beliefs are evidence of the widespread anthropocentric presumption and pretention that we humans are supreme within 'creation'; that we humans are uniquely special within the universe; and that we are inherently deserving of whatever whim we can imaginative and arbitrarily dream-up and desire. This feels extremely pretentiously, narcissistically self-indulgent and grandiose. Many religious, new-age and conspiratorial beliefs assume that exclusively particular humans are the chosen ones, the cosmological elite, ultimate divine beings, the hub if creation, God's favourite beings in the entire universe — and that all other humans are sinners, infidels, gentiles, lost souls, unsaved, doomed, unenlightened — and so and so and so. Forgive me, but again, WTF! This stuff feeds like delusional grandiosity of the egoically narcissistic, male mind of Mr Hyde and his whimsical, uncritical, irrational, factless followers.

Not What We Need

My suggestion to you is that we don't need the titillation and left hemisphere self-indulgences of imagined, narcissistic, grandiose make-believe religious, new-age and conspiracy notions about humans being special and elite. The grandiose hubris that arises from such inane presumptions takes us deeper and deeper into projective left hemisphere fantasy and fiction; and farther and farther away from rationality, facts and reality. Fanciful beliefs lead us into delusion and away from sanity. They lead us toward dreamy fictional projections, and away from critical thinking. Fanciful beliefs lead us away from being grounded in the facts of the grittiness of our earthly existence.

Many of our imagined, fantastical left hemisphere ideas lead to problematic delusions of superiority about the specialness of one group, and the inferiority of another group. Imagined ideas predispose Hyde-like left hemisphere supremist beliefs, judgemental attitudes, pathological actions, and spurious justifications for war, genocide, totalitarianism, sectarianism, racism, misogyny, and abuse of the vulnerable. For example, far-right fundamentalist left hemisphere theology assumes and asserts God-ordained white superiority and inherent black-inferiority. Colonisation, decimation of culture, genocide, slavery and centuries

346

of degradation and injustice are the flow-on consequences of contrived 'white Anglo-European', God-ordained, righteous, left hemisphere racial supremacy and entitlement. Again, forgive me, but WTF!

Who and What We Are

Collectively and equally, we are neither humanity nor being. We are the species, Homo sapiens. We are not mystical ethereal beings. We are chemical and biological entities. You and I, and all 7.9 billion of us, are animals. Our species, including you and me, is the result of evolution, in exactly the same way as all other species of plants and animals resulted from evolution. The evolutionary origins of our species are about 200,000 years old. Our species is not ethereal or eternal. It evolved from Homo erectus, which evolved from primates. The first lifeforms appeared about 3.5 billion years ago. The earth is about 4.5 billion years old. The universe is about 13.8 billion years old. This timeline is intended to ground us in reality, and free us from inane fantasies and baseless whims. Nothing is eternal and ethereal because there is no such thing. The ideas of — a divine sky-god, heaven, hell, timeless, boundless, other worldly eternity and the divine creation of human beings — is a wildly dreamy, imaginative fantasy; a made-up fallacy; a contrived fiction; an arbitrary, imagined delusion; a huge, fantastical lie.

We don't need any of these contrivances to feel the dignity and wonder of existence. I smile very widely at the chemical and biological wonder of our evolution. Homo sapiens, and our fellow species, and our complex, homeostatic ecological systems are mind-blowing marvels of evolution; and are the spectacular phenomena of existence; ultimately, they are the mind-blowing reality of life on earth. And, because of our intelligence and consciousness, we get to observe these wonders, and to learn about them in excitement and awe. What an extraordinary gift. We don't need to add inane whims and fantasies to this amazing situation. Reality is more than sufficient to excite, motivate and enthral us.

And yet, as a highly intelligent and highly creative species, we use our abstract mental capacities to massively over-interpret many phenomena, and to distort many realities. We assume that the combination of — imaginative intelligence and sophisticated and complex technology, institutions, cultures, systems, structures and language skills — equate to a special, enlightened, spiritual status. The simple reality and irony are that we use our imaginative but arbitrary, grandiose and fanciful mental capacities to contrive the baseless, narcissistic notion that we are not just the ultimate spiritual creation on the planet; but that we humans are also the centre of the entire universe that consists of billions of solar systems, stars and planets. Seriously! We use our imaginative left hemisphere intelligence to pretend and confabulate that we are the quintessence of God; the image of God, the special ones of universe. I can't think of anything dumber, more psychotic, more narcissistic, and more preposterous. We don't need to do this stuff. We are a wonderful species that has the exceptional good fortune to live on a wondrously complex and bountiful planet.

Pause and Embrace Reality

It will be worthwhile to pause, to be open, and to realise that the vast majority of our esoteric left hemisphere presumptions, pretentions and whimsical ideas are utterly egoic — utterly arbitrary, fantastical, fictional, ignorant and dishonest. Our whimsical ideas and idealisms are completely ill-conceived, ill-informed and illogical. They are incorrect. They are unnecessary. Much more importantly, they are highly problematic. From an evolutionary perspective, myths are only beneficial if they promote the perpetual relational, communal and ecological existence of the species that devises them.

Many First People stories fit this criterion. While mythical, not literal or factual, First People stories promote very long-term, harmonious relational, communal, biological, ecological, environmental and 'whole of earth' harmony and homeostasis. These are the elements and prerequisites of the perpetual biological existence. They are the elements for the continuance of life; including human life. Human-centred, religious and ideological egotism is not a driver of 'whole of earth' harmony, symbiosis, homeostasis and evolutionary perpetuity. It is an egoic driver of ignorance, disharmony, suffering and death for peoples, our fellow species and the earth.

If our imaginative, fantastical ideas are detrimental to perpetual, ecological continuance of our species, ecologies and the earth, then they are not evidence of how special and superior we are. They are evidence that we are utterly, mindlessly sadomasochistic. As Forest Gump famously said: "Stupid is as stupid does … and does and does". Cast your mind of the litany of utterly, mindlessly sadomasochistic historical and contemporary stuff we post-indigenous humans have done, and done, and done in the name of human superiority, human entitlement and human dominance; all of which are assumed and inherent in

348

Western culture, religion and ideology. Does our massive historical and contemporary hodgepodge of left hemisphere humancentrisms define us as stupid and mindless? Significantly, yes!

In 2022, our fanciful and delusional religious and ideological left hemisphere proclivities actually threaten the sustainability of human existence. They are patently counter-evolutionary. On its current trajectory of sadomasochism, Homo sapiens seem unlikely to continue to exist for thousands of years; perhaps not even for hundreds of years. Our species has existed for about 200,000 years. We have existed for about 70,000 years with our current level of intelligence. During the past 100 years we have damaged the biosphere so extensively that we may be lucky to exist 500 years into the future. Mr Hyde's narcissistic and sociopathic religious, political, industrial and economic humancentric madness will kill us.

Does that sound special, enlightened, spiritual, intelligent or superior?

Do these patterns qualify us as special, God-made, centre-of-the-universe, ethereal 'beings'?

Is delusional, sadomasochistic destructiveness the hallmark of a species that deserves an award for esoteric enlightenment or evolutionary excellence?

Is a propensity for wonton violence and environmental destructiveness evidence of cosmic design, divine intention, spiritual consciousness, redemption or salvation?

Or, are narcissistic, sadomasochistic violence and destructiveness indicative of a crazy, ignorant, projective masculinised god whose name is ego?

Can you imagine us humans letting go of fantastical, egoic, anthropocentric ideas and coming to peace with the reality that we are animals; that we are the highly intelligent but incredibly stupid species Homo sapiens?

Can you envisage us embracing the reality that we humans are not as god's children, and are not enchanted, cosmic beings of the universe?

Breathe, and imagine us letting go of these whims and fantasies. This is our only hope for sanity, efficacy and survival.

Can we do better by letting go the whimsical fantasies that are highlighted in this chapter?

Can we do better by embracing dignity and rationality as our standards and hope for societal evolution and for the survival of our species, the survival of our fellow species, and for the healing of the earth.

Populism, Our Most Recent Expression of Dumb and Dumber

This chapter is about an escalating, toxic, delusional 21st century left hemisphere political culture that is obliterating dignity and rationality by influencing too many of us to be extraordinarily fantastical, dumb, ignorant, irrational, dysfunctional, dishonest, dangerous and destructive. It is astounding that so many 21st century humans are embracing patently crazy, egoic, sadomasochistic ways to be dumb and destructive.

Governments have always struggled to be informed, rational and dignified. They have always struggled to stay abreast of strategic issues, science and technology. Governments struggle to implement intelligent, rational, evidence-based and purposeful societal and environmental policies. They struggle to be dignified, congruent, transparent, integrous and accountable. Typically, governments struggle to be grounded in facts, truthfulness and reality. Governments of all persuasions struggle to identify and maintain strategic communal and ecological priorities and directions. They struggle to be systems-focussed and systems disciplined. Governments struggle not be toxic and self-destructive. These common masculinized inabilities and limitations are highly constraining and problematic; but it gets much worse.

With the rise of populism, typical political and governance shortcomings have escalated to an unprecedented post-WWII level of stupidity and toxicity. Since about 2016 there has been an observable rise in — wilful political delusion, wilful and deceitful ignorance, the flagrant dishonesty of big lies, and blatant mismanagement of human and environmental issues. Populism is inherently, intransigently and pathologically dumb, delusional, narcissistic and sociopathic. Populism is inherently mad, corrupt and criminal. It is the 21st century political incarnation of the egoic, left hemisphere toxicity at its worst. Populism is obnoxious, blundering, quixotic Mr Hyde at his most ridiculous and most diabolical.

The Drivers of the Popularity of Populism

Populism feeds off the frustrations and disillusionments of middle-class, blue collar and rural citizens, who rightly feel that their voice and everyday needs are being ignored by mainstream political parties, and by traditionalist democratic governments. Populist leaders and governments have risen to prominence because traditional post-WWII neoliberal governance and democracy are increasingly seen to be failing due to entrenched elitism, arrogance, individualist ambition, complacency, indolence, incompetence, greed, and corruption. Populism flourishes due to deeply-felt disenchantment with the shameless self-servingness, profiteering and power-obsession that has become endemic in traditional, mainstream political parties over the past seventy years; but most particularly over the past twenty years.

Opportunistic, Machiavellian, extremist populist left hemisphere politicians assert that traditional neo-liberal democracy has lost its way, and should be replaced by patriotic, right-thinking, dynamic, aggressive, can-do leadership. Populism claims to truly represent the needs of the 'silent majority' of 'real patriots'. More and more people are believing these claims, and are joined the populist revolution. The populist revolt is fuelled by widespread negative perceptions of mainstream governments.

Populism is being embraced by many as a timely and necessary alternative to mainstream policy failings, an alternative to the conceit and arrogance of corrupt, detached and incompetent traditional neo-liberal, democratic governments. Populism is rising to prominence because of perceptions that traditional governments have lost their 'love of country'; and have lost connection with the mythical 'good old days'. Populist market these romanticised, jingoistic, nationalistic clichés to entice those who identify as patriots and lovers of their national ethos and identity.

This is typified by Trump's clarion call to "make America great again". Populists assert the extreme idea that those who disagree with them — hate their history, hate their country and hate their culture. Populists assert that 'they', traditional politicians, are the evil, unpatriotic haters of country and tradition who have abandoned and betrayed their national identity and cultural purity. Populists accuse non-populists of wantonly destroying the fantastical, romantic notions of nobility, beauty and the pride of a glorious, mythical national past. Populists assert that alleged leftist, anarchical America-haters want to destroy their nation and free enterprise; and want make America a socialist outpost of Communist China. These spurious, paranoid, delusional conspiratorial claims and allegations are the basis and justification for far-right vitriol, baseless anti-socialism paranoia, bitterness, hatred, and threats of violent revolution; which culminated in the storming of the Capitol. Tens of millions of Americans have embraced these crazy, paranoid claims. Populist is flourishing in the USA; along with its bedfellow, Christian fundamentalism.

Populist Expedience, Madness and Indecency

Typically, with an attitude of righteous, expedient left hemisphere vindication and self-justified urgency, populist governments cut red tape, and side-line scientists, authentic experts, public servants and other qualified advisers. Populist leadership ignores bureaucratic and administrative checks and balances. They force and rush through policies and changes. Populist governance tends to dismiss and ignore protocols, procedures, processes and contrary evidence. Populism — manipulates information; appoints ambitious sycophants to positions of authority and influence; aligns with religious fundamentalists and extreme conspiracy theorists; fosters and utilises wilful deception and agnotology; side-lines and denigrates legitimate scientists and genuine scientific evidence; promotes pseudo-science and quackery; supresses debate; berates difference; circumvents the rule of law; crushes decent within its own ranks; and rationalised; condones domestic terrorism; and incites sedition. This diabolical, toxic list of madness resulted in the storming of the Capitol.

Populism demonises difference and opposition as unpatriotic; for example, as being 'un-American'. Populism is inherently highly conflictual, divisive and alienating. It is disparagingly and stridently anti-intellectual and anti-academia. Populism is wilfully ignorant, agnotological, fundamentalist, conservative, conspiratorial, paranoid, delusional and combative. With these dispositions and defaults, populist governance and populist cultism are inherently highly irrational and reactive. Populist leaders incite quixotic rallies and protests, and are hell-bent on violent revolution. Inherently, unavoidably, the delusions and aberrance of populism obliterate decency, sanity, evidence, integrity, lawfulness, transparency and accountability.

If political and religious delusions are plentiful; and decency, sanity, integrity, lawfulness, transparency and accountability are in short supply, or missing altogether — what takes their place? The answer is — unchecked left hemisphere madness, tyrannical empire building, obscene and grotesque uses of power, hyper-greed, blatant unconscionable dishonesty, complete absence of ethics, bare-faced resistance to decency, sanity and the rule of law, unconcealed manipulation of institutions, overt and unchecked 'big lies, corruption and criminality. Populists possess, and are possessed by this dangerous conglomeration of crazy, toxic traits. Populists are utterly mad and bad. It is utterly malignant. Populism is an extremely dangerous political, cultural, religious and nationalist version of Mr Hyde.

The Rise of Populist Power and the Demise of Dignity and Critical Thinking

In 2017, Mr Hyde populist politics toppled mainstream politics in the USA, and rose to prominence and power in a range of European and some South American countries; and now, in 2022, in the Philippines. In the USA, populist governance plummeted from being amusingly dysfunctional to being pathologically dishonest and explosive; from dumb to dumber; from mad and bad to madder and badder. Trump is a quixotic Mr Hyde, populist, left hemisphere architype of extreme hatefulness, insanity, toxicity and unrestrained narcissism and sociopathy.

Tump's blatant mismanagement of the COVID pandemic, Black Lives Matter issues, and destructive wildfires showcased his inanity, incompetence and complete lack of decency, knowledge, rationality, judgement, integrity and accountability. He is utterly devoid of rational, integrous custodianship, leadership, eldership, statesmanship and character. Trump is utterly and irredeemably flawed. He is utterly and incurably toxic and malignant. He is a quintessential populist. And, although trump is rat-cunning and massively self-aggrandising, he is the dumbest of the dumb.

Trump's profile encapsulates 21st century populist traits that block rational, decent, intelligent, competent, strategic, relational and ecological management of big picture issues, such as human rights, human suffering, and environmental vandalism. Dignified, reasoned, competent, integrous, strategic ecological acumen is conspicuously and disastrously absent in populist governance.

Contemporary populism has the potential to derail decades of hard-won post WWII inter-governmental collaboration. It is a highly destabilising global influence. Populism is at least as confounding as Christian fundamentalist and extremist Islamism. Conservative and fundamentalist left hemisphere religion and populism are enmeshed and mutually reinforcing. Often, they are mutually crazy and corrupt. Populism and religion are enmeshed in crazy, dysfunctional political and religious conservatisms, fundamentalisms and extremisms. 21st century populism parallels and is on par with the toxicity of 20th century left hemisphere Nazism and Cold-War Communism. Trump's populism is the American equivalent of 21st century Chinese Communism and Russian Putinism.

The Popularity of Populists and the Lure of Populism

Globally, 21st century citizen-voters are electing populist leaders in increasing numbers, despite the evidence that populism is massively floored. In many cases, blatantly corrupt, incompetent and completely mad-bad populist candidates are elected by a majority of citizens because we citizens fail to recognise the toxic nature of the person and the ethos for whom we are voting. Voters fail to see massive irrationality, policy-competence, ethical impropriety, lack of integrity and disrespect for the rule of law. Voters fail to recognise that populist leaders are utterly devoid of character and sanity. Astonishingly, voters fail to recognise the dangers of electing blatantly narcissistic and sociopathic populist criminals to positions of great power.

Citizen-voters are hoodwinked by blustering hubris and patently fantastical, false and crazy conspiratorial left hemisphere information about societal issues and opposition politicians. Citizens fall for shallow reformist rhetoric, and for insane stuff about aliens, worldwide, baby-eating paedophile rings. Voters naively believe inane, dumb, dishonest, glib, trite traditionalist motherhood assertions; and are hoodwinked by mindless, fervent fundamentalist religiosity. Many 21st century voters fail to recognise 'the most recent cult of Mr Hyde' in populist form.

Questions

Have mainstream political parties become so irrelevant and unpalatable that citizens prefer to vote for nutcases, narcissists, sociopaths, fraudsters and extortionists?

Can mainstream parties do better and win back the confidence of populist converts?

Or, are we citizens too — unaware, uninformed, fanciful, naïve, indifferent, ignorant and undiscerning that we cannot recognise religious and political criminals when the evidence is strong and clear? Can we do better than this?

Why do apparently intelligent citizens believe, trust and elect utterly dishonest, ignorant, untrustworthy, incompetent populist candidates?

Why are we so easily hoodwinked by blatantly inane cliché, jingoistic motherhood assertions, conspiracy theories and populist cultism? Can we do better by being more aware and discerning?

How is it that ignorance, bias and naivety trump decency, facts and sound judgement? Can education dispel ignorance so that citizens can do better?

Are you and I able to learn to recognise a 'nutcase shyster' when we see one?

Can we learn to recognise an insane, cultist sham?

Can we learn to recognise 'big lies' and blatantly insane, conspiratorial cultism?

Or, are we too easily sucked in by fantastical smoke-screens, projection, rhetoric, baseless claims, hollow promises, and groundless rhetoric?

What causes so many to willingly and fervently believe populist narcissists and sociopaths?

Is it that the fanciful voter ego is easily fooled by the Machiavellian populist ego?

Is the dysfunctional citizenry ego naturally attracted to and beguiled by the dysfunctional populist ego? Can we learn not to be beguiled?

Are there sane, decent, credible, integrous and competent non-populist candidates who are worthy of our trust, respect and confidence?

Or, is there a dearth of traditional credible, dignified, integrous and competent political stewards and leaders of democracy who are worthy of election to political service? How do we inspire credible role models to step forward so that politics can do better?

Has neoliberal politics deteriorated to such a level that blatantly crazy, dishonest and corrupt candidates are widely perceived as a better option than traditional candidates?

What impact is all this having on dignity and rationality for us citizens and our communities?

Has the two-party adversarial system become an irredeemable lamb duck?

What are the alternatives to the two-part adversarial model?

Can democratic institutions, structures, systems and processes be reformed and transformed so that they can do better?

Australia

In Australia, right-leaning parties are imploding from a left hemisphere void of character, integrity, accountable leadership, dignified statesmanship and mature eldership. Until the change of government in May 2022, the Australian government was characterised by salesmanship, marketing ploys, bluff and bluster, unflinching denialism, pathological aversion to honesty, stubborn refusal to be factual, rampant individualistic ambition, incompetence, and blatant dirty deals with 'mates' in big business.

This combination of factors reduced parliamentary processes and governance to cynical, Machiavellian power-mongering, individualism, careerism, transactionalism, greed and empire building. These traits obliterated decent, integrous stewardship, effective service and ethical, competent governance. This resulted in opportunistic back-room deals with sycophants, power-brokers, factions and 'mates' in big business. These factors obliterated integrity, accountability, parliamentary decency and dignity, and destabilised fact-based, rational, integrous, competent, accountable strategic management of big-ticket issues; especially climate change. The extent of blatant unscrupulous conniving, manipulation and rorting was staggering.

Then, in May 2022, the Australian people showed their awareness and astute judgement by resoundingly removing the Morrison populist government. En masse, Australians voted for integrity, decency, competence and accountability in the prioritisation and management of big-ticket issues, and for ethical propriety. Let's hope the new government will be worthy of citizens' vote of confidence, trust and hope.

Perhaps the 2022 Australian election shows that it is realistic for us citizens to envision and vote for decency, integrity, rationality, competence, transparency and accountability in governance?

Astute voters showed that we can do better than the sham of populism.

Destabilisation – The Hallmark of Populism

The botched and corrupted Brexit plebiscite cast Britain into prolonged political turmoil, and dragged Europe into Britain's mess. This destabilised situation gifted Russia with the opportunity to facilitate the rise of populist instability to unprecedented levels in Europe, including in the European parliament. In the USA, the failure of Clinton's campaign, aided by Russian cyber-attacks, gifted Trump the opportunity to make his own chaotic and corrupt populist mess.

In Britain, Europe and the USA, destabilisation of parliamentary processes opened the gate for populist candidates to proliferate 'big lies', paranoia, racism, 'anti human rights', anti-immigration anti-science and climate-change denialism. At that time, the decline of quality parliamentary and governmental processes in Australia also allowed China to infiltrate our markets, as well as professional and educational institutions; and to establish dangerous footholds in a range of South Pacific islands; most recently in Solomon Islands.

Around the globe, the quality of neoliberal, democratic governance is being destabilised by a critical mass of profoundly fanciful, ignorant and incompetent power-obsessive left hemisphere narcissism that may be very difficult to reverse. Governance is also being eroded by increasing Machiavellian corporate opportunism, corruption and criminality.

This has opened the door for the meddling, exploitation and violence of opportunistic exceptionalistic rogue states; most particularly, Russia and China. Russia's populist opportunistic and exploitative invasion of Ukraine has shattered Ukraine's safety and peace; has bolstered populism in Russia; and had significantly destabilised economics, gas and oil supplies in Europe and food security in the Western world.

Inept and corrupt democratic governance has also predisposed a rise in Islamist theocratic violence, religious absolutism, ideological cultists, and political totalitarianism. The 2021 invasion of Afghanistan by the Taliban Islamists is another recent example of destabilisation. This web of factors has brought decay and death to decency, critical thinking, integrity, accountability and strategic competence. Issues in Eastern Europe and Afghanistan have also resulted in the decay of European and global stability.

What We Can Do

The situations outlined in the chapters on populism behove us citizens to — slow down, to observe, to read widely and intelligently, to ask penetrating questions, to examine policies, to scrutinise political candidates for sanity, ethics, factfulness and competence; and to vote on the basis of informed, reasoned intelligence and critical thinking. These situations behove you and me not to vote with uninformed or ill-informed, reactionary and conspiratorial ignorance. Informed intelligence begets informed intelligence. Dumbed-down, fanciful, arbitrary, reactive, egoic ignorance begets more and more crazy, stupid, dumb, ignorant, egoic, incompetent, destructive governance.

We, modern individuals, and contemporary society, can either spiral slowly upwards toward reverence, rationality, decency, intelligence, integrity, accountability and strategic ecological competence. Or, we can destabilise and spiral downwards toward escalating inanity, egoism, ignorance, apathy, cultism, destabilisation and destruction. You and I need to be aware of the factors that drive these contrasting directions so that we can choose to be informed citizen-voters; as well as to be rational, decent, conscious, intentional, effective and integrous in our custodian responsibility and in our various societal roles.

That's what this book is about — personal, citizenry, custodian and societal stewardship through the dignity and rationality of awareness, integrity, and informed reasoned factual and strategic intentionality. Sane, competent, integrous stewardship in governance can only come from a critical mass of sane, competent, integrous stewardship of citizen voters. There's a saying: 'We get the governance we deserve'. To get good governance, we citizens need to be worthy of good governance. We need to know what we are looking for; and know what we will not vote for or tolerate. I am looking for sane, values-based, decent, integrous, rational, factful, accountable, strategic, ecological governance. I will not tolerate crazy, indecent, narcissistic, conniving, sneaky, dishonest, untransparent left hemisphere incompetence and corruption.

Now is the time imagine and envision new values, principles, priorities, systems, structures and governance accountabilities that may restore sanity, honesty, decency, rationality, integrity, transparency, respect, trust, efficacy and stability?

How do you feel about this analysis?

In what ways can we citizens and voter do better?

The next chapter looks at the dumbest of the dumb, and the worst of the bad.

The Mad and the Bad

In 2022, across the globe, there is a relatively small percentage of governments that are — genuinely sane, sensitive, socially aware, dignified, empirically informed, integrous, responsible, accountable, compassionate, intelligently strategic, and highly competent. So, it's a rarity for governance to be reverent, dignified, sensitive, socially aware, empirically informed, rational, integrous, responsible, accountable, compassionate, intelligently strategic, and highly ecologically and systems competent. How does it feel to absorb this reality? Finland, New Zealand, the Nordic countries, Canada, Holland, Scotland and Switzerland are among the countries that tick most of these boxes. Australian has the potential to join this group of decent, sane, integrous and competent governments by breaking free from its former left hemisphere populist government. This small band of countries are the extremely functional end of the continuum. Hopefully the new Australian government will enable Australia to join this band of integrous and competent countries.

There is a collective of countries that tick some of the boxes; but just below the surface they lack crucial traits such as rationality, compassion, ecological awareness and accountability. Most countries sit in the middle of functionality continuum.

The Decline of Sanity and the Rise of Madness

At the negative end of the continuum, there is a global mishmash of highly deluded, dysfunctional, dangerous and destructive political and religious leaders, cults, cultures, governments and states. This chapter raises our awareness about this messy mix of 21st century toxic left hemisphere dysfunctionality. I refer to highly dysfunctional, toxic and dangerous leaders, cults and cultures and governments as — 'mad and bad'. Being mad and bad usually incorporates the hazardous combination of inanity, 'big lies', wilful ignorance, anti-science, narcissism, sociopathy, Machiavellian opportunism and complete unaccountability. 'Mad and bad' is political and religious ego at its most pathological. It is the masculine ego at its most crazy, dysfunctional, dangerous and destructive. Mad and bad is ego at its most toxically destructive. Mad and bad is Mr Hyde doing his masculine, crazy, quixotic and destructive cultural, political and religious worst.

Mad-Bad Threats to Long-Term Stability

Traditional two-party liberal democracy seems to be devolving and imploding, while globally, mad-bad political, religious and cultural insanity, criminality and instability may be gaining momentum. The 21st century is morphing into a hotchpotch of crazy, cultish, renegade influences that are filling the democracy vacuum, the sanity vacuum, the decency vacuum, the competence vacuum, and the accountability vacuum. Renegade categories include the rise of a strange conglomeration, including Chinese Communism, Russian post-communism Tsarism, far-right extremism, crazy populist cults, Islamism, Christian fundamentalisms, corrupt mega-rich and powerful corporations and oligarchs, and a disparate mix of renegade, nutcase religious and nationalist left hemisphere empire builders. This is quite a disturbing international hotchpotch. Across the globe, there is a risk that traditional democratic governance could be supplanted by this disparate mishmash of extreme 'mad-bad' influences.

The critical mass of Western populism + China + Russia + extremist theocracy + renegade states + cults + powerful corrupt corporations + corrupt billionaire power-brokers does not bode well for sanity, peace, justice, stability and constructive collaboration into 21st century. All the players in this destructive left hemisphere conglomeration are notoriously unamenable to calls to factuality, decency, rationality, science, negotiation, international cooperation, strategic ecology, and accountability with respect to big-ticket issues; such as human rights and environmental protection. Mad-bad players and left hemisphere states are — ignorant, paranoid, rabidly self-protective, passive-aggressive, extremely idiosyncratic, delusional, egoically self-seeking, utterly unethical, impulsive, projectively accusative, and completely self-justifying. Individually and collectively, they are beyond sanity, decency, diplomacy and rationality. Each of them is Mr Hyde. Together, they are a Hyde-like medusa, with many terrifyingly crazy heads and dangerous flailing arms.

Individually and collectively, toxic, mad-bad narcissistic and sociopathic left hemisphere psychopathologies render these people unable to empathise, respect or be decent, rational and integrous. Mad-bad psychopathologies predispose incorrigible corruption and diabolical internal and international criminality. If it weren't for the rule of law and other institutional systems of accountability in advanced democracies, the syndrome of mad and bad would much more significantly undermine and unravel democracy throughout the world. The erosion of democracy and possible impending collapse is almost on par with threats of climate change. As a prime example, mad and bad forces unhinged the USA and destabilised democracy during the Trump presidency. Only the rule of law saved America from collapse into complete left hemisphere insanity, chaos and anarchy.

Sadly, and horribly, decency, rationality and the rule of law have not protected Ukrainian people from Putin's utterly mad-bad invasion, mass-murder terror and destruction.

Does some or much of this ring true?

Do you see Mr Hyde in this mad-bad syndrome?

Are Trump, Putin and Xi the extremes of mad and bad?

Are Trump, Putin and Xi the most dangerous men on the planet at this juncture in history?

Could any of these sociopathically toxic men, or a combination of them, completely destabilise the globe?

Is man-made global destabilisation occurring as you read this book?

Should we be very concerned?

Are you concerned?

Can you suggest how we might manage and mitigate the mad-bad intentions and actions of Trump, Putin and Xi?

Can you I and a critical mass of mindful citizens mitigate the machinations of smaller scale mad-mad players, such as Kin Jong-un.

Locally and globally, how can you and I and 7.9 billion of us nurture and build sanity, reverence, dignity, decency, rationality and integrity in citizenship, culture, politics and governance?

Sanity and Dignity

This chapter starkly contrasts lucid, gracious mindfulness and inane, boorish, toxic mindlessness in high office.

I have watched many interviews with former President Obama. I am struck by his consistent reverence, dignity, decency, integrity, emotional intelligence, clarity, humility, eloquence, statesmanship, grace and command of strategic issues. My observations are that Obama is entirely suitable for high office in terms of his sanity, character, reverence, sensitivity, poise, intelligence, sophistication, professionalism, character, congeniality, collegiality, leadership and strategic ecological acumen. He is a person of dignity, intelligence and critical thinking — par excellence. My conclusion is that his qualities and skills are far beyond all American presidents that I have observed in my lifetime. Obama was entirely suitable to be President of a great liberal democracy.

While I watched the interview, I was shocked by the contrast between former President Trump and former President Obama. In stark contrast to President Obama — President Trump is — inane, irrational, arrogant, bombastic, boorish, utterly self-seeking, inarticulate, mindlessly simplistic, insensitive, personally unaware, undignified, unstatesmanlike, ill-informed about the facts of issues, an habitual liar, insidiously and incorrigibly Machiavellian, reactive, erratic, offensive, conflictual, divisive, judgemental, derogatory, denigrating, devoid of empathy and compassion, utterly vindictive, totally lacking in grace and statesmanship, a bully, and completely lacking presidential stewardship and leadership qualities and skills.

Reread these contrasting profiles of traits.

I cite these two 21st century leaders to highlight the extreme contrasts between dignity and narcissism; between sanity and insanity; between decency and sociopathy; and to highlight the contrasts between a truly inspired, decent and rational democratic leader and typical populist, cultist narcissist and sociopath. Obama is an exceptionally dignified and competent 'statesman-custodian-president'. Typical of populist leaders, Trump is an appalling human. Just below the surface, populist leaders tend to be abominable; and the vast majority are narcissistic and/or sociopathic left hemisphere men. Populism and Mr Hyde populists are killing sanity, decency, integrity, dignity and critical thinking in governance. They are the worst of toxic masculinity at the highest level of governance. And they are yours and my present reality. In so many ways, 21st century populists are the reinvention of Hitler; the abominable Mr Hyde of the 20th century.

So that we might do better, what can you and I, and billions of our fellow citizens, do to foster decent, honourable, statesman-like qualities, and to deter toxic pathologies in 'our' politicians?

More on Russia and China — Their Extreme Expressions of Mad and Bad

Russia and Putin

21st century Russia is at the top of the mad and bad list of sociopathic renegade states. Russia is caught in a strange anachronistic, Tsarist, imperialist, post-communist, post-cold war, nationalist, exceptionalistic, pseudo-revivalist mindset. Russia is led by an obsessive, ruminating, entirely conservative, traditionalist, grandiose, narcissistic, sociopathically Machiavellian enigma. Putin is a bizarre 'Tsarist communist religious populist oligarch'. He sees himself as absolute, as God-appointed commander in chief, as the people's emperor, and as Russia's messiah and saviour of an imaginary, post-cold war, divine, Tsarist, Motherland Empire.

Putin shares power with a highly pathologized criminal patchwork of fellow sociopathic, power-obsessive oligarchs. At the same time, Putin juggles a messy mix of modern reformists, angry and bitter vengeful old-school communists, and nostalgic, Tsarist imperialists. Criminality, corruption and incompetence are rife within this this pathological mix of noxious bedfellows. Decency, integrity, sanity and accountability are conspicuous by their total absence.

In 2022, the bulk of the world's governments and peoples condemn Putin's Russia as a diabolical international pariah. Until 2022, in addition to the brutal decimation of swages of Syria, Russia's power and pride were channelled through periodic opportunities to destabilise the USA and Europe through cyber-attacks. Russia meddled and destabilised just for fun; just because it could; but mostly in retaliation for the sting of smug Western judgemental schadenfreude in the face of the failure and collapse of the USSR and Russian Communism.

Until 2022, Putin's 'populist Russia' was a bitter-and-twisted, failed superpower and a failed communist state. Putin desperately wants retribution for smug, contemptuous mocking by the West in response to a range of obvious post-cold-war failures. These include fiscal incompetence; the plundering of state coffers; violent human rights violations; brutal suppression of freedom of speech; and aggressive, prideful, nationalistic expansionism in Chechnya and Crimea. As mentioned before, Russia flexed its military muscles and revealed its shameless cruelty in Syria.

Until 2022, Russia had devolved into a botched pseudo-communist left hemisphere superpower that was defined by corruption, nationalistic pretence, passive-aggressive malice, and pathetic face-saving. Until 2022, Putin and Russia are lost in a dark, angry, resentful, vengeful, political no-man's-land. Then, early in 2022, Putin catapulted Russia into a disgraceful, murderous war. Now, Putin and Russia are defined by the most abhorrent sociopathic military violence and destruction since WWII.

As a pathetic, pathological macho traditionist, Putin is ever-desperate to flex his 'small-man' political and military muscles, and to prove to the world that 'his' imperial Russia is still a powerful macho force to be reckoned with. Putin is desperate to be a mighty man of Russian history. He is desperate for the world to submit to him as unrelentingly formidable, steely, fearless, ruthless, totally in control, and able to bluff, dominate and destabilise the motherland's traditional enemies. Putin is a person of extreme obsessive-compulsive, grandiose, narcissistic, masculine left hemisphere egotism. He is defined by and exemplifies 'the worst tyrannical extremes of angry, try-hard, little man, victim syndrome'.

Putin lives in a highly idiosyncratic, massively pathological, and utterly egoic, deluded and malignant world. Putin sees himself and his Russia as victims of Western subterfuge and evil intent. He sees himself as the gallant rescuer and liberator of his Motherland and empire. Typical of the self-justifying, pathological victim mentality, Putin believes and asserts that any means justifies the ends of reborn, reinvigorated nationalist pride. For the ruminating, vengeful, deluded Putin — any means justifies the rescue of the Motherland from nationalistic death, and liberation from the black heart of the West.

In all his paranoid, delusional, sociopathic ideation, the macho Putin has zero awareness of reality and decency, and zero inclination to be respectful, integrous and accountable. Putin, the self-deceived, unconstrained victim-rescuer, is utterly, ruthlessly diabolical, incorrigible and unaccountable. Putin's mindset is the same as the sick, coercive, violent man who kills and wife and children; because, if he can't have them, no one will. Such pathological men, often contrive and assert that that they are the misconstrued innocent victims of unrequited love, misunderstanding, betrayal and conspiracy. Clearly, in so many ways, Putin is completely mad and bad. Putin is an unimaginably pathological and hellish modern-day Mr Hyde.

Russia's, China's and America's incarnations of My Hyde

It is sickening to realise that Putin is Trump's model man. Trump who asserts an array of deluded victim contrivances, greatly admires and idealises Putin. At the same time, Putin and Xi are good friends, confidants and allies. They are enmeshed in their paranoid mistrust and hatred of the West, especially, the USA. Xi also contrives that China is a victim of the West, and therefore is justified to assert its cultural purity and nationalistic prerogative; by any all means.

These three psychopaths are entangled in pathological populist ideations of grandeur and megalomaniacal obsessions, entitlements and desires. Individually and together, they are driven by deluded left hemisphere victim mindsets that justify and fuel their unrelenting personal and nationalistic ambitions; and by which they execute their unrestrained, sociopathic, Machiavellian means and ends. Individually, they are massively dangerous. Enmeshed, they are likely to be unstoppably lethal.

China and the Chinese Communist Party

The Chinese Communist Party (the CCP) is ruthlessly mad and bad and toxic; but in very different ways to anachronistic Russia. China's very detailed and very long-term 'belt and road' intention is to proactively, systematically and inexorably exploit every relationship, to fill every vacuum, and to unflinchingly assert its will; culturally, politically, economically and militarily. China is now the second largest economy in the world, and is a burgeoning, dominant technological force. The Chinese Communist Party abounds in strategic clarity and strategic opportunism in its drive toward global control. While utterly pathological, China is exceptionally visionary, calculating, focussed, determined, patient and unrelenting.

While Putin is fighting a repulsive, reactive, pathetic, face-saving war, Xi is on the global strategic front foot militarily, economically, technologically and culturally. Putin is an insane, desperate reactionary who is clinging to the post-cold war fragments. Xi is a clear-minded visionary who is leading a far-sighted, cohesive, unflinching, determined strategic China toward unprecedented global ascendency. Xi is a clear-headed, power-obsessed, long-sighted political genius.

He is an inexorable, evil Mr Hyde genius, but a genius, nevertheless. Xi is totally, purposefully focussed on the ruthless, unwavering absolutism of the Chinese Communist Party; not for the dignity of humankind, but for unlimited cultural, economic, technological and military expansion; all to achieve global imperial dominance of the Chinese Communist Party.

Chinese Communist Party attitudes and actions are classically egoically macho and sociopathic. The CCP is without empathy, compassion, conscience or compunction. China has no concern for the victims of its ambitions, opportunisms, deceptions, exploitations, bullying, manipulations and crimes. China, the historical victim of Western imperialism and the contemporary victim of Western attitudes of superiority. As a victim, China feels totally justified in using undiluted, resolute, sociopathic Machiavellian pragmatism to achieve its grandiose, nationalistic ends. China is uncompromisingly, pragmatically and strategically sociopathic. What a mind-blowing assessment and profile. The CCP's and Xi's China are sociopathic, left hemisphere Mr Hyde on super-steroids.

Mr Hyde — Then and Now

There is no dignity or decency in political, economic, technological and military sociopathy. The murderous tyranny of 20th century Nazism and Communism, and Russia's 21st century murderous war, have shown us that unchecked, unrelenting personal and political sociopathic ambition obliterates dignity, decency and integrity. China's and Russia's sociopathic intentions are a clear and present threat to decency and dignity on a scale not seen since the egoic madness and murderous tyranny of Nazism and 20th century Cold War Communism. Putin's 21st century Russia is Mr Hyde reborn as a murderous, maniacal left hemisphere maniac. The CCP is Mr Hyde reborn as a Chinese Godzilla juggernaut.

Postscript

Until recently, the vast majority of the malignant rich and powerful men and institutions were white Anglo-European-American. In the 2100s, many are Chinese. China's rising machoism may soon surpass powerful wealthy white Western male dominance. Soon, we won't refer the malignant 'white' elite. Whoever the elitists are, it will be the same result for the poor and the powerless, for indigenous peoples, and for the environment. Too soon, the earth may be under new left hemisphere management, but not for the better. China could make previous 'Anglo-European-USA empires', Christianity and Islam look insipid, incidental and inept. Unless a critical mass of the people and nations says "No!", an unprecedented level of global, Hyde-like tyranny may soon emerge.

Does this analysis ring true?

How might the rest of the world respond to the potential rise and rise of China?

How might a critical mass of mindfully decent, integrous and intelligent Chinese people do better than subservience to sociopaths and compliance with sociopathy?

In the meantime, Putin's Russia threatens to catapult the globe into WWIII and nuclear oblivion.

How might a critical mass of decent, intelligent, integrous Russian citizens, leaders and statespersons prevent catastrophe, and restore decency, integrity and sanity?

Postscript Question

What might this problem look like if China and Russia were to cut a deal, and pool their resources?

This is very disconcerting prospect.

How can we, a global critical mass of billions of sane and decent peoples, prevent this?

Yours and My Place in Big Picture Issues and Future Possibilities

Macro and micro problem definition and issues analysis are complete. Hooray!

From this point onward, we will explore how you and I can nurture micro priorities, principles and values; how can we nurture, build and proliferate core values such as dignity and rationality. We will explore how a prioritised and elevated system of right hemisphere values can liberate and empower 'us everyday people' in our roles as local and global citizens, custodians and leaders.

This book doesn't ask you and me to try to manufacture solutions. But it does ask us to be informed, aware, dignified, rational, integrous, engaged, constructive and accountable in family, friendships, at work and business; and in our local and global community, citizenry, custodian and leadership roles and responsibilities. This book asks us to consider and participate in constructive alternatives to religious conservatism, fundamentalism and extremism, sociopathic political Machiavellianism, cultist populist madness, commercial media madness and inane social media inanity. What a sick and dangerous mix of sociopathic and narcissistic bedfellows.

My hope and aspiration are that we humans will mindfully and actively strive to be the best we can be through life-giving, lived-values; and through strategic, rational intelligence. My desire is for us humans to aspire to evolve a critical mass of Yin-based emotional intelligence, critical thinking, integrity and accountability as our chief standards, priorities, intentions and guides for us as family members, workers, professionals, citizens, stewards, custodians, leaders and elders.

What might your roles be in these hopes, aspirations and priorities?

The Companion Workbook will help you respond to this invitation.

Dignity, Reason and Character — In Contrast to Ego

The next three chapters will shift our thinking from global macro issues — to micro individual, personal and relational issues and opportunities. The purpose of these few chapters is to ground you and I in dignity and rationality at personal and relational levels by presenting four real-life characters. One of these is a person of ego. The other three are persons of mindfulness through conscious dignifying values and rationality.

Our egoic person is defined by typical, 'modern' egoic ambition and self-promotion. He is intelligent, ambitious and capable; but lacks the dignity of sensitivity, and is noticeably prone to ends-driven ethics. The other three people are mindful exemplars of principle, sensitivity, decency, integrity, critical thinking and accountability. These three people are humble, gracious, intelligent, impeccably ethical, very capable and highly accomplished.

The profiles below contrast typical modern-day egoic, masculine bluster, against the rarity of dignified, sensitive, rational, gracious, integrous, unassuming, mindful efficacy. The profiles also contrast questionable and egoic character against conscious, integrous depth of character. These contrasts highlight two starkly different ways of being in the world of relationships, work and community; the sensitive, integrous mindful way in contrast to egoic way of relative unawareness, insensitivity and situational ethics.

Bill – A Person of Ego

Here is our example of an egoic person whose groundedness, awareness, sensitivity, dignity and integrity were somewhat compromised because of his overriding egoic left hemisphere drives to appear clever, important, influential and successful.

Years ago, I worked with a fellow whom I will call Bill. He often told thinly veiled self-aggrandising stories. Bill often fantasised and overstated the results of his work. This gentleman was what my colleagues called a 'FIGJAM'; meaning — "fuck I'm good, just ask me".

Bill was quite oblivious to his patterns of fantasising, overstating and thinly-veiled boasting. Bill automatically assumed that people loved hearing him talk about himself; about 'his' amazing ideas, superior expertise and spiritual enlightenment. He was also blissfully unaware that many saw him as loose-with-truth and prone to put himself an excessively good light. And yet, Bill often talked about values such as mindfulness, awareness, honesty and integrity. People would say: "He's a really bright guy, but I'm not sure that I trust him". There was a question mark over Bill's character, his personal insight and his skewed grasp of reality. But Bill was so caught up in his imagined, self-advancing grandiose story that he was unaware of why people reacted to him with caution. He had a vague idea that he put people offside, but didn't know how or why. I think Bill assumed that he was rational, brilliant, right and righteous; and that we lesser beings couldn't quite get his genius and enlightenment.

Many people observed incongruities between Bill's espoused values and the pattern of his behaviours and actions. People commented behind his back, but few dared to openly disagree with Bill; nor to challenge his self-assertions and questionable behaviours. Occasionally, when someone questioned him, gave feedback or challenged Bill, he reacted defensively and argumentatively. Bill could be belligerently self-justifying. Bill was always right; and often, was aggressively righteous. Bill assessed those who disagreed with him as unenlightened and/or as jealous of his ability and success.

For Bill, humility, self-awareness and resistance to collegial accountability were barriers to achieving his lifelong desire to be admired as brilliant and successful. Bill was desperate to be exceptional. He was desperate to be authoritative and famous in his field of endeavour. Bill constantly tried to influence his friends and colleagues to join his confabulated narrative of how impressive he was; and he strongly resisted communication that was contrary to his confabulations, self-image, desires and narratives.

Brilliance and persuasiveness were Bill's left hemisphere substitutes for awareness, grace, sensitivity, integrity and dignity. In Bill's mind, intellectual power and verbal cogency were his salvation from his existential dread of being insignificant and invisible. Pursuit of adulation was his protection from his subconscious fear of not being noticed and venerated. Deep down, Bill dreaded the prospect of being average, ordinary and unremarkable. For him, at a subconscious level, these were tantamount to egoic oblivion as a person, failure as a professional, and invalidation in family and in peer groups.

The Need for Approval

Because we are social creatures, similar to Bill, to some extent, egoically, many of us fear disapproval, invalidation, disqualification and rejection. To be affirmed and included, many of us construct semi-fanciful, self-promoting stories and contrived personas to minimise the risk disapproval, failure, nullification, alienation and exclusion. It is common for us moderners to employ egoic strategies to secure internal and communal confirmation. To some extent, most of us use egoic ploys to present and bolster our left hemisphere value and to seek social and peer validation and inclusion. Typically, egoic ploys include narratives of fantasy, wishful thinking and confabulations.

Internal Locus vs External Locus

It is quite liberating when you and I identify the unnecessary sham of our egoic approval-seeking confabulations, narratives and ploys. When we identify and own our fanciful, self-promoting manoeuvres, there is the possibility of distancing ourselves from our mind-made egoic self-contrivances. And, with insight, there is hope that we can move toward an unforced, uncontrived 'internal locus of authenticity'. When this happens, the approval-seeking voices and stories of ego become less dominant. Pretending, posturing and performing tend to subside as our egoic approval-seeking personas and ploys abate. When our externally-referenced ego abates, there is potential for an internal locus of reality, authenticity, peace, contentment and joy to arise.

The stronger our internal locus of right hemisphere confirmation, the less we need external, worldly, egoic substitutes; such as wanting friends and peers joining our fanciful, self-promoting success-stories of brilliance, achievements, materiality, wealth and/or power. Internal confirmation is closely related to personal and relational authenticity, and is the essence of depth of character. When you and I see ourselves through the confirming eyes of 'an internal locus of grace' we can recognise our inherent, innate quality. With an intuitive or deeply-felt awareness of grace, we can accept and embrace ourselves as we are;

including our mix of assets, quirks and shortcomings; warts and all, as the saying goes.

With the confirmation of an internal locus of grace, we don't need to contrive or conjure or fantasise an impressive external persona in order to establish or prove our desired value or standing. When we don't need to perform, we don't need to make up convincing, self-promoting narratives, rationalisations and justifications. Joy of joys, we can stop fearing, doubting, fantasising, contriving, telling, selling, spinning, convincing, defending and compensating. An 'internal locus of character' can emerge when our compensating, self-promoting egoic left hemisphere stories fade; and when externally-referenced performances and personas abate.

In the absence of self-promoting fantasies and stories — peaceful internal confirmation and grace-imbued depth of character can become our way of right hemisphere engaging with the world of family, friendships, work and community. Internal confirmation can free us from the stress and angst of contriving reality and earning acceptance through imagined external measures of left hemisphere justification, achievement and success.

Internal confirmation and depth of character are our best options to being grounded in grace, that is, in the reality, peace, contentment and fulfilment in our own skin. Authentic, internal confirmation is an honest, peaceful, dignified and confident foundation for enjoying relationships and pursuing endeavours. Authentic, grounded internal confirmation is a positive driver to relate, participate and work peacefully and effectively. Internal, grace-derived confirmation and internally-inspired depth of character give us the potential to leave a legacy of respectful, mutual relationships, groundedness, fine achievements and good deeds; the combination of which arise from a blend of unforced peace, reality, awareness, goodwill, dignity, sensitivity, integrity and competence. This blend is a superb foundation for all relationships, roles and endeavours.

Back to Bill

But, an abiding internal-grace-locus of intrapersonal confirmation eluded Bill, and undermined his capacity for insight, reality, peace and achievement. As said before, just slightly below the surface, Bill was a very insecure person who habitually compensated for self-doubt and fear of ordinariness. He compensated by defaulting to self-aggrandising fantasises; including exaggerated claims about himself as a highly evolved person, and as a superior professional. All this worked against him personally, relationally and professionally. There was potential for irony to reveal this situation, because Bill talked a lot about mindfulness; but he refused to be silent, to listen, to be sensitively self-aware, and to be gently aware of others.

The paradox was that all Bill's effort was unnecessary. He was very intelligent, an original thinker, creative and innovative; and, he was often well-intended. He was very good at what he did. But this was not enough for his insecure, fantasising, over-compensating, externally-referenced ego. And that's what the egoic mind is: fantastical, insecure, externally-referenced and endlessly compensating for ill-conceived, arbitrarily illusory measures of personhood. Ego has no awareness of the unforced ease, acceptance and confirmation of grace. Ego knows about fear, insecurity, compensation and effort; but not about the unearned embrace of grace.

In desperation, Bill convinced himself that to be okay he had to be enlightened and successful. He proffered a fantasised persona and exaggerated wisdom and ability, in order to achieve popularity, adoration, glory and fame. The reality was that he was already a very capable and highly talented. Bill worked against himself through unnecessary, self-sabotaging left hemisphere delusions of grandeur that became thinly-veiled narcissism. The fantastical grandiosity of narcissism is thinly-veiled egoic desperation. Hunger for grandiosity is a symptom of over-compensating masculinised egoic desperation. This hunger is very common for us Yang-conditioned moderners who are almost entirely unaware of the grace of Yin-mindfulness.

Bill was too busy blowing his own trumpet to discern or intuit the resonance and confirmation of an internal Yin locus of grace, dignity and character. His was oblivious to the reality that fanciful Yang bluff-and-bluster were unnecessary, unbecoming, undignified and unhelpful. And so, Bill substituted boasting and inflated claims-to-fame as egoic facades for a grounded, peaceful internal locus of confirmation and authentic awareness. He substituted presumption and pretention for realistic, peaceful trust in his capacities, and for the ease of humility.

Alas, the ease and peace of grace eluded Bill. At the same time, his default to overcompensate was inherently self-diminishing and self-sabotaging. This sort of unhelpful, fanciful, masculine egoic try-hard stuff is very common. It is the 'way of the modern masculine egoic world' in which we work and play.

Commonly, fanciful, egoic try-hard stuff is the way of the contemporary masculinised egoic mind.

Parallels Between Bill and Us

In our various ways, and to varying degrees, most of us are like Bill. We are deeply impacted by aspects of our family background and a range of egoic developmental and environmental influences. All of us are greatly conditioned by peer groups and work relationships. Under the sway of an array of worldly influences, we take-on and intensify masculine egoic beliefs, opinions, ideals, wishes, wants, hopes and behaviours. Under the sway of the various masculine egoic cultures in which we are immersed, we try to compensate for unawareness of the confirmation that is inherent in an internal locus of mindful, sentient grace and dignity.

Ironically, we decompensate through our habitual left hemisphere over-compensation. This means that, all too often, our efforts to achieve and impress, work against us and undermine us, not for us. Unwittingly, we diminish and sabotage ourselves by concocting whims and fantasies, by inventing personas, by over-performing, and by acting-out confabulated narratives and roles that we mistakenly intuit will impress those whom we want to like us, approve us, include us, and recommend us. All this typical of the masculinised left hemisphere ego; in men and women.

Fantasised and imagined externalities are our substitutes for internal confirmation of grace and dignity that are inherent in all persons; in men and women. Thankfully, grace and dignity also don't play favourites. They are ubiquitous. Grace and dignity are a level playing field. All of us, women and men, can enjoy the peace, joy and freedom of a right hemisphere internal locus of grace and dignity.

However, we act out egoically because we do not intuit, discern or feel the inherent confirmation of simply being a peaceful, gracious, dignified and integrous person. In the absence of atunement with inner confirmation, we default to various egoic dispositions; including, seeking approval, favour, advantage, influence, popularity, position, profit, power and control. Look at yourself and those around you. Look at our religious, political and corporate worlds. Do you see these egoic compensations at play; in men and women?

Egoic Roles

Common examples of compensatory egoic left hemisphere fantasies, aspirations and roles that we fall into, include: powerful politician, champion sportsperson, brilliant student, accomplished professional, successful business person, high-status executive, admired public figure, important community member, amazing parent, superb lover, loyal friend, wonderful son or daughter. The list of compensatory egoic roles and defaults is endless. We do our best to act out assumed personas, and to perform our roles sincerely, faithfully and effectively.

But, often, they are in compensation for unawareness of the validation of right hemisphere grace dignity and character. We can be a terrific person and achieve amazing outcomes 'from the inside out'; that is, from an internal locus personhood. We don't need to make up personas and act out roles to compensate for who we misperceive are not. Nor do we need to perform to compensate, and/or to perform to impress and earn approval and inclusion. Contrary to the assumptions and ways of ego, we don't need to 'sing for our psychological supper'; and certainly not for our spiritual supper.

'Singing for our supper' is compensatory left hemisphere stuff. In it, our unconscious masculinised egoic hope is that we will somehow perform well enough to be 'good enough' in the eyes of those who we want to impress. Our subconscious hope is that our scripts, personas, roles and achievements will win the acceptance and inclusion of the people whose 'judgements' are pivotal to our identity and personhood. Almost undetectably, the very common, underlying egoic left hemisphere hope is that if we perform well-enough, we will be approved in the social domains of family, friendships, peer groups, professions, work and society.

Striving for imagined egoic left hemisphere validation is an extremely common modern-day existential malaise. Approval-focussed pursuits of the Yang ego are a universal, modern-day distraction from the internal peace of graceful sensitivity, awareness and integrity. Egoic-drivenness blinds us to the beauty and ease of graceful internal locus of authenticity, simplicity, contentment and gratitude. Egoic drivenness distracts us from the inherent dignity and grace that we were born with.

All impression management, identity management, posturing, status seeking and power agendas are the work of worldly, egoic, compensatory left hemisphere thought patterns. All of these are counterfeits and substitutes for an inner sense of right hemisphere grace, dignity, reason and character. All are arduous substitutes for the ease and joy of simplicity, contentment and gratitude. All approval seeking is 'the way of our man-made egoic world'; in which, and by which, we are immersed, conditioned and programmed. In this stuff, each and all of us are products of egoic priorities. Unless we are aware of and choose an internal locus of dignity, your egoic-mind and my egoic-mind will be extensions and copies of the man-made egoic world by which we are conditioned; and in which, unawares, we too-easily become absorbed, enmeshed and consumed.

The Individual Ego and the Ways of the World

The individual ego and 'the ways of the world' are opposite sides of the same left hemisphere coin; they are enmeshed as one. Each person's ego and the egoic world are 100% enmeshed, 100% mutually co-dependent. The masculine ego and the masculine world are the co-authors of a web of personal and collective left hemisphere arbitrary, fanciful stories and narratives. Bill was enmeshed with the masculine egoic ethos of family, workplace, society and world. In the decades I have known Bill, he never found a way through his egoic left hemisphere maze, nor a way out of his imagined, confabulated, self-aggrandising, compensating egoic left hemisphere stories. The best Bill can do is to wander from chapter to chapter of his self-written masculine egoic fiction. The best he can do is to haplessly reinvent himself as the main character in an unfolding assortment of self-aggrandising fantasies, claims, narratives and roles.

But — To No Avail

All egoic left hemisphere roles, stories, claims and narratives are to no avail, because sentience, grace, dignity and character cannot be found in the masculinised stories, posturing, performances, fictions and left hemisphere fantasies of ego and world. Right hemisphere, Yin sentience, grace, dignity and character are felt in the depths of sentient intuition; and in quiet, still, mindful, meditative discernment. They are felt and discerned when mindfulness and faith quieten the desperate blustering of our masculinised-egoic-mind. Intuiting and discerning grace and faith is evidenced through the outworking of a right hemisphere internal locus of a peace, authenticity, simplicity, contentment, gratitude and joy.

Faith is a peaceful, mindful state. Faith is a way of thinking, speaking, acting and living from a base of unforced peace and presence. Grace is experienced as an absence of fear, guilt, shame and judgement toward oneself and others. We become the completed package when we look inside and see and trust the right hemisphere imbuements and core values of who we are and what we do. A network of other liberating and empowering values will automatically arise when values and rationality are the silent, internal grace-faith-reference of our consciousness and existence. These right hemisphere internalities and values have nothing to do with espoused religions or new-age beliefs or spirituality. Internal values are the fruit of mindful graceful and faithful awareness and sensitivity.

Feel and embrace an internal right hemisphere network of mindful, graceful, faithful, peaceful, confirming values within yourself.

The person profiled in the next chapter shows us the possibility of an internal locus of grace, faith and values; and an internal locus of quiet, peaceful, gracious rationality and groundedness. This man consciously embraced a Yin orientation; and consciously stepped away from a Yang orientation.

Alan — A Person of Character, Grace and Dignity

Let's have a brief look at a peaceful, graceful contrast to Bill's futile egoic left hemisphere posturing and touting. Let's look at a profile of Alan — a mindful, soulful and reverent person of right hemisphere faith, grace, dignity, reason and character; within whom sentience is strong and ego is minimal. Note the inverse relationship between sentience and ego. When sentience is prominent, ego falls silent. The same relationship exists between mindfulness and ego, grace and ego, faith and ego, dignity and ego. When any of these is conscious, ego abates. Ego decreases most when a network of these inner states is unpretentiously and unobtrusively present. This the essence of mindful, peaceful, humble confidence. Alan exemplifies a network of values. They are his 'internal locus of personhood'; his internal locus of who he is and what he says and does.

Alan was a long-term executive manager in a not-for-profit organisation. During the almost-forty years I have known Alan, he has always been calm, sensitive, peaceful, clear-minded, non-judgemental, and deeply aware. Alan lives a quiet, unassuming faith. He is gently and unobtrusively devoted to his experience of family, work and community. Alan is unwaveringly committed to stewardship, leadership and service. He is comfortable and peaceful in his own skin. Alan consciously and consistently dignifies and respects his family, colleagues, friends and those whom he serves and leads. He has much to give, little to say, and nothing to prove. Reread the previous sentence. Alan shows us faith through sentience, peace, presence and a conscious, internal orientation toward trust in the midst of what is. He shows us how to be gracious and graceful, dignified and dignifying; from the inside-out.

Alan is naturally and calmly rational and quietly confident. He is very comfortable with a wide variety of people, and with humanity as a whole. Alan is gracious toward human frailty; his own and others. He is widely confirming and widely confirmed. Alan is deeply and sincerely personable. He is a peaceful and highly competent as a husband, father, friend, citizen, practitioner, mentor, manager and leader. Alan is widely and highly respected as a steward, statesman and elder in his industry and beyond.

Alan is a normal, wise, humorous, capable and grounded human being. This is because he is attuned to the integrity and compassion that flows from depth of character. Alan embraces the oneness of dignity and grace within himself and others. He sees the oneness of dignity and grace within humankind. He is peacefully at home in the world, but clearly not moulded by its egoic influences. Alan is a person of ease and trust; not of the effort of egoic struggling and striving. He seems not to have a story. Alan doesn't need to hear the sound of his own voice. He epitomises the saying: 'still waters run deep'. Alan is the quintessential quiet, unpretentious achiever.

All this amounts to the quintessence of right hemisphere orientation. Alan is a right hemisphere person.

Alan is a rarity, not because he was born special or gifted, but because, for decades, in a multitude of domains, relationships and roles, he mindfully — purposefully and consistently discerned, chose, embraced, internalised, prioritised, was faithful to, and was grounded in — awareness, sensitivity, integrity, grace, rationality, kindness and generosity.

In decades of work in the helping professions, I have only met a few people with Alan's depth of presence, grace, clarity and character. It seems that a mindful, internal locus dignity and reason is 'the road less travelled'. Mindful sentience and presence of Alan's ilk are relatively rare in today's fanciful, blustering, presumptuous, pretentious, try-hard, pontifical, religious and new-age neoliberal, political, economic, commercial, transactional, material, mechanical, technological, social media, conspiratorial world. This paragraph is worth rereading.

Imagine and envisage an internal locus of sentience, presence, grace, faith and dignity.

What can you and I can learn from Alan that can help us do better?

For now, breathe, and sit in silence and feel the peaceful, joyful unassuming inner resonance of grace and dignity.

Allow these qualities to trickle to surface as awareness, sensitivity, kindness, respect and integrity.

Michael and Joan

Here is one more example of peaceful, humble, capable everyday right hemisphere role models.

Michael and Joan have been married for about 35 years. They are mindful — values-based people; humble, unobtrusive, gracious, welcoming and inclusive. For decades Michael and Joan have been my role models of personal dignity, and of dignity in relationship.

At about age 40, after 25 years in a trade, Michael became a massage therapist. While developing his profession, Michael studied other modalities. He also looked closely at a bunch of research, and eventually synthesised a sophisticated approach to body-work that he hoped would be very effective at treating structural issues that are difficult to remedy. Over years, Michael increased his theoretical knowledge, and refined the practical application of his steadily emerging expertise.

Because of the efficacy of Michael's model, more and more practitioners became curious about his evolving expertise. Michael decided to develop his model into a training program. A few workshops lead to many. Soon, there was a flood of requests for him to train physiotherapists and other practitioners in Australia, and internationally. The rest is history. His teaching and consulting roles grew rapidly.

Michael is a superb role model for all of us. He is a humble, mindful man who is guided by an array of interlinking right hemisphere values and qualities — including — dignity, intelligence, grace, vision, drive, creativity, analytical thinking, integrity, humility, self-confidence, aspiration, openness, patience, persistence, resilience and wisdom. Note this balanced mix of attributes; some soft, some strong, some intellectual, some theoretical, some clinical, some of character, some of professionalism, and some are visionary and aspirational. In his late sixties, Michael is a mentor, leader and statesman in his profession. With all this, he remains unpretentious, grounded and modest. From his blend of right hemisphere values and attributes, Michael achieves a high level of success in community service, in clinical practice, and in business. While ever-gracious and dignified, Michael is not a pushover or submissive. He is clear about his guiding values, and about his boundaries.

In all this, wonderfully, Michael is not highfalutin; he is an ordinary, everyday Australian man. With all his insight, learning, personal development, effort, professional standing and success, Michael is a person of authenticity, simplicity, contentment, gratitude and peace. He is internally referenced by a clear and congruent network of priorities, principles, processes, values and aspirations.

Michael and Joan love and respect each other. They are peaceful as individual persons, and in their marriage. They rejoice in each other, and in what they share. Michael and Joan confirm and support each other. Conscious, intentional values guide their personal and shared attitudes, aspirations, discernments, choices, life-direction, relationship and sense of community. Michael and Joan do this with 'delightful ordinariness'. In this, they are role models of what it is to be relatively free from the fantasy, fear, insecurity, pretention and over-compensation that are so often seen in today's worldly, egoic left hemisphere struggling and striving.

What are the key learnings for you from Michael and Joan?

Alan, Bill, Michael and Joan — Four Excellent Role Models

Many family members, friends and colleagues are my teachers. Politicians, business persons, sportspeople, journalists and criminals are my teachers. Many have shown me who and what I don't want to be and do. A diversity of people has helped me discern who, what and how I want to be and do. Ultimately, they have helped me clarify my preference and aspiration to be a gracious person of dignity, sensitivity, integrity and accountability. When I encounter grace and mindfulness, I feel peaceful; and I feel the joy of being human. When I encounter grounded, mindful people, I feel the ease and joy of internal authenticity, simplicity, contentment and gratitude. Consciously and purposefully, I draw close to clear-minded, gracious people. I observe them, listen to them, ask open enquiring questions, and absorb their disposition and wisdom.

Alan, Michael and Joan

The example of Alan, Michael and Joan teach me a lot about the ease, joy, peace and freedom of mindful right hemisphere humility, dignity, character, integrity, and 'grace under pressure'. Significantly, they rarely 'tell' me anything. Unless asked, these three rarely talk about themselves, their knowledge, aspirations and accomplishments. All three are consistently truly present, humble, gracious and graceful; as friends, fellow professionals and fellow-earthly human travellers. In various ways, they role-model sentience, purpose and strength of character. Their intuitive and mindful expressions of this blend of right hemisphere qualities and capacities is what I have alluded to as 'soulfulness'. Soulfulness is mostly unspoken. It is not about having a soul. But is 'mindfully lived' — mostly unspoken, gentle, unassuming — presence, sentience, awareness, listening, connection, discernment and wisdom.

384

By their example, Alan, Michael and Joan show me that — it is possible to be content with simplicity, to be present in relationship; to be focussed in service, stewardship and leadership; to be satisfied with modest materiality; to be aspirational, but to be free from the lure of selfish ambition and narcissistic aggrandisement; and, to be peaceful and present in the midst of turmoil and stress. Alan, Michael and Joan show me that it's possible to be consistently gracious, dignified, calm, reasoned, prioritised, purposeful, committed, disciplined and effective in a range of domains, roles and endeavours. These three human companions show me the mindful, soulful road least travelled; not by what any of them say, but by walking it, for decades. Alan, Michael and Joan are three of a handful of role models who help me discern the contrast between the soulful right hemisphere ease and the drivenness and futility of masculinised egoic left hemisphere struggling and striving.

Bill

As amazing as Alan, Michael and Joan are, Bill is probably one of my best teachers. Bill teaches me that people see right through egoic blustering and the futility of fanciful, wilful, noisy compensation. He shows me that my insecure, doubt-based, fear-driven efforts to impress, are smoke screens. Bill shows me that clever explanations and impassioned justifications don't fool many people. And, most crucially, wilful, noisy compensation doesn't nurture an internal locus confirmation, depth of character, and the discernment of grace and dignity. The Bills of this world show me that unaware, insightless, fear-driven compensatory effort only digs us deeper and deeper into an egoic pit.

Bill and those of similar egoic ways, show me that we don't fool many people by presuming, posturing and pretending; nor by blustering, pontificating and boasting. We don't become more complete through self-promoting fanciful, grandiose, ambitious endeavours and forced worldly success. The opposite is more likely. This is because, in our pretentious, self-serving worldly striving, we tend to lose ourselves in the narcissism, obsessiveness and dishonesty that are inherent in the politics and power-plays of chasing egoic worldly success and accolades. And, pretentious, self-serving, egoic worldly striving also tends to stymie our potential quality, credibility, standing, service and leadership.

Usually, there is only one person who is taken in by egoic fantasising and bullshitting, and that is the one who is trying to sell the sham. Often, the person telling the stories and spinning the narratives is the only one who believes them.

Others smile politely and think, "whatever". In Australia, we refer to egoic, self-deceived story-tellers as bullshitters, wankers and dickheads. Harsh, but apt.

Teachers, Role Models and Exemplars in Your Life and My Life

I have rubbed shoulders with thousands of Bills; but only a handful of people of the right hemisphere ilk of Alan, Michael and Joan. Nevertheless, rational, values-based exemplars and role models are out there. When you come upon mindful, soulful persons of grace, dignity and reason, they are gold in your life. Draw close to them. Be silent. Observe their stillness, sentience, values and character. Absorb their ethos. Learn from their example. When you encounter the Bills of the world, try not to judge them. From them, learn what not to say and do, how not to fantasise, pretend, posture and perform. From them, learn what and who not to be.

Feel free to pause and reflect.

Reflect on Bill. Can you identify aspects of egoic compensation and futility in yourself?

Reflect on the mindful, soulful example of Alan, Michael and Joan.

Can you imagine or sense the possibility of intuiting the peace and ease of an internal locus of grace, dignity and reason?

Can you envisage blending the disciplines of factfulness and critical thinking with the unobtrusive, quiet, gentle discernments and mindfulness of faith, grace and dignity?

This is a classic head-heart blend.

Another Exemplar and Role Model

Let's read about another real-life exemplar of grace, dignity and integrity.

Uncle Bob

Here is a true story that has the potential to help you recognise, choose and nurture right hemisphere grace, dignity, integrity and rationality.

When my dad died in 1964, Uncle Bob, his younger brother, stepped-in and raised us kids; Rob then 16, Margaret 12, and myself, 9. Uncle Bob fulfilled a wartime promise to look after Dad's family if anything should happen to him. Uncle was a living example of the principle that 'the greatest love is to give your life' — to put aside your ambitions, wishes and wants; to give your time; to give your money; to give all you have for family, friends and strangers. This true story of love and giving will unfold over the next six pages.

Uncle Bob didn't marry. And, after Dad died, he gave up his desire to return to farming. Uncle secured a job as a clerk in the federal public service to ensure a reliable income with which to support his adopted family. Uncle Bob put aside all his hopes and plans so he could devote himself to his brother's children. He also supported my Mum financially. This is how my uncle loved his brother, and his brother's children.

What Uncle Bob did was far from easy. Mum resented his presence. She struggled with depression and the effects of a traumatic — abusive, repressive and destabilised childhood. Mum was not able to provide our parenting and financial needs. Uncle Bob saw this, and, as unobtrusively as possible, he brought wisdom, perspective, good judgement and financial stability to our family. Uncle Bob respected Mum, and did his best to show her dignity and empathy. Nevertheless, the politics between mum and uncle was always tricky; and often, was strained.

In the face of an awkward and tense situation, Uncle Bob was very clear about his priorities for his surrogate children. He maintained clarity and purpose with unswerving grace and wisdom. Uncle considered and respected Mum, while focusing on what was best for us kids. With hindsight, I can see that his judgement, leadership and long-term priorities were entirely appropriate and necessary.

What is even more amazing, is that, year upon year, Uncle's 'grace and dignity under pressure' showed his depth and strength of character. Uncle Bob was an ordinary man of extraordinary commitment to a few key right hemisphere values. In tandem with values, his sense of priority was clear, rational and uncompromising; but was never forceful or harsh. Uncle Bob was often firm, but never disrespectful. The more I think about that, the more amazed and awed I am. Uncle Bob is my 'Gunga Din'; the one who showed me exceedingly rare clarity, reason, purpose, strength of character, and constancy of dignity and grace under pressure.

The previous paragraph is a snapshot of the essence of Can We Do Better. It describes on ordinary person showing extraordinary character through right hemisphere values and rationality. Not through brilliance or great skill, but through clarity and consistent application of priorities, principles and values. Pay attention this theme throughout this chapter.

Uncle's formal education was meagre. He left school after Grade Seven. But Uncle was an avid reader, a keen observer, and a thinker. The bulk of his work was as a farmer. Uncle Bob survived the deprivations of the great depression by eating meagre produce from his farm, and by hunting rabbits. He was content to have a roof over his head and sufficient to eat. In 1939 Uncle Bob and Dad enlisted in the army and served in active duty for the six years of WWII.

For decades after the war, Uncle Bob suffered from depression and PTSD. When I was a child and young teenager, Uncle and I shared a room. Many nights I woke him from nightmares about the war. Uncle accepted his mental illness with dignity and resilience. He was philosophical about life's challenges and adversities. Uncle Bob also minimised his dispositions to gambling and alcoholism that he acquired during the war. It was very rare for him to relapse; and never in ways that impacted on the family.

This true story of Uncle Bob shows you and me that 'ordinary frail people' can also be exemplars of right hemisphere grace, dignity, awareness, reason, discipline and integrity. Through these qualities, Uncle was an edifying and enriching role model. Throughout my adult and middle-aged years, Uncle Bob's example enabled me to make sense of decades of study and the application of spirituality and psychology; at home, at work and in our local and global human communities.

Uncle Bob's physical health was poor. He had smoked since he was child. In 1965 he was diagnosed with pulmonary fibrosis; which had severely affected one his lungs. Soon after diagnosis he had surgery to remove a large part of the badly affected lung. This greatly reduced his physical robustness. Uncle Bob was in constant pain, was short of breath, and was prone to infections; such as pneumonia. In the midst of these difficulties, he had only one priority — to live long enough to raise his brother's children. I never witnessed any hint of self-pity, victimhood, regret or resentment. Uncle Bob suffered his ailments with poise, cheerfulness and resilience. Another wonderful combination of right hemisphere qualities in a simple, ordinary man.

This longish paragraph is a summary of the family dynamics that Uncle Bob had to navigate. During Rob's teenage and young-adult years, he resented but tolerated Uncle's presence. Rob coped by joining a surf lifesaving club so he could be away from home as much as possible. Uncle Bob empathised with Rob and respected his choice to distance himself from the family. Many times, Uncle stood between Rob and me. Rob was easily infuriated by his annoying little brother, and was prone to lashing out. Marg was not close to Mum, but adored Uncle Bob. She sheltered under his gentle, calm wisdom. Marg needed guidance to deal with tense family dynamics, and to parry the advances a string of would-be boyfriends. Mum resented that Marg turned to Uncle Bob for advice. Marg's relationship with Mum was strained. This created a difficult, triangulated tension. I was an 'Attention Deficit Disorder' (ADD) kid, whose misdirected energy got me into plenty of trouble; at home and at school. Looking back, it seems that I struggled to make sense of Dad's death and Mum's depression. As a child and a teenager, it seemed to me that mum didn't care that Dad died. I couldn't understand why she was sullen, resentful and angry much of the time. Mum didn't have anyone to turn to; she was isolated within the family. One image I have of Mum is her sitting on the edge of her bed, staring at the floor, and smoking. Anger, frustration and sadness defined Mum. It also defined us three kids. Rob and I channelled our anger into sport. After she left school, Marg, a champion sprinter, didn't have a sporting outlet for her anger. She became a dedicated nurse and channelled her mental and emotional energy into work. Thankfully, anger did not define Uncle Bob. He was mostly calm and clear in the midst of our very tricky, and often tense family dynamics; and in the face of his ongoing post-war mental and physical health issues.

In the midst of family machinations, Uncle Bob was clear about his priority to be a positive role model for Rob, Marg and me. He was consistently present, patient, measured, generous and wise. Through these lived-right-hemisphere-values, Uncle Bob was an exemplar of respect and reason. Looking back, I am amazed at Uncle's foresight. He persuaded the Department of Veteran Affairs to finance a War Widow's loan in Mum's name to purchase a home in crime-free suburb. He did this to move us out of a high-crime Housing Commission area, that was a safety risk for Marg, and a crime risk for me. The home loan was in mum's name, but Uncle Bob made the payments until he retired, soon after I finished high school. For almost ten years, Uncle brought much-needed stability to our family.

Uncle Bob directed my boundless childhood and adolescent energy into sport, fishing and camping. I ran, swam, surfed, played footy and cricket, fished and camped. Uncle bought a small boat, a tent and some basic camping gear. We fished most weekends and camped on long-weekends, and during school holidays. This was a perfect channel for my 'often-misguided energy'. Uncle Bob also helped me with schoolwork and steered me toward some routine in my study. Typical of kids with ADD, I had difficulty focussing on school work; and struggled academically. Uncle supported me with structure, but did not pressure or judge. From time to time, he said: "You'll be okay; you'll fall on your feet and find your way". This was his 'positive self-fulfilling prophesy' for me. This was Uncle Bob's unwavering right hemisphere faith in the unfolding of a child and teenager who is guided supported by a consistent and congruent ethos of confirmation, support and firm, respectful guidance.

Uncle Bob was absolutely correct. I fell on my feet. As a young adult, I found my intelligence, focus, discipline and maturity. Ultimately, I completed two university degrees, gained a bunch of other minor qualifications and professional accreditations, and worked in a range of helping-profession and managerial roles over several decades. Considering my poor school performance and behavioural issues, no one could have imagined that I would succeed at university, or in a professional career. Uncle Bob trusted when others (family members and teachers) judged and despaired. He dignified me, and reasoned with me; when, otherwise, dignity and reason were in short supply. Again, this is extraordinary for 'an uneducated bachelor farmer' with no prior parenting experience. Uncle Bob was able to do this because he was guided by loving right hemisphere values, reason, clear priorities, unwavering purposeful intentions, and faithfulness to his purpose.

Again — unwavering clarity about priorities, principles and values.

From time to time, Uncle Bob also supported elderly and sick family members by making room for them in our small house. We all fitted; and it just worked. During my high school years, uncle also supported a few of my school mates whose families were in turmoil. Uncle Bob made room in our home for lads who needed brief respite from family conflict and dysfunctional parents. One schoolmate lived with us for almost many months in our final year of high school. I have stayed in touch with these chaps over the decades since our school years. When we catchup, they often express their gratitude for Uncle Bob's simple, unpretentious kindness and generosity. Uncle paid for all our holidays and treats. He always included my friends, and never did so begrudgingly. Again, always with grace and generosity. Uncle Bob didn't judge, and was consistently inclusive. These are more examples of his intuitive wisdom; and of his 'reason and values in action'.

Uncle Bob and I talked lots while fishing and camping. We processed family and kid stuff. He told me stories from his childhood, his family, the farm, the Great Depression, and the war. We hung out inseparably for almost a decade until I finished high school. After high school, I started work, and then went to university; and Uncle Bob retired to his dream-shack on Hope Island, near the Gold Coast. His promise to my dad was fulfilled. Us kids were safe and getting on with life as responsible, self-sufficient adults.

Uncle Bob was my mentor and role model well into my young-adulthood. He continued to be unwaveringly patient and present; even when, in the grip of 'the misguided certainty of youth', I became an insensitive and annoying 'fundamentalist religious zealot'; and insulted the beauty of his Anglican spirituality. Thankfully, I realised my insensitivity and ignorance in time to apologise well before he passed away in 1988. Also, luckily, I recognised my insensitivity and judgment toward Mum. I apologised, and we became great friends.

After retirement, Uncle Bob also continued to be a superb father-figure and mentor to Marg, my 'big sister'. Uncle and Rob made their peace and became quite close. Rob, a carpenter, built uncle's modest retirement home. This was Rob's way of saying thanks; and, I love you. Rob's, Marg's and my relationships with Uncle Bob matured to into a grateful awareness of his wisdom, generosity and sacrifice. Now, as a man in my late-sixties, my affection, respect and appreciation for Uncle Bob's character, wisdom, guidance and nurturance continues to deepen.

I don't recall Uncle Bob saying he loved me. He loved Rob, Marg and me with much more than words. He loved us with right hemisphere respect, sensitivity, understanding, patience, perseverance, integrity and wisdom. It was Uncle's profound sense of integrity and reason that motivated his clarity and congruence. Uncle's right hemisphere congruence encompassed a host of positive traits and qualities, including — awareness, presence, sensitivity, constancy, self-sacrifice, respect, empathy, gentleness, generosity, kindness and fairmindedness. With all our many and difficult foibles and issues, Uncle Bob did not judge Mum, Rob, Marg or me. Even when frustrated and perplexed, he always tried to confirm and honour us. Reverence and graciousness were his inmost character. Reverence, grace, dignity and reason were 'who' Uncle was; inmost and foremost. They were the elements of his mindfulness; the elements of his personal and relational intelligence.

Uncle Bob rarely spoke about integrity and character. He never spoke explicitly about grace, dignity and reason. He role modelled them, and unobtrusively nurtured them in his kids. An intuitive, mindful, soulful right hemisphere expression of grace, dignity and reason was the source of Uncle Bob's exceptional reverence, perseverance and resilience in the face of grief, loss, adversity, difficult personalities, family politics, frustrations, ill-health and trauma. Whatever his circumstances, Uncle was clear about his priorities, and lived them with faithfulness, coherence and consistency — from situation to situation, from relationship to relationship, from day to day, and from decade to decade; until he died in his mid-seventies. All who knew Uncle Bob loved and respected him. Many were touched by his quiet, good nature. All were drawn to his simple, unpretentious ordinariness.

Uncle Bob was a devout Anglican. From his experience of religion, he drew right hemisphere elegance, trust, peace, modesty, charity and insight. As with all other domains of his life, Uncle's religious beliefs and experiences coalesced into dignity, grace and integrity. While the circumstances of his life were difficult, this blend of qualities gave Uncle Bob reality, perspective, proportion, priority, compassion, discipline, duty and endurance; all of which are the fruit of his expression of right hemisphere mindfulness. Uncle Bob was a true elder; a very rare gift in family and community. For Uncle Bob, these qualities were both rational and soulful; both reasoned and intuitive. Conscious, pragmatic wisdom and soulful sentience guided all his personal and relational priorities, decisions, choices and actions.

It's no surprise that a blend of right hemisphere values and reason have become the touchstone to which I aspire. The qualities described in this chapter were role modelled by an ordinary, frail and somewhat quirky man. Please, pause, and reread the previous sentence. Note the words: ordinary, frail and quirky. You and I can be ordinary, frail and quirky; while being dignified, gracious, integrous and reasoned at the same time. Frailty and foibles need not be barriers to you and I being clear, sensitive, faithful, integrous and congruent; and being guided by depth and strength of right hemisphere character. Frailty and foibles are inherent in 'the grace of ordinariness'.

How lucky am I? And, how lucky are you, too? You are reading about a real-life example of gracious, dignified personhood at its unegoic, practical, soulful best. For you and me, and for all who read this book, Uncle Bob's example and legacy are an abiding source of right hemisphere clarity, perspective, reality and possibility. Uncle Bob showed me how to blend shadow and grace. He showed me that all I need is unwavering clarity, strategic perspective, faithfulness to values and commitment to accountability. He showed me the right hemisphere peace, joy and fulfilment of simplicity, contentment and gratitude. In this, Uncle Bob helped me to glimpse, intuit and discern right hemisphere faith and grace. And he showed the beauty of unpretentious right hemisphere values, principles and rationality. Uncle Bob showed us that ordinary, quirky people can be kind, generous, humble, rational, wise, disciplined, strong, resilient, enduring and effective.

Sometimes, it rained while Uncle Bob and I were fishing. He would smile and say: "At least no bugger is shooting at us; and, we're catching fish". Uncle had a wonderful way of bringing me back to right hemisphere joy, reality, perspective and priority. My eyes fill with tears of gratitude every time I revisit this chapter. It's no surprise that I spent my working life in the helping professions. And it no surprise that values and rationality are the focus of this book.

Perhaps, reread this beautiful true story about Uncle Bob, then respond to the following question.

What practical priorities and principles have you gleaned for yourself from this chapter?

From Now On — Values and Rationality

If not God, religion, ideology, new-age fantasies and conspiracy theories ... then what?

The answer is simple. All we need to guide personal, local and global human existence is a network of mindfully-chosen right hemisphere values and critical thinking that imbue us with an internal locus of awareness, sensitivity, decency, integrity, responsibility and accountability.

Values and critical thinking can apply equally and fully to one and all — to family members, friends, citizens, workers, students, community leaders, business people, corporate executives, industrialists and politicians. Values and critical thinking can be the common standard, priority and measure of what is appropriate, reasonable and acceptable — for one and all — all persons, relationships, communities, cultures, institutions, nations and the global human collective.

Dignity

The word dignity has been a frequent and prominent strategic priority in Can We Do Better. Dignity has been promoted as a pivotal means and end; as a core principle and a fundamental process. Let me clarify some aspects of what I mean by dignity.

Dignity is central to each person's inherent right hemisphere worth and value. Dignity does not arise from race, nationality, skin colour, religion, culture, political orientation, occupation, wealth, materiality, position, status, role or achievement. Weather obvious to us or not, dignity is innate in each and all. But not all persons, groups and institutions think, speak and act from a place of mindful dignity. Perhaps those who read this book may be more mindful of the innateness and universality of dignity. That is my hope.

Relational and societal right hemisphere dignity is experienced when we exist in safety, kindness, freedom, peace, sufficiency, well-being, mutuality, empowerment, equality and justice. Personal dignity is experienced as right hemisphere awareness, decency, sensitivity, compassion, integrity and accountability. Mindful reverence, inclusion, welcoming and honouring help us feel and discern our inherent dignity; and the inherent dignity of others. There is dignity in simplicity, contentment and gratitude. Right hemisphere dignity is the antithesis of left hemisphere disparagement, judgementalism, prejudice, rejection, exclusion and alienation.

By mindfully embracing dignifying priorities and principles, we can nurture our capacity to moderate negative and destructive egoic tendencies. An inner awareness of dignifying principles stimulates a confirming awareness of self and others; and arouses sensitivity toward self and others. Awareness and sensitivity help facilitate dignity by reducing inclinations to judge, project, criticise, blame and react disparagingly to self and others. They help us to be peaceful, considered and measured toward self, others and situations. The awareness and sensitivities of dignity help us not to act out with negative or harmful attitudes, emotions, behaviours and actions. Awareness and the application of sensitive, reverent, dignifying principles also help us to nurture the reverence, respect and esteem for self and others; including our fellow species and our Mother Earth.

All persons, peoples, species and ecologies are inherently deserving of right hemisphere dignity and reverence. Conscious, intentional, strategic dignity and reverence help us be appropriate and effective in our relationships with each other, with our communities, with our fellow species, with our environments, and with the earth.

A strong, abiding inner awareness, sensitivity and reverence also show up as mindful, dignified right hemisphere citizenship, custodianship, stewardship and leadership. Dignity and reverence serve the common good, and nurture the greater good for one and all. An internal locus of right hemisphere dignity and reverence does not flow from religious or ideological left hemisphere dogma, but from an internal locus of right hemisphere awareness, atunement and sensitivity.

There is much more that could be said about dignity, but this provides sufficient clarity for now.

Reason, Rationality and Critical Thinking
As is the case for dignity, the words reason, rationality and critical thinking

appear many times in this book. They are crucial strategic components of our right hemisphere quest for the common good of the vast majority. As for dignity — reason, rationality and critical thinking are a means and end.

Reason, rationality and critical thinking have repeatedly and strategically been promoted in conjunction with dignity and reverence. My rationale is that these five priorities are inextricably connected; and are core conjoined components of mindful right hemisphere management of human and environmental issues.

Reason and rationality are characterised by aware, honest, informed and disciplined right hemisphere critical thinking — which enables us to intelligently identify, assess and prioritise information, issues, problems, needs, ideas, options, choices, decisions, behaviours, responses, strategies, policies and actions. Reason and rationality are based on awareness and utilisation of the evidence of data, facts, logic and critical analysis. Reason and rationality equip us to strive to optimise mindful objectivity in issues-management and problem-solving in relationships, roles and strategic endeavours.

Reason and rationality can also help us apply mindful — consciously chosen, cogent, values-based and disciplined right hemisphere mental processes. Mindful-critical-thinking is reason and rationality in action. Reasoned and rational critical thinking is process-guided and process-disciplined. It relies on rigorous, logical, analytical processes, with the intention of maximising strategic clarity and objectivity — to maximise outcomes for the common good of the greatest number.

The right hemisphere greater good includes safety, fairness, equality, justice, reverence, dignity, decency, integrity and accountability. The goal and intent of reason and rationality is to nurture and build the common good for the widest possible and most inclusive diversity of persons, peoples, species and environments. As I present them, right hemisphere reason and rationality aren't inherently exclusive, self-leveraging or transactional; but are inherently inclusive, relational, communal and ecological. In all this, reason and rationality are also intended to help us to be mindful — conscious, values-based, values guided, principled, maximally objective, intentional, purposeful and strategic.

Right hemisphere — reasoned and rational critical thinking processes are guided by all the values emphasised throughout this book. My logic and rationale are that a network of right hemisphere values guide and motivate reason and rationality; and, that, reciprocally, reason and rationality guide and motivate values-based, priorities, principles and processes. Reason, rationality and values are mutually inter-dependent, and mutually reinforcing. Woven together, they are mutually and reciprocally mindful. When we nurture, build and reinforce reason and rationality, we automatically and consciously nurture, build and reinforce values-based mindfulness. As is the case for values, there is no place for left hemisphere dogma and ideology in reason and rationality. Decency, integrity and accountability are the means and ends of critical thinking. All right hemisphere critical thinking principles and priorities and all empowering values promote and build the common good for the greatest number.

The Mutuality of Values

Right hemisphere values — including awareness, dignity, reverence, sensitivity, kindness, integrity and accountability — are interconnected and mutually reinforce each other. Each value contributes to the others, and all contribute to one. The interplay and networking of values is inherent in an internal locus of right hemisphere — personhood, relational responsibility, citizenship, custodianship and leadership. This network of values helps us moderate our egoic human disposition toward arbitrariness, selfishness, exclusion and transactionalism. Inter-complementary right hemisphere values help us be purposefully aware, to focus on strategic relational, communal and ecological priorities, and to live constructively and intentionally.

A network of values is the heartbeat of mindfulness. It arises from mindfulness; and nurtures and builds right hemisphere mindfulness. Reasoned-rational, values-based mindfulness gives us humans the capacity and potential to and be better and do better.

For example — simply, crucially and specifically — reasoned, valued based right hemisphere mindfulness can help us be kind — to act in a kindly way toward people, our fellow species, and the planet. A simple, singular, principled, reasoned focus on kindness is fundamentally and radically pragmatically strategic. The inherent dignity and rationality of kindness-in-action can guide us all our attitudes, communication, behaviours and responses to small and large needs, issues and problems. Mindful — reasoned-rational right-hemisphere-kindness-in-action — helps us prioritise and act with maximum intentional, dignity and decency toward people, our fellow species and Mother Earth. Simply and practically — mindful, strategic kindness-in-action can help us discern and create a viable and sustainable right hemisphere future where all are safe and have what we need to exist with dignity, justice and sufficiency on this planet. Without mindful right-hemisphere-kindness-in-action, we humans and our fellow species face a terrible and frightening future due to the ongoing web of left hemisphere unkindness discussed in Chapters 4–7.

A network of mindful and mutually reinforcing values such as kindness, doesn't require left hemisphere dogma, dreamy mystical fantasies or opinionated beliefs. To the contrary, mindful, rational values can help us be aware of and to moderate the pervasiveness of left hemisphere patriarchal dogma and chauvinism. A mindful network of mutually reinforcing, reverencing, dignifying and reasoned values, such as kindness — give us the potential to be consciously, intentionally and purposefully less egoic. That is, a mindfully chosen network of reasoned-kind-right-hemisphere-values-in-action can help us be consciously and strategically inclusive, caring, fair, just and empowering.

Carefully chosen values and conscious rationality aren't perfect or absolute, but they provide us with the potential to prioritise unifying and strategic relational and ecological vision, standards, templates and guides. Unifying strategic right hemisphere values and rationality have the capacity to guide us humans toward respectful, integrous, intelligent awareness; and toward kind and rational choices, policies, actions and accountabilities. The combination of universal values and ubiquitous rationality has the capacity to inspire and guide consciously dignifying and just decisions, priorities, intentions and actions.

Right hemisphere relational, communal and ecological values and rationality are simply a means of highlighting and nurturing empowering strategic — clarity, priorities, vision, purpose, mutuality, perspective, coherence, congruity and harmony.

As emphasised before, the point is that, unifying, strategic values and rationality have the potential to be a universal guide for all humans. Mindful, right hemisphere values and rationality have the potential to be a universal sounding board and a benchmark for all of us. They have the potential to be a yardstick for 'our', for 'all of our', common good. A rational values-based network of priorities can help us focus on and nurture kindness and goodwill toward oneself, friends, strangers, fellow species, and the earth. Strategic, mutual, shared values; plus strategic, mutual shared reason; can lead us to think, speak and act with decency, rationality and efficacy; over and over and over; as often, whenever, wherever; for as long as and what circumstances we need to be accountable for being kind and rational.

A Way Forward

Thus, the mutuality of right hemisphere values and reason gives us humans the potential to lead ourselves out of the mire of our current tired, ailing and failing man-made societal, political, religious and economic models. The mutuality of Yin-based, right hemisphere values and rationality is a viable way forward toward an inclusively just and decent human world. The mindful marriage of values and rationality, is our practical hope, our potential future. Entwined, values and critical thinking, are our guideposts and signposts. A shared internal locus of personal, relational, communal and ecological values is our best hope for a creating and sustaining a safe, kind, peaceful, fair, fulfilling personal relational, ecological and global future. This is the thesis of this book — that right hemisphere values-based decency and rational clarity are our only alternative to the constraints and problems of our individual and collective masculine egoic left hemisphere mind and our egoic left hemisphere world.

My best understanding and conclusion are that mindful values and mindful rationality are our best hope; perhaps our only hope. They are my best recommendation to facilitate societal evolution, and for the healing of the earth. For this reason, the plea of this book is for 'us', for you and me, and a critical mass of us, to nurture a mindfully-chosen network of values and steadfast rationality — within ourselves, within our families, in our relationships, in our workplaces, within and throughout our local communities, within and among our political systems, corporations and industries; and, ultimately, throughout our global community.

My vow, is to commit my remaining days on earth to embrace and apply myself to promoting core values and critical thinking as our most viable ways of being a person and being a local and global community. Values and critical thinking are my preferred, intentional and most recommended way to be human in the 21st century and beyond.

Choose and Embrace the Value that Resonates for You

So far, the values we have repeatedly emphasised, include the following extensive list. Read this list, and choose <u>one</u> value that you consider is pivotal to the evolution of human attitudes and behaviours. For you, which <u>one</u> of these values is the key to nurturing other values?

Awareness; reality; reverence; sensitivity; grace; faith; trust; peace; clarity; decency; kindness; compassion; honesty; integrity; responsibility; transparency; accountability; relationship; community; ecology; simplicity; contentment; gratitude; generosity; hope; justice; education; stewardship; custodianship; leadership; eldership; eldership; role modelling; congruence; consistency; humility; relational honesty; vision; aspiration; the common good; silence; stillness; factfulness; reason; rationality; critical thinking; strategic discipline; data-based evidence; science; empirical processes; open-mindedness; creativity; imagination; respect; freedom; hope; faith; possibility; accurate problem-definition; self-reflection; self-honesty; ordinariness; irony; paradox; mindfulness; faithfulness; delayed gratification; sanity; nurturance; awareness by all, but especially by men; humility by men; integrity by all, but especially by men; accountability by all, but especially by men.

Which value stands out for you as pivotal to all other values?
What is your logic and rationale for choosing this particular value?
What other key value is not in the paragraph above?
What will your chosen value enable you to do?
What might it enable 'us' to do?
How will you nurture, apply and role model this value?

Envisage

The word, envisage, has occurred many times throughout this book. To envisage means — to consider, contemplate, conceive, embrace and envision. Throughout this book I have invited you to envisage, aspire and move toward a range of interconnected right hemisphere priorities and principles.

- Envisage possibilities and aspirations that may help create a desirable future for yourself, your family, your community and humankind.
- Envisage how small and big issues might be managed, minimised and resolved through a network of priorities and processes that can help us nurture dignity and rationality as the norms for relationships, communities and ecologies.
- Envisage values and rationality as the norms for leadership, custodianship and governance. And, I have invited you to envisage values and rationality as strategic norms, principles and priorities for policies and governance in all domains, levels and endeavours.
- Envisage the rise of a respectful and kind ethos of reverencing and dignifying one another and all peoples. I have invited you to envisage a rational ethos of respecting and honouring our fellow species; and to envisage a rational ethos of reverencing, restoring and healing Mother Earth.
- Envisage the rise of a widespread, purposeful ethos of integrity and accountability to lessen and supersede spurious, arbitrary, contrived, artificial, dishonest left hemisphere barriers to fulsome and equitable empowerment and justice for all peoples, our fellow species, and the biosphere.
- Envisage an emerging orientation of strategic, ecological, homeostatic, systems-based holism that may become the conscious, common mindset

of the vast majority; for the common good of all peoples and species who share the earth.

- Envisage an evolving mindfulness of biological holism and systems oneness of species, habitats, ecosystems, environments and Mother Earth.
- You have been invited to envisage the emergence of a profound, unbounded, undivided relational, communal and ecological orientation to life on earth.
- Envisage human existence based on loving values and kind, decent use of power; for one and all.

These possibilities are worthy of our best imagination, desire, hope, curiosity, intention, purpose, intuition, discernment, creativity, intelligence, rationality, integrity, congruence, faithfulness, problem-solving, sustained effort, delayed gratification, sacrifice, duty, strategic intent and accountability.

Right now, please pause and envisage the potential the network of possibilities and aspirations listed above.

Pause and envisage an evolving global ethos and universal culture that exemplify these right hemisphere values, principles, rationalities, qualities, priorities, capacities and hopes.

As asked earlier in the book, will you envisage falling in love with the diversity of humankind; falling in love with the macro and micro kaleidoscope of our fellow species, both domestic and wild; and falling in love with Mother Earth.

Imagine if a critical mass of us falls in love with Mother Earth, her ecosystems, her species, and her peoples.

Here is one a bunch of poems I have written about envisaging and aspiring to do better.

Fall in Love

Fall in love with ourselves, one-another, our fellow species and Mother Earth. Let go all that is not of love.

Fall in love with biological and ecological systems as the tapestry of life. Let go all that separates and divides.

402

Fall in love with the oneness and inclusion of diversity of Mother Earth. Let go arbitrary exclusions.

Fall in love the holism and the whole. Let go arbitrary man-made fragmentation and disconnection.

Fall in love with symbiotic, homeostatic ways. Let go me versus you, and us versus them. Let go all that is parasitic.

Fall in love with him and her, they and them. Let go egoic, arbitrary, ignorant judgementalisms.

Fall in love with one humanity. Let go toxic, masculinised, exceptionalistic, adversarial tribalism.

Fall in love with the oneness of intercomplementarity. Let go fear and aversion to difference.

Fall in love with the hopes of an open and curious mind. Let go subjective rigidity and mindless absolutism of opinions and beliefs.

Fall in love with reality. Let go arbitrary, mindless, factless imaginings, myths and conspiracies.

Fall in love with facts and actualities. Let go baseless, fanciful whims and fads.

Fall in love with science and process-discipline. Let go easy-lazy presumptions and pretentions.

Fall in love with education. Let go easy-lazy, superficial, uncritiqued, arbitrary ignorance and baseless pontification.

Fall in love with critical thinking. Let go arbitrary, wishful flights of fancy, contrived beliefs and uncritiqued opinions.

Fall in love with values and principles. Let go arbitrary dogma, confabulated esoteric stories and fictional claims.

Fall in love with honour, honesty and truthfulness. Let go self-serving connivance, deceit and lies.

Fall in love with humility. Let go posturing, pretence, pontification, arrogance and conceit.

Fall in love with sensitivity, kindness, respect, integrity and accountability. Let go disrespect, self-serving, ends-driven ethics and self-justification.

Fall in love with the art and nuances of mindfulness. Let go the glib, obtuse oblivion of ego.

Fall in love with the awareness and sensitivities of the Feminine Mother. Let go all forms of toxic masculinity.

Fall in love with stewardship. Let go the masculine ways of ambition and wanting for me and mine.

Fall in love with custodianship of Country. Let go entitled possession and exploitation of nature.

Fall in love with relationship, community and ecology. Let go me-centred, transactional giving-to-get.

Fall in love with eight billion of us. Let go of the male illusions of my country, culture and religion.

Fall in love with interwoven, interdependent diversity. Let go arbitrary, exceptionalistic separation.

Fall in love with grace. Let go millennia of toxic, malignant, arbitrary man-made judgementalisms.

Fall in love with unspoken, peaceful sentience and presence. Let go noisy, voluble, pompous pretences and assertions.

Fall in love with hope that is founded in facts. Let go arbitrary fantasies, illusions and delusions.

Fall in love with the peace and joy of simplicity, contentment and gratitude. Let go insatiable wanting.

Altogether, fall in love with kindness and grace-in-action. Let go all that is not of kindness, grace and love.

With what else might we fall in love so that we can do better?

Ahead are several chapters that have the potential to help you and me understand, envisage and embrace the possibilities, vision, aspirations and capacities expressed in this chapter, and throughout this book.

A Revolutionary, Mindful, Enlightened and Evolved Culture

The following several chapters have the potential to help contemporary humankind to recognise, learn from, and envisage a genuine and viable example of mindful, cultural dignity, reverence, rationality, integrity and strategic enlightenment.

The next group of chapters began with a trickle of clarity; then, over several months, unanticipated details poured forth. As a non-indigenous person, I feel great apprehension in writing about the beauty, genius and enlightenment of Australia's First Peoples. As an outsider, I am aware of my profound ignorance and inadequacy to write about a time and a culture that is not within my experience and expertise. Nevertheless, 'looking from the outside in', I will be true to my observations, discernments and understandings.

My hope and trust are that, with all their inadequacies, the forthcoming chapters might stimulate awareness, curiosity, openness, learning, hope and vision. Ultimately, my long-term intention is to stimulate a network of constructive conversations and to promote engagement about strategic principles and priorities that have the capacity to ensure the future of humankind and our fellow species; and to heal and restore Mother Earth; which birthed all species, and sustains all species; including us humans.

This chapter profiles right hemisphere humankind at our most mindful.

A Dignified, Rational, Effective and Enduring Culture

Australia's pre-settlement First Peoples, with their vast and interconnected nations and clans, were not completely unegoic, but perhaps, were as relatively unegoic and as mindful as have ever existed. Australis's First People cultures were not perfect or romantically utopian; but evolved to become relatively highly peaceful, harmonious, socially cohesive, ecologically effective and enduring. As you read, this and the next chapter, try to absorb the extensive network of mindful, strategic awareness, vision, reason, values, principles and priorities that characterised Australia's First Peoples as highly ecologically evolved, profoundly systems attuned, highly intelligent. exceptionally culturally mindful, and highly species successful.

Reread the previous sentence. It encapsulates a blueprint for ecological harmony, emotional and spiritual intelligence, sustainability and endurance.

In previous chapters, I've made the point that 'mindless' — egoic, left hemisphere religious myths greatly contribute to ignorance, misjudgement, human suffering, and environmental damage. Well, here is an example of a homogenous culture that incorporates mindful, strategic right hemisphere mythical stories that are actually values-based, principled, congruent, constructive, instructive, highly adaptive, purposeful and harmoniously ecological. My personal perspective is that First Nation stories aren't factual. However, while mythical and symbolic, First People stories are extremely educational, because they help people intuit, discern and learn how to meld and evolve interwoven relational, communal, biological and ecological systems, networks and processes. This is Spirituality 101.

The purpose of First Nation stories was, and is, to create and sustain mindfully peaceful and effective symbiotic and homeostatic networks among humans, and between humans and their ecosystems. The strategic purpose of these networks is to sustain human life by sustaining the species, ecosystems and environments within which they exist. And, ultimately, to sustain the earth — their Mother — life-giver, provider, role-model, nurturer and teacher. Sit with, ponder, absorb and envisage that revolutionary level of mindfulness and purpose.

For millennia, Australian First Peoples used 'strategic, mystical stories and songs' to moderate ego, and to dispel ignorance. First Peoples used strategic mystical stories and songs to — nurture and sustain relational, communal and ecological awareness; to foster the common good for greatest number; to maximise intra- and inter-tribal peace; to be one with their environments; and to do minimal harm to themselves, the land, the waters, the air, and their follow species.

Over eons, First Peoples became better and better at fastidiously observing biological and ecological systems with which they needed to be in synch. In tandem with their extraordinarily detailed, practical ecological and biological observations, First People discerned and crafted mystical stories and songs that helped to educate and unify 'one and all' with respect to environmental intricacies, survival imperatives and ecological continuity. They did this with the conscious-strategic-purposeful-intentional view to ensuring human sustainability in synch with the sustainability of the Country and Mother Earth. Note their exceptional blend of conscious-mindful-strategic-purposeful-intentionality — in perpetuity. This is enlightenment 101.

First People combined the very best of — pragmatic environmental learning, esoteric intuition, values-in-action, principles-in-action, story-making, story-telling, education, enculturation and logical 'reason-in-action'. This way of 'being human' not only built on, but went well beyond, primordial hunter-gatherer-forager knowledge and practices. Australian First People ways of being human exemplified and greatly surpassed the very best of hunter-gather-forager wisdom. Much more significantly, First People ways are vastly different from and exceedingly superior to modern Western-Anglo-European-American-Asian models of culture, religion, education, politics, economics, agriculture, industry, technology, bureaucracy and governance.

The previous paragraph is a crucial aspect of the thesis of this book. Read it again. Sit with each element. Then, as you read on, absorb the genius and enlightenment of mindful — purposeful ecological rationale, principles, priorities, intentions, vision and strategies — again, astonishingly — in perpetuity. First People strategic mindfulness is the gold-standard archetypal model and blueprint of ecological and biological sustainability. It is mindful ecological and biological intelligence par excellence. It is by far the best model of human existence to which we can refer for education and guidance. First People wisdom is 'Perpetual Strategic Ecological Mindfulness 101'. This wisdom, enlightenment and genius is the right hemisphere revolution that I hinted at and alluded to in earlier chapters. First People mindfulness is profoundly revolutionary.

The evolution of a seamless, functional model for interface between Australia's First People's spiritual stories and their environmental pragmatism is unparalleled cognitive illumination and unparalleled relational and ecological intelligence. It is immeasurably more dignifying, principled, intelligent, rational, congruent, grounded, integrous, pragmatic and visionary than the power-obsessive, greedy, materialistic, empire building narratives and transactional ways of left hemisphere Anglo-European-American 'take and break' attitudes and actions. I venture that Australia's First People's enfolded spirituality and pragmatism are even more holistically mindful, and more relationally, communally and ecologically evolved, far reaching, encompassing and practical than Eastern philosophies, such as Buddhism and Taoism.

So far, what is this chapter saying to you?

Are there several principles or priorities that capture the quintessence of this chapter?

For me, the standout, is the mindful — conscious, intentional evolution of extremely detailed observations, holistic ecology, enfolded synergy, seamless homeostasis, and universal education with respect to timeless systems principles and perpetual existence priorities? As said before, First People values, principles and priorities are profoundly revelatory and revolutionary.

Can you envisage us moderners embracing the revelation and the revolution of First People holistic systems ecology, enfolded synergy, seamless homeostasis, and universal education with respect to the principles and priorities for perpetual sustainability? First People principles and priorities for 'perpetual sustainability' are a complete game-changer. They are our greatest hope in the 21sr century and beyond.

Ecological Oneness – Not Take and Break

Crucially, First Peoples learned not to impose themselves on the intricate and delicate biological and ecological systems, cycles and processes of their environments. They didn't make up dodgy, man-made, transactional, self-leveraging, self-justifying left hemisphere stories to suit their fantasising, greedy, empire building, power-amassing, consumptive, land-acquiring and money-making agendas. Again, crucially and instructively, First Peoples evolved Yin-based stories and songs that enabled systems thinking, critical thinking and strategic thinking. Their stories and songs arose from observation of their right hemisphere Mother Earth.

First Australian mythology and pragmatic knowledge evolved in tandem to help our pre-settlement ancestors 'consciously learn from' and 'consciously meld with' their environments. Their genius was 'mindful, intelligent learning and melding', not mindless, dumb presuming, wanting, taking, possessing, exploiting and damaging. Ultimately, profoundly — First Peoples learned that they belong to the land; that the land did not belong to them. They learned that the earth was Mother; the bearer, nurturer and sustainer of all life; including human life. Australia's First Peoples learned to love, protect and preserve the

408

land as living, breathing Country — their living, breathing Mother. This real-life example of learning and enlightenment is our hope for learning; our hope for revelation, enlightenment, revolution and evolution.

My conclusion is that Australian First Peoples observed and learned from initial prehistoric extinctions and other detrimental issues caused by over-hunting and other insensitivities during their early millennia in the new island home. They learned from initially being less in tune with systems and cycles. From a range of early environmental misjudgements and mistakes, our Ancestors progressively learned to recognise and be in synch with life-cycles, biological patterns, ecological systems and habitat homeostasis. Ultimately, First Peoples — learned not to reduce the sustainability of food sources by not disturbing the rhythm of ecosystems; by not to disturbing natural cycles; and by not disrupting the homeostasis of ecosystems, habitats and species. First Peoples' finely-tuned consciousness and way of homeostasis is our hope for revolution in human existence.

Mindful, right hemisphere — loving, observing, melding, educating, learning, adapting and evolving define Australia's First Peoples. These six primacies enabled them to steadily and surely become one-with lands, rivers, oceans, animals and plants; one-with Country and Mother, which is totality and whole of geography, ecology and biology; including all humans. Ultimately, these primacies enabled our First Peoples — 'not to be against' their fellow creatures and systems; not to dominate them, not to subjugate them; not to distort them; not to own them; not to damage them; and not annihilate them.

It the contrast between First People Yin and White-man Yang; the contrast between them and us, ringing any bells?

Being one with systems and Country is the essence of highly educated, highly enlightened, highly adapted, highly evolved, highly relational, highly communal, and highly ecological intelligence. With a view to perpetual sustainability, relational, communal and ecological intelligence is the highest expression of human intelligence. Ecological intelligence exemplifies mindful — rational and enlightened right hemisphere systems custodianship. Being 'one with' is exceptional revelation and revolution. It is exceptional common-sense. Mindful systems principles and priorities are 'Sustainability 101'. This revelation and revolution are the common sense we need to grasp, do and make common. We modern humans must imbue, embrace and apply this common sense as our new 21st century ecological normal.

Us

In contrast to First People enlightenment, our egoic, masculinised Western philosophies and land-management practices are highly systems-ignorant and systems-averse. Western philosophies are not 'one with'. They are 'over' and 'one-down'. Typically, and commonly, the left hemisphere Western mindset dominates nature, exploits nature, works against nature and damages nature. Western egoic attitudes and ways are the epitome of being mindlessly — adverse, exploitative, destructive ignorance of the unaware, unreflective, insensitive, ill-informed, irrational and dumb.

First Nations learnings and evolution are in extreme contrast to hundreds of years of mindless — repeated, intransigent and ignorant 'take and break' environmental destruction of white post-settlement agriculture and animal husbandry. To a huge extent, we post-Anglo-Europeans are making the same strategic ecological miscalculations, misjudgements and mistakes in 21st century agriculture that our forebears made hundreds of years ago. The issue is that, unlike our First Nation ancestors, we post-settlement and modern white left hemisphere Australians fail to be mindful — fail to be aware, fail to observe, fail to discern, fail to meld, fail to learn, fail to educate, fail to adapt, fail to evolve, fail to love Country and Mother.

We egoically masculinised, agricultural, industrial, technological, economic post-First People humans, have not imbued the 'sophisticated mothering sustainability' priorities of nurturance, and the mindful intelligence of 'being in strategic harmony with'. We have not imbued 'nature's feminine art and science' of strategic mutuality, congruence, symbiosis and homeostasis. Insanely — from about 10,000 years ago, we Anglo-Europeans demoted, dethroned and usurped the timeless, iconic right hemisphere Yin Mother. In her place, we agricultural, religious, political, economic and industrial men, promoted and ensconced the mechanical, data-obsessed, administrative, legalistic left hemisphere, Yang, bean-counting number-crunching male, left hemisphere ego to CEO of the world and the earth.

Masculinised, Abrahamic, white, Western 'take and break' male models. assume, impose, inculcate and enforce masculine entitlement and dominance. Through these models, we men impose our loveless, mindless — harmful arbitrary, self-serving, presumptions, preconceptions, beliefs, whims, wishes and wants throughout the past several hundred years of global colonisation. and entitlement.

However, there is another way to be human and male. There is an alternative and a solution.

Dadirri

Here is an explanation of a revolutionary, mindful spiritual and psychological orientation that is completely different from assumed, mindless, egoic, Western, masculine arrogance and superiority. As you read this section, note the contrasts between purposeful right hemisphere Yin mindfulness and short-sighted, left hemisphere Yang mindlessness.

Dadirri is the name given to a many millennia-old meditative and mindfulness practice of the First People of the Northern Territory in Australia. It is a strategic process that involves the practise of intentional and systematic silence, stillness, presence, sentience, attentive listening, and calm, peaceful discernment. Dadirri is a process that nurtures peace within the person, peace within human relationships, peace between human communities, and peace between humans and the environments which sustain them. Inherently, Dadirri also nurtures sensitivity, awareness, perceptual acuity, strategic clarity, atunement to natural processes. Dadirri nurtures deeply-felt reverence for, and relationship with, Country and Mother. Dadirri is another revolution and revelation. Dadirri is hope.

First People explain that Dadirri sharpens, deepens and consolidates their awareness of and respect and reverence for natural biological and ecological networks and systems. Dadirri mindfulness enables First Peoples to understand that humans are inherent and integral within biological and ecological networks and systems. It and helps humans understand and embrace our roles and responsibilities as 'conscious, intelligent and accountable caretakers, custodians and stewards' of Country and its local and global ecosystems. Dadirri enables First People to discern and imbue a mindful awareness of being 'with and within' nature. It enables them to discern how not to interfere with, work against, or harm natural ecological and biological systems, cycles and processes.

Dadirri is 'a way of being human' that blends the mindfulness of — presence, reverence, dignity, sensitivity, intelligence, integrity, responsibility and accountability. It is a way of discerning, joining, relating and educating. Dadirri mindfulness facilitates conscious, purposeful revelation and learning, adjustment, adaptation, education and evolution. It is an extremely effective way to minimise the dispositions of the masculine ego; and to maximise the mindfulness of — peace, respect, reverence, engagement, harmony, dignity, reason and intelligence. Dadirri is enlightened genius that predates Eastern meditative practices by many millennia. Importantly, Dadirri is not complicated and constrained by rigid hierarchies and complex dogmas that tend to be problematic in Eastern philosophies, such as Buddhism, Taoism and Zen.

First People emphasise that Dadirri is not exclusive to them, but is a universal mindfulness process that can by learned, imbued an applied by all peoples in all cultures and contexts. First People women have been facilitating Dadirri seminars and training for the wider Australian community for many years.

Can you see the relevance, value and application of Dadirri mindfulness for all 21st century peoples?

Can you see that Dadirri is revelation, revolution and evolution?

Can you see the connections between Dadirri and the Breath Meditation process that is emphasised and encouraged throughout this book?

Can you see the connections between Dadirri and peace, dignity, clarity, purpose, human efficacy, integrity, relational, communal and ecological harmony, longevity and sustainability?

First People — Empiricists and Spiritualists

Through meditative and mindfulness practices such as Dadirri, First Peoples were the first humans to evolve and meld a unique and highly effective 'spiritual empiricism'. We moderners must learn to be meditative and mindful. We must learn to become 'spiritually empirical' and 'mindfully soulful'. We must envisage and blend highly detailed — evidence-based 'ecological pragmatism' with a reverence-based, sensitivity-based 'ecological spirituality'. This is a systems-based spirituality. We must envisage and craft a highly-detailed pragmatic, relational, communal and ecological ethos. We must envisage and craft highly detailed awareness, evidence-based knowledge, boundless inclusive mutuality, and unrestricted inclusive ecological relationship among humans, with our fellow species, and with Mother Earth. 'Spiritual empiricism' is the revolution that we 21st century humans must internalise and utilise — or perish.

As 'spiritual empiricists' we must embrace an ethos of oneness with each other; oneness with our fellow species, oneness with environments, with ecosystems; and, ultimately, oneness with Mother Earth. We must come to recognise that the human expression of existence and life is but one expression among an intricate, interconnected and boundless network of micro and macro lifeforms and systems.

Relatively and absolutely, First People 'Spiritual Empiricism' is the exceptional delicacy, process-discipline, focus, sophistication, elegance, intelligence, responsibility, grace and enlightenment that we must envisage, and to which we must aspire.

We must evolve a unified, sustaining system of awareness, reverence, sensitivity, reason, ecology, harmony, congruence, discipline, rationality, responsibility, collaboration, mutuality, functionality, efficacy and accountability. These are the elements of First People revelation, revolution and evolutions. They are the elements of First People 'Spiritual Empiricism 101'.

In the 21st century, the blend of First People 'Spiritual Empiricism' and Dadirri mindfulness the prerequisites for 'Modern Human Evolution 101'. Note the blend of uncorrupted Yin and Yang capacities, priorities, processes and principles. Note the words — delicacy, elegance and grace. These are the Yin qualities to which we modern humans must be drawn; which we must embrace.

Absorb this blend of Yin and Yang realities, priorities, values, principles and possibilities into your consciousness. They are the revolutionary benchmarks of mindful 21st century personhood, relationship, citizenship, custodianship and leadership to which we, modern humankind, must aspire and evolve. If we modern humans cannot or will not envisage, attune, aspire, adapt, evolve and become mindful stewards and custodians, we will continue to rapidly decline; and likely, will perish. It's that simple and stark.

Questions

Does First People Spiritual Empiricism — relational and ecological reverence — and pragmatic ecological intelligence — look like an excellent model for 21st century human existence? Is it a model that can help us to do much better?

Might Dadirri meditative and mindfulness practices help us internalise and apply Spiritual Empiricism?

Might this mindful blend help us to do better.

Have First Nation Peoples shown us that humans can observe, envision, imbue, collaborate, meld, educate, learn, adapt, aspire, evolve and become? Might we learn from their example; and do better?

Can we embrace the revelation and revolution of First People priorities, values, principles and processes?

Can personal, relational and ecological, awareness, sensitivity, values, principles and priorities become the new human intention and purpose; our evolving enlightenment; our revolution; our new normal?

The next chapter contains a comprehensive network of dot-points that maps the spiritual and practical relational, communal and ecological principles of First People mindfulness and spiritual empiricism. The next chapter presents the components of a revolutionary model for human elegance, intelligence, enlightenment, efficacy and potential perpetuity.

Practical Learning from Australia's First Peoples

For tens of millennia, Australia's First Peoples endured and thrived for many reasons, some of which were mentioned in the previous chapter. To build on this encapsulation, read the following extensive, interconnected and overlapping network of dot-points. Observe the detail. 'Join the dots'. Make a profile of humankind at its dignified, rational, intelligent best.

Read slowly, carefully, and openly. Read with a sense of curiosity and possibility. My observation is that any one of these dot-points could revolutionise us 21st century peoples; individually and collectively. Together, this network of priorities, principles and practices contains potential beyond the experience and imagination of most of us contemporary peoples. Each and all of these points have the potential to be a revelation and a revolution mindfulness for us modern, Westernised humans. They contain the seeds of hope for human evolution and hope.

First-People Gifts to Us

These Yin-principles are First People's right hemisphere gift to us in the 21st century. The following extensive network of principles are what all of us 21st human can recognise, envisage, imbue, learn, apply and consolidate.

- Critically, ultimately, First Peoples learned not to make the same serious mistakes and misjudgements over and over. They 'learned to learn'. If they had not, it is likely that our ancestors would have perished, along with some species that they drove to extinction during their very early millennia on this island. But our First Peoples did learn; and for that reason, they did not perish. At the time of the First Fleet, Australia's First Peoples were flourishing; and had been so for tens of thousands of

415

years. Australia's First Peoples are superb exemplars of learning, adaptation, evolution and education at their best; as evidenced by many thousands of years of mindful — peaceful, sustainable, strategic ecological management par excellence.

- Crucially, over eons, Australia's First Peoples used their learnings to became less and less destructive, and to become more and more aware, ecological and strategic. They became less and less an ecological aberration. That is, they became less and less ecologically unaware, insensitive, short-sighted, clumsy, dysfunctional, harmful and self-sabotaging. First Peoples learned not to plunder resources, and not to disturb or damage ecosystems. Over millennia, their ecological awareness, sensitivity, education and adaptation incrementally networked and evolved into highly effective cultural-mindful — spiritual atunement, which included strategic ecological knowledge, priorities, principles, systems, structures, processes and disciplines. That network is the gold standard in pragmatic ecological spirituality. We don't have to reinvent spiritual model or 'the ecological wheel'. First Peoples can educate us. Their spiritual atunement, values, principles and priorities can revolutionise us. We can attune to, learn, absorb and apply the priorities and principles of First People spiritual and ecological mindfulness with a view to adaptation and sustainability.

- First Peoples weren't empire builders, powermongers, status-seekers, materialistic, consumer obsessive, competitive, individualist, self-leveraging, transactional, greedy or adversarial. First Peoples embraced reverence, relationship, ecology, simplicity, subsistence and sufficiency as their priorities and principles; their currencies; and their capital. They weren't trapped by egoic individualistic and tribal ambition, wanting, getting, possessing, accumulating, hoarding or controlling. Nor were they lured by the ego of politics, wealth, social power, position or status. Imagine being guided by individual, relational and societal values, principles and priorities that are non-egoic; that not dysfunctionally masculinised. That is, being motivated and guided by ways which are not political, not money-obsessive, not material and not consumed by craving, wanting, perusing, getting, hoarding and protecting. Sit for a moment with these priorities and principles. They are an exceptional revelation and a life-changing, life-giving revolution.

- Australia's First Peoples grasped and applied the three-way principles of: 1. delayed gratification; 2. disciplined strategic prioritisation; and 3. Enshrining the common good of the greatest number for the perpetually long-term. This is an extremely empowering grouping of principles and priorities. Imagine if we modern humans delayed gratification, and applied disciplined strategic prioritisation for the common good of the greatest number for perpetual long-term of the earth, environments, species and the entirety of humankind. Imagine that. Envisage that. Absorb that revelation and revolution into your consciousness. Seriously, meditate on that way of being human.

- Ultimately, First Nation peoples learned to seamlessly harmonise with and meld within their fellow species, habitats, ecosystems and environments. They learned to be one-with fellow plant and animal systems and processes. They sustained themselves by blending 'with and within' their enduring, perpetual, holistic, biological and ecological environments. They became 'seamlessly part of', and in sync with the biological and ecological perpetuity that had already evolved and existed for hundreds of millions of years. First Peoples learned the art and science of 'everlasting seamless synergy'. That's the benchmark that we can envisage, and to which we can aspire. Imagine and absorb the benchmark of 'everlasting seamless synergy'.

- The evolution of First People consciousness resulted in the profound awareness that humans don't own the land, but the land owns us. We don't own environment, but are stewards of resources, caretakers of ecosystems, and custodians of living, breathing, life-giving, life-sustaining Country. They learned to be mindful caretakers and networkers of relationship, ecology and biological systems and cycles. Absorb the revolutionary intelligence of being mindful caretakers, nurturers and networkers of ecology, relationships, systems and homeostasis. This is the epitome of cultural-mindful — purposeful awareness, intelligence and enlightenment. Imagine and envisage a revolution of that depth of consciousness. Meditate on it. Absorb it into your awareness. Let it become central to your emerging mindfulness.

- First Nation spirituality became truly holistic. It became minimally individualistic, minimally self-leveraging and minimally transactional. All priorities became relational, communal and ecological. 'One and all' were educated to be fully conscious of the common good of all peoples, of all land, and of the entirety of Country. This was the lived-experience of the principle of: 'all for one and one for all'. Spirituality gave rise to priorities that weren't egoic, me-oriented, selfish, nationalistic or exceptionalistic. Ultimately, it wasn't about what 'I' or 'my-group' or my country want; and bugger the rest of you. 'Intentional holistic synergy' for 'the greatest good for greatest number for the longest time' emerged as the highest priority; the supreme ecological capital; the ultimate investment in the future as 'timeless perpetuity'. Envisage a revolutionary ecological model of 'timeless perpetuity'. First People had no interest in short-term, individualistic material, political or economic capital; nor in amassing power as capital. There was minimal consciousness of the self-leveraging, transactionalism, superiority, exclusivity or our empire. Imagine if contemporary spirituality was much less short-sighted, individualistic, self-obsessed, self-leveraging, transactional, superior, exclusive, fundamentalist, pie in the sky, exceptionalistic, power obsessive, thing oriented and possessive. Sit in silence and envisage the evolution of an unbound, all-inclusive, egalitarian, relational, communal and ecological spirituality-culture-mindfulness. I have joined these because they are one.

- First People consciousness isn't linier, bounded or fragmented. It is cyclical, boundless, seasonal, and inextricably interconnected with and within 'the seasonal and cyclical tapestry of networks and systems of the whole'. That is: the whole of time; the whole universe; the whole earth; and whole environments, ecosystems and habitats; including the whole network of all peoples who comprise the earth, tribes, families and persons. This is exceptional holistic mindfulness, and exceptional systems inclusiveness. Imagine if we contemporary humans were conscious of 'whole of earth' human and environmental networks; without arbitrary man-made boundaries, divisions or chauvinistic fragmentations. Imagine if were learn to be completely inclusive and enfolded systems thinkers. Envisage this culture-mindfulness for us.

- First People are mindful of being pragmatically inseparable from and entwined within boundless, naturally occurring structures and processes that encompass and interconnect the whole of country, land, oceans, waterways and species. There are no barriers, no divides, no separations, no exclusions, no greater or lesser, no major or minor, no in and out. There is exquisite diversity and wondrous difference. There are carefully mapped personal, family, communal and ecological roles, functions, responsibilities and accountabilities; but no hierarchy of being — not among humans; not between humans and other species; and not between humans and ecosystems. 'Being' is intuited and discerned as 'the inherent, inclusive oneness of diversity'. This is an exact parallel of the human body, which is a manifestation of the inherent oneness of the diversity of chemistry, physiology, anatomy and microbiology. Imagine and envisage an ethos of 'the oneness of being' through oneness of diversity, oneness of interdependent purpose, oneness of interdependent relationships, oneness of systems and ecologies, and oneness of interdependent ecological roles. Pause and envisage a 'cultural mindfulness of oneness of diversity and seamless, interconnected interdependence'. Absorb this revelation into the depths of your consciousness.

- Thus, First Peoples discerned that existence and life are 'seamless, enfolded wholeness'. Unbroken wholeness and holism are fundamental to belonging to and 'being within' highly functional, unbounded and everlasting biological systems and networks, interwoven roles, interconnected collaborations, mutual responsibilities and shared accountabilities. First Peoples discerned this many millennia before the emergence of Eastern Philosophies. Sit with that extraordinary reality.

- In contrast, the non-indigenous religious and political mindset is filled with — boundaries, borders, barriers, divides, divisions, separations; 'ins-and-outs', binaries and dichotomies of lesser-greater; elitisms, arbitrary inclusions and arbitrary exclusions; structural advantages and structural disadvantages; systemic injustices and alienations; fragmentations and reductionisms; conflicting dogmas, competing ideologies and countless self-serving individualist opinions and beliefs — and — a tangled web of muddled, self-defeating, competing, oppositional priorities. Reread and sit with the components of that long and telling sentence. Inherently, modern-day fragmentation, religious and political dividedness, and institutional competitiveness are vastly less functional than seamless, ecological, collaborative, societal and ecological wholeness. The distinction between the holism of First People right-hemisphere 'consciousness' and the fragmentation of left hemisphere Western 'thinking', is stark and telling. The distinction is a profound revelation and a life-changing revolution. Envisage us moderners doing better than arbitrary fragmentations, exclusions and adversarialism? Imagine us evolving to become the reality of the revelation and revolution of wholeness and oneness.

- First People spirituality-culture and subsistence pragmatics are geared toward simplicity; but are not simplistic. The spirituality and practices of subsistence are extremely complex, sophisticated, highly nuanced and wholly integrated. But, they are not complicated, confusing or self-confounding. Subsistence philosophy and practices are clear, detailed, congruent, consistent and cohesive. Again, this is in stark contrast to the confused, complicated, illogical, conflictual, and inherently unavoidably disparate and self-confounding hotchpotch of competing contemporary cultures, religions, pseudo-spiritualities, ideologies, politics, economics, commerce and conspiracy theories. Can we 'modern' humans envisage, embrace and integrate elegant complexity, graceful simplicity and sublime sophistication?

- With respect to subsistence agriculture and aquaculture, First Nations peoples learned to harmonise with a myriad of interconnected cycles of fertilisation, reproduction, growth, death, regeneration and repopulation. Note the four words: 'learned to harmonise with'. First Peoples learned not to ignore, meddle with, disrupt or go against these cycles; nor to impose themselves on them. They learned to observe and blend with a vast, interconnected network of systems and cycles of perennial and perpetual biology. As said before, the revolutionary elegance, delicacy, sophistication, logic and rationality of this is hugely instructive. Sit with the words: elegance, sophistication, delicacy, logic and rationality. This blend is so instructive. Add relational grace to this blend. Sit with that blend and let it soak into your consciousness.

- First Peoples learned how to be strategically mindful — strategically congruent, strategically ecological and strategically disciplined. They seamlessly blended culture, spirituality and mindfulness so that three were one and the same. They did this, despite being tribally diverse and geographically widespread over the largest island on the earth. Over millennia, many intersecting and interconnecting clans developed a very functional level of 'purposeful harmony' throughout a geographically vast and tribally diverse island continent. Are we contemporary humans capable of 'mindful — purposeful, strategic harmony' — that which First Peoples call — culture?

- Crucially, the list of previous dot-points shows that, contrary to the myth of First Peoples being simple-minded, unintelligent, hapless, wandering, disparate, wretched, inane, itinerant 'Stone-age Savages' — there is abundant evidence that Australia wide, First Peoples 'became, were and are' exceptionally mindful — purposeful, intelligent, socially sophisticated, highly organised and highly skilled community members, land-managers, agriculturalists, aquaculturalists and engineers; and have been so for tens of millennia. Let the truth of this emerge and saturate the mind of contemporary humankind.

- As was appropriate within their various environments, First Peoples hunted, harvested natural grasses such as wheat and other simple crops, dammed rivers and dug wells. And, as was functional, they built settlements. In some areas, structures included grain storage barns, animal enclosures, ceremonial sites, huts and wells. Some communities managed stock (kangaroos and emus) and constructed elaborate fish-traps. At the time of settlement, throughout the continent, First Peoples cared for Country and very effectively managed highly diverse environments. They did so mindfully-culturally — knowingly, intelligently, sensitively, delicately, systematically, ecologically, skilfully and strategically. Land-management included purposeful, timely, sophisticated, skilful and delicate use of fire. Once again, note the words: purposeful, timely, sophisticated, skilful and delicate. Imagine if we modern humans exemplified these attributes. Can you envisage this? Can we 21st century humans learn and evolve to be purposeful, timely, sophisticated, skilful and delicate?

- Most of the evidence of sophisticated land-management and effective engineering was dismissed, trampled, destroyed or stolen by explorers, settlers and the government officials within decades of settlement. In great part, this was because the legitimacy of British occupation was contingent on proof of Terra Nullius, the philosophy of empty, undeveloped, unorganised, unmanaged land. Evidence of intelligent, purposeful land-management, strategic organisation, and learned social and cultural complexity, would have negated the legalities of settlement, occupation and possession. Settlement with the illusion of Terra Nullius would and did amount to the criminal acts of invasion, dispossession, wholesale theft of lands, cultural decimation, and widespread extermination.

- In extreme contrast to Terra Nullius, and in complete contrast to Anglo-European cultures, unique in human history, Australia's First Peoples learned how to be individually different and tribally diverse, but to exist with a high level of collaboration for the greater good of Country, and for the common good of massively diverse peoples and tribes. They did this with a mindful view to the perpetual existence of 'their common world of the vast community of peoples and Country'. To exceptional effect, this was 'rational and enlightened societal organisation in action'. This was Culture. Until occupation, common cultural principles of lore, consciously harmonious inter-tribal relationships, sustainable strategic management of Country hundreds of First People clans to exist effectively and in relative peace for tens of millennia. By today's standards, that is extraordinary. In absolute terms, it is unique. Soak in the realities, lessons and revolutionary adaptations mentioned in this paragraph. Envisage the evolution of an equivalent level of cultural and societal enlightenment and efficacy for us contemporary humans going forward.

- In contrast to Anglo-European-Celtic agricultural and industrial peoples, and against the potential for egoic self-servingness, First Nation peoples learned to blend idiosyncratic tribal identity with relatively functional levels of strategic inter-tribal peace, collaboration and efficacy. Commonly, tribes shared detailed knowledge of overlapping lands and resources. They shared bloodlines. Intersecting tribes shared many cousins, grandchildren and great grandchildren. Many in each tribe were related to people in neighbouring tribes, and far beyond. That's partly why, today, many greet each other as 'cuz', and why older women and men are 'aunty and uncle'. Imagine and envisage us modern peoples being bonded to and reverent toward a vast network of groups and nations; near, far and wide.

- Some First People were multilingual. Neighbouring tribes shared stories and were purposely interconnected by overlapping and interconnected

422

Song Lines. First Peoples went to great lengths to create and consolidate common spiritual bonds, with the strategic intent to minimise issues that might provoke damaging divisions, enmities and conflict. To attack a neighbouring tribe would risk disrespecting Song Lines and Culture; and to risk harming many generations of cousins, nieces, nephews, grandchildren and grandparents. How mindful; how spiritually-mindfully and pragmatically sophisticated; how disciplined and functional is that? Can we moderners learn the strategic value of far-reaching respect? Can we learn and internalise Culture-Spirituality-Mindfulness?

- Unlike most ancient and contemporary cultures, very commonly, Australia's First Peoples strived to settle differences and disputes with minimum violence; and with a strong consciousness of the common good of an interconnected network of tribes; a consciousness of the wider-greater good of the collective of all peoples; and a mindfulness of the common shared consciousness of the sacred universality of all peoples who are interwoven into the life and being of Country. Imagine and envisage an equivalent level of strategic clarity and discipline today.

- Even in the light of some strong inter-tribal differences, for the most part, First Peoples learned to minimise inter-tribal violence, and, for the most part, to avoid all-out war, mass-murder and genocide.

- In contrast to agricultural and industrial mindsets, Australia's First Peoples learned how to blend individuality, loyalty to tribe, awareness of being diverse Nations of Peoples, reverence for Country, and the ethos and discipline of boundless common good of Country; which inherently included a vast diversity and tapestry of clans and environments. Again, this is exceptional culture-mindfulness-spirituality. It is unique in the ancient and modern history of humankind. Can you envisage the revolutionary possibility of a mindful — holistic appreciation of 'the oneness of the vast diversity as an interwoven tapestry of peoples' — for us in the 21st century and beyond?

- Amazingly, and in contrast to Anglo-European cultures, Australia's First Nation Peoples learned how not to be destructively ego-centric, humancentric, ethnocentric and anthropocentric. Again, this is exceptional. As far as I know, it is unique. Can we achieve that level of strategic rationality, intelligence and dignity? Can we recognise that these values are profoundly strategic and mindful?

- First Peoples learned how to reverence and be accountable to each other, to their eldership, to tribal and gender roles, to their spiritual values, to Cultural Lore, to the processes of nature, and to their roles as custodians and stewards of Country. Imagine and envisage an equivalent level and extent of sophisticated, purposeful awareness, reverence, dignity, discipline, integrity, responsibility and accountability. First People reverence and accountability are very powerful systemic values-in-action.

- Personal, relational, tribal and environmental awareness, respect, responsibility and accountability evolved to become primary and inviolable strategic values, priorities and realities. They evolved to become universal, absolute and sacrosanct. Beliefs served strategic holistic values, principles, priorities and strategic purpose. Beliefs weren't arbitrarily, idiosyncratic, individualistic, self-serving, incongruent, divisive or destructive. Nor were they dysfunctionally exceptionalistic, nationalistic, sectarian, fundamentalist, exclusive or conflict-ridden. Neither were they narrow-sighted or short-sighted. Envisage that level of cultural-mindful purpose and strategic insight and foresight.

- By modern Western standards, some punishments for infringements of societal principles were harsh, but were designed to minimise destructive anti-social behaviour; especially, to minimise destructive behaviours associated with narcissism and sociopathy. Imagine a world with much less religious and political narcissism and sociopathy. That would be a revolution and transformation of human existence.

- For the most part, it seems that the First Nation equivalent of the rule of law was applied effectively. It appears that justice processes and punishments were consistent, equitable, timely and functional. Justice processes fostered prosocial behaviours and curbed antisocial behaviours and disruptions of reverence, lore, cohesion, stability and strategic priorities. First and foremost, criminality and violence were minimised through systematic enculturation, education and training. Antisocial and 'unloreful' attitudes and behaviours were not tolerated; and it seems, were relatively rare. A deeply-imbibed and mindful-cultural philosophy and education of Dreaming, Totems, Song-Lines and Kinship were nurtured and consolidated as sacrosanct cultural norms of reverence, dignity, sensitivity, integrity, discipline, simplicity, contentment and gratitude. The systematic internalisation of pro-social Dreaming-Cultural-Spiritual priorities, values, principles and norms minimised dysfunctional and antisocial propensities.

- Individually, relationally, socially, politically and culturally, the vast majority First People learned how not to be governed by ego in the form of self-serving, individualistic arbitrariness, ambition, impulsiveness, pride, recalcitrance, ignorance, and wilful transactional self-leveraging. Note how starkly different this is from our contemporary masculine individualistic ethos, and from our self-serving, self-leveraging, transactional Yang tendencies. Can we envisage the revolution of being primarily relational, inclusively communal and sensitively ecological?

- Within First Nation culture, there is little evidence of the rampant egotism, ambition, transactionalism, elitism, nationalism and exceptionalism that have driven us Anglo-Europeans to horrendously damaged many non-indigenous cultures for many centuries. How respectful, dignified, peaceful and pleasant would that be?

- First Nation spirituality and culture became relatively free from the ignorance, insecurities, dominance and deviance of individual and collective masculinised egoic dysfunctionalities that were detailed and explained in earlier chapters.

- Predominantly, our ancestors learned to exist authentically and harmoniously; and to be symbiotically communal. They learned how to be individually and collectively mindful-spiritual — reverential, relational, ecological and homeostatic.

- In stark contrast to us material, fiscal, consumptive, industrial, technological moderners, First Peoples learned how not to be greedy, parasitic, sadomasochistic and chronically ambitiously sadomasochistic.

- I am not aware of evidence of destructive sectarianism, or religious violence in First People history. In contrast to many Middle Eastern and Western Abrahamic institutional religious cultures, they learned how to be devout and socially coherent; but not to be institutionalised, fundamentalist, conservatist, or pathologically theocratic and tyrannical. Imagine and envisage a world without combative and violent cultural, religious and political conservatism, fundamentalism, and adversarialism; and a bunch of other problematic and harmful religious isms.

- To a great extent, First Australians evolved by mindfully — seamlessly blending mythology, symbolism, ritual, music, dance, reason, lore, subsistence pragmatism, and a soulful reverence for life and Country. This was their 'conscious, blended, seamless Spirituality-Culture-Dreaming and existence-pragmatism in perpetuity'. Mindfully integrating spirituality and systems pragmatism is the epitome of purposeful, timeless, ecological enlightenment. It is as mindful and unegoic as has ever existed. Can we comprehend, appreciate and embrace this revelation of mindful — sane, principled, values-based, constructive, functional spirituality-culture.

- In contrast to Abrahamic myths and Hindu mysticism, First Nation spirituality was predominantly egalitarian and respectful. For the most part, First People spirituality was not chauvinistically pathological, violent, elitist, incongruent, divisive, repressive, misogynistic, degrading and destructive. That list is a profound contrast to the overt and prolific chauvinistic pathologies of our White, Asian and Middle-Eastern cultures, religions and political systems. First People psychology is a revolution of dignified spiritual and cultural functionality and efficacy.

- Shared, devoted, strategic, ecological and relational consciousness prevented peaceful, soulful spirituality from decompensating into dysfunctional political, divisive, ethnic, sexist, combative, destructive religiosity. Australia's First People epitomised holistic, congruent, inclusive, respectful, peaceful, pragmatic spirituality-culture. Sit with that for a moment. Envisage us modern humans embracing and being guided by a holistic, congruent, inclusive, respectful, peaceful, pragmatic spirituality. Imagine this becoming the norm for us.

- It seems that the spirituality and mindfulness of Dreaming, Song Lines, Culture, inter-tribal marriage and pan-tribal Kinship prevented pathological despots and populists from seizing power, abusing the masses, damaging culture, destroying environment, and from inciting enmity, sectarian violence, genocide and war. Again, this is in stark contrast to historical and contemporary Western, Asian and Middle

Eastern experiences. Imagine the plight of narcissistic sociopaths, such as Trump, Putin and Xi, in pre-settlement First People times.

- There were strong and explicit links within First People networking of reverence for Country, mythology, genealogy, tribal roles, gender roles, relationship principles, community roles, stewardship, custodianship, leadership and eldership. These elements evolved and integrated to become a holistic system of spiritual, cultural, relational, communal and ecological intelligence and wisdom. These were the crucial elements of extremely effective education and enculturation for one and all; from early childhood to old-age; from tribe to tribe, throughout their island continent.

- All these linkages arose from a blend of stillness, sensitivity, intentional conscious awareness, systematic structured observation, and shared conscious integrity, responsibility and accountability. These values and practices were fully and equally of all; were internalised by all; and were applied consistently to all, by all, for the benefit of all. First People ethos and practice became egalitarian and utilitarian excellence that sustained and prospered them for many millennia. Was this the First People version of liberty, equality and fraternity?

- Thus, it seems that First Nation spirituality, stewardship, custodianship, citizenship and governance evolved to be of the people, by the people, for the people.

- It seems that gender roles were mostly respectful, equitable and functional. Women were able to be heard, and were highly active in spirituality, culture-building, leadership, stewardship, custodianship, lore-enforcement, decision-making, responsibility and accountability. Women were reverent and practical, nurturing and strong, harmonising and authentic. Women were clear, capable and active stewards, leaders and elders. Women were also clear and assertive voices of reverence, dignity, respect, rationality, integrity, congruence, discipline, responsibility and accountability. They were prominent in all aspects of family, community and ecology. Women were a very positive force in First People families and communities. This is a revolutionary possibility for us.

- Gender equality was unlikely to be ideal as we politically-idealistic Westerners imagine it 'should' be. But, in contrast to Abrahamic and

Hindu religions, women seemed not to be institutionally and culturally lesser, repressed, degraded, exploited and abused. It seems that women freely and effectively contributed to all community functions and endeavours; far beyond the stereotypical role of child rearing. As well, as necessary, women were fierce, warrior-like defenders of their safety and respect. Women were not to be disrespected or messed-with.

- As is the case in contemporary First Nation society, women were key voices of purpose, reverence, dignity, safety, well-being, vision, reason, justice, social cohesion, and cultural purity. Again, this is a revolutionary possibility for us in the 21st century.

- Elderly women and men were-are greatly respected and esteemed as elders, leaders, sages and experts.

- Spirituality, kinship, culture, relationship and ecology were valued and positioned above patriarchal, chauvinistic, misogynistic and narcissistic gratifications of individualism, sexism, agism, tribalism, exceptionalism and nationalism. The relative absence of harmful isms is a revelation.

- Socially, the priorities of spirituality-culture, kinship, culture, relationship and ecology were prized in lieu of egoic mindsets of chauvinism, patriarchy, materiality, wealth, consumerism, prestige, position, power and politics. Another extraordinary hope for revolution.

- To a great extent, the positive and pragmatic strengths of spirituality and culture enabled tribes to manage strong or aberrant personalities; to minimise potentially destructive politics; and to avert destabilising and destructive narcissistic and sociopathic power-plays — within tribes, and among tribes. Imagine this level of potential safety, sanity, decency and integrity in our modern world.

- The priorities of First People collective-spiritual-cultural consciousness became the explicit and implicit mindful common good' of 'the whole, diverse multitude' that made up the whole Nation of Peoples. This holistic ethos arose from consciousness of the whole of the Island as the sacred space of Country; including the inviolability of nature's systems, networks and processes that comprise the entirety of the island. Imagine this level of holistic consciousness as a mindful guide for us global citizens moving forward.

- The values of mindfulness-culture-spirituality — atunement, reverence, dignity, humility, sensitivity, integrity, simplicity, contentment and gratitude were purposefully and systematically educated, socialised, internalised, integrated, networked and maintained as congruent, coherent, holistic life-sustaining spiritual and pragmatic imperatives and accountabilities.

- This network of values, principles and priorities evolved, integrated and consolidated over a 60,000-year timeframe; ultimately, to form the 'internal locus of collective consciousness' of Australia's First Peoples.

- These cultural-spiritual-mindful — cohesive highly functional values, principles and priorities were their individual, familial, social, collective and ecological consciousness at the time of settlement.

- As said before, to legitimise settlement, evidence of a highly conscious, widespread, sophisticated society had to be removed from history. To this end, evidence of sophisticated, holistic, pragmatic, functional consciousness was largely obliterated. False evidence to support the fraudulent myth of Terra Nullius was very effectively proffered and proliferated. Over 230 years later, a growing body of legal, archaeological, historical and cultural evidence is resoundingly refuting the myth Terra Nullius. Evidence is revealing the truth of sophisticated tribal governance; and is building increasing hope for reality, dignity, respect, justice, empowerment and healing.

- However, there has not been unreserved, sincere, comprehensive acknowledgement, contrition, accountability and effective remediation for the indignities, travesties, injustices, lies, disparagements and crimes of history by successive British or Australian Federal and State governments, institutions and peoples. This situation leaves a massive blot on British and Australian history; and a gaping, bleeding, infected wound in Australian society. Despite legal president and mounting evidence, previous and current elitist white political, religious and societal institutions have shown slow, inconsistent and superficial inclination toward unreserved recognition, contrition, responsibility, accountability, reconciliation and healing of intergenerational trauma. The May 2022 change of government and its revolutionary make up, heralds an aspiration and commitment for Australia to do much better by way of Constitutional Recognition, Treaty, Voice to Parliament and Truth-telling.

- Australia's First People situation and hope for truth, dignity, justice, empowerment and healing is paralleled throughout the globe. Worldwide, First Peoples thirst for these fundamental and essential imperatives.

Breathe, Digest, Absorb, Apply

That's a lot of revelationary, revolutionary and evolutionary cultural awareness, principles and learning to digest and absorb. Remember, any one of these dot-points has the power to educate, enlighten, transform and revolutionise us. Each dot-point is greatly instructive for you and me, for all Australians, and for 21st century humankind. Also, just as with empowering values and principles that are discussed throughout this book, all the nuanced dot-points in this chapter overlap, interconnect and mutually reinforce each other. When we apply the priorities and principles from one dot-point, we position ourselves to appreciate and apply the priorities and principles from all other dot-points.

Therefore, reread each dot-point, slowly, meditatively and open-mindedly. Sit with respective themes and interconnected themes in silence. Absorb the revelations, values, principles, priorities, intelligence, wisdom, enlightenment, pragmatics, potential and possibilities of each dot-point; and of the whole chapter. Feel free to stay with points that resonate strongly. Let them soak into your consciousness. Let the values, principles, rationalities and priorities of Australia's First People spirituality become part of your personal, relational, citizenry and community intelligence and mindfulness. Let relational, communal and ecological values and principles lead you toward a purposeful, values-based, rational, sophisticated and strategic appreciation of existence; including human existence.

How are you feeling? What are you thinking?

Are you ready to contribute to conversations, and to help strategize a mindful way forward toward evolving — awareness, decency, dignity, respect, sensitivity, rationality, integrity and accountability?

By your future contributions, are you ready to do better?

In a spirit of decency, integrity and accountability, in Australia and globally, it is time for Recognition, Voice, Treaty and Truth-telling.

Breathe; and sit with this imperative.

Principles, Priorities and Aspirations

Here are seven interconnected aspirations that crystallise how we might learn from the previous two chapters on First People enlightenment; in Australia and globally. These aspirations are built on awareness, respect, decency, integrity, rationality and accountability. They are crucial prerequisites for ongoing evolution of humankind and for the healing and rejuvenation Mother Earth.

1. **In the spirit of Avatar, 'see' First Peoples**. Love them for who they are. Love them as they are today. Afford them unconditional and everlasting compassion in the light of hundreds of years of degradation, devastation, morbidity and death. Graciously reverence and embrace their enduring dignity and resilience. Mindfully and compassionately understand and empathise with their enduring wounds and post-settlement trauma.

2. **Confirm First Peoples** by honouring them as highly esteemed forebears, elders, leaders, role models, custodians, stewards and leaders. Confirm them as creators and curators of timeless ecological knowledge, truths, values, rationality, principles, priorities, wisdom and enlightenment. Confirm them as original, authentic and competent custodians of Country and Mother Earth.

3. **Respect First Peoples** as legitimate, credible and sovereign. Respect them as original, authentic, rational and uniquely gifted. Respect them as relational, communal and ecological exemplars, role models and statespersons. Respect First Peoples as highly esteemed human kin and human elders.

4. **Embrace First** holistic systems and harmonious, functional networks of communities, ecologies, customs, lore and governance. Embrace First Peoples models as mindfully attuned relational, communal and ecologically peaceful, symbiotic and homeostatic ways of being human.

431

Embrace First People consciousness as a revelation of harmony and peace, and as a revelation of how not to be sadomasochistic and destructive.

5. **Defer to First Peoples** by actively and strategically seeking their relational, communal and ecological wisdom and guidance. Engage and listen purposely, attentively, constructively, humbly and non-defensively. Make very few statements, while asking many sensitive, searching, inquiring questions. Actively and openly learn from timeless, archetypal First People enlightenment. Actively and openly absorb and follow their counsel about strategic ecological values, issues, priorities, principles and processes. In particular, inquire of and be open to the 'feminine mother wisdom' and the enlightenment of indigenous women. Defer to these archetypal women and men as loving and wise elders, custodians, mentors and teachers.

6. **Heal with First Peoples** through unreserved repentance for historical and contemporary colonial harms. Ask First Peoples what we need to do to heal and rejuvenate humankind and Country. Collaborate with First peoples as friends, mentors, leaders, elders and healers.

7. **Move forward with First Peoples** by committing to internalise their consciousness of perpetuity — their purpose, perspective, reverence, grace, dignity, integrity, rationality, responsibility and accountability. Aspire to evolve by embracing the 'oneness in diversity'. Internalise and be guided by seamless, 'holistic, inter-complementary homeostasis'. Aspire to imbue and apply a locus of relational, communal and ecological reverence and discipline Move forward with First Peoples by embracing and supporting Recognition, Voice, Treaty and Truth-telling.

What is resonating for you that might help you and us do better?

Women's Voices and Women Role Models

In addition to hearing the voices of First People, another crucial aspect of the way forward is that we men tune into 'the feminine voice'; and the archetypal voice of 'Mother'. Humankind needs to recognise, embrace, listen to, and encourage wise and gracious women as role models, mentors, stewards, elders and healers. We need to hear 'the feminine voice' of critical thinking and strategic awareness. We need to observe the 'rational mother feminine' in action. We need to embrace the Yin feminine to balance and remediate the millennia of the dysfunctional and destructive dominance of the Yang masculine.

Women, please, tell us men what we need to hear. Teach us how to be respectful, dignified, gracious, nurturing, protective, strategic and sustaining. Please, teach us to be much less short-sighted and narrow-sighted. Teach us how to be less and dysfunctional and destructive. Humankind needs wise, clear-minded and gracious women to help all of us learn to be intelligently relational, communal and ecological. The world needs a 'wise mother perspective and loving mother ethos' to help moderate millennia of the destructive, arbitrary, masculine will to power. We men need to incorporate 'a wise and loving feminine-mother voice' to moderate our habitually inept, clumsy, chauvinistic, patriarchal, paternalistic heavy-handedness.

My hope is that many wise and gracious women — Grandmothers, Mothers, Wives, Aunties, Daughters, Sisters, Nieces and Cousins will rise to be exemplars, role-models, champions, educators, leaders, elders and nurturers of dignity and critical thinking. May many more women initiate and lead intelligent conversations about the core values of awareness, sensitivity, reverence, integrity, relationship, community, ecology and accountability. I will be inspired and heartened to hear the voices of hitherto unseen, unheard and unknown women stewards, custodians, leaders, elders, teachers and role models. The voice of Amanda Gorman, the young African American poet, is such a voice.

Name other women voices. Listen to them. Read about them. Learn from them. Be educated and inspired by them. Join them. Work with them.

The entirety of the world and every country are replete with actual and potential women role models and women leaders who are ready to rise to the fore. In Australia, as in all countries, we are blessed with many older and younger woman voices of clarity, dignity, respect, rationality, courage and hope. Across the globe, may many more women role-models and leaders speak to us, challenge us, inspire us, inform us, nurture us, guide us and lead us in the ways of dignity and rationality.

A Word of Caution

A word of caution — women, be careful not to be seduced by a long list of masculinised, egoic, left hemisphere proclivities. Women, consciously and steadfastly avoid the following age-old masculine inclinations — shallow and crass ambition; pathological will to power; obscene self-aggrandization; unabashed self-promotion; uncensored transactional leveraging; unconscionable greed; shameless empire building; out of control lust for materiality; narrow-sighted over-reliance on technological solutions to complex, soulful human issues; and refusal to be aware, sensitive, decent, integrous and accountable. Women, in your aspirations, contributions and rise to influence — beware these masculine proclivities, and minimise them. They are death to aware, sensitive, decent, integrous, competent and accountable stewardship, leadership and eldership.

Potential women leaders, don't become female versions of the worst of cultural, political and religious masculinity. Don't become female versions of Mr Hyde. Beware the subtle and sneaky proclivities of the ignorance and ego that explained in earlier chapters. Beware the gravity of deceptive and projective, self-defending and self-promoting egoic blind spots, biases and groupthink. Listen to irony, and learn from her. Beware the dumbness of anti-science and aversion to critical thinking. Beware the inanity, delusions and deceptions of new-age fads, junk-science, pop-psychology and conspiracy ideations.

Beware pathetic, narcissistic, masculine longing for approval, inclusion, fame, status and prestige. Beware egoic self-pity and victimhood. Beware egoic preciousness, indignance, anger, resentment and bitterness. Beware egoic presumptions, pretention and pontification. Beware masculine propensities for narcissism and sociopathy. Beware Machiavellian sociopathic big lies,

434

corruption and the criminality of masculinised politics and religion. Beware populism and populists. Beware the lure of religious, political and new-age conspiracy cults. Beware a legion of pitfalls of egoically masculinised institutions and structures.

Women — Be vigilant. Be aware. Be informed. Be sensitive. Be compassionate. Be respectful. Be rational. Be non-defensive. Be critical thinkers. Listen attentively and reflectively. Be open to feedback. Be disciplined in thoughts, words and deeds.

Such breadth and level of mindfulness are rare among us humans; especially among highly egoic, masculinised men. My sense is that 'the feminine' and the 'wise, loving Mother' have much more potential to imbue and channel the dignity and rationality of mindfulness, than does the contemporary world of entrenched egoic masculinity.

How might women and the female collective, exercise the voices of dignity and reason to the greatest effect?

In particular, what and how might First People women and Women of Colour contribute to evolutionary and revolutionary enlightenment, leadership and eldership by women.

Men, what do we need to do to support women in their rise to local and global stewardship, custodianship, leadership and eldership?

What must we men be careful <u>not</u> to do so as to not sabotage this cultural evolution?

In what ways will you, woman and men, support our evolution toward the feminine and mother?

I have written a number of poems that crystalise priorities and possibilities of leadership by First People, Women of Colour and other women. The poems, this book and the Companion Workbook are intended to help you and me and a critical mass us to do better.

Here is one of these poems.

Women of Reality and Hope

Women of reality and hope ...
Speak your truth, tell your stories and share your vision.
Speak to be clear and forthright, but not to judge and stereotype.

435

Speak to us men patiently and persistently; because many of us are very slow to learn, mature and evolve.

Speak to enlighten us about man-made issues and harms, including those of malignant masculinity; be truth-tellers.

Speak to catalyse awareness of long-overdue facts, critical thinking, reason and logic.

Speak to men who desire to understand the nuances of disenfranchisement; and the experiences of the disenfranchised.

Speak to men of power who may not desire to understand, but who must listen hear, understand, mature and evolve.

Speak to help us let go a vast array of arbitrary fantasies, biases and delusions.

Speak to highlight realities that must be understood for humankind to evolve and survive.

Speak to help us imbue a vision of humans at our best.

Speak to nurture the priorities and principles that will enable us to build decency, integrity and ethical propriety.

Speak to create and nurture possibility and possibilities.

Speak to educate us about the plight of vulnerable, disempowered peoples and endangered species.

Speak, to inform and educate men about the harms of ignorance, insensitivity and disrespect.

Speak to spur us away from wilful ignorance and toward love and grace in thoughts, words and deeds.

Speak to proclaim the power of conscious, kind, respectful values-in-action.

Speak to nurture and build freedom, autonomy, inclusion, equality and justice.

Speak to liberate women and men from subservience to dominant, egoic men in an egoic man's world.

Speak to enable women and men to step away from patriarchy, paternalism and misogyny.

Speak to stop chauvinistic, malignant and toxic male coercion, violence, abuse and all the cause trauma and suffering.

Speak to create safety and respect in family, relationship and community.

Speak to nurture dignity within each one and among us all.

Speak to nurture joy, peace, contentment and gratitude within each of us and among all of us.

Speak to convey your womanly grace and feminine authority as custodians, leaders and elders.

Speak to enlighten men and women with revelation of what was, what is, and what must be.

Speak to inspire a revolution of awareness, reality, priority, wisdom, integrity and accountability.

Altogether, speak to nurture a revelation, revolution and evolution of kindness and sanity.

What aspects of this poem have spoken to you?

My Acknowledgements and Commitments

In the light of all that is written in this book, I give my unreserved and heavy-hearted acknowledgement of our man-made history of indignities and injustices through gross insensitivity, exploitation, degradation, abuse and violence toward our fellow species, the earth, women, children, First Peoples, people of colour, the poor, the defenceless, and other disenfranchised peoples.

I acknowledge that we men can do much better in terms of authentic, intentional love through dignity, respect, sensitivity, decency, reason, empowerment and justice for these groups; and, I conform that decency and integrity call us to do so.

I commit to nurture and promote reverence, dignify and decency for all peoples, but particularly to reverence and dignify First Peoples, women, children, people of colour, and other disempowered and disenfranchise peoples.

I commit to advocate for dignity, respect and justice for the greater good of all peoples, for the good of our fellow species, and for the good the planet.

I commit to be guided by science and by legitimate and credible research processes, evidence gathering and critical analysis.

I commit to be guided by First People wisdom, the wisdom of Peoples of Colour; feminine wisdom, and the wisdom of the archetypal Mother.

I commit to foster critical thinking and to nurture integrity, rationality, factuality, sanity, competence and strategic relational, communal and ecological intelligence within persons, corporations, institutions, systems and governments.

I commit to nurture relationship, community and ecological systems awareness in all domains and at all levels.

I commit to contribute to and nurture awareness, reflection, honesty, transparency and accountability in relationships, citizenship, stewardship, custodianship, leadership, eldership and governance in all domains, and at all levels.

I commit to lifelong learning about the issues, values, principles, priorities and possibilities contained in this book.

I commit to embrace legitimate and empowering revelation, revolution and evolution.

I commit to speak and write about hopes and possibilities with all the mindful — factful awareness, clarity, reverence, dignity, courage, integrity and intelligence I can muster.

These are I my hope and commitment to do better.

Which of these paragraphs have resonated for you?

To what will you commit?

Your Acknowledgements

To male readers, will you pause for a moment, and acknowledge our man-made history of degradation, abuse and violence toward our fellow species, the earth, women, children, First Peoples, people of colour, the poor, the defenceless, and the disenfranchised?

If you are a religious person, will you pause and acknowledge thousands of years of suffering caused by patriarchal arbitrariness, fantasies, contrivances, chauvinism, misogyny, dogmas, impositions, lies, corruption, degradations, criminality and other toxic and malignant aspects of man-made religion?

If you are an ideologue or a politician, will you pause and acknowledge hundreds of years of suffering from the man-contrived arbitrariness, narratives, spin, propaganda, lies, corruption, criminality, incompetence, degradations, violence and other toxic and malignant aspects of masculinised politics and ideology?

If you are an industrialist, corporatist or are rich and powerful, will you pause and acknowledge hundreds of years of man-made suffering from misuse of power, greed, empire-building, exploitation, contrivances, lies, corruption, criminality, degradations, violence and other toxic and malignant actions toward people, other species, and the earth?

For me, the legacy of our patriarchal, paternalistic and chauvinistic history is unavoidably and painfully obvious. I feel honour-bound to pause and acknowledge this reality. I feel inwardly compelled to imagine and envisage how we men might adjust and evolve and do better personally, relationally, communally, ecologically, spiritually, professionally, institutionally, politically and culturally.

Men, do you feel honour-bound to acknowledge this reality?

My fellow men, do you feel honour-bound to do better than the harms of patriarchy, chauvinism, misogyny and toxic masculinity?

Do you feel honour-bound to contribute to the dignity of humankind, to the protection and rejuvenation of species, and to the healing and revitalisation of the earth?

Men, are you open to ways that women, First Peoples, peoples of colour, and disenfranchised peoples can rise to the fore and help all of us fulfil these commitments, aspirations, intentions and hopes?

Here is another poem that might help us men to do better.

Men — It's Time

Men — it's time to listen, hear and respond with love and grace.
It's time to listen to women, to hear their stories, to understand their
perspective.
It's time to listen to the truth about violence, fear, harassment, sexism,
inequality and disadvantage.
It's time to listen to First Peoples and Peoples of Colour, to hear their voices,
to absorb their stories and feel their trauma.
It's time to talk with First Peoples about the devastation and trauma of
colonisation and industrialisation.
It's time to talk with Peoples of Colour about slavery, exclusion, racism,
persecution, disadvantage and other traumatic degradations.
It's time to talk with refugees and hear their stories of persecution, dislocation,
deprivation and trauma.
It's time to talk with marginalised peoples in poverty, severe illness and great
mental strain.
It's time to hear about cultural and racial harms, including systemic and
structural disadvantage and injustice.
It's time to open your hearts and minds to those who endure so much harm and
terrible suffering.
It's time to embrace facts, to embrace the realities of a toxic web of man-made
horror and pain.
It's time for truth-telling, to hear the truth of so many truths.
It's time to empathise with peoples who suffer, to sit with them in reality, love,
grace and hope.
It's time to be present, compassionate and kind through loving attitudes, words
and values-in-action.
It's time to let go unkind, unhelpful, and unfounded prejudiced opinions, beliefs
and judgements.
It's time to let go the presumptions of ignorance, to listen to understand, care,
restore and heal.

It's time to replace judgement with a consciousness of awareness, sensitivity, respect and generosity.

It's time to recognise, call-out and stand against corruption, criminality, narcissism and sociopathy in religion and politics.

It's time to stand against all expressions of sectarianism, racism, misogyny, sexism and chauvinism.

It's time to choose decency, integrity and accountability for what we men said and say, did and do.

It's time to stop judging and pontificating about pain that you have not experienced and do not feel.

It's time to ask many open-minded, enquiring questions; to listen with humility, courage and compassion.

It's time to seek facts and truths; to listen and listen and listen to facts as our core truths.

It's time to embrace the primordial, archetypal ways of the Feminine Mother holism and homeostasis.

It's time to exemplify symbiotic relational, communal and ecological priorities, values and principles.

It's time to dignify, respect and honour the wisdom of women, First Peoples and Peoples of Colour.

It's time to dignify, respect and join the strength and resilience of poor and alienated peoples.

It's time to be present, sentient, decent, integrous and accountable as you listen, learn and mature.

It's time to encourage your fellow men to love through grace-filled listening, values, words and deeds.

It's time to reform and transform societal institutions, and to purge them of presumption, prejudice and corruption.

It's time to be men of awareness, sensitivity, decency, integrity and accountability.

It's time for us to be men who listen, speak and act with grace-in-action and love-in-action.

Breathe

As with the previous chapters, if you are reacting defensively to what you have been reading, my best-guess is that the voice of ego saying: 'Not me. This is negative. This is wrong. It's not my fault. Don't blame me or my group for what happened throughout thousands of years of history. I am a good man. How dare you!'

Take sixty seconds to listen to your breath; and to feel the rise and fall of your chest. As your indignation, resistance and defences fade, it's possible that awareness, sensitivity and accountability may emerge.

What has resonated for you?

An Internal Locus

A central message of this book is that you and I and other readers can choose to blend an internal locus of dignity and critical thinking that will give us the inner capacity to be decent, rational and competent in relationships, roles and endeavours. We can choose and commit to and internalise values and analytical skills that will help us be appropriate, constructive and effective in family, at work, in local and global communities; and in our relationship with Country and Mother Earth. Women and men — each and all of us can choose to internalise a blend of values, principles and priorities that will enable us to be effective stewards and leaders in all areas of our day-to-day life.

We can choose to absorb, internalise and nurture mindful — strategic relational, communal and ecological awareness and sensitivity that will equip each of us, and 'the collective of us', in personhood, citizenship, stewardship and leadership.

We can choose to nurture an internal values and robust thinking processes that will help rise above egoic apathy, cynicism, ignorance and institutionalisation. We can choose values that can enable us to rise above egoic small-p political power-games, peer pressure, social media superficialities, new-age pop-psychology fantasies, shallow hip-spirituality, junk-science, and conspiracy paranoia.

An internal locus of conscious, purposeful values and rationality can be our individual and collective inner reservoir of dignity, clarity, freedom and autonomy. An internal locus of values and rationality can be our reservoir of personhood, citizenship, stewardship and leadership.

Not Beliefs

Very importantly, as emphasised before, note that the values, principles and priorities explored in this book have nothing to do with beliefs. In this book, I'm not suggesting that you 'believe' or 'believe in' anything. In fact, repeatedly, I suggest that you stop saying: "I believe this or that"? Stop saying: "My belief is this or that". Frequently, I exhort you to stop defaulting to, referencing and clinging to cultural beliefs, religious beliefs, political beliefs, new-age beliefs, social media beliefs and conspiratorial beliefs. Many times, I have emphasised that beliefs, along with opinions, are inherently arbitrary, baseless, fantasised, made up, biased, parochial, prejudicial, exclusive and divisive. Beliefs are substantially unhelpful. They are much more a part of the problem, than part of the solution; because, beliefs divert us from facts, evidence, critical thinking, values, principles and priorities. And, beliefs dispose us to egoic, arbitrary, inductive, self-serving judgements and ignorance.

Again, and again, I have suggested that you and I demonstrate our values and rationality by the decency, sensitivity, integrity and efficacy of what we say and do — from person to person, from situation to situation, in every relationship, in every encounter, in every role, and in every endeavour. Over, and over, I have said, don't get sucked into made-up religious, political, new-age or conspiratorial fantasies, opinions, beliefs, ideas, stories, narratives, rationalisations, defences and justifications.

We give ourselves the potential to do better if we choose, internalise and live through values-in-action and principles-in-action.

A Final Recap of Principles for Values and Rationality

Here is a final recap and ready-reference of twenty practical principles that may help you move forward and do better. Read each one slowly. Highlight the ones that resonate for you.

1. Nurture an internal locus of dignity, sensitivity, reverence, , rationality, integrity and accountability through your application of the following principles.

2. Speak and act with awareness, decency, kindness and compassion; and with factfulness, reason, integrity, transparency and accountability.

3. Integrate and apply these values and priorities in all your relationships, roles, endeavours, choices, decisions and aspirations; and apply them within your spheres of concern and your spheres of influence.

4. Be mindfully intentional, congruent, coherent and consistent. Nurture these purposeful attributes as the pillars of who you are as evidenced by what you do. Apply mindfully intentional, congruent, coherent and consistent values as pillars of your personal integrity, your depth of character, your relational maturity, your ecological clarity, and your societal credibility.

5. Be less self-serving, less self-leveraging, and less transactional. Instead, be more relationally aware, focussed, gracious and bighearted. Give much more than you expect, want, take or get. In the way of Uncle Bob — love faithfully, simply, freely, practically and generously.

6. Confirm and nurture your commitment to reality by being factually informed through accurate, reliable data; by the processes and disciplines of authentic, credible research and science; and by disciplined critical thinking.

7. Consciously minimise arbitrary, wilful and fanciful ignorance; and minimise distortion through denial of reality, contrivance, deception and dishonesty.

8. Nurture reality by not indulging the shallow, dreamy, romantic whims of egoic fantasy and wishful thinking.

9. Nurture reality by steering clear of arbitrary religious myths, political spin, pop-culture fads, social media memes and conspiracy falsehoods. Nurture reality by steering clear of egoic arbitrariness, fantasies, fictions, fads, beliefs and opinions — in all their forms.

10. Gravitate toward and internalise the peace, joy and freedom of simplicity, contentment and gratitude.

11. With this network of values, principles and priorities in mind, actively and purposefully cleanout, shed and prune. Intentionally discard arbitrary, non-factual, bullshit — fantasies, beliefs, opinions, judgements and biases. And, don't replace old arbitrary clutter with new arbitrary clutter and bullshit.

12. Be open to possibilities, and be available to contribute, but don't get caught up in trendy new-age optimism; and steer well clear of quixotic conspiracy theories.

13. Be discerning, and be open to intuition, including the meditative calm of sentience, presence and equanimity, which are inherent in mindfulness and in an attitude of grace. But, be careful not to stray into romantic, fanciful, wishful, whimsical make-believe.

14. While being mindful of self-respect and legitimate personal feelings and boundaries, embrace difficulties, adversity and personal suffering. Let them burn-away egoic arbitrary, self-servingness, fantasies, entitlements, resistances, scripts and insecurities.

15. Recognise, treasure and nurture our unbounded, undivided community of peoples, the abundance and diversity of species, and our boundless interdependence of the oneness of the multiplicity of the ecologies and systems of the earth. Nurture and apply your awareness of interconnected symbiosis and homeostasis of relationships, communities, ecologies and systems. Commit to and apply purposeful, strategic, relational, communal, ecological systems priorities and principles in all domains.

Ponder the human body as a ready exemplar of oneness through intercomplementarity and interdependent systems of diversity. Your hand doesn't judge your eyes; or want to be your brain. And, visa-versa. Instead, they work together in the beauty and brilliance of seamless systems of hand-eye coordination, anatomical intercomplementarity, and bodily harmony and systems ecology.

16. Absorb First People revelation of strategic reverence, awareness, perspective, symbiosis and homeostasis. Learn from and embrace the example of First People sentience, values, principles, priorities and disciplines. You and I can share in the mindful dignity, reason, genius and enlightenment of First People approach to relationship, community and ecology. Use your citizenry intelligence to nurture strategic relational, communal and ecological priorities that will enable First Peoples, environments and the earth to heal, recover, rejuvenate and continue. Follow the lead of First Peoples by falling in love with Country and Mother-Earth; her systems, and her species; including her diversity of peoples. Reverence First Peoples. Embrace them Protect them. Nurture them. Learn from them. Support and ensure their dignity and continuance.

17. Embrace and nurture the Yin-wisdom of women and the potential of the-feminine and Mother. Embrace and nurture the strength, sensitivity, resilience, stewardship, leadership and eldership of women. Welcome, nurture and imbue the grace, dignity, intelligence, reason and resilience of womanhood in all relationships, roles, institutions, systems, and governance.

18. Identify and draw close to mindful, reverent, sensitive, intelligent, integrous and wise roles-models, mentors, custodians, stewards, leaders and elders. Absorb and emulate their network of perspective, awareness, sensitivity, dignity, rationality, integrity, knowledge, maturity, vision and discipline.

19. Use your compassion, integrity and intelligence to contribute to the reduction of structural and systemic injustice and suffering. Support and nurture solutions to human issues; at home, at work, in community, and globally. Protect the poor. Feed the hungry. Heal the sick. Nurture respect, dignity, freedom, equality and practical justice for all peoples.

Nurture unbounded common good for the unbounded collective of humankind.

20. Every day, for the rest of your life, breathe consciously. Every day, practice the silence and stillness of listening attentively to and feeling the rhythm of your breath. Practice mental timeout through Breath Meditation. May Dadirri Mindfulness and Breath Meditation arouse, internalise and channel the core values and qualities of reverence, dignity, sensitivity, awareness, reason, perspective, rationality, responsibility and accountability; within you, through you and among you.

Remember, the Companion Workbook can help you clarify and action values and intentions.

Be the Difference to Make a Difference

Thank you for your goodwill and perseverance. Thank you for asking, 'Can we do better'? Thank you for aspiring to do better. Thank you for aspiring to help others to do better. Thank you for being the difference that will make a difference.

Our Final Questions

What are you feeling?

What will you do to move forward with dignity and rationality?

What do we humans need to do to move forward?

At home, locally and globally, in what ways might you contribute to the evolution of humankind?

What is the next step for you?

What's the next step for us humans?

I would be happy for us to connect and discuss possible ways forward?

Appendix 1 – Definition of Terms

It is important that you know 'what I mean' when I use particular terms. Use this section as a ready-reference of what I mean when using these terms; and for the purpose of clarification. In this book, all these terms interconnect to create my understanding of current human dispositions, issues, risks, possibilities, and hopes for societal evolution.

Mind is a universal reference to the complex networks of the brain. It is an arbitrary, universal, easy-lazy, simplistic, vague, nebulous, convenient, generic, broad-brush, shortcut, substitute and reference for enormously the brain's complex neuro-chemical mental processes and networks. The simplistic notion, 'mind', is an easy, grab-bag term for apparent, mental activity and patterns, including interwoven networks of perceptions, thoughts, emotions, imaginings, beliefs, judgements, and opinions. Mind is a shorthand reference for the myriad of electrochemical intricacies and interconnected anatomical complexities of the human brain. The actual human brain is vastly more complex than our 'automatic-easy-lazy-simplistic-arbitrary-abstraction', mind. In this book, mind means the apparently common stuff we think, and typical ways we process information and issues.

Mindfulness is a peaceful state of conscious, undistracted awareness, presence and sensitivity. Mindfulness is being fully aware and present in the here and now. It is about be tuned-into what is happening within yourself – e.g., your thoughts, emotions, anxieties and bodily sensations. It is about being tuned into your relationships and what is happening for others. It is about being tune-into the kaleidoscope of what is happening around you; sights, sounds, smells, activities, problems, tensions, conflicts, harms, pain, suffering, joys and possibilities.

Values are standards for behaviours, actions, relationships, and roles. Values enable us to discern priority options, standards, choices, decisions, contributions, endeavours and plans. Values are the basis of personhood, relationship, citizenship, stewardship and leadership. Values advocated in this book include awareness, reverence, honesty, sensitivity, graciousness, kindness, decency, compassion, integrity, critical thinking, logic and accountability. These are encapsulated in the foundational and overarching values of dignity and reason. The thesis of this book is that conscious, intentional values give us clear awareness and concern about the issues and consequences that arise from an absence of value-guided actions. It is values that need to be our priorities and guides; not opinions, beliefs, confabulations, and dogma.

Principles are fundamental 'values-in-action' that guide attitudes, behaviours, actions, relationships, roles, systems and processes. Principles are foundational to all vision, standards, benchmarks, aspirations and endeavours. This book recommends principles based on and guided by dignified and reasoned criteria, such as 'kindness-in-action', 'respect-in-action' and 'logic-in-action'. Typically, principles give us clear awareness and concern about the issues and consequences that arise from an absence of rational, integrous, guiding values.

Internal Locus is a perspective or orientation that one's guiding values, principles and rationality arise from within the person, not from other people or external influences, such as religion or political ideology. A conscious intentional internal locus tells us that we can purposefully identify and choose our guiding values, principles and priorities, such as an and internal locus of reverence, internal locus grace, an internal locus of dignity, an internal locus of reason, an internal locus of freedom, and an internal locus of responsibility. An internal locus is guided by conscious, intentional awareness, and by sensitivity toward issues and consequences; to which we can choose to respond with an internal locus of decency, integrity, critical thinking and accountability. Often, our internal locus is called our conscience. But, it is more than that. Internal locus is also our inner compass, our network of ethics, our sense of boundaries, our sense of responsibility, and, very importantly, our commitment to transparency and accountability.

Stewardship is our values-based, dedicated, dutiful, careful, responsible accountability for the custodianship, care, management, protection and nurturance of something valuable that is entrusted to a person or a group. Stewardship is guided by values and reason. Typically, stewardship is motivated by a strong awareness, reverence and concern for the issues and consequences that arise from a failure of stewardship. Stewardship is motivated by concern for issues that arise from an absence of decency, care, integrity, duty, protection, nurturance, responsibility and accountability. This book invites readers to be stewards of values, rationality, relationships, roles, responsibilities and endeavours.

Leadership is the action of leading people; hopefully, toward ethical and high-quality standards, goals and desired outcomes. Leadership is a network of processes that nurtures a sense of belonging to a team, and belong to community. Leadership is inherently communal. At its best, leadership nurtures positive and constructive communal values, principles, priorities, responsibilities and accountabilities. Leadership engenders a sense of common ground and common good. It enables individuals and groups to meld their thoughts and effort into a unity of values, purpose and effort. In that, leadership is inherently purposeful, strategic and systematic. It creates a shared or team or community focus on big picture and long-term priorities, hopes, direction, outcomes and goals. Leadership is also ecological; that is, it is systems-oriented, network-oriented, and strategically future oriented.

The next sentence is long. Leadership enables individuals to focus, to delay personal gratification, to contribute knowledge and skills, to make sacrifices, to work together, to persist, to be resilient, and to endure long periods of effort with the shared conscious intention to work together toward a shared communal priority, and to achieve agreed-upon desired values, hopes, and strategic ends for the common good of the vast majority.

To do this, leadership informs, supports, inspires, harnesses collaboration, and enables people move forward toward a desired future. Leadership requires and imbibes clarity and vision about values and strategic priorities. It imbibes an uncompromising desire, intent, aspiration and willingness to work smart and work hard for years and decades; perhaps for an entire lifetime, and over ensuing generations. Leadership is shared by people with a diverse range of knowledge, skills, roles and responsibilities. Leadership instils a shared internal locus of values, priority, desire and intention. It melds 'the diversity of us' into unity of mind and intention. Leadership melds oneness and wholeness, and moves 'a unity mind and muscle' forward, as one. I invite you to contribute to leadership in family, at work, and in local and global community.

Integrity is a blend of awareness, honesty, decency, responsibility, discipline and accountability that enables people and institutions to think, speak and act with congruence, consistency and coherence. Integrity guides and drives communication and actions that are values-based, principles-based, and ethics-based. Integrity is an inner voice that strongly urges us to be honest, decent, respectful, responsible and accountable. Integrity is motivated by reverence, dignity and reason. Typically, integrity has a clear awareness and concern about the issues and consequences that arise from an absence of integrity; from an absence of honesty, care, stewardship, leadership, strategic discipline, and accountability.

Note the network of linkages between values, principles, and internal locus of intent, stewardship, leadership and integrity. This network is interwoven throughout this book.

Revelation is surprising, unexpected and previously unknown awareness, facts and understandings that become a conscious and are integrated into knowledge, wisdom, good judgement and action.

Revolution is an unexpected awareness that catalyses the embrace and application of dignifying and rational energy, values, principles, priorities and aspirations to empowering stewardship and leadership.

Evolution is the steady, progressive, incremental intentional development and improvement.

Grace is conscious but unforced and uncontrived reverence, dignity and equanimity. It is an unspoken inner preference to be gracious, which is an inclination to be sensitive, compassionate, patient and kind. Grace is an inner disposition to welcome, embrace and honour difference and diversity. Grace is inherently inclusive. It is a natural disposition and preference not to be judgemental toward people and situations. Grace is also peaceful surrender to the reality of data and facts. It is a peaceful and kindly expression of reason and rationality. Grace is a basis for respect, decency and compassion. Grace gives us a clear awareness of the issues and consequences that arise from an absence of conscious intentional peace, dignity, decency, respect and compassion. Grace enables us to be clear, concerned, focussed, firm, determined, patient and kind in the ways we deal with people and situations; and in ways we work toward priorities and goals.

Reverence is deep and abiding mindfulness of loving, respecting, valuing, knowing, dignifying and embracing of peoples, Land, Country, our fellow species and Mother Earth. It is doing only that which shows sentience, awareness, sensitivity, decency, integrity, responsibility and accountability.

Dignity is inherent and innate personal value and worthiness. Dignity includes reverence, sensitivity, respect, honour and esteem; irrespective of beliefs, education, position, wealth, ethnicity and social status. Dignity is inherent in sensitive and reasoned communication and actions. Typically, dignity has clear awareness and concern about the issues and consequences that arise from an absence of respectful, reasoned and respectful priorities, communication and actions.

Reason consists of a network of mental capacities that enables us to explore ideas and possibilities through logic and systematic analysis. Reasoning contributes rationality to discussion, prioritisation and problem-solving. *The 'voice of reason' strives to explain and support ideas, and to critique with respect, fairness, mental discipline, facts and evidence.* The voice of reason is guided by grace and dignifying values. Inherently, reasoned thinking is sensitive, factual and realistic. Inherently, reason gives us conscious, intentional awareness and concern about issues and consequences that arise from lack of facts, evidence, logic and critical thinking.

Critical Thinking is an intellectually and mentally disciplined process of analysing and weighing information, data, facts and ideas. Assessing and weighing observation, experience, reflection, and discussion are involved in critical thinking. These processes help form values, principles, conclusions, priorities, actions and goals. Critical thinking gives us conscious awareness and concern about issues and consequences that arise from the absence of values, reason and critical analysis. Critical thinking is a key component of one's internal locus of discernment and judgement.

Rational Thinking is a process of weighing variables and values. It assesses data, facts, information, judgments, opinions and beliefs to form sound logical and defendable rationale for choices, decisions, priorities, goals and actions. Rationality is about maximising objective ways to define issues and problems, and to draw the most factual conclusions we can muster. Rationality is guided by values, reason, pragmatic principles, and disciplined investigative and analytical processes. Rationality equips us with conscious, intentional awareness and concern about issues and consequences that arise in the absence of data, facts, reason and critical thinking. Reason, critical thinking and rationality are close cousins.

Accountability focusses on being transparent and answerable for values, reason and actions in our attitudes, communication, actions, choices, decisions, responsibilities, outcomes and consequences. Accountability is guided by values and facts. It is motivated by conscious, intentional awareness and concern about the issues and consequences that arise when we are not answerable for our values, attitudes, beliefs, opinions, choices, decisions, behaviours and actions.

Ecology is interconnected interdependence. It is a network of factors, and a system of features. For us humans, being strategic ecological requires us to be guided by values, principles, reason and strategic priorities. Inherently, ecology has conscious, intentional awareness and concern about issues and consequences that arise from an absence of ecological awareness, and that arise from diminished ecologic prioritisation of roles, responsibilities, goals and accountabilities. We are as effective as we are strategically ecological. Ecological thinking, prioritising and planning is fundamental and systemic.

Strategic means a very long-term, purposeful, big picture, future orientation, perspective, vision, ideal and priority. We are strategic when we are consciously and intentionally guided by crucial values, data, facts and critical analysis of issues and priorities. Being strategic requires a high level of awareness and concern about issues and consequences that arise from lack of strategic awareness and prioritisation. There is strong link between data, facts, rationality, critical thinking, values, ecological goals, stewardship and strategic ecological leadership. This linkage is strongly emphasised in this book.

Fundamentalism is a strict, rigid, narrow, absolute, exclusive and judgemental system of ideas, beliefs, opinions and interpretations of religion, ideology, and culture. Whatever its cultural, political or religious expression, fundamentalism is not guided by reverence, dignifying values, critical thinking or wider societal accountability. Typically, fundamentalism has minimal awareness or concern about the issues and consequences of being irreverent, undignified, narrow, rigid, prescriptive, judgemental and exclusionary. Fundamentalism is highly problematic for individuals and society. It dumbs us down and incites judgementalism, divisions, exclusions, enmities and conflict.

Fundamentalists are people, groups and intuitions who impose righteous, strict, rigid and narrow religious, political and cultural ideas, opinions and beliefs. Inherently, most fundamentalists are not guided by reverence, dignifying values, critical thinking or social accountability. Typically, fundamentalists show minimal awareness or concern about the issues and consequences of their fundamentalist beliefs, judgements, impositions and acting out.

Quixotic alludes to the ways of Don Quixote. Quixotic persons and groups are idealistic, short-sighted, blinkered, unrealistic, and blundering. Often, such persons and groups are enthusiastic and well-intended, but, typically, arc

456

misinformed, misguided, clumsy, ham-fisted and inept. In the spirit of Don Quixote, quixotic people 'tilt at windmills' by being ill-informed, and by acting with 'zeal but without wisdom'. Quixotic people are religiously, politically and/or culturally assumptive, pretentious, one-eyed, over confident, under-informed, partisan, ignorant, misguided, blustering, insensitive, and ill-equipped in terms of reverence, dignity, knowledge and skills. This blend of dispositions causes quixotic people to be silly, glib and greatly unsophisticated. Typically, quixotic ideologues, quixotic religious fundamentalists, quixotic new-age enthusiasts, and quixotic conspiracy theorists are not guided by relational sensitivities, data, facts and reasoned critical thinking processes. Commonly, they show minimal awareness or concern about the issues and consequences that arise from their ill-considered and ill-fated blundering and acting out. All expressions of fundamentalism are quixotic. Many are harmful to people and destructive of environment.

Institutions are renown religious, political or societal organisations, systems or structures. Institutions tend to be ensconced, traditionist, conservative and rigid. Institutions establish or entrench conventions and norms which become inherent in the culture of organisations, governments, nations and cultures. People who are uncritically under the sway and control of institutions are said to be enculturated or 'institutionalised'. Institutions tend not to be guided by data, facts or critical thinking. They tend to be guided and governed by masculine norms, roles, rules and culture. Institutional culture is 'the way we do things around here'. Typically, institutions have minimal awareness or concern about the issues and consequences of their traditions, norms, rules, culture, influences and controls. Institutions tend be insular, and 'a law unto themselves'. Historically, most institutions were established by men, are controlled by men, and are mostly for the benefit of men.

Masculine refers to abilities, qualities and values which are traditionally associated with being strong, capable, courageous, ambitious, determined, aggressive and 'powered by testosterone'. Overt masculinity tends not to be guided by nurturing values; but by self-serving and self-gratifying, transactional drives, and by power motives. Typically, the masculine mindset has limited awareness, sensitivity or concern about personal and relational issues and consequences associated with the Yang-driven ambitions, aggression, manipulation, control and forcefulness. At its rare best, masculinity is aware, sensitive, strong, courageous, determined, integrous and accountable. At its common worst, masculinity is insensitive, uncaring, unempathic, prejudiced, institutional, nationalistic, aggressive, Machiavellian, determined, forceful and violent.

Feminine describes abilities, qualities and values which are traditionally associated with being nurturing and protective. At its best, the-feminine is sensitive, supportive, selfless, cooperative, empathic, kind, helpful, devoted, and understanding. The-feminine is not about being weak, timid or passive. At its best, being feminine is about being strong, determined and courageous in non-aggressive and non-harmful ways. The-feminine is rarely violent. It tends not to be individualistic, institutional, nationalistic or exceptionalistic. At its best, the-feminine tends to be more relational than transactional. The-feminine mindset and ethos aren't perfect or egoless, but, compared with overt masculinity, it is relatively less ambitiously exploitative, and is relatively less overtly harmful. At its best, the feminine is reverent, aware, sensitive, relational, integrous, strategic and ecological. At its worst, the feminine tends more to be passive-aggressive than overtly aggressive.

Humans are at their best when they blend the best of masculinity and the best of femininity. This may occur through the idea of androgyny, which is the blending of male and female traits within individuals. But this blend is most likely to occur through conscious intentional collaboration between men and women who are guided by dignified reasoned strategic ecological values, principles and priorities. The emergence of active, strategic, dignified and reasoned collaboration among women and men is a prominent hope of this book.

Men and women readers, I invite you to use this book to help you think about how you will participate in a constructive, strategic collaboration, stewardship and leadership to increase justice, and to reduce the causes of harm, suffering and environmental damage. I invite women and men readers to use this book to stimulate your thinking, and to identify ways that you can nurture constructive, strategic collaboration toward strategic relational and ecological ends.

Country is term used by Australian First Peoples. Country encompasses all lands and waterways. Symbolically and literally, Country is 'Mother'; the giver of life. 'She', Country, is 'the one' who forms us, births us, feeds us, carries us, sustains us, nurtures us, protects us, teaches us. Country is Mother's womb, Mother's breasts, Mother's arms, Mother's embrace, Mother's voice, Mother's kiss, Mother's touch, Mother's unconditional love, Mother's sustenance,

Mother's protection, Mother's nurturance, guidance and discipline. Country is creator.

Patriarchy and Patriarchal are societal mindsets, systems, institutions, and governance in which men hold power, status and control; and where women are largely restrained, diminished and excluded from recognition, respect and influence. Patriarchy isn't guided by dignified and reasoned values that empower men and women 'equally, as equals'. Patriarchy tends not to be guided by values such equal decency, fully, and for all. Nor is it guided by integrity, transparency and accountability for all. Typically, patriarchy has minimal awareness or concern about the issues and consequences it generates for women, children, First Peoples, the poor, the powerless and the earth. The inherent purpose of patriarchy is to benefit men; most particularly, powerful, wealthy, elitist men; who are 'the dominant patriarchy'. Patriarchy is not inclined to robustly self-critique its assumptions, pretentions, pontifications, motives, biases and resistance to accountability. It strongly resists critique by women and the-feminine.

Chauvinism consists of biased claims, authority and dominance of a sex, group, institution, system or cause. Most commonly, it is generated and driven by patriarchal men, masculine groups and male-dominated organisations. Chauvinism is masculinity at its worst. It isn't guided by reverent, dignified and reasoned values; nor by decency, integrity, transparency and accountability. Typically, chauvinism has minimal awareness or concern about the issues and consequences of disrespect, indignity, irrationality, coercion, exclusion, dominance and alienation. Chauvinism is inherent in narcissistic and sociopathic leadership, power, and empire building.

Patriarchy and chauvinism go together. Enmeshed, they resist the inclusion of the-feminine from the formulation of governance based on dignifying values, priorities, policies and strategies. Patriarchy and chauvinism dismiss, diminish and poohoo the feminine. Typically, they diminish and subjugate women. The ethos of chauvinism and patriarchy remain prominent in the 21st century systems and structures of religion, government, commerce and industry. They are much more part of present-day problems and harms, than they are part of solutions and of societal evolution toward fulsome respect, dignity, reason, integrity, equity, justice and accountability.

Basically, chauvinistic and patriarchal men hold most the key cards that determine the future of humankind and the planet. The track-record of chauvinistic men for causing harm and suffering is obvious. This book confronts these issues, and asks readers to contemplate and investigate how we can nurture reverence, dignity and reason in order to reduce the harms and suffering of unbalanced, unrestrained, chauvinistic masculinity.

Ego, Egoic-Mind and Egoic-Self are synonymous, and consist of patterns of thoughts and beliefs that are oriented to me, I, mine, and what I want, deserve and must have. Ego is identified by self-benefiting and self-promoting mental patterns and processes. Egoic patterns and processes form a mindset that places the personal me, the political me, the corporate me, the religious me, and the new-age me; before others. The egoic-mind assumes that 'I am more right and more righteous' than others; I am more important than others; I am better than others; and, and I am more deserving than others. Egoic-thinking tends not to be guided by dignified and reasoned values; and tends not to be subject to the logic and evidence of critical thinking. Typically, egoic thinking has minimal awareness or concern about issues and consequences caused by egoic attitudes, priorities and actions. Ahead, are a number of chapters that explain various aspects of ego.

Confabulation, Confabulations and Confabulating are about making-up, inventing and falsifying information, stories and narratives that we believe to be true; or that we want to be true. Confabulations may be apparently overconfident versions that are either unintentionally incorrect or distorted, or are wilfully fabricated. Confabulations unconsciously and intentionally misinterpret memories and versions of oneself, others, relationships, experiences, circumstances, situations, and history. Often, confabulation is closely connected to assumed beliefs, pretentious opinions, and biased agendas.

Confabulations range from subtle misrepresentations of facts, to wilful ignorance, to outrageous distortions, to deceptions and lies, to agnotological manipulation. At the very least, confabulations are desired, idealised, optimistic, wishful, self-justifying versions of reality. But they are not reality. Confabulations are at least somewhat imaginary, contrived or delusional versions that erode and stifle truthfulness, facts, reason and critical thinking. Typically, confabulations have minimal awareness or concern about the issues and consequences of misrepresenting the facts of history, relationships, situations, and reality.

Cognitive biases are a web of irrationalities and anomalies of judgment and understanding. Individuals and groups create their own distorted realities from

460

ill-founded ideas and beliefs which have little or no basis in data, science or facts, and have minimal basis in reason or logic. There are many cognitive, emotional and group biases. All of which distort, contrive and deny the facts of reality, and which cause people to be misguided, misdirected, irrational, clumsy, and quixotically blundering. Most of our everyday opinions and beliefs tend to be based on various cognitive biases, which are much more prominent than most of us are aware. Typically, cognitive bias renders people unaware of alternative perspectives, issues and consequences that arise from bias, prejudice, distorted facts, and lack of logic and critical thinking. All these effects are enmeshed with and drive prejudice, religious and new-age distortions, and conspiracy proneness.

Opinions are attitudes, judgements and conclusions that tend not to be based on data, facts, critical thinking or tested knowledge. Mostly, opinions are not guided by dignity and reason. Typically, they have minimal awareness or concern about issues and consequences that arise from 'making up stuff', judgementalism, self-serving bias, and ill-informed spruiking. In Australia, some might say that we pluck opinions from our arse. This is crude, but apt.

Beliefs are ideas that we assert to be true, real or actual, but without supporting data, facts, logic, reason or rational analysis. Typically, 'believers' have minimal awareness or concern about issues and consequences that arise from assertions of belief in the absence of proof and critical thinking. Again, typically, we pluck beliefs from the air. We just make them up, imagine them, contrive them, assert them, defend them, and accumulate them. Beliefs are arbitrary.

Arbitrary, Arbitrariness and Arbitrarily consist of imagining, believing, asserting an idea, opinion or belief on a self-serving personal whim, a group whim, a religious whim, an ideological whim, or an institutional whim. Arbitrary choices, decisions and actions are made not on the basis of values, ethics, evidence or a logical rationale; but commonly, are made up on the basis of an assumed or preconceived self-serving desire or aim. Typically, arbitrary choices, decisions and actions occur with minimal awareness or concern about issues and consequences that arise from being baselessly whimsical and fantastical. Arbitrariness and self-servingness go hand in glove; as do arbitrariness, opinions, beliefs and fantasies.

Fantasy and Fantasising arise from arbitrarily imagining, wishing and wanting an idea or belief to be true and real, even if it is impossible, irrational, or an extremely unlikely. Fantasy is not guided by facts or reason. Typically, it has scant awareness or concern about issues and consequences that arise from making things up on a whim or a fancy. Fantasies are arbitrary. They are not factual or rational. Fantasies are extremely common, and they are problematic because they undermine facts and sound judgement, and they generate fads, misinformation, lies, cons and conspiracy theories.

Fads and Faddism are popular arbitrary and fanciful ideas that have minimal basis in facts, science or logic. Fads are akin to crazes, that typically, tend to come into vogue, then disappear. Typically, faddish ideas and superficial fashions and fancies are usually short-lived, and are 'in vogue', until superseded by the next fad or craze. Fads aren't guided by reason. Typically, fads have minimal awareness or concern about issues and consequences that arise from factless, fanciful, fictitious and fallacious claims.

New-age is a patchwork of hip ideas and trendy, modern, quasi-spiritual beliefs and pop-culture practices that emerged out of alternative culture revolution, that began in the 1970s and has continued into the 2000s. New-age ideas, fantasies and fads aren't based-on or guided-by data, science, facts or reason. Typically, new-age stuff has minimal awareness or concern about issues and consequences that arise from arbitrariness, fanciful ideas, baseless beliefs, pop-psychology, junk-science, dodgy practices, and conspiracy theories.

Junk-Science consists of untested, unproven, unprofessional ideas and bogus theories that masquerade as empirical science and scientific facts. Junk-science isn't guided by legitimate credible data, facts, critical analysis or empirical processes. Typically, it has minimal awareness or concern about issues and consequences that arise from the distortions and deceptions of dumb science, bad science, false science, and fraudulent science. Junk-science isn't science, it's junk.

Pop-Psychology consists of trendy, untested, unproven, unprofessional, fantastical, simplistic and often bogus ideas that become urban myths and memes, which are widely popular and held to be true in new-age circles. Pop-psychology isn't based on credible research, facts or critical analysis. It is shallow and simplistic. Typically, pop-psychology has minimal awareness or concern about issues and consequences that arise from insubstantial, unsubstantiated pseudo-psychology that is arbitrary, naïve, egoic and self-serving.

Conspiracy Theories are popularised, untested, unproven and dubious, ideas, beliefs, claims and assertions about allegedly clandestine collusions and ulterior motives by allegedly corrupt, self-invested influential people, organisations, corporations, institutions and governments, who are responsible for allegedly dangerous or unexplained events that will benefit the conspirators and harm others. That was a long sentence, but it captures the elements of conspiracy theories and conspiracy theorising, which aren't guided by facts, legitimate science, critical thinking, integrity and accountability. Typically, conspiracists have minimal awareness or concern about the harmful issues and consequences that are caused by their arbitrary, contrived, false, spurious, fraudulent and patently incorrect beliefs, opinions, claims, accusations and distortions.

Ideology is an arbitrary system of political, economic and societal values, beliefs and ideals which stipulate the priorities that should govern human communities. They may or may not be guided by dignified and facts or dignifying values. Typically, ideologies have minimal awareness or concern about issues and consequences that arise from of lack of facts, doggy logic, exaggerated and misleading claims, and spurious accusations about competing ideologies. Ideologies tend not to be formed and guided by critical thinking, and are generally are not amenable to critique, transparency and accountability. Ideologies tend not to be aware or concerned about the issues and consequences of their lack of congruence, logic, evidence and critical thinking.

Dogma is an arbitrary system of 'right and righteous' beliefs and rules compiled by self-declared and self-appointed cultural, religious or societal authorities that presume to contrive and stipulate what they deem to be absolutely and incontrovertibly true, righteous, moral and required for right-thinking, right-believing, right-opinions, right-behaviour, right-belonging, just rewards, and inclusion in a group or institution. Another long sentence, but is in keeping with the nature of dogma. Dogma is not formed, guided by, or answerable to values, facts, science, critical analysis, integrity or accountability. It usually lacks logic, proof, congruence, consistency and coherence. Very commonly, dogma lacks dignified and compassionate values. Typically, it has minimal awareness or concern about issues and consequences of rigid, irrational, absolutistic, disparaging, exclusive judgemental beliefs, claims, assertions and accusations.

Transactional leveraging are personal and interpersonal mechanisms that seek self-serving benefits from relationships and interactions. The transaction ethos is 'only give to get'; you scratch my back and I'll scratch yours, but only if I have to; 'tit-for-tat'; and an eye-for-an-eye. Transactional priorities are: always try to gain more than you give; apply leverage to get and edge, to press an advantage, to build influence, and to increase power. Transactional leveraging is not guided by dignified relational values. Transactional leveraging is ends-driven. Ends justify any transactional means; including unethical and corrupt means.

There is a strong relationship between egoic thinking and transactional leveraging. It is inherently and unapologetically egoic, self-serving and me-focussed. Typically, transactional leveraging has minimal awareness or concern about issues and consequences that arise from relational insensitivity, relational dishonesty and relational exploitation.